SPECIAL OPS LIBERATORS

DEDICATION

*To all those that served with
223 (Bomber Support) Squadron
in 100 Group during World War II,
especially the aircrew who gave
their lives in the losses of
Liberators TT336, TS520 and TS526*

SPECIAL OPS LIBERATORS

223 (Bomber Support) Squadron,
100 Group, and the Electronic War

Dr Steve Bond and Richard Forder

Grub Street • London

Published by
Grub Street
4 Rainham Close
London
SW11 6SS

Copyright © Grub Street 2011
Copyright text © Dr Steve Bond and Richard Forder 2011

British Library Cataloguing in Publication Data
Special Ops Liberators : 223 (Bomber Support) Squadron and
   the electronic war.
  1. Great Britain. Royal Air Force. Bomber Command. Group,
  No. 100. 2. World War, 1939-1945 –Aerial operations,
  British. 3. World War, 1939-1945–Radar. 4. Air bases–
  England–Norfolk–History. 5. World War, 1939-1945–
  Regimental histories–Great Britain.
  I. Title II. Forder, Richard.
  940.5'44'941-dc22

  ISBN-13: 9781908117144

Cover design by Sarah Driver
Edited by Sophie Campbell
Designed by Roy Platten, Eclipse, Hemel Hempstead
roy.eclipse@btopenworld.com

All maps credited to TNA Air 14/3412.

Printed and bound by MPG Ltd, Cornwall.

Grub Street Publishing only uses
FSC (Forest Stewardship Council) paper for its books.

Contents

FOREWORD

The history of Bomber Command during World War II is an ongoing subject for analysis by a wide variety of authors. Within that huge subject there are many detailed and vital aspects which have been given far less attention than they deserve. The radio counter-measure (RCM) battle between allied and German air forces is one such aspect. There was virtually no precedent for this battle, most certainly nothing approaching the scale of activities developed and practised by the opposing air forces and their support services, including their national intelligence services, technical research and production resources. In the opinion of the commander of the German air defence service, "The task of forming a picture of the emerging air situation, during a bomber raid using supporting radio counter-measures, was one of the most exciting and difficult functions of command." The RAF began to use ground-based RCM in the defensive battle against the German bombers during the Blitz, to counter the German use of radio beams to guide their bombers to targets within the UK. This gave rise to the RAF formation of 80 Wing in October 1940.

As the offensive bombing campaign by the RAF against German targets developed during 1940/41, there was a growing need to find ways to minimise the loss rate of bombers at the hands of the German defences. This gradually saw the fielding of operational RCM. Initially these counter-measure equipments were installed into individual bombers in addition to their normal bomb payloads. However, as the equipments became more capable so did the penalty on those individual bombers in terms both of their available bomb load and the need for operators to control the counter-measure equipments. During the summer of 1943, Bomber Command recognised the benefit of creating a specialist RCM unit that would provide direct support to the Main Force bomber operations.

This unit was formed in November 1943 under the command of Air Vice-Marshal Addison, with the initial title of 100 (Special Duties) Group. The group absorbed the existing 80 Wing and the title changed a little later to Bomber Support. This group was eventually equipped with thirteen RAF squadrons and one United States Army Air Force squadron.

At the end of the war, the Bomber Command signals staff declared their professional opinion that the use of RCM and the related Bomber Support operations had saved at least 1,000 bomber aircraft and their aircrews. In addition, those techniques and operations placed a very considerable strain on the enemy's radio research and production organisation. Another unseen dividend was the impact on the morale of the enemy air defence fighter aircrews and the supporting ground operating staffs, as the performance and effectiveness of their equipments and control communications were progressively degraded.

The squadrons within 100 Group were made up from heavy four-engined bombers and lighter twin-engined aircraft, especially Mosquitoes. The heavy bombers delivered major radio and radar jamming support and the twin-engined aircraft provided specific aggressive support, much of which was as intruder forces to penetrate enemy territory and attack their airfields and aircraft as they recovered from air defence sorties. The integrated tactics of the Main Force and the counter-measure support forces, often with spoof raids and other diversions, were a matter of constant evaluation and variation to achieve the greatest impact on the enemy air defence system.

This book examines the formation in August 1944 and subsequent activities of 223 Squadron, one of the heavy RCM squadrons which was based at Oulton and equipped with American Consolidated B-24 Liberator aircraft. That expansion of 100 Group was given added urgency by intelligence that Germany's V2 rocket-powered weapon was fitted with a radio guidance system; this was subsequently seen to be incorrect but was a key target for 100 Group jamming operations at the time, under the code-name 'Big Ben'. 223 Squadron's Liberator RCM installation included the Jostle T.1524 radio-jamming equipment; this was a massive device weighing some 600 lb and using 10 KW of electrical power. In the final stages of the conflict, Boeing B-17 Fortresses were introduced in place of some Liberators.

Later chapters in the book provide a fascinating insight into the day-to-day activities covering a wide remit across the domestic aspects, the technical engineering support work, the planning and the conduct of operations with subsequent post-operation de-briefing. In particular, there is a detailed account of bomber operations on the night of 20/21 March 1945 which includes the loss of a 223 Squadron Liberator. There are numerous photographs including operational aircrews and the various RCM equipments. Annexes provide a full list of 223 Squadron's operational sorties with summaries of the operational task and the Main Bomber Force objectives for each night.

The book is an original and valuable addition to the documentary history of 100 Group. It records the role of 223 Squadron in the combined bombing offensive by RAF and USAAF air forces, illuminated by personal accounts from squadron personnel.

John Stubbington, Wing Commander
Chairman, 100 Group Association

Preface & Acknowledgements

It is a sunny afternoon in the late summer of 1944; the place, the quaintly named Turkey Tump, a small collection of houses in the parish of Llanwarne in Herefordshire. A small boy riding a tricycle, accompanied by his aunt, had just left the cottage of his grandparents. They were in the unpaved lane, an old drovers' road that ran along the side of the cottage when they were joined by an airman in his RAF uniform. The airman lived next door and proved to be very friendly giving the boy some of the old toys that had belonged to him and his late brother. He passed the time of day before mounting his smart red racing bike with its drop handle bars and white mudguards. He set off down the lane before turning right to join the road which crossed the lane and would take him to nearby Wormelow. The small boy was me and the airman was Sergeant (Sgt) Edward David Thornton Brockhurst. This was the last time I was to see him, but I never forgot him.

I had often wondered what had happened to David and what he had done in the RAF. Finally in 1987, and now in the RAF myself, I decided I must find out. I was able to establish some very brief details from the RAF Records Office that recorded that David had been a sgt air gunner and had served with 223 (Bomber Support) Squadron. My interest was immediately aroused. 223 was no ordinary squadron but had been involved in the very secretive war of radio counter-measures (RCM). What was equally fascinating was that the squadron had flown Consolidated B-24 Liberators – in fact the only squadron in Bomber Command to do so. This was an uncanny coincidence as I had personal interest in the Liberator.

I was born in Malta GC just after the war broke out in September 1939. My father was in the army and had been posted there in 1937. Eventually, as things started hotting up in the Mediterranean wives and families of service personnel were evacuated, but not all. My mother and I were among those that remained. We survived the Malta blitz until things calmed down in 1943 when we were evacuated, leaving my father on the island.

On the morning of 3 June 1943 we were driven by car to RAF Luqa and to a dispersal at the bottom of the sloping airfield, where Consolidated Liberator II AL523 of 511 Squadron was parked. I looked up the slope across the airfield and was surprised to see a lot of old vehicles on the airfield. I was later to learn that they were part of the anti-invasion measures. My mother and I climbed up a shiny ladder through the ventral hatch and into the rear fuselage. We were then guided forward and stepped down into the bomb bay. The vertical bomb beams had been removed and a wooden floor installed. There appeared to be bench or locker seating along each side of the bay. All the seating was taken up so my mother and I had to lie on the floor on an old green bedspread that we had brought with us. That was our only luggage apart from a fabric bag my mother carried.

I was the only child on board and one of the RAF crew took me by the hand and proceeded to show me over the rear of the aircraft. I remember being very impressed by the belts of ammunition fed into the guns of the Boulton Paul rear turret. The rounds reminded me of the shell cases I used to find in the back garden of our house in Melita Street. At that moment the engines were started and the rear end began to shake, accompanied by a terrific noise. I immediately let the side down and began to cry – in retrospect I had probably detected a 'mag drop' on one of the engines. I was promptly returned to mum in the bomb bay, but I do not remember having any further qualms. Once we were at altitude and straight and level there seemed to be freedom to move about and I can remember standing by the ventral hatch gazing down at the North African desert below. The hatch was constructed with triangular dished clear panels and occasionally I would catch sight of vehicles. We landed at Gibraltar after a flight of seven hours and twenty minutes. It was this early flight that obviously sparked my life-long passion and involvement with aviation. Many years later in February 1975 I was returning from the Far East in Nimrod MR1 XV255 when we landed at Luqa for a refuelling stop. We were directed to the old Strike Command V-Bomber dispersal site at the bottom of the airfield. I stepped out of the aircraft almost on the spot where I had climbed aboard the Liberator thirty-two years previously. AL523, by the way, was to achieve lasting and controversial fame just four months after my flight when it crashed on take-off from Gibraltar on 4 July 1943 killing the Polish leader-in-exile General Sikorski.

Returning to David Brockhurst and 223 Squadron, after some initial research I established that David had lost his life in B-24H, TS526 (T) as a member of Fg Off N S Ayres' crew. A big break-through occurred in 1993 when my aunt, Mrs Violet Smith, in Herefordshire sent me a cutting from the local paper from someone seeking information about David. This was Len Davies who had entered the RAF with David and gone right through training with him until they both joined 223. They shared a hut together at Oulton but flew in different crews. I now had David's service history, with the marvellous bonus that Len introduced me to the 100 Group Association that had just been formed. So it was with great anticipation and excitement that I attended the first reunion in Norfolk in May 1994 for the unveiling of a memorial on the edge of the old Oulton airfield and a book of remembrance at St Andrews Church adjacent to Blickling Hall. The highlight for me on this memorable weekend was the gathering held on the Saturday evening in the town hall. This was a most appropriate venue as it had been the site for wartime dances. It was obviously an emotional and joyful evening for those attending, many of whom were meeting fellow squadron members and wartime pals whom they probably had not seen for nearly fifty years. It was also a special night for me as Len introduced me to the 223 Squadron members including the late Jamie Brown, Dr Peter Lovatt and the late Bob Lawrence who had been in David Brockhurst's first crew (Flt Lt Hastie). My only regret was that my knowledge of 100 Group and 223 Squadron was pretty rudimentary at this stage and therefore I was unable to ask the right questions during this unique opportunity. Many of those I met that weekend and at subsequent reunions were to become special friends through the following years.

With a good understanding of David Brockhurst's early life in Herefordshire from my aunt and other people who had known him, I extended my investigation to the other members of Fg Off Ayres' crew, and I also wrote to the Bürgermeister of Wolfhagen, the nearest town to where TS526 had come down. The latter provided another major leap forward when my letter was passed to local historian Bernd Klinkhardt. Bernd had served his national service in the Luftwaffe and was immediately interested in my request to track down the crash site of TS526 and establish the circumstances surrounding the loss and the existence of any local witnesses to the event. Bernd in turn, introduced me to Hans-Joachim 'Hajo' Adler, an internationally-recognised authority on wartime cash sites in the Hessen region and much more. Pooling our respective knowledge we quickly identified the crash site and established that Hauptmann (Hptm) Johannes Hager had shot down TS526. This was not straightforward however, as I outline in the book. Unfortunately Hager had passed away before his identity was established, but my German friends traced and enabled me to correspond with Walter Schneider, Hager's radio/radar operator, concerning their three victories claimed on the night of 20/21 March 1945. Dirk Sohl, one of Hajo's fellow historians was able to provide copies of the relevant combat reports. My investigations in Germany over three visits in 1997, 2000 and 2003 aided by Bernd and Hajo enabled me to establish crucial information, including a thorough examination of the crash site. I would like to acknowledge here the exceptional hospitality provided by Bernd and Hajo and their wives Waltraud and Waltraud during our three visits. I should also mention the assistance, including translation, provided by Bernd's uncle, the late Werner Pinn and his wife Elizabeth. Werner served in the Luftwaffe as a radio/radar operator during the early part of the war. He was shot down in a Ju 88 of 4(F)122 (a long-range reconnaissance unit) on 7 December 1940 and spent the rest of the war as a POW in England and Canada. After the war he was awarded the OBE for services with the British Embassy in Bonn, and was a regular contributor to the *Luftwaffen Revue* magazine for many years.

Meanwhile another breakthrough stemmed from Aunt Violet in Herefordshire. She forwarded to me a letter that had arrived at David Brockhurst's old address at Turkey Tump requesting information about him. The writer was Rodney Vowler who was engaged in the same quest as me, and was trying to trace friends and family of Ayres' crew. Rodney's uncle, Leonard Vowler, had been David's fellow waist gunner in the lost aircraft. Rod was to prove an invaluable help through the years assisting me with tracing 223 Squadron members from its Bomber Support era. Since 1995 he has passed on any information, photographs or details which he believed were relevant to my research. A member of the 100 Group Association for many years he has beavered away behind the scenes keeping in touch with wartime members, and in recent times has acted as a valuable member of the association committee, and is the official standard bearer.

Initially, my intention was to produce a small book covering the crew of TS526 and the circumstances of its loss. However, as time passed and my researches and knowledge increased, it prompted me to consider extending the proposed book to include a history of 223 Squadron in its Bomber Support period. Unfortunately, various diversions, some of them major, delayed the achievement of this project. Finally, the old enemy procrastination played its part with *anno domini* inevitably exerting its influence, and

I realised that something had to be done. My greatest concern was that the delay was letting down all those that had helped me through the years. So in 2010 I asked my old RAF colleague and friend Dr Steve Bond if he was interested in a collaboration to complete the book. The timing was good as Steve had just finished his book *Heroes All,* also published by Grub Street. When discussing the project we agreed that in producing a history of the squadron and its part in the electronic war we needed to put it into the context of Bomber Command's battle with the German defences. Steve has done that in the opening chapter. We also agreed that the story would be incomplete without covering the battle as seen from the German view. Again Steve has provided this element drawing on his research for *Heroes All*, and most importantly his valuable interviews and correspondence; in particular with Peter Spoden and Heinz Rökker, two very experienced Luftwaffe night-fighter aces. I am deeply grateful to Steve for enabling *Special Ops Liberators* to achieve publication, and for taking on the onerous task of final editing and pulling it all together ready for publication. He was also able to tie up a number of loose ends through further visits to The National Archives on my behalf. We both acknowledge our thanks to Wg Cdr John Stubbington RAF (Rt'd), chairman of the 100 Group Association who kindly agreed to write the foreword to the book.

However one great regret remains in that there is no coverage of the essential ground staff involvement in 223's operations. This is not a lack of recognition of their crucial role, simply that no technical ground staff ever responded to my published requests for information. Additionally, no ground crew from Oulton have ever contacted the 100 Group Association, although we have been lucky enough to have had members from 192 Squadron.

There are many people who are due acknowledgment for their help, and I have already mentioned some of them. However I cannot ignore the special contributions of the following:

Ron Johnson for his friendship, assistance and encouragement of many years; and for his permission to draw on his book, *A Navigator's Tale*, for details surrounding the loss of his aircraft TS520. Ronnie Simmons for his tolerance with my many questions over the years, and for his permission to produce extracts from his unpublished autobiography. Mrs Mervyn Utas, and her son Bryan, for their kind permission to reproduce extracts from her late husband Mervyn's unpublished memoirs.

Andrew Barron for his friendship and outstanding help and advice over many years, not least in providing real time information from his archive collection of navigation charts and plots relating to his 223 Squadron operations.

Peter Matthews for his help and permission to use material from his correspondence and private memoirs.

Dr Peter Lovatt for all the valuable personal experience details he has provided, and for the many hours of fascinating discussions we have enjoyed. Peter has done extensive research into 100 Group operations which was the basis for his Doctorate and finally, for his permission to draw on his own publication *Ordinary Man, Super Pilot – The Story of Flt Lt Roy Hastie DFC*.

Leslie Boot DFC DFM for permission to use extracts from his unpublished memories of his wartime service, and for his valuable input in our correspondence and many discussions relating to his duties as a special operator.

Gp Capt John Mellers DFC RAF (Rt'd) for his personal account of the loss of TT336.

Flt Lt Didier Hindryckx, Belgian Air Force, for assistance with details of the crash of TT336.

John Reid, The Stirling Association, for details of Sam Silvey's operations with 149 Squadron.

223 (Bomber Support) Squadron

Rex Arnett, the late Arthur Anthony, Bob Belton, the late Jim Bratten, the late Jack Brigham, the late Jamie Brown, Peter Cameron, Len Davies, Walter Gatenby, Bob Lawrence, Leslie Matthews, the late Professor Tony Morris, the late Don Prutton, the late George Simons, R J Smith, 'Mick' Stirrop, Ken Stone, the late 'Bill' Sykes, Ralph Tailford, Reggie Wade, Tom Wallis, Derek Wilshaw and last but not least Peter Witts. Peter, a good friend and stalwart supporter of 100 Group Association reunions since they started, generously funded the production of the association's standard.

Friends and Relatives of 223 Squadron Personnel

D Swingler, brother in law of Gerry Schutes and Martyn Thomas, son of W H G Thomas. Mrs Jean Anthony for permission to use extracts from her late husband Arthur's book *Lucky B-24*.

Family and Friends of the Crew of TS526

The following friends and relatives of the crew of TS526 were all most helpful and I am eternally grateful for their willingness to assist me in obtaining some RAF Records of Service, and loaning photographs and flying log books together with similar memorabilia. Their memories of the individual crew members were most valuable.

Mrs S H Siddall – aunt of Norman Ayres; the late Charles Bramley – cousin of Norman Ayres; Alf Ridler – housemaster of Norman Ayres; Mr Edmund Rhodes – boyhood friend of Norman; Mr M E Bellamy – son of James Bellamy; Mr G P Finnerty – James Bellamy's skipper on 115 Squadron; Mr G W Hoing – friend of Sam Silvey; Stan Smith – boyhood friend of David Brockhurst; Mr George Holley – friend of David Brockhurst; Mrs Jennie Taylor – daughter of Alfred Cole; Mr Peter Cole – step-son of Alfred Cole; Mrs E Wilson – sister of Joseph Cairns; Mrs Doris Hulbert – widow of Harold Hale; Bob Lewis – cousin of Harold Hale; Harry Gumbrell – Harold's skipper on 101 Squadron; Mrs Josephine Mitchell – cousin of Arnold Redford; Mrs Muriel Godley – cousin of Dennis Marsden; Maurice Fellowes who remembered the Marsden family.

I am also deeply indebted to the following RAF and Luftwaffe aircrew for providing memories of their part in operations on the night of 20/21 March 1945:

50 Squadron

Ted Friend, who has also completed his own detailed research of Bomber Command operations on the night in question, and who has provided raid documentation and an account of the loss of his aircraft.

227 Squadron

The late Bert Allam and his son Peter, Mervyn Croker DFC, Wyn Henshaw (WOp) who provided recalled essential details of their attack by Hauptmann Joahnnes Hager on the night of 20/21 March 1945.

Ray King RAAF, who kindly provided information concerning the loss of his aircraft and gave permission for details of his part in the Böhlen raid to be drawn from his account in *Ops Are On To-night*.

619 Squadron

The late 'Jasper' Miles and David Thomas who were invaluable in providing their memories of events surrounding the shooting down of their Lancaster.

4./NJG I

Hauptmann Fritz Lau KC, staffelkapitän.

6./JG 1

Unterofficier Walter Schneider, radio/radar operator for Hauptmann Johannes Hager KC.

From Germany

Frau Jospha Bals, Frau Wickmann, Horst Willensteine, Stephan Sandor and Werner Ruesmann.

If I have failed to recognise any help or contributions by individuals I can only apologise and stress that it has not been intentional. Information sources and photographs are credited to their original owners wherever this has been possible; with apologies for any we may have missed.

Last and by no means least my special thanks to my wife Janice for her support for this project over many years, not to mention her tolerance for my long absences at The National Archives and other sources. Her first-class German has been invaluable for the translation of German documents and the many letters from my German friends that have arrived through the last seventeen years. Perhaps her devotion to the cause is best summed up by a postcard that she wrote on one of our German visits which read:

'……. I have enjoyed better days than standing in a dark, damp, German forest translating a technical discussion on the relevant merits of electrical and mechanical propeller pitch control mechanisms.'

No greater love…?

Richard M Forder
Sheffield
June 2011

For my part, I have watched Richard bringing together all the many and varied threads of this story since we first met in the early 1990s when, while both serving in the RAF, we worked together in the Ministry of Defence in London. I was delighted when he asked me to help him complete the task and bring it to publication, and I must also pass my thanks and appreciation to those whose experiences and counselling I have drawn on for the parts of the book that Richard entrusted to my care. If I have inadvertently missed anyone out I apologise, but you know who you are.

RAF
Jack Bromfield; Eric Clarke; George Cook; John Elliott; Ron Hall; Peter Langdon; Henry Payne; Michael Wainwright.

Luftwaffe
Willi Reschke; Heinz Rökker; Peter Spoden.

Steve J Bond
Milton Keynes
June 2011

CHAPTER ONE

The Bomber War & 100 Group

Of all the major campaigns during the air war between 1939 and 1945, the most prolonged and arguably the toughest for both sides, was the allied bombing of Germany. The first operation was flown on the opening day of the war, with the final major attack taking place on the night of 25/26 April 1945. In 1940 Winston Churchill said: "The fighters are our salvation but the bombers alone provide the means of victory." By the time of the German surrender on 8 May 1945, Bomber Command alone had flown no fewer than 364,514 operational sorties for the loss of 55,573 aircrew (over 40% of those who took part) and 8,325 aircraft.

The Unites States Army Air Force's (USAAF) 8th Air Force also paid a very heavy price for its daylight bombing effort from England, suffering a further 26,000 casualties. As with the RAF, the initial thinking was that heavily-armed bombers could protect themselves, but it was not until the advent of long-range escort fighters, in particular the P-51 Mustang, that the USAAF was able to start bringing down their loss rate.

From humble beginnings with handfuls of aircraft acting almost completely independently, and individual crews free to decide their own take-off times and routes, the RAF's bombing campaign grew to a massive scale; tightly organised and technically highly sophisticated. The cost both in terms of human sacrifice and materiel losses was enormous, and it was largely a recognition of the need to develop specialised measures against German defences in order to minimise those losses, that 100 Group Bomber Command was brought into being.

The Early Stages of the Bomber War

Following Germany's invasion of Poland, general mobilisation of the Royal Air Force commenced on 1 September 1939, and bomber squadrons were ordered to disperse their aircraft and prepare for immediate operations, with the expectation of primarily targeting aerodromes in north-west Germany. At RAF Wyton in Huntingdonshire, Flying Officer (Fg Off) Andrew McPherson of 139 Squadron and the rest of his crew were put on standby to operate if required. They were given the order to go just one minute after Great Britain's declaration of war against Germany at 11 o'clock on the morning of 3 September, and their lone Blenheim IV light bomber took off at 12 o'clock to undertake Bomber Command's first operational sortie of the conflict. Piloted by McPherson, the rest of the crew comprised Commander Thompson RN as observer, and Corporal Vincent Arrowsmith, wireless operator/air gunner (WOp/AG). They flew to the north of

Wilhelmshaven to photograph airfields and German shipping in the Schillig Roads, which included the battleship *Admiral Scheer* and the cruiser *Emden*. For this action, McPherson was awarded the Distinguished Flying Cross (DFC) a week later, only to lose his life on 12 May 1940 when his Blenheim was shot down by Bf 109s from 2./JG 1 and 3./JG 27 during an attack on armoured columns in Maastricht, Belgium. By a strange twist of fate, the Blenheim he was flying at that time was the same one (N6215) in which he had carried out the first operation eight months previously.

Also dispatched on the first day of the war, a small force of eighteen Hampdens and nine Wellingtons went out to search for German warships, but no attacks were made. The size of Bomber Command at this time was simply not capable of supporting anything more ambitious, in addition to which, the targets allocated were very much constrained by pre-war thinking about rules of engagement and what constituted a legitimate target. From this very modest beginning, the Bomber Command war effort gradually grew as the force evolved its tactics. Initial raids on Germany during the so-called 'Phoney War' in late 1939 and early 1940, tended to concentrate on small-scale attacks on many targets in one night, together with a great deal of leaflet dropping, known as Nickel raids, which was all that was allowed over the German heartland at that time. The aircraft available were also a factor, with types such as the Hampden, Wellington and Whitley being restricted in range and payload.

Both daylight and night raids were being carried out, as there was still considerable faith in the ability of a concentrated formation of bombers to defend themselves from fighter attack through their combined defensive firepower. This theory was quickly called into question, as loss rates during daylight attacks quickly approached 5% of the attacking force, which had been calculated as the maximum sustainable loss rate that could be tolerated, given the limitations of the replacement system for both aircrew and aircraft. At this early stage of the war, night raids were more successful in this regard, with a typical loss rate of about 2.5%.

Following the German air attack on Rotterdam on 14 May 1940, restrictions on Bomber Command targets were eased the following day, and it was authorised to attack targets east of the Rhine. This allowed targets on the Ruhr such as oil refining plants, steel works and so on, to be attacked, and this marked the start of the strategic bombing campaign.

Few raids were provided with any fighter escort at this stage, not least because the fighter force was spread very thinly with campaigns in France and the Low Countries, plus of course, the Battle of Britain. Indeed, there was little thought about pre-planned assembly of bomber forces, with squadrons and even individual aircraft captains deciding their own take-off times and routes to the targets. It should also be remembered that there were few navigation aids available, and coupled with limited experience, finding their way to the target was by far the biggest challenge facing the crews. WOp/AG Sergeant (later flight lieutenant) Eric Clarke flew his first operations in Hampdens with 49 Squadron at Scampton in Lincolnshire, and remembered his first trip suffering from this very problem:

"I did not get airborne on an operation until 12 October 1941, actually 00:10 on the 13th. I had not been informed that I was flying that night until Flight Sergeant

Gadsby told me at tea time to be at briefing at 18:00. After take-off I heard the navigator give the pilot a new course, we were crossing the Norfolk coast, goodbye England, hopefully just for the time being. I think we were at about 10,000 to 12,000 feet, and the navigator sounded crisp and confident and the WOp reported 'nothing from group'. Throughout the trip the WOp must listen out to group HQ every fifteen minutes from the hour in case of recall or diversion. W/T silence was observed except in case of emergency and only used with the pilot's permission. As we approached the enemy coast the pilot warned us that we were in a night-fighter zone but there was now a lot of cloud and I could see nothing. The Air Ministry report reads: 'Hampden AD979 Sergeant Robinson, 10/10th cloud at Wesel on ETA, set course for target, dropped flares without success for twenty-five minutes at 2,000-4,000 feet looking for target, spending fifty minutes in area. Essen and Ruhr under 10/10th cloud, bombed 'drome and flarepath in Holland on return.' We landed at base at 07:50; we had been airborne for six hours and twenty minutes."

Although the Luftwaffe had some night fighting capability from the start, it too was unsophisticated at first and the main threat to the bombers came from anti-aircraft artillery – 'Flak' (an abbreviation of the German word *Fliegerabwehrkanone*, meaning aircraft defence cannon). When fighter escorts began to get underway in 1941 and early 1942, particularly in support of daylight attacks against military targets by the light bomber force in 2 Group, it was done as much to attempt to draw Luftwaffe fighters into combat as to protect the bombers.

The Beginnings of Electronic Counter-measures
Recognising the need to provide counter-measures against Luftwaffe navigation aids for their bombing attacks on the United Kingdom, a decision was taken by the Air Ministry to set up an organisation dedicated to the control of radio and radar counter-measures (RCM). Accordingly, 80 (Signals) Wing was established on 14 October 1940, under the leadership of Wing Commander Edward Baker Addison OBE, who had been transferred to the technical branch from the Directorate of Signals on 24 April 1940. The wing had the very appropriate motto 'Confusion to Our Enemies', and was initially based at Aldenham Lodge, a requisitioned country hotel near Radlett in Hertfordshire. This location was chosen primarily because of its close proximity to the main London to Birmingham general post office (GPO) trunk cable, which eased the problem of communication with remote outstations.

With a modest staff of around 200 servicemen and women, the wing's task was the identification and subsequent jamming of the German very high frequency (VHF) blind-bombing system known as Knickebein (crooked leg) after the shape of the ground transmitter aerials used. The first of these was set up at Stollberg in northern Germany in 1939, with others following close to the Dutch, French and Swiss borders. After the fall of France, further transmitters were erected on the French coast near Dieppe and Cherbourg. Knickebein, which was codenamed Headache in Britain, was a radio-based navigation aid that guided enemy bombers through a system of electronic beams which converged over the intended target, and culminated in a signal being sent to the aircraft when they were over the bomb-release point.

The existence of the beams was first discovered on the night of 22/23 June 1940, when they were intercepted by an Anson aircraft of the Blind Approach Training and Development Unit, flying from Wyton. It was Scientific Intelligence Officer Reginald Victor 'RV' Jones and his team in the Secret Intelligence Service at the Air Ministry, who correctly identified the true nature of the Knickebein system after analysing equipment found in a downed German bomber. Together with secretly recorded conversations by German prisoners-of-war, this indicated the equipment found was an aid to bomb aiming. Initial jamming efforts by 80 Wing consisted simply of transmitting 'noise', but this was quickly superseded by a higher-powered jamming signal known by the codename Aspirin, which transmitted imitation Knickebein signals in an attempt to confuse the bomber crews. Beam signals were also intercepted and re-broadcast using an adapted 50-watt beam-approach beacon under the codename Masking Beacon, or Meacon, and this proved to be more effective. The beacon was initially set up at Wyton before being moved to a dedicated site in Norfolk, as part of what came to be known as the 'Battle of the Beams'.

It was not long before the Germans realized that counter-measures were being employed against Knickebein, and as a result they adopted a number of strategies in an attempt to overcome the jamming. These included reduced-power signals that could no longer be re-transmitted and many changes of frequency, and transmissions at irregular times. In addition, development of more advanced beam systems was already well under way, and these emerged during late 1940 and into 1941 in the form of X-Gerät (Apparatus) and Y-Gerät.

Both these systems used much higher frequencies, were considerably more accurate than Knickebein, and introduced additional intercepting beams to give a countdown to target indication which consequently led to much more precise bombing. One report suggested that X-Gerät had an accuracy of between ten and twenty yards over London. It was primarily carried by Heinkel He 111 aircraft of Kampfgruppe (KGr) 100 which was based at Vannes in Brittany, under the command of Hauptmann (Hptm) Friedrich Aschenbrenner, and was first used on 13 August 1940 during an attack on the Spitfire factory at Castle Bromwich, Birmingham. Y-Gerät also introduced voice messages to be transmitted to the bomber crews on the same frequencies as the beams, and was more difficult to jam. It was first fitted to the He 111s of Major Viktor von Lossberg's III./KG 26 at Poix-Nord in the Pas de Calais. The counter-measures used against the new systems, in the 'Battle of the Beams', used the codename Ruffian, and consisted of pulse and wave transmitters.

Flying Officer Alan 'Tommy' Thomsett was a Wellington pilot on 1473 Flight and later 192 Squadron, who flew sorties to try and intercept the German beams and understand how they functioned:

> "We had Wellington Is and IIIs. Our main job was to locate the beams coming out of Holland and France in particular and track them, then ring up Radlett *[80 Wing]* and say: 'We won!' Then we had to provide a plot indicating what exactly happened

on the night. How much of a use that really worked out to be I'm unsure, but I believe it helped somewhat, but it was quite tricky actually locating it.

"The other part of the job was to come in with the German bomber stream and check the efficiency of the ground signals. We tracked them from our base at Ford and then rushed into the sky at an enormous rate of knots, clambered up there and then followed the beam. I remember it was unreadable at Crawley but of course from there you could see London, so it would only require one incendiary or one flare and then they had the target illuminated.

"We intercepted their bomber stream from behind, I imagine…although I had no way of knowing at the time. All you would get was a telephone call saying there's a radar image of a gang approaching from France; so get up there quickly with an approximate location and just patrol the sky until you hit the beam. Since you knew where the beam was coming from as it had been tracked, it generally wasn't too difficult.

"Also there was a detachment, three aircraft went up to Turnhouse for the winter where we trialled 'jamming'. It meant going out and gradually climbing up to maximum altitude way out over the North Sea to check the efficiency of the jamming transmitter which was based in the aircraft. That was very interesting, actually."

The Build-up of Bomber Command

By 1942 it was clear to the British Government that the bombing effort needed to be substantially stepped up in order to hasten the satisfactory conclusion of the war, and in that year the cabinet agreed to a major change in bombing policy. The government's leading scientific adviser on the subject was Professor Frederick Lindemann, who had a seat in the cabinet. He presented a paper advocating the area bombing of German cities. This essentially meant targeting the major industrial centres; not just industry itself, but also destroying residential areas in order to displace the workforce. The plan was controversial from the start, but it was agreed that such large-scale bombing was the only possible course of action to attack Germany directly, since a land invasion was still years away. In addition, the Soviet Union was pressing hard for more effort to be made to relieve the pressure on the Eastern Front.

This was accepted by cabinet and in February 1942 the Area Bombing Directive was issued to Bomber Command to carry out the task of identifying fifty-eight major industrial centres. In order to facilitate this, it had already been recognised that much larger aircraft were needed with the capability of carrying heavier bomb-loads deeper into enemy territory and accordingly, the Halifax, Lancaster and Stirling four-engined bombers were brought into service. The whole strategy and operating philosophy of Bomber Command also needed a thorough overhaul. The man charged with carrying this policy through was Air Marshal Sir Arthur Travers Harris, who was commonly called 'Bomber' Harris by the press, but his crews usually referred to him as 'Butcher' or simply 'Butch'. Harris had taken command of 5 Group at the outbreak of war, and he was promoted to commander-in-chief (C-in-C) of Bomber Command in February 1942, reporting to Air Chief Marshal Charles Portal, who was chief of the air staff.

F/L Stan Woodward's crew with Liberator TS529 (C) 'Circe'. Rear L to R: Ground crew, F/L Stan Woodward, F/S H Harding, F/O S F McCrae, Sgt John McClaren, W/O 'Rex' Greatorex, U/K, F/L C D Forrest, F/O A Featherstone. Front L to R: Ground crew, ground crew, Sgt Les Matthews, F/S Aubrey Ward *[C L Matthews]*.

With this major increase in bombing activity, involving considerably higher numbers of aircraft attacking together, the established system of uncoordinated squadrons or groups operating autonomously had to be improved. A major part of this change was a move away from random penetration of enemy defences by small formations of aircraft to, what came to be known as, the bomber stream – a single, very large, force of aircraft, stretching over many miles, and penetrating enemy air space at one point. This allowed for much better coordination of effort, more concentrated bombing and had the added advantage of the ability to swamp the Luftwaffe night-fighter radar screen, which at that time was still inhibited by a very restrictive area defence network usually referred to as the Kammhuber or Himmelbett system, which is described on page 28.

On the night of 30/31 May 1942, Harris launched the first 1,000-bomber raid on Cologne (a change of the intended target from Hamburg, due to bad weather). In the event 868 aircraft bombed the primary target, with a further fifteen attacking secondary targets for a loss of twenty-two from the main force. Harris conceived this as proof to both the Germans and Britain's allies, that Bomber Command had reached the point where it was able to begin inflicting severe damage on the enemy's ability to wage war, both by seriously impeding industrial production and by diverting substantial Luftwaffe resources to the defence of the homeland. These raids were considered to be successful in their primary objectives, even though a significant contribution was required from aircraft and crews at operational training units (OTUs) to make up the numbers. Sergeant (later flying officer) George Cook who, having survived thirty-three operations with 49 Squadron, was a staff instructor on Hampdens at 14 OTU Cottesmore, was among those called:

"After your tour of ops you were given, what they called, a rest period and I went to Cottesmore in 1942 as a screened instructor and safety wireless operator, still on Hampdens. While I was there, the 1,000-bomber raids were introduced, and they made us staff partake as well, so I went on the raid to Cologne and to Essen *[1 June]*. On the Essen trip, we were attacked by an Fw 190 night fighter, but fortunately he was a poor shot."

Eric Clarke also took part in this 1,000-bomber raid, by which time 49 Squadron had re-equipped with the Avro Manchester:

"On 30 May we were briefed for the raid on Cologne, but I do not remember any particular emphasis on the number except that some OTU crews would be taking part. 49 Squadron supplied thirteen Manchesters and 83 Squadron *[also at Scampton]* supplied twelve Lancasters. The raid was fully reported as a boost to morale and that we were now taking the war to the enemy.

"The report reads 'Manchester R5775 Pilot Officer Jeffreys. Took off 23:03, landed 04:57. Light and visibility excellent, no cloud. Load dropped on target and bursts seen. Successful in every respect.'

"I recollect that when we arrived at the target there were a great many fires and palls of smoke. Our bombing run seemed strangely devoid of flak, although there were many searchlights. Of those aircraft that failed to return, 49 Squadron lost two, its first Manchester casualties. The second 1,000-bomber raid (actually 956) took place on 2 June and the report reads 'Primary attacked from 9,000 feet at 02:03 on 40 degrees true. Light and visibility excellent, bombs seen to burst in target area and large fire started.' To me the raid seemed quite uneventful – 49 Squadron lost one Manchester. It turned out to be my last operation in the Manchester, and the squadron's last Manchester operation was on 25 June to Emden."

By this time research activity was focussed on improving bombing accuracy, since a very high percentage of bombs dropped were falling at a considerable distance from the intended target. A 1941 study revealed that only about 30% of bombers were finding their way to within five miles of the designated target. This was primarily due to the combined effects of darkness, very basic navigation aids and bad weather. To compound the problems, accurate meteorological forecasting was still in its infancy, as Lancaster pilot Squadron Leader (Sqn Ldr) Pete Langdon of 207 Squadron, Waddington recalled:

"On my first ten trips I was diverted six times. Every time you came back in '42, you were diverted. Everyone was, not just me, because we used to go off and the met men never really knew what the weather was going to do. When you eventually got out of the aircraft at your diversion airfield you never had anything you needed, and there was nowhere to get it from. Finally someone said that diversion kits were needed for these chaps. We then were issued kits which included a towel, bar of soap and a toothbrush – still pretty primitive."

Clearly work needed to be done to introduce navigation and bombing aids, and to improve existing expertise. The Pathfinder Force was activated within 8 Group on 15 August 1942. Their aim was to solve the navigational problems by establishing squadrons manned by experienced crews who flew ahead of the bomber stream and marked the targets with coloured parachute flares called target indicators (TIs). The Pathfinders were also the first to receive newly-developed navigation aids including GEE, Oboe and H2S.

Navigation & Bombing Aids

GEE

The GEE system (an extension of the code letter G for grid, since that is what the lines on a GEE chart resembled), was a British invention, developed by Telecommunications Research Establishment (TRE) at Malvern. It provided navigators with equipment to receive signals from two ground stations. These signals presented readings on a cathode ray tube display which were read off by the navigator and converted by the issued codes to plot the aircraft position on a special map with lattice lines related to the converted readings. It was a very accurate tool to enable the navigator to establish the aircraft's position, but was subject to heavy jamming by the Germans interrupting the radio signals from England. Certainly prior to the invasion of Europe the value of GEE was seriously diminished when flying over continental Europe, since its range was limited to about 300 miles for an aircraft flying at 10,000 feet, after which it began to deteriorate. The first operational use of GEE took place on the night of 8/9 March 1942.

Oboe

Oboe (known to the Germans as *Bumerang*) was a more accurate extension of the GEE principle and was first used by Mosquitoes of 109 Squadron from Marham, Norfolk, during an attack on a power station in Holland on the night of 20/21 December 1942. Developed by Frank Jones at the TRE and Alec Reeves at the Royal Aircraft Establishment (RAE), it was again based on signals from ground stations, and was so-named because the tone heard by receiving aircraft sounded like the musical instrument. With 'Oboe' the aircraft re-transmitted the signal back to England, which enabled its position and progress to be continuously monitored. The pilot received signals from one of the transmitting stations if he deviated from his intended track, and from the second station, which was measuring his ground speed, when he had reached the correct point for bomb release. As with GEE, the effective range was about 300 miles, and as the ground stations could only control one aircraft at a time, Oboe was mainly used by Pathfinder Force aircraft leading the main bomber stream. The effective range of Oboe increased after the Normandy invasion in June 1944, when transmitters could be erected on the continent.

G-H

Coming into operational use in December 1943, G-H was an advanced version combing elements of both GEE and Oboe, in which the bomber transmitted radio pulses to two ground stations which then sent them back to the aircraft. Measurement of the time gap between initial transmission and reception of the return signal allowed the navigator to direct the pilot and calculate the point of bomb release with considerable accuracy. Although 300 miles remained about the limit of its effectiveness, the fact that the controlling factor was with the bomber rather than the ground stations, meant that a number of aircraft – up to eighty with one pair of ground stations – could use the system at the same time. Warrant Officer Jack Bromfield was a wireless operator on 158 Squadron, flying Halifax aircraft from Lissett in Yorkshire in 1944-45:

"I don't remember exactly too much about G-H, but it was a system of marking, and one Lancaster would be equipped with it and three or four others would follow him. His accurate navigation under G-H was key; there was a camera fitted over the H2S screen, and when the leader dropped his those behind then dropped theirs."

H2S

The first use of an airborne ground-mapping radar system was known as H2S. It was put into service in January 1943, with the first attack using the system for blind-bombing taking place at Wilhelmshaven on the night of 11/12 February. The origin of the name is unclear, with different versions coming from people involved at the time. One claim is that it stood for 'Height to Slope', whilst another says 'Home Sweet Home'. Whatever the reason for the name, a large parabolic dish was mounted in a fairing beneath to map the surface and display the results on a cathode screen. With the ability to show the ground even during cloudy conditions, this was a major breakthrough for navigation accuracy, even though the display was not particularly clear, with coastlines, large rivers and major built-up areas showing up best. The drawback to H2S was the fact that as it was an active radar, its signal could be detected by the enemy which thus enabled night fighters to home in on it. Nevertheless, although it was at first fitted to Pathfinder aircraft only, the use of H2S rapidly became widespread throughout the main force.

Even as late as October 1944, H2S was still not without its problems, as a 4 Group letter[1] that month explained.

'In using the H2S set there is considerable difficulty in using the three controls, "Brilliance", "Focus" and "Gain", as the optimum picture depended on the setting of all three controls. In general navigation the method taught is to pick out a particular town and then turn down the 'Gain' until this town is easy to pick out with reference to the rest of the picture and the fixes are taken. The point is that no effort is made to use all three controls…for accurate mining or marking it may be important. It is suggested that in your report you deal fully with this problem and give a drill for the use of these three controls.'

During a raid on Cologne on the night of 2/3 February 1943, H2S-equipped Stirling R9264 MG-L of 7 Squadron from Waterbeach, flown by Sqn Ldr William Smith, was shot down by the night fighter of Oberleutnant Reinhold Knacke from Nachtjagdgeschwader (night fighter wing) NJG 1, and the Germans were able to capture the H2S set sufficiently intact to uncover its secrets. The Germans used the codeword Rotterdam for the equipment, since it was near there that the Stirling had come down; and as a result of this find, they developed the Funkgerät (W/T equipment) FuG 350 *Naxos* radar detector, a passive homer which allowed night fighters to recognise the H2S signal. It was developed during the summer of 1943, and entered service early the following year.

Defensive Aids

As the Luftwaffe defences increased in sophistication and effectiveness, Bomber Command responded with the introduction of a variety of defensive aids to help protect the bomber streams from fighter attacks.

Window

Probably the best known of all the anti-radar counter-measures employed by Bomber Command, Window was first used during the major raid on Hamburg that took place on the night of 24/25 July 1943. The basic principle was extremely simple; small metallic strips, (which could be varied in length to provide varying signal returns depending on the radar frequencies), were ejected in very large quantities from bombers to be picked up by German radar and interpreted as large numbers of aircraft, also confusing the German radar operators as to the true location of actual aircraft. About 2,000 strips would result in a radar-echo on the FuG 65 *Würzburg* radar replicating a heavy bomber. The results were instant, with a significant reduction in the bomber loss rate as enemy radars become increasingly blinded to Bomber Command's intentions. The United States Army Air Force's 8th Air Force, which used the name 'Chaff', first made use of Window on 22 December 1943 during daylight raids on Münster and Osnabrück.

There had, in fact, been lengthy debate over whether or not to use Window at all, since it was expected that as soon as the Germans started to pick up the strips on the ground they would realise what was happening and use the same idea on their own raids against Britain. The Germans did already have the technology, but had not used it for exactly the same reason. Harris argued that the use of Window would save lives, and it remained a major radar counter-measure for the rest of the war, although after a time it was known that skilled German radar operators, both on the ground and in the air, developed the ability to differentiate the Window returns from actual aircraft. Jack Bromfield:

"We threw out little strips like the tinsel we use at Christmas. Window came in two sorts, wide and narrow, and was contained in bundles wrapped in poor quality cardboard with a string pull attached. When you had to drop it, there was a hatch in the floor and you held the bundle in the opening, tugged hard on the string, which released it, and then shut the hatch quick, otherwise all the Window blew back inside! You had to have a piece of plywood or something to put over the hole, because if not it all came back in again. At one time it was dropped out of the flare 'chute I believe. Then it became apparent it was much easier for the wireless operator to drop it out. At time on target (TOT) minus one hour, we would start dropping it and we would often find strips of Window trapped in the engines after an op as there was so much of it flying about."

In addition to causing confusion amongst the night-fighter defences, Window also had a significant effect on anti-aircraft artillery. The system used searchlight beams to identify target aircraft which were then coned by other lights to provide supplementary target data for the radar-directed flak guns. With the introduction of Window a 4 Group report[2] on its effectiveness commented:

'The lateness of engagements on coned targets has been noticeable, especially compared with pre-Window operations when there was no waiting period once the cone was properly formed or even forming.

'This delay is probably attributable to the fact that the gunner does not now obtain any fire control data until the cone is properly formed. Previously the cone was supplementary to the gunnery data already possessed. Now the gunner has become dependent on the cone in the absence of other fire control equipment in action.'

Tinsel

This was a jamming device carried on each bomber and was first used on the night of 2/3 December 1942. A microphone was fitted in one of the engine nacelles in order to pick up engine noise, which the wireless operator then transmitted on the frequencies used by the German night-fighter controllers. Jack Bromfield explained how it was used.

"When we went to briefing for the night raid I went to the wireless briefing, and I was given a few kilocycles *[usually a band of 150 kilocycles]* on my dial to search. My job was to listen out for transmissions at set times, recalls, diversions, or any information. Normally you'd hear nothing, just a long dash and a time signal, and in between those ten-minute segments, you were given a section of the 1155 dial to search. Just backwards and forwards, only a few kilocycles, and one night I heard, *'Achtung Nachtjager, Achtung Nachtjager'*, and he was giving a course to the fighters to intercept the bomber stream – some of the crews said they had occasionally heard a female fighter controller. So I tuned my transmitter exactly to my receiver, pulled the switch and pressed my Morse key, and the transmitter was then connected to a carbon microphone in the right outer engine nacelle so that they couldn't hear us anymore. Then he would just get engine noises, so he would have to change frequency."

Fishpond

This was an extension of the H2S radar system, designed to give warning of night fighters approaching below the bomber, and it was intended to have an effective range of up to thirty miles. Jack Bromfield found it tricky to use due to its location in the WOp's compartment:

"It was downward looking only and the screen was divided into zones, so that aircraft returns would be reported as, for example, port quarter, quarter deep, or fine, depending on their angle of attack. I was kept very busy; the left eye watched the Fishpond screen, the right eye was on the TR1154 receiver scanning the frequency range I was given to search, plus looking after Window drops. Every night op I flew we encountered fighters, and when you got a return indicated on Fishpond, you pressed a button which brought up radius rings indicating the range from our aircraft from 300 to 900 yards. Any large returns that kept station with you were other bombers in the stream, but if you saw a smaller dot moving about relative to you, then you knew it was a night fighter. You would tell the crew, for example, 'WOp – contact Fishpond – port quarter deep – 1,000 yards'. After that it was up to the rest of the crew. Immediately, the tail gunner would turn his turret in that direction, while the mid-upper would turn the other way in case there was a second fighter. The trouble was that the fighters could home onto both Monica [*described below*] and H2S signals. You knew the night fighters were about when the tail gunner would come on the intercom and say 'the flak's stopped!', that really made every one nervous."

On 5 December 1944, 1 Group HQ sent a report to Bomber Command detailing an account of operational experience with Fishpond reported by 460 Squadron RAAF (which flew Lancasters from Binbrook in Lincolnshire), during an attack on Aschaffenburg.

'Fishpond switched on 19:35. Two blips picked up immediately, range 1,500 yards on port quarter flying parallel course to own aircraft. Both blips continued to follow for approximately six minutes. On turning to port for homeward journey, after bombing run, both blips closed in to 800 yards, one on port quarter, and the other on port beam. Both gunners were informed by WOps of positions and approximate distance.

'Port quarter blip, closed in to attack, rear gunner gave evasive tactics and visually identified aircraft as a [*Messerschmitt*] Me 110, at approximately 19:42. During evasive action, blip appeared again on screen, at 2,000 yards, on port quarter. Blip on port beam closed in to attack immediately behind port quarter attack. This aircraft was sighted and visually identified by both rear and mid-gunners as an Me 210.

'During these attacks bomber was in strong evasive action, but both attacks were broken off without enemy aircraft opening fire.

'At 19:43, approx, WOp picked up second blip again, near blip already seen on screen on fine port quarter at 1,200-1,500 yards. Owing to poor visibility, gunners could not see aircraft until they closed in to attack.

'On all attacks, Fishpond showed the blips closing in on the bomber. At 19:46, approx, attacks ceased, and no further contacts were reported by WOp, or sightings by gunners.

'WOp's reports Fishpond screen clear, and contacts easy to pick up and follow.'

Monica
Fitted to the extreme tail of Halifax and Lancaster aircraft, ARI 5664 Monica was an active radar operating on 300 MHz frequency to give warning of the approach of night

fighters from behind, and was introduced in 1942. It featured a double-dipole type aerial fitted to the back of the aircraft under the rear turret to give both visual (a blip on a screen) and oral signals when an aircraft was detected making a tail attack. Flying Officer John Elliott was a wireless operator on Lancaster-equipped 550 Squadron at North Killingholme in Yorkshire, and he described its use:

"Early Monica sets had two screens, one showing a vertical scale, and the other a horizontal scale, but later they were combined into one unit. Other bombers could easily be identified as large dots on the screen, whereas a fighter made rapid movements on the screen. The trouble was the fighters could home in on it too!"

A letter dated 8 August 1943[3] from 4 Group to Bomber Command HQ, outlined some of the operational issues being experienced with Monica, not least the difficulty of distinguishing between enemy fighters and other bombers.

'In this group the present use of Monica is at 600 yards range. On operations when the concentration is large there are still numerous "friendlies" and thus the crews are not taking violent evasive action immediately. Ideas vary considerably from pilot to pilot but the present general tendency is for a gentle evasive action to be started which will become more violent if the pips continue and it is not possible to secure a visual on a friendly bomber.

'I find that gunners tend to regard Monica as an aid to visual sighting and it is difficult to convince them that at times the visual range is very short.'

Another concern was the potential for Window to affect Monica, such that crews might not be able to distinguish between returns from their own Window and those from enemy aircraft. This was tested on 7 October 1943, using a 76 Squadron Halifax V DK151 (MP-Q) from its base at Holme-on-Spalding Moor, Yorkshire[4].

'Tests were made at a height of 10,300 feet, flying straight and level at an IAS *[indicated airspeed]* of 160 mph. Mr Lloyd sat in the bomb aimer's position and observed the wireless operator as he dropped the Window, using a stop watch to time the pips on the Monica screen. Plt Off Wilkinson was at the rear of the aircraft, and observed the Window through the rear under blister. He checked the times with another stop watch.

'In general there was a solid mass of pipping from 2.0 seconds to 5.0 seconds approximately, then a slight break for about 0.5 seconds, then a further mass pipping for about another 1.0 second, and a final two or three separate pips fading away. The last pip was usually between seven and eight seconds from the time of release.

'The pilot, Flt Sgt Fulgate, who is an experienced pilot having completed nineteen operational sorties, was most surprised, and stated that he had never heard anything approaching this amount of reaction. The rest of his crew confirmed this statement.

'Conclusion. As the set warmed up, resetting was necessary to keep the set operating at maximum efficiency. If a Monica set is working efficiently then Window may be expected to give continuous pipping for a period of at least three seconds.'

Boozer

Boozer was a further attempt to give warning of approaching night fighters and was first trialled by 7 Squadron at Waterbeach in November 1942. In this case, lights on the pilot's instrument panel would light up when the passive system detected that the aircraft was being tracked by radar, either the ground-based Würzburg, or airborne Lichtenstein radars, prompting the pilot to take evasive action until the light went out again. A later double-channel version was able to distinguish between Würzburg interception and Würzburg flak-control radar signals. However, the system was not very successful as it tended to trigger false alerts due to the increasingly large amount of various radar signals, both enemy and friendly, any one of which could trigger the lights to illuminate, and it was discovered that Boozer and Monica signals could interfere with each other. 'Boozer' Mk I was also ineffective at ranges above 1,500 yards and it was withdrawn in September 1944.

Airborne Cigar (ABC)

Cigar was a radio/telephony (R/T) jammer developed to block enemy night-fighter controllers' VHF radio transmissions to the aircraft. In order to extend the range, the first airborne use of the system, thus known as Airborne Cigar (ABC), was in 101 Squadron Lancasters flying from Ludford Magna in Lincolnshire; an eighth crew member – a German-speaking special operator – was responsible for monitoring frequencies and carrying out the jamming activity. The first use of ABC was on the night of 7/8 October 1943; it comprised a receiver and three transmitters combined into a Jostle transmitter, which enabled the frequency being used by the fighter controller for his running commentary to the night fighters to be identified and then jammed. The controller immediately knew and would then change frequency, so it became a cat and mouse game between the two, constantly switching frequencies. The first use of Cigar was on 22 September 1943 during a raid on Hannover. A further version of the system was developed to jam fighter-bomber controllers' communications to counteract the increasing numbers of intruder raids on south-east England; this system was known as Cigarette. From the spring of 1944, the US 8th Air Force also had German-speaking extra crew members in a small number of B-17s.

The enemy employed a variety of measures to counteract the effects of ABC. These included the use of female R/T operators, captured ABC transmitters, and the speeding up and shortening of R/T transmissions. Despite this, the use of ABC continued, and in March 1945, Halifax-equipped 462 Squadron RAAF, based at Foulsham in Norfolk took over the role from 101 Squadron, which had flown a total of 2,477 ABC sorties for the loss of seventy-seven aircraft.

RAF Air Intercept Squadrons

As early as 1940, the RAF had introduced airborne radar to detect enemy aircraft as a counter-measure to increasing Luftwaffe night raids. Initially fitted to night-fighter versions of the Blenheim light bomber, air interception radar AI Mk IV was an active system that detected aircraft by bouncing a radar signal off them. Trials during the summer of 1940 led to the first successful use of AI radar on the night of 22/23 July, when Fg Off Glynn Ashfield and his crew of a fighter interception unit Blenheim, flying from Tangmere in Sussex, brought down a Dornier Do 17Z of II./KG 3 piloted by Leutnant Kahlfuss, which came down in the sea off Brighton.

Sqn Ldr Michael Wainwright flew Blenheim IF night fighters with 64 Squadron from Church Fenton in Yorkshire, and found it to be less than satisfactory in the role:

"It wasn't meant to be a night fighter then, although we had radar in the back, AI gear it was called. All we had was four machine guns under the belly. Those were Mk I and we started to use Mk IV; it was a nice aeroplane but no bloody good for fighting a war. We used to do sweeps over the North Sea and when we found there was not much doing, we went in search of action if we had enough fuel, so we'd go from a place like Leconfield when we were at Church Fenton as that was nearer the coast, and fly to a place called Borkum, a German island in the North Sea. At Borkum the Germans had some biplane aeroplanes with the floats – seaplanes – and we'd go and shoot them up."

Recognition of the limitations of such a basic air intercept system led to the development of Serrate, which was introduced in Beaufighters in late 1943, and was a homing device capable of reading radar transmissions emanating from the enemy aircraft.

The idea was to use both systems together, with Serrate detecting the enemy at longer range, and then handing over to AI Mk IV for the final close-in and interception. Two cathode ray tubes were used by the operator to cover both systems, and they were switchable from one to the other as required. In order to avoid the possibility of confusing radar returns from friendly aircraft, an identification friend or foe (IFF) interrogator system was also carried.

The initial success of Serrate led to the establishment of three dedicated night-fighter squadrons: 141 at Wittering, Cambridgeshire; 157 at Castle Camps, Cambridgeshire, later moving to Predannack in Cornwall; and 169 at Little Snoring, Norfolk. All were progressively transferred to the newly-formed 100 Group from the end of 1943 by which time they were equipped with Mosquito NF II aircraft which, although of superior performance to the Beaufighter IIF, initially suffered from poor reliability, especially with the engines.

However, early in 1944 it was apparent that the Luftwaffe had become aware of the Serrate danger, as the number of radar transmissions being detected started to decline significantly. The Germans had developed a new radar, Lichtenstein SN2, operating on a different frequency band, embedded within the range used by their ground stations, a ruse which successfully confused the RAF fighters, which had difficulty identifying night-fighter signals among a host of other returns. In addition, the Germans had also managed to find an effective method of jamming the AI Mk IV radar.

As a matter of great urgency, the Mk IV version of Serrate was brought into service, which was able to home in on the SN2 radar. The system fitted to the Mosquito could now produce a high-pitched aural signal to the navigator, which filtered out the ground-based Funkmessgerät FuMG 401 Freya radar, as a series of dots and dashes that could be interpreted as an indication of a night-fighter's presence, direction and range. The fight was also being taken to the enemy, and Serrate Mosquitoes roaming around the night skies over Germany became an ever-increasing problem for the Luftwaffe.

The German Defences

When the war started there was effectively no organised Luftwaffe night-fighter force as it was not considered that there was any significant threat of air attack on either the German homeland or any of the occupied territories, and it was felt that any such attacks could easily be dealt with by anti-aircraft artillery. This situation changed rapidly as 1940 progressed and Bomber Command became increasingly active.

In the summer of that year Hptm Wolfgang 'Wolf' Falck submitted a report on the theory of night interception techniques to the Luftwaffe hierarchy. At that time he was based with Zerstörergeschwader (Heavy Fighter Wing) I./ZG 1, a Messerschmitt Me 110 unit at Aalborg in Denmark, and as a result of his report, he was ordered by Albert Kesselring, general field marshal of the Luftwaffe, to return with his unit to Düsseldorf and develop night-fighting tactics. Consequently, Major Falck has become known as the father of the Nachtjagd (night-fighter force) and he began his command of the first dedicated night-fighter unit NJG 1, on 26 June 1940. He led the unit for three years, during which time, in concert with general of the night fighters Josef Kammhuber, he was instrumental in developing the core tactics that were to stand the expanding NJG network in good stead for much of the remainder of the war[5].

As far as aircraft equipment was concerned, the Me 110 virtually chose itself. Having been designed and introduced into service as a long-range day fighter, it suffered a bad mauling at the hands of the RAF in particular, being no match for the opposing Hurricanes and Spitfires. However its availability in significant numbers made it an obvious choice to redeploy in the night role, where speed and manoeuvrability were less important than they were for day fighting. The other principal types pressed into early service with the NJG units were adaptations of the Dornier Do 217 and Junkers Ju 88 bombers, with the latter ultimately proving to be the most successful through almost constant upgrades. Hauptmann Heinz Rökker, who scored sixty-four victories with NJG2, certainly liked the Ju 88:

"I only had a short time flying the Me 110. I only claimed one shoot down with an Me 110, it was a Lancaster or Halifax in Berlin. I preferred the Ju 88; it was a very safe aeroplane. I think I could even fly it now!"

Hauptmann Peter Spoden, who scored twenty-four night-fighter victories with NJG 5 and NJG 6, had much the same opinion:

"I liked the Ju 88 more than the '110. Not all night-fighters preferred it however, and stayed with the '110. In my opinion, the Ju 88 had certain advantages; firstly, there were four in the cockpit and we all had contact. We could help each other when wounded, and were not separated like in the '110. Secondly, we had two radio operators, one for radar and one for navigation. With eight eyes you can see much more!

'The engine handling (one lever) was better than in the '110, and the Ju 88 was better with one engine out. The emergency exit, which was below, was better than the difficulty of jumping out in the '110. I moved to the '88 in early summer 1944 from Me 110 G-4 to Junkers 88 G-1, and later on G-4."

Nevertheless, the Me 110 remained a significant element of the Nachtjager until the final days of the war. Indeed, the highest scoring night-fighter ace of all, Major Heinz-Wolfgang Schnaufer scored every one of his 121 victories flying the Messerschmitt with NJG 1 and NJG 4.

The Himmelbett System

The so-called Himmelbett (variously interpreted as meaning sky-box or four-poster bed) system of night-fighter defences was established by the Luftwaffe to counteract the early Bomber Command strategy of random and uncoordinated penetration of German-controlled airspace by relatively small formations of bombers. Largely credited to Josef Kammhuber, the system has taken its common name from the fact that the defences were split into four main elements. Within each tight geographic area, or box, were located one Freya long-range radar to acquire the bombers, one (later two), Würzburg radar, one to track the incoming bombers and the second to control the night fighter, plus a number of radio direction finding (RDF) controlled searchlights (usually three) and the night fighter itself. The searchlights would illuminate the detected bomber in order to guide the night fighter in for an interception, although this was less effective in anything more than 6/10ths cloud cover, and the introduction of Lichtenstein airborne radar in the spring of 1942 gradually removed the need for searchlight illumination of targets.

The first Freya installation identified by the photographic reconnaissance unit (PRU) at RAF Benson, Oxfordshire, was spotted late in 1940 at Cap de la Hague on the Cherbourg peninsula, and by May 1941 sufficient information had been gathered to identify a German early-warning system that extended from the West Frisian Islands to Brest and could even be continuous from Denmark to the Spanish border. Each *Freya* radar was estimated to have an effective range of up to 100 miles for an aircraft flying at 5,000 feet. At about the same time, further radar installations were detected both along the coast and inland, and these turned out to be for Würzburg.

The fighters were required to patrol and attack only within their designated Himmelbett box, with three or four boxes combining under the operational control of a Nacht Jagd Raum Führer (NJRF – night fighter control room), who had control of the operational night-fighter gruppen. Although this system was initially fairly effective, it lacked depth, as once the fighter belt had been penetrated there were few control mechanisms further into German airspace. An increase in depth was therefore made, with additional sites in front and behind the original boxes, and equipment was upgraded to allow the simultaneous control of two night fighters. Himmelbett was known to the allies as 'The Kammhuber Line', and Heinz Rökker had considerable experience of the system:

"With Himmelbett, fighters were led to the enemy by radar from the ground; all over the coast. It was the idea and work of Kammhuber. When the big bomber stream came it was not very effective because it was only a little piece of equipment on the ground that led you to one fighter. Then when Window was dropped you could not follow the fighter to the target as it was overwhelmed."

As Harris developed the Bomber Command tactics to incorporate larger bomber streams, these soon flooded the Himmelbett system. Matters came to a head with the major raid on Hannover in July 1943, when night-fighter crews could clearly see they were out of position but were refused permission to leave their designated patrol areas to attack bombers within their visual range. Peter Spoden flew that night:

"I was patrolling in the area codenamed Reiher (Heron) to the east of Lübeck. We could see the target burning, a huge red glow in the sky, although Hamburg was 100 kilometres away. All our radars were being heavily jammed; there were flickering signals everywhere, but no readable echoes, so the fighter controller could not find a target for me. We begged our controller to allow us to leave our area; I told them I could see many bombers and I could get them, but we were refused. The controller said 'No, that is outside my area, that is a flak area'. We had to stay where we were and watch the terrible bombing. I was not allowed to go for them; I should have simply disobeyed the order. I landed at Parchim completely exhausted."

This single attack caused huge consternation in the German hierarchy and a radical rethink of defensive tactics. A new solution was demanded, and the urgency was further enhanced by the onset of effective jamming of both Freya and Würzburg, supported by Tinsel and ground-based Cigar against R/T communication.

Before the Hannover raid, the Luftwaffe had been considering the use of single-engined fighters, freed from restrictive ground control, against the bomber stream, and the onset of Window accelerated this idea. Peter Spoden:

"A highly-experienced officer and excellent bomber pilot, Hajo Herrmann [Oberst Hans-Joachim 'Hajo' Herrmann], the sort of old campaigner that wars have produced since the dawn of time, had advised Göring and the senior echelons of the Luftwaffe that in addition to the twin-engined night fighters, singled-engined Me 109s and Fw 190s should go into action above the burning targets. This then, was Wilde Sau (Wild Boar) and Zahma Sau (Tame Boar), which often enough put the fear of death into us twin-engine men by their pilots' wild manoeuvring. Both systems would cause the RAF great trouble during the next months."

With Wilde Sau, each aircraft operated autonomously within the target area, and were given a running commentary on the raid situation from central operational HQ. Specialist Wilde Sau units were formed, including Jagdgeschwader JG 300, JG 301 and JG 302, using a mixed fleet of Fw 190 A and Bf 109 G aircraft, and arrangements were made to restrict flak batteries to certain maximum altitudes to avoid the risk of the fighters being shot down by their own side. It was highly effective during the late summer of 1943, but became less so with the onset of winter and bad weather conditions. It also relied heavily on the controllers' ability to identify the intended main force target in good time, so an obvious counter-measure swiftly adopted by the RAF, was to conduct simultaneous decoy raids against a number of potential targets to cause as much confusion as possible about which the actual target was.

Zahme Sau took the idea a stage further and allowed the freeing up of twin-engined night fighters to leave their boxes and engage in long-range pursuit of bomber targets. It took some time for crews to acclimatise to their new found freedom, but once they did, they found the running commentary system aided them considerably, and increasing success ensued. Large numbers of night fighters (up to fifty-five could be controlled centrally at any one time) were scrambled and told to orbit navigation beacons while the bomber stream's target was identified. Jack Bromfield recalled how his crew saw the night fighters operating:

"The fighters mostly worked in pairs and used the 'Wild Boar' system of fighters operating independently but in areas indicated to them to await the bomber stream. They usually waited 2,000 feet above the highest bomber in the stream. The fighters attacked us once when flak was still coming up, so whether the Germans had a communications breakdown I don't know. Their tracer was all red and much closer together than ours. We used alternate tracer, ball, incendiary and armour piercing in our ammunition, but I don't think the Germans used ball rounds in theirs.

"The Germans used visual means of identifying our location for the Wild Boar aircraft, such as a radar-directed searchlight which was bright blue. If it caught an aircraft it would stay on it until the normal white searchlights had picked it up, then move off and look for another one. The blue one was for the fighters to follow.

"With their Schräge Musik (slanting or Jazz music) upward-firing cannons they attacked us from underneath of course. Otherwise, they would approach at your level from about 45 degrees off the beam, lay on their deflection, and then breakaway underneath, because they knew we had no defensive armament there. Sometimes you might only see his exhaust. If it was daylight, whoever saw him would count down his range in yards, '900 – 800 – 700 – 600 – 500 go!' Our aircraft would then break away hard, as the effective range of our Browning 303s was only 400 yards."

The RAF's response to the new tactics included more jamming of radars and voice communication, but it also introduced Corona, a system also referred to as the 'ghost controller', whereby fluent German speakers would transmit misdirections to the night fighters to mislead them about the bomber stream's intended target. First used during a raid on Kassel on the night of 22/23 October 1943, contradicting broadcasts had to be handled very carefully to avoid unintentionally giving away the true location of the intended target, and with changes to VHF transmissions and control of night fighters by individual units rather than centrally through NJRF, the effect of Corona declined quite rapidly and was of little use beyond the spring of 1944.

Other anti-jamming measures adopted by the Luftwaffe included the Anna Marie programme, named after the German forces radio station in Stuttgart. Music programmes broadcast during the evenings began playing music related to the suspected Bomber Command target areas, for example if the target was thought to be Munich, Bavarian folk music would be broadcast.

Luftwaffe Radar & Counter-measure Advances

By late 1943 Germany had started to counter the effect of Window and electronic jamming by providing Würzburg radars with a second frequency band, adding a third a year later. At the same time, a Wismar adapter was provided to facilitate quicker frequency changes as jamming was encountered. This enabled frequencies of up to 100 Mhz to be used, which required five-metre lengths of Window suspended under a small parachute in order to fully maintain its effectiveness. This was produced under the codename Rope, but its weight and bulk were a major drawback to its use, which was limited to a small number of squadrons and operations.

Other ground-based jammers were introduced to counter navigation and bombing aids. GEE was jammed by Heinrich transmitters, and Oboe by Anti-Bumerang D which transmitted false pulses to the aircraft which were then repeated to the ground station to destroy accurate navigation. The H2S ground-mapping radar was countered by Roderich transmitters, which were capable of blanking out H2S screens in the bombers at a distance of forty kilometres, although it is not clear to what extent this system was introduced[6].

On 13 July 1944, Junkers Ju 88 G-1 Wnr.712273 4R-UR belonging to III./NJG 2 based at Twente in Holland, landed at the emergency landing ground at Woodbridge in Suffolk. The pilot Obergefreiter John Maeckle, had become lost and running low on fuel, had little option but to land at the first airfield he saw. The aircraft was an absolute gift to British understanding of the latest German technology, as it was equipped with three types of radar; FuG 220 Lichtenstein SN2 airborne interception search radar, plus FuG 227 Flensburg and FuG 350 Naxos radar-warning receivers, the last two of which were previously unknown. The aircraft was flown on evaluation exercises by pilots from the wireless and electrical flight at RAE Farnborough, and it was discovered that FuG 227 honed in on signals transmitted from a bomber's H2S set, and FuG 350 recognised Monica signals. As a result, Bomber Command tactics were immediately altered, minimising the use of H2S to what was absolutely essential, and stopping the use of Monica altogether.

On 31 August 1944 John Elliott and the rest of Flight Lieutenant Jim Lord's crew flew a fighter-affiliation exercise against this same Ju 88.

"We carried out a practice exercise, testing radar equipment, with a captured Ju 88. We were flying in another of those very rare birds which were to go on to complete over 100 sorties, in this case B-Baker 'Phantom of the Ruhr' [EE139 BQ-B]. As soon as I switched on my Monica set, the Ju 88 knew where we were, so we had to switch it off again."

The Formation of 100 Group

An analysis of Bomber Command losses carried out in August 1942, came to the conclusion that an effective system of RCM could reduce the loss rate by between 30% and 60%, and recommended the urgent development of both counter-measures to be used by bombers in the target area and for airborne interception. A subsequent meeting at Bomber Command HQ at High Wycombe, Buckinghamshire, on 6 October 1942, endorsed the recommendations, specifically targeting action against Freya and Würzburg radars. Throughout the following year, it became evident that such specialist operations needed to be flown by dedicated and suitably-equipped squadrons operating under a separate control structure from the main force.

Matters came to a head in August 1943, when Harris sent a letter to the Air Ministry contending that a concentrated effort to disorganise the German defences was an essential requirement to enable further weakening of the enemy. He proposed three key elements to achieve this objective: RAF night-fighter operations; bombing intruder operations; and RCM against the German R/T system. He went on to propose that all three needed to come under the umbrella of a dedicated Bomber Command group, and that the operation of specialised jamming devices should be carried in a small number of aircraft capable of barrage jamming the entire German defensive system.

As a result of this proposal, a conference was held at the Air Ministry on 29 September 1943, attended by senior RAF and USAAF personnel[7], and it was decided that:

1. The proposed dedicated organisation should be established.
2. Fighter Command intruder squadrons and other established units should be transferred to the new organisation.
3. A development unit should be established to continue research work on RCM.
4. The new organisation should carry out both air and ground jamming.
5. The new organisation should be under the operational control of Bomber Command, and the technical control of the Air Ministry.
6. The USAAF should be asked to supply a number of B-17 Fortress aircraft for development work and commencement of operations.

The authority to set up the new organisation was issued on 28 October 1943 by the secretary of state for air, and on 8 November instructions to form 100 Group were issued. Temporarily, the group was to form at West Raynham, Norfolk prior to moving to permanent accommodation at Bylaugh Hall, East Dereham, Norfolk, which at that time was occupied by 2 Group, 2nd Tactical Air Force. Ten days later, the new group absorbed 80 Wing into its structure and Air Commodore Addison was appointed as its first commanding officer. Existing units which were transferred to the new group were[8]:

141 Squadron, West Raynham, Norfolk. Mosquito II.
169 Squadron, Little Snoring, Norfolk. Mosquito II.
192 Squadron, Foulsham, Norfolk. Halifax V, Mosquito IV, Wellington X.
239 Squadron, West Raynham, Norfolk. Mosquito II.

515 Squadron, Little Snoring, Norfolk. Beaufighter IIf, re-equipping with Mosquito II.
1473 Flight, Little Snoring, Norfolk. Anson, Mosquito, Wellington.
1692 (Radio Development) Flight, Drem, East Lothian. Beaufighter IIf, Mosquito II.

The request for B-17 Fortress aircraft for new 100 Group units was based on the premise that there would be two such squadrons, one RAF (214) and one USAAF, each with an establishment of twelve aircraft plus two reserves. Among the reasons for selecting the Fortress was its ability to carry an H2S set in the nose position, normally occupied by the chin turret, and room to fit a Jostle jamming transmitter. 214 Squadron was formed at Sculthorpe, Norfolk, and by early February 1944 thirteen aircraft had been received from USAAF stocks.

The specific roles of 100 Group were defined in a Bomber Command directive issued on 21 March 1944 as follows:

(a) To give direct support to night bombing or other operations by attack of enemy night-fighter aircraft in the air, or by attack of ground installations.
(b) To employ airborne and ground RCM apparatus to deceive or jam enemy radio-navigational aids, enemy radar systems and certain wireless signals.
(c) To examine all intelligence on the offensive and defensive radar, radio navigation, and signalling systems of the enemy, with a view to future action within the scope of (a) and (b).
(d) From the examination of this intelligence, to plan for use in future operations means of disorganising the enemy offensive and defensive radio systems.
(e) To provide immediate information, additional to normal intelligence information, as to movements and employment of enemy fighter aircraft to enable tactics of the bomber force to be immediately modified to meet any changes.[9]

The group was not only unique in its blending of both bomber and fighter aircraft operating units under the same operational control, but also by having control of a USAAF unit, 803 Bombardment Squadron (which became 36 Bombardment Squadron) equipped with B-24 Liberators, a type which was to play the major role in the Bomber Support RCM operations described in the chapters that follow.

Notes:
1. The National Archive: Air 14/3229 ORS General Correspondence 4 Group
2. Ibid
3. Ibid
4. Ibid
5. *Gefechtsstand of Jägdabschnittsführer Dänemark.* Colonel Michael 'Ses' Svejgaard www.gyges.dk
6. Ibid
7. *The Second World War 1939-1945 Royal Air Force, Signals Volume VII Radio Counter-Measures.* Air Ministry 1950, reprinted by MLRS 2011
8. Ibid
9. Ibid

CHAPTER TWO

The Early Days of 100 Group

Air Commodore (Air Cdre) Addison faced a heavy workload as he stepped up to command the newly-formed group. 'Cometh the hour cometh the man'; a very true saying in Addison's case. Born on 4 October 1898 he joined the RFC for service in 1917 leading to a commission in the newly formed RAF on 22 July 1918. Trained as a pilot he was selected to study for a degree at Cambridge University in the early post-war years, and later attended the RAF specialist signals course. In the inter-war period he saw service in India and the Far East. A wing commander at the outbreak of WWII, his specialist signals background made him an obvious choice for the newly-formed RCM branch set up in the Air Ministry in 1940. When 80 Wing was formed as a result of the 'Battle of the Beams' on 4 September 1940 Addison was appointed to command. 1942 saw him return to the Air Ministry as a group captain eventually becoming director of signals. He now faced his greatest challenge: to form the new group and develop the tactics required to minimise Bomber Command's losses in the growing war of attrition with the German air defences. Fortunately for the RAF Addison grew with both the responsibility of command and the developments in technology that his new post demanded.

He was initially hampered by the diverting battle to establish his new HQ. It had been decided that 100 Group HQ should occupy Bylaugh Hall in Norfolk in close proximity to the airfields allocated to it. Unfortunately, the existing occupiers, 2 Group, 2nd Tactical Air Force, under the legendary Air Vice-Marshal (AVM) Basil Embry were somewhat tardy in moving to their own new location at Mongewell Park, Wallingford, in Berkshire. Addison suffered the handicap of establishing a temporary HQ at RAF West Raynham in December 1943, before finally making the move to Bylaugh Hall on 8 January. He could now concentrate on agreeing and defining the operational tactics for the new group, and equipping and organising his allotted squadrons. He brought with him his already experienced 192 Squadron from 80 Wing. 192 based at RAF Foulsham was to be one of his largest squadrons, absorbing 1473 Flight to become a three-flight unit equipped initially with Wellington X, Halifax III and Mosquito B IV aircraft. Their role would continue to be electronic intelligence (ELINT) and would now include jamming operations with the Window force. [*The activities of the Window force will be covered later.*]

There were to be two main elements of the group. The heavy squadrons which would form the Window and Mandrel (a device for jamming Freya radar) forces and carry the heavy-jamming equipment, and ultimately a total of seven Mosquito squadrons for intruder operations. The latter would provide high-level bomber escort cover with and around main force, and low level operations to patrol around German night-fighter bases and night-fighter marshalling beacons. An Order of Battle for 100 Group is shown at Appendix One.

With the heavy elements, the first units to join the group after 192 Squadron were 214 (Federated Malay States) Squadron and 803 Bombardment Squadron (BS) of the USAAF. 214 Squadron had its origins in the Royal Naval Air Service (RNAS) in the Great War. It had been originally formed at Coudekerque in France as 14 Squadron on 9 December 1917 and operated as a heavy-bomber unit equipped with Handley Page 0/100 and 0/400 aircraft. On the formation of the RAF on 1 April 1918 it was renumbered 214 Squadron and was disbanded on 1 February 1920. With the threat of remilitarisation in Germany 214 Squadron was reformed at Boscombe Down on 16 September 1935 with the venerable Vickers Virginia Mk 10 'heavy' bomber. It eventually went to war with Vickers Wellingtons serving in 3 Group of Bomber Command, re-equipping with Short Stirlings in April 1942.

After distinguished service with 3 Group, 214 was one of the assets transferred to form 100 Group, where it was scheduled to re-equip with the Boeing B-17 Fortress, arriving at RAF Sculthorpe, Norfolk, in January 1944. The Fortress had been selected for 214 Squadron's new role because of its ability to fly at higher altitudes than its RAF heavy-bomber counterparts. The design of its vertical-style bomb bay would enable it to carry one of the proposed large jamming transmitter units, Jostle IV, which could not be accommodated in British bombers. As described in Chapter 1 the USAAF and the Air Ministry had agreed to the provision of two Fortress squadrons for operations in 100 Group in the RCM role, the provision of the aircraft and the associated attrition reserves to be shared between the two air forces. The establishment of the American squadron was approved by Washington in December 1943. However, problems arose in equipping the proposed British squadron. The RAF only had two squadrons, both in Coastal Command, equipped with Fortress aircraft. The aircraft required for the 100 Group squadron would have to come from the future allocation of Fortress aircraft scheduled for delivery during 1944.

The urgency to get the two RCM Fortress units in operation as soon as possible prompted a request from the British for an allocation from existing USAAF stocks to be replenished later from the RAF's 1944 deliveries. Although the Americans agreed to the request there were further problems. The initial deliveries to 214 were B-17G models which featured a chin turret which was the only practical location for the H2S blind bombing and navigational aid, and so these aircraft had to be exchanged for Fortress II or B-17F models. Ironically, the squadron was to re-equip with the B-17G (Fortress III) models anyway as they eventually received further aircraft from the RAF Boeing production line, the B-17F (Fortress II) model production having finished. It is assumed that the later aircraft rolled off the Boeing line with the chin turret deleted, allowing the H2S radar and scanner fit to be completed at the Scottish Aviation plant at Prestwick in Scotland, prior to delivery to the squadron. Scottish Aviation provided engineering support for Fortress aircraft models in RAF service in the UK.

With the arrival of the Fortress II the urgently required conversion of crews commenced. The change from Stirlings to Fortresses generated a requirement for larger crews. The basic crew of pilot, air bomber, navigator, flight engineer, wireless operator and two air gunners would require two extra gunners and a special operator to man the jamming equipment, making ten in all. The squadron's commanding officer (CO), Wg Cdr Desmond J McGlinn remained in charge into the Fortress era. Some of the aircraft were used for conversion training and the remaining aircraft were fitted out with the initially agreed RCM and operationally required kit. The initial RCM standard included ABC communications jamming equipment as an interim fit. This equipment was designed to jam German defensive radio/telegraphy transmissions in the 38-42 megacycles/sec (Mc/s) frequency band. As has already been described, this equipment had been employed in 5 Group's 101 Squadron Lancasters to overcome the declining effectiveness of the earlier jamming device, Tinsel, employed by Bomber Command. The 214 Squadron aircraft would also be fitted with Monica III tail-warning radar to notify crews that their aircraft had been 'painted' or picked up by an enemy night fighter. A GEE navigation aid was included in the standard fit.

803 BS was the American element of the proposed RAF/USAAF RCM Fortress-equipped force. The initial element, of what would become 803, comprising a number of aircrew and ground engineers were posted from USAAF 8th Air Force units for detached service with the RAF at Sculthorpe, arriving on 17 January 1944. This small number under the command of Capt G E Paris initially provided much needed assistance to 214 Squadron to ease conversion of aircrew to the B-17, and to give similar training and guidance to the ground crew. On 2 March this nucleus was incorporated in the formation of the USAAF RCM Fortress unit designated 803 Heavy Bombardment Squadron under the command of Lt Col Clayton A Scott with Capt Paris assuming the position of squadron executive officer. Six crews and their B-17G aircraft were detached in from the 96th BS at Snetterton Heath, Norfolk, where they had been employed on RCM duties starting in the previous month. Serious preparation now began to work up the squadron in its RCM role for joint or individual operations in support of RAF Bomber Command and the USAAF 8th Air Force as directed. The requirement to support Bomber Command operations posed an additional challenge for the American crews as they were now required to train for night operations. This requirement also involved modifications to the B-17s including the fitting of flame dampers to the engine turbocharger exhausts to minimise the giveaway to night fighters, and changes to subdue cockpit lighting. The squadron's aircraft were equipped with Mandrel, and in some cases, Carpet jamming transmitters. To assist in the conversion of 214 Squadron crews to their new aircraft type 1699 (Fortress Training) Flight was established at Sculthorpe with an establishment of three Fortress aircraft.

199 Squadron, another 3 Group Stirling III unit, transferred to 100 Group in May to operate from North Creake and be equipped with Mandrel. The Stirling's operational limitations were well known and 199 would eventually replace the type with the Halifax III in February 1945. The squadron would be joined in September by 171 Squadron with Mandrel-equipped Halifax III aircraft. Mandrel was developed by TRE and was used by the two squadrons to jam the German early-warning radars.

May also saw the move of the two Fortress units, and 1699 Flight, to Oulton. They were accompanied by the Sculthorpe station commander, Gp Capt T C Dickens. Dickens, a pre-war regular RAF officer had commanded 103 Squadron equipped with Fairey Battle aircraft in the disastrous days of the Battle of France in 1940. A popular and well-respected man, Dickens was to prove an ideal commander of an operational airfield with acknowledged attention for the welfare of his personnel which ensured a happy station and excellent relations with the USAAF squadron. Not long after their arrival at Oulton the two squadrons became operational. 214 Squadron was the first to do battle dispatching four aircraft in support of Bomber Command operations against targets in France in the build up to the D-Day invasion. This culminated in flying intense Window sorties over the English Channel in a successful attempt to confuse German radar and mask the presence of large numbers of troop-carrying and other aircraft on route to Normandy. Operations using small numbers of aircraft continued through the summer months, but not without cost. Pilot Officer A J N Hockley RAAF, in Fortress SR384, failed to return from a main force attack on Antwerp on the night of 24/25 May, the squadron's first casualty in their new role. The squadron was to lose sixteen aircraft on operations by the end of hostilities.

Meanwhile 803 BS were to break their operational duck on 3 June by flying a single B-17F, 42-3518, escorted by no fewer than twelve P-51 Mustangs, on a daylight monitoring of British ground radar stations while flying in Belgian airspace. Night-time Mandrel sorties with four aircraft followed on 5 June, the eve of D-Day. The task was to create an electronic screen to blind the German long-range Freya early warning radars. They were supported in this task by eighteen aircraft from 199 Squadron from 100 Group. The screen would be achieved by adjacent pairs of aircraft flying a race track pattern with individual aircraft being located at opposite positions on the race track.

A major change for the squadron occurred in July following a USAAF decision that the B-24 Liberator was a better platform for RCM operations. This decision was probably influenced by the greater capacity of the B-24's bomb bay for the carriage of the special equipment and associated operator. It is also suggested that the Fortress was favoured by the USAAF for European theatre operations, and as such the B-24 became available as 8th Air Force squadrons converted to the B-17. The first sortie with the B-24 was flown on 12 July with conversion being completed by the end of the month.

Royal Air Force Oulton

RAF Oulton opened as a grass airfield satellite for nearby RAF Horsham St.Faith on 31 July 1940 in 2 Group Bomber Command. The airfield, which had taken up land occupied by three farms, lay on the edge of the small hamlet of Oulton Street on the Cawston Road. In September 1943, the road was cut by the main east-west (29/11) runway and was closed for the duration of the war. The airfield passed briefly under the control of 3 Group before undergoing major works to create a Class A bomber station with three hard runways, four T2 hangars, and a new bomb store site, together with supporting technical, administration and domestic buildings. The domestic accommodation was located on three dispersed sites together with officer, SNCO and WAAF accommodation in the grounds of the nearby Blickling Hall.

On completion in February 1944 the airfield was reallocated to the newly formed 100 Group. 214 (Bomber Support) Squadron was the first flying unit to arrive at the newly revamped station from RAF Sculthorpe in mid May together with 1699 Flight. The squadron would initially occupy the northern spectacle dispersals with 1699 Flight using the north western (see airfield plan on page 55). 214 Squadron were joined in very short order by 803 BS. 803's time at Oulton was destined to be brief. In July the unit had been joined by a detachment from 858 BS, and further reorganisation took place in August when 803 and the 858 detachment were officially disbanded and, together with the 856 BS from North Pickenham, Norfolk, were amalgamated to form 36 BS RCM. The new unit formed at Cheddington in Buckinghamshire when all personnel and aircraft started assembling on 14 August, assisted in setting up by RAF personnel from Oulton. Despite its new designation 36 would continue to operate in support of Bomber Command until January 1945. During that time, the unit had an aircraft establishment of thirty-six Liberators, all fitted with Jostle IV equipment, and suffered the following five aircraft losses[1]:

10 November 1944, B-24J 42-51226 R4-L crashed following an engine fire near Boucly, France; Lt Joseph Hornsby.

15 November 1944, B-24H 42-51219 R4-I crashed immediately after take-off on a Mandrel mission; Lt Norman Landberg.

22 November 1944, B-24J 42-51232 R4-J 'The Jigs Up' abandoned out of fuel three miles south west of Valley, Anglesey, during a diversion; Lt Harold Boehm.

5 February 1945, B-24J 42-51239 R4-C 'The Uninvited' failed to return from an RCM patrol over the North Sea; Lt John McKibben. Although there were no 8th Air Force or Bomber Command main force operations that day, German records show that a night-fighter crew claimed a victory over an unidentified aircraft, possibly of RAF Coastal Command, in the waters between Denmark and Norway[2]. Given the general location and the fact that Coastal Command also operated Liberators, it is possible that this was in fact Lt McKibben's aircraft.

19 February 1945, B-24H 42-50385 R4-H 'Beast of Bourbon' crashed near Cheddington shortly after take-off on a training flight due to instrument failure in poor weather; Lt Louis McCarthy.

Notes:
1. *Secret Squadrons of the Eighth* Pat Carthy, Ian Allan 1990.
2. *Nachtjagd War Diaries* Dr Theo E W Boiten & Roderick J Mackenzie. Red Kite Books 2009.

CHAPTER THREE

223 (Bomber Support) Squadron

The next heavy aircraft squadron to form in 100 Group was 223 (Bomber Support) Squadron. Like its sister squadron at Oulton, 223 had started life as a RNAS unit in the Great War. Details are sparse but the squadron had its origins in B Squadron of 2 Wing RNAS when it was renumbered 223 Squadron at Stavros in the Aegean on 18 September 1918 under Major A B Gaskell DSC and is believed to have operated de Havilland DH 4, DH 9 and DH 9a aircraft until it disbanded at Mudros on 21 May 1919. It reformed in December 1936 at Nairobi, Kenya, initially equipped with Fairey Gordons which were to be replaced in fairly short order by Vickers Vincents. The squadron remained in Kenya until just before the outbreak of WWII when it moved to the Sudan by which time it had re-equipped with the Vickers Wellesley, which it used in the East African campaign. It remained in the Sudan until April 1941 when it moved north to Shandur in Egypt. It then spent a year in a secondary role operating as a temporary OTU converting crews to the Martin Maryland for the Desert Air Force.

223 Squadron then resumed operations in April 1942 flying Martin Marylands supplemented later with Martin Baltimores together with Douglas Bostons. It then joined the North African campaign operating these types and established a fine reputation continuing into the Sicilian and Italian era. On 12 August 1944 the unit was renumbered as 30 (South African Air Force) Squadron. The squadron's number plate finally made it to the UK for the first time on 23 August when it was allocated to a new squadron forming in 100 Group at RAF Oulton.

The expansion of 100 Group heavy squadrons by the addition of 223 was given added urgency from intelligence that suggested that Germany's V2 rocket-powered weapon was fitted with a radio-guidance system. This intelligence resulted from examination of the remains of a rocket, believed to be a V2, discovered in Sweden and made available to the allies. The examination revealed that the debris contained elements of a receiver-transmitter and other items that could possibly be used for radio control. Eventually, this proved to be incorrect and it is believed that the rocket in question was a test vehicle being used to test items for the Wasserfall anti-aircraft missile. However, the possibility that the V2 was radio controlled generated significant and urgent action to investigate and prepare counter-measures. 192 Squadron therefore flew sorties to try and identify and clarify further intelligence on the controlling frequencies.

Additionally, 214 Squadron which was in the process of being equipped with the Jostle IV transmitter to provide jamming of the Luftwaffe ground control interception HF and

VHF frequencies, was tasked with an additional role in the investigation. These ops were given the codename Big Ben. The squadron's Jostle system was quickly modified to enable a special operator to detect any frequencies in the likely V2 controlling band then back-tune the powerful Jostle transmitter to the detected frequency. This modification involved installation of a receiver, indicator signal modulator and oscillator. The mod was also designed to include an ABC panoramic receiver to allow the later universal Jostle to be used for spot jamming as well as barrage jamming of frequencies. In Martin Streetly's book *Confound and Destroy*[1] he records that in service Jostle appeared to be referred to as Jostle IV when used for spot jamming, and as VHF Jostle when used for barrage jamming. This raises the question, what were Jostle I, II and III used for? It is assumed that they were a family of communications jammers, but only references to Jostle II and IV seem to exist. Jostle II was designed in 1941 for jamming enemy tank communications in the 38 to 30 Mc/s VHF band. Installed in Wellingtons of 109 Squadron, they were operated in the Middle East with some success.

The introduction of 223 was therefore given extra urgency and the Air Ministry authorised the formation of 223 (Bomber Support) Squadron with effect from 23 August 1944. The unit was to be equipped with the Consolidated B-24 Liberator supplied from the USAAF 8th Air Force in UK. It is interesting to speculate why it was the B-24, and not the B-17 already in service with its sister squadron at Oulton. Logic would point to the obvious logistic and operational advantages of standardising on one type – so why not? In the authors' opinion the problem of supply of B-17 aircraft experienced in the setting up of 214 was probably a strong factor. It would also appear likely that Bomber Command and 100 Group were strongly influenced by the USAAF's recent decision that the B-24 was the better platform for the RCM role. Certainly, there was a strong bond of co-operation between the RAF and the USAAF during this early period of RCM development.

The aircraft provided by the USAAF were B-24H and J types from various model blocks and built by a variety of American aircraft firms; a full breakdown of the twenty-eight aircraft supplied to 223 and 1699 Flt is included at Appendix 4. There has been quite a lot of confusion over the years concerning the RAF mark that has been quoted in various published sources. It is most likely that this originated from reference to the aircraft movement cards (Air Ministry Form 78). The clerk maintaining the cards for 223 Squadron's aircraft seems to have had his own difficulties with identifying the correct mark with inconsistent usage of Mark IV and Mark VI. Most sources seem to have accepted that Mark VI is the correct designation to cover both H and J models. However, the authors believe this was initially incorrect having discovered the following statement in a note of action dated 22 August 1944 on file at the National Archives which reads:

'Whilst at Air Ministry on 21/8/44, I made enquiries regarding the proposal to form a new Liberator squadron in 100 Group. W/Cdr Jasper, (O.A.3) was, however, unable to give me any very definite information other than the fact that it will form to an establishment of 16 U.E. Liberators with either Mark VI (J) or Mark IV (H) aircraft.

'The squadron will be known as 223 (B.S.) Squadron, and the Servicing Echelon, 9223 will form concurrently.

'No definite information could be given regarding the provision of training aircraft, but the possibility of initially obtaining crews from Coastal Command was mentioned. This is at present under investigation, but so far, very little headway regarding this matter appears to have been made.'

This minute was written by the wing commander (organisation) 3 Bomber Command to Air Commodore T Fawdry, his senior equipment staff officer. Apart from clarifying the correct mark designation for the two Liberator models, it indicates how quickly things were moving as this was just the day before 223 Squadron was authorised to reform at RAF Oulton.

There is little variation between the H and J models, the only obvious external differences being the nose-wheel doors which extend outside the airframe on the H variant when the nose wheel is lowered, and it is believed that some H models featured enclosed waist positions. What became clear very early when the aircraft began to arrive from Prestwick was that they had seen considerable operational service. Flying Officer Ron Johnson recalls the comment from one of the USAAF delivery pilots:

"Jesus, you mean you're actually going to fly these goddam clapped-out old crates over Germany?"

Some of the aircraft had flown over 300 hours and one over 500, a very large number for an operational wartime aircraft.

Officers' quarters at Blickling Hall. L to R; F/L Roy Hastie, F/O Mervyn Utas, F/O 'Soapy' Hudson, F/O Chris Spiver [Hastie collection].

The establishment of the new squadron would be based on that of 214 Squadron to support an aircraft establishment of sixteen aircraft. Servicing would be carried out by 9223 Servicing Echelon. The squadron was allocated domestic accommodation recently vacated by 803/36 BS; most of the SNCO aircrew being located in the Nissen-hutted 3 Site. Officer accommodation would be in Nissen huts in the grounds of Blickling Hall which lay to the north-west of the airfield. The rush to set up the new squadron resulted in the appointment of a temporary CO on 23 August, the experienced Wg Cdr Desmond J McGlinn, 214 Squadron's CO who conveniently became tour expired as the new squadron formed. Flight Lieutenant B James was posted in from the Bomber Support Training Unit at Great Massingham to fill the post of adjutant. A list of officers that held executive positions in the squadron are listed in Appendix 3.

What of the crews destined to form 223? Bomber Command was extremely fortunate in its urgency to form its first and only Liberator squadron. The timescale coincided with the timely availability of a surplus of such embryo crews in Coastal Command as the command gained the upper hand in the U-Boat war. Coastal Command Liberator crews were converted to the Liberator at 111 (Coastal) OTU at Nassau in the Bahamas. The unit comprised three flights. The course consisted of two phases. Initial flying was carried out at Oakes Field with A and B Squadrons on the twin-engined North American B-25 Mitchell. Its advantage was of familiarising pilots with the, then, relatively uncommon nose-wheel layout. A Squadron trained pilots, co-pilots and navigators before passing them on to B Squadron where they were joined by wireless operators and air gunners to form the basis for a crew. They would also become acclimatised to local flying before proceeding to C Squadron at Windsor Field to commence the conversion to the four-engined Liberator also with a nose-wheel undercarriage. The aircraft at Windsor were mainly Liberator GRVs. Pilot, Fg Off Mervyn Utas, RCAF recounts his experience at the OTU:

"I still remember our first day in class when we got the usual welcome greeting from the commanding officer along with an outline of the course. The CO explained to us what a demanding job coastal command flying was; he told us that it involved long patrols of up to fourteen to sixteen hours all over water. Also that it required accurate knowledge of weather systems and precise navigation and piloting skills. He told us that the reason we were there was because we were older, more experienced aircrew. I was bit amazed and thought that if at the age of nineteen and with 210 hours of flying I was an older, more experienced pilot, then what would an inexperienced pilot look like? I was paired with the most senior pilot, a RAF flight lieutenant who had been instructing in Canada. I think he had been instructing on single-engine aircraft as he had considerable difficulty with the B-25 and got an awful lot of the flying time.

"As usual we started out with some ground school mixed with flying. We continued with navigation training, ship recognition but also had to study the B-25 Mitchell's systems. We had to learn about hydraulic systems, electrical systems, armament systems, bomb sights, radio gear and emergency procedures for such things as manual undercarriage lowering, engine failure, engine fires and electrical failures. The armament part was interesting. They had gun turrets mounted on platforms on the gunnery range, each turret was fitted with two 0.5 in calibre Browning machine guns and even we pilots were required to get into a turret and fire a few rounds at stationary targets.

"We then got checked out on the B-25 which was a very nice aircraft. Shortly after that we were formed into crews. Then we started more serious training, such as how to attack a submarine with depth charges. Since it would not have been wise to use real depth charges against a target which was being towed about 100 yards behind the boat, they came up with a unique solution. Our depth charges were wooden logs, about one yard long and eight to ten inches in diameter. They drove a large staple in to it so that it could be hung in the bomb bay. You usually attacked a submarine from an angle offset about 15 degrees from his line of travel. It was a low level attack from thirty to fifty feet altitude, and a stick of three depth charges was dropped. I do not know why we studied how to use a bomb sight as the attack was visual. The idea was to release the depth charges (or logs) so the first hit just at the back of the sub, the next near the prow and the third slightly ahead of the line of travel. The theory was that by the time they blew the sub would have moved ahead so that the last charge would be by his prow, the second one about his middle. If the attack was head on you would release a bit earlier so the first would be by the prow instead of the third one. I had to admire the fellows in the tow boat as every once in a while one or all of the logs would hang up or be slow in releasing and crash down near the tow boat. The depth charges were released by the pilot who had a switch on his control column.

"When the B-25 phase was completed, captains were selected and crews were put together. I was called to the flying instructor's office and found my instructor there. I was told I had done very well on the ground school and flying, but because of my age they were not going to select me as one of the captains. They felt I would have difficulty in putting a crew together. Instead, they said I had probably realised that the RAF flt lt had some difficulty but because of his rank and seniority he would be a captain. They were hoping that I would agree to provide support by crewing with him. I am afraid I did not endear myself when I said that if I were to be killed in the war I would prefer it to be at the hands of the enemy and not an ally. Shortly afterwards Fg Off Tony Morris approached me and I agreed to join his crew. With the initial phase completed, it was to move to C Squadron at Windsor Field for conversion to the B-24 Liberator. Now we were going to have four mighty engines with turbo charging to manage.

"Once again on the ground to learn about the aircraft, we also had final exams in navigation and meteorology. The pilots had to sit the same exam as the navigators and to our navigator's dismay I got a higher mark than he did. I never let him forget it! Once we were checked out on the B-24 we did a lot of practice depth-charge attacks against towed targets. We also did long over-water navigation trips lasting eight to ten hours. On some exercises we did actual ship escort duties using live depth charges. There were always oil tankers coming out of the Gulf of Mexico loaded with oil and headed for New York, Boston or Halifax to join a convoy for England. The Germans would send subs into the area to try and sink them, so they put our training to good use and had us escort them.

"However, our stay in this tropical paradise had to end. We were posted to England by way of Canada, so Moncton was our first destination and I figured I was a cinch to get at least two weeks leave since so far I had had none, and had also been out of the country for four months. Our group by this time consisted of both RCAF and RAF personnel. 111(C) OTU was an RAF unit, which explains why we were sent to the RAF Repatriation Depot at Moncton. My first stop was station HQ to explain that I was a Canadian in the RCAF, and that I was entitled to some leave and should not be repatriated to England as I had just been repatriated to Canada. Well five days later I was standing on the deck of a ship steaming out of Halifax harbour exclaiming loudly 'you have made a terrible mistake; I am in the RCAF not the RAF so you cannot repatriate me and I am entitled to leave in Canada'.

"They certainly knew how to put me in my place. When we arrived in England I did not go to the RCAF Reception Centre in the south of England but was hauled, kicking and screaming, to the RAF Reception Centre in Cheltenham. Then just to rub more salt in my many wounds we were assembled on the parade ground for the usual welcome and the CO welcomed us all 'home' and stated that since we had all been away suffering in other countries, we were all entitled to two weeks leave to get reunited with our families."

There were a number of changes before the crews were finalised. A number of the OTU instructors, very experienced Coastal pilots, were tour expired and elected to return to the UK instead of possible postings to the Far East. As a result some of the instructors took over as aircraft captains. Fg Off Ronnie Simmons was a navigator in Flt Lt Levy's crew. He describes the formation of his crew:

"I had joined the RAF under a combined navigator (whom we called observers), bomb aimer and air gunner scheme. We were posted to 111 OTU, Nassau destined ultimately, we thought, for Coastal Command. There were three general groups of us, pilots, navigators and wireless operators, and we were left to encounter each other in the mess and make overtures. As navigators we thought of the newly graduate pilots as being our skippers and without prior knowledge of their flying capabilities, we each had to make our own judgement calls.

"Our flying instructors had each completed a tour of operations with Coastal Command and, with the end of the course at Nassau, were to be put back into the fray as aircraft captains. I teamed up with 'Joe' Boaden as my pilot and Wilf Bridgeman as wireless operator on his second tour; Mark Levy was our primary flying instructor. My duties comprised navigation, bomb aiming and gunnery; we had no other gunners at that time. Mark Levy eventually teamed up with us as our captain which was a great delight to me.

"We picked up the rest of our crew in the UK. 'Taffy' Pryce was our flight engineer for the duration and Archie Rudd was our faithful and reliable tail gunner on his second tour. Archie was a professional golfer who one day took us out to a beautiful golf course on the north Norfolk coast to teach us the rudiments of playing the game, but we made a sorry mess of it in front of the club house. He was to stay with us to the end of December 1944 and was then sent, I believe, on a rest course; we did not see Archie again. His place was taken by Fg Off J R Wolff; I never knew his first name and he was always known as 'Wolfy', a very reliable and competent tail gunner on his second tour. *[Jack Raymond Wolff had already completed a tour on Wellingtons with 70 Squadron in the Middle East, and had originally been posted to Oulton as 223 Squadron's gunnery leader on 28 August. He did valuable work in setting up and organising the gunnery section, and was awarded the DFC in September 1945.]*

"Wilf Bridgeman, our wireless operator, during our high altitude decompression tests, apparently developed a severe haemorrhage and was hospitalised from flying until about November 1944. I believe his place was taken temporarily by Sgt Bryant. *[F/O Bridgeman returned to ops with the crew on the night of 26/27 November. The other air gunners in the crew were Sgts N S Pearson, J E Nicholls, W R Turpie and R McEwan. The latter three were all graduates of 10 Air Gunnery School (AGS).]* Fg Offs Stephens and Gamble were our regular special operators."

The crews arrived in England at the end of July and were sent to 7 Personnel Reception Centre (PRC) at Harrogate where they kicked their heels awaiting their postings. Eventually they were given the news about 223 Squadron forming at RAF Oulton in 100 Group, Bomber Command. This was certainly a culture shock to the Coastal veterans – Bomber Command, and where the bloody hell is Oulton? They were soon to find out.

The penultimate day of August 1944 saw the first arrivals for the new squadron consisting of eighteen officers and eighteen non-commissioned officers (NCO) of the RCAF, all ex-Coastal Command. They were closely followed the next day with the arrival from Harrogate of thirty-three officers and senior non-commissioned officers (SNCO), mainly consisting of the 111 OTU graduates. The first day of September produced an initial batch of experienced second tour wireless operators who would assume the role of special operators. One of these, Fg Off Leslie Boot DFM, had completed a tour with 61 Squadron on Hampdens. He had hoped to rejoin 61 Squadron with his first tour pilot who had dropped in to his screen tour base at Seighford to recruit him. He described his move to Oulton:

"However, Hodgkinson's request to Bomber Command must have alerted the 'powers that be' who as usual, being bloody minded, immediately posted me to 223. Nobody knew where it was, but eventually it was found to be at Oulton in Norfolk. I had a 1936 Austin 7 which I had acquired for about £20 and so Tommy Thomson, Les Green and another whose name I cannot remember, piled into the 'jalopy' – quite a squeeze with all our gear – and proceeded to find our way to the mysterious 223 Squadron. Our first tours had been in 5 Bomber Group, but we discovered that 223 was in 100 Group, about which little was known, it being known as a 'hush-hush' group. Oulton was about three miles from Aylsham, and we were to be billeted in Nissen huts in the grounds of Blickling Hall. I was allocated to a hut with about nine other commissioned WOp/AGs on their second tour."

The next arrivals on 2 September were thirty-eight air gunners direct from 96 Course at 10 Air Gunnery School (AGS), Walney Island (listed at Appendix 3), described by Flt Lt James as all above average and very anxious to start their first operational tour. Eager they may have been but many had suffered the bitter disappointment of being compulsorily remustered from pilot to air gunner as the result of a pilot surplus. The disappointment was made more acute by their having achieved solo standard on the Tiger Moth at their respective elementary flying training schools (EFTSs). One of their number, Leslie Matthews, described passing the Oulton airfield just before they reached their Aylsham destination. From the train they could see the Fortress aircraft of 214 Squadron looking very sinister in their predominately black heavy-bomber camouflage finish with disruptive dark earth and dark green upper surfaces. Arriving at Aylsham they were met by motor transport (MT) to take their kit whilst they formed up and marched back to Oulton. As with other SNCO aircrew, they would be accommodated mainly on 3 Site, recently vacated by the departing 36/803 BS. The same day also saw the arrival of seven young flight engineers straight from their specialist course at 4 School of Technical Training (S of TT) at St. Athan in South Wales; not all the 111 OTU crews had arrived with flight engineers.

223 Squadron crew outside their hut on 3 Site at Oulton. L to R, back: F/S Vic Green, F/S Jamie Brown, Sgt Aubrey Ward, U/K, F/S Arthur Anthony, U/K, F/S Jim Bratten; L to R, front: F/S H Harding, U/K *[Jim Bratten]*.

Three aircraft had already arrived at Oulton on 25 August to be taken on charge by 1699 (Fortress Training) Flight which it had been agreed would take on the responsibility of training and converting future 223 Squadron crews. Initially, the aircraft TS537 X, TS538 V and TS539 Y were loaned to the squadron and used for check circuits and familiarisation; this was done by personnel of 36/803 BS who had stayed behind after the move to RAF Cheddington in order to assist 223, Lieutenants Curtis and Sheldon helping with this early flying training. To reflect these changes, on 24 October 1699's title was changed to 1699 (Training) Flight.

All founder members of 223 in these first days confirm that all aircraft received by the squadron and 1699 Flight were finished in the standard Bomber Command heavy bomber camouflage and markings. This consisted of disruptive dark earth and dark green upper surfaces (as previously mentioned), and black (night) fuselage sides and under-surfaces. The highly secret nature of the squadron's role has resulted in very few complete aircraft photos available today. A study of these and various crew photos showing parts of aircraft indicate that the demarcation between the disruptive upper-surface camouflage and the black surfaces was not always a sharp line. The black finish also appears to vary; in some shots it appears dull, in others relatively glossy. The dull finish may be down to erosion during the airframe's service, or the quality of the photograph. By this time in the war the official finish would have been a semi-gloss. Experiments earlier in the war at RAE Farnborough had shown that a semi-gloss night finish reflected light and broke up the outline of the aircraft at night. The earlier dull or sooty black finish did not reflect light and resulted in the aircraft showing up in silhouette. The squadron code 6G (1699 Flight's code was 4Z), the individual aircraft code letter and the aircraft serial were finished in the standard matt dull red colour. The aircraft code appeared on both sides of the nose below the cockpit side window, and the squadron code on the rear fuselage to the rear of the waist gun positions. The aircraft featured dull red and blue B type roundels on the main plane upper surfaces and dull finish C1 roundels on the fuselage sides forward of the waist hatch locations. Later when operations started each operational sortie was recorded on the port side of the nose as a lightning flash in the same dull red finish. It is of interest that flight entries in flying log books (FLBs) for this early period gave the aircraft identification as just the aircraft code letter and/or the last three digits of the USAAF aircraft serial number. This continued in some FLBs well into the late autumn and, in one case into December. The USAAF aircraft serial number and aircraft model information continued to be stencilled on the port side of the nose in 223 service.

The working-up of the squadron continued as more personnel arrived and the embryo 111 OTU crews were brought up to strength and revised as necessary. The thirty-eight Sgt air gunners from 10 AGS were allocated to crews nominally in threes, in alphabetical order according to Peter Lovatt and Mick Stirrop who joined 'Jock' Hastie's and Tony Morris's crews respectively. The original crew make up on the squadron consisted of pilot, 2nd pilot, navigator, flight engineer, wireless operator, front gunner, mid upper gunner, two beam or waist gunners and a tail gunner. Two special operators made up the crew of eleven. The 2nd pilot had long been deleted from Bomber Command with the introduction of the heavy bombers. The reasoning behind the decision to retain the Coastal Command two-pilot arrangement is not known, but it is significant that if a 2nd pilot left the crew for any reason he was not replaced, and replacement crews provided by 1699 Flight later did not contain a 2nd pilot. This change was good news for the poor flight engineers who would now have the luxury of a seat instead of standing on the steps up to the flight deck or crouching down behind the pilots. The crews were very large by comparison with the normal Bomber Command heavy bomber crew of seven. Some members of the squadron who had served earlier tours felt that this resulted in crews not being as tightly knit. Leslie Boot felt this quite keenly having been in a Hampden crew of five:

> "I did not find the same friendliness or camaraderie as on 61 Squadron except amongst the special operators – maybe the crews were too big – although I did get along with the pilot and waist gunners on my crew, and also with the ground crew of the aircraft, one of whom kept me supplied (unofficially) with 100 Octane fuel for my car."

Another strange anomaly on the reforming of the squadron was the arrival of a number of air bombers, not least because the squadron would not be dropping bombs. Perhaps this was an administrative error by the P (personnel) staff at Bomber Command who possibly assumed that a heavy bomber unit must require bomb aimers. Possibly it was thought that they could assist the navigators, perhaps helping with GEE readings or manning the front turret. Whatever the reason they tended to be spare hands in the crews they flew with and were reposted away by the end of the year; there was, in any case, a surplus of navigators. In Nassau there were some who had trained as 2nd navigators, probably another example of Coastal Command practice. Fg Off Andrew Barron found himself in this category:

> "111 OTU was quite different for me. I have no recollection of being 'crewed up'. I think that I and 'Pop' Hedges (so called because of his advanced age of twenty-six or so) were earmarked right from the start to be 2nd nav and 2nd pilot to an operationally-experienced captain, 1st nav and wireless operator in the form of Fg Off 'Scotty' Steele, Plt Off Freddie Freake and Plt Off Norman Giles. As far as I was concerned I only flew about half as many hours as Fg Off Ron Johnson *[Fg Off Thompson's navigator]* quotes in his own account."

Andrew flew his first four operational flights with Steele's crew as a front gunner. He then transferred to Fg Off Morris's crew as the result of unfortunate circumstances described later. The surplus of navigators saw the departure of Plt Off S Perkins RCAF and Warrant Officer (W/O) C Ashworth to 192 Squadron on 21 September.

The special operators tended to be a breed apart from their fellow crew members. Due to the high security aspect of their job and the special equipment they operated they were forbidden to talk about their work. They were also accommodated separately from other aircrew, and this applied even if they landed away when diverted. Although special operators did have good relations within crews the division was obvious. It may also seem surprising that the special operators did not receive any specialist training before arrival on the squadron. However, at this stage not all the special equipments that the 100 Group squadrons, including 223, would operate were generally available. Leslie Boot again:

"A day or two later we found out that we would be flying in Liberators and had to wait until the aircraft had been fitted with some special radar equipment. Furthermore, it was heavily emphasised that it would be a Court Martial offence to talk to anyone about the equipment or our work, and that it was only permitted to complete our log books with date, crew, time off and back and target. The only other description allowed was 'Ops as detailed'. Our sister squadron (214) would be doing similar work but on Fortresses. No private notes or diaries to be kept of the work we would be doing.

"Meantime we had one of the mysterious radar sets [Jostle] rigged up and we were taught how to operate it, although that did not take very long. It took about four or five weeks for the aircraft to be fitted with the radar transmitter/receivers etc.

"However, the time came when we were crewed up and ready for take-off. I was crewed with Sqn Ldr McKnight, a Canadian. He got off on every op possible, which was great, and between 22 September and 24 February 1945 I had completed my second tour of twenty-five sorties making sixty-one altogether."

With the squadron's work-up underway it is of interest to hear what Mervyn Utas found on his arrival at the start of his first operational tour:

"RAF Oulton was rather different as it was spread over several locations a few miles apart. The aerodrome was on a farm with some of the farm buildings still in use by the farmer. The airmen's quarters and mess were a couple of miles away near a small village [Oulton Street]. The non-commissioned officers' quarters and mess were in a different area about four miles from the aerodrome. The officers' mess was in the grounds of Blickling Hall, an impressive estate which was supposedly the birthplace of Anne Boleyn.

"The officers' mess building and several Nissen huts were spread around the grounds near a small lake. There was a formal lake in front of the hall. Everyone thought it would be very cool to get quarters in Blickling Hall. Most of the rooms were already occupied by 214 Squadron officers as they had been there for a few months. There were a few rooms left which went to some of the more senior individuals on 223 Squadron. I ended up in a Nissen hut right beside the lake. However those who were in the Nissen huts wound up as the winners as the winter turned out to be very cold. The lake near our hut froze solid and some of the local people had never seen this happen before. Although the huts were cold, the hall was even colder as many of the rooms did not have a fireplace and the stone walls were so thick that even when it warmed up outside it took a few days before the interior got warmer.

"Even so the huts were no bargain. They were semi-circular structures made of tin and were not lined by any material. There were four cots down each side with a small wooden locker at the head of the bed. In the middle was a tiny circular stove about twelve inches in diameter, which was supposed to burn coke but was a miserable failure at that task. We were rationed how much coke we were given during a week, which came nowhere near filling our needs during the winter. Our coke was supplied from the compound near our huts. It was an area about twelve feet square surrounded by a ten foot wall topped with barbed wire. When we really got desperate for some additional coke instead of raiding Germany we would raid the coke compound. Because I was the tallest in our hut I was appointed as the inside man. It was my job to scale the wall, not get impaled by the barbed wire and get inside the compound. Once inside I would throw pieces of coke over the wall and my partners in crime would try to find them in the dark. I usually had a lot of help getting into the compound but when it came to get out I was on my own and could only get verbal assistance.

"Our bathroom facilities were a bit unique and combined with the cold winter, ensured that we would not waste much water taking showers. In the midst of the huts was our bathroom, which was a concrete pad with a roof but no walls. There was a row of wash basins with mirrors for washing and shaving. There were stalls, open above and below some with toilets and some with showers. A person did not spend too much time meditating on the 'throne'. Showers were not too frequent when it was cold and even on good days you might only get very lukewarm water out of the shower head."

The aircrew and ground crew SNCOs were also accommodated in Nissen huts with the same 'healthy' open air ablutions as Flt Lt Ian McPherson's flight engineer Don Prutton describes:

"The seven of us *[flight engineers straight from training at 4 School of Technical Training, St. Athan]* arrived at Oulton somewhat miffed. We had elected to do our type training on Liberators; one of the attractions was that the only conversion unit (i.e. flying training) was Nassau in the Bahamas. In fact when we reached Oulton there were the crews, fresh and tanned from the Bahamas, just needing flight engineers *[plus special operators and some extra air gunners]*. Our flying training consisted of a few circuits and bumps, and we were on ops.

"We shared a Nissen hut from our arrival until the end of hostilities in May 1945, in which time we lost Dennis Marsden and Bob Hartop, and we did not replace them. We endured the Norfolk winter of 1944/5, and the one central solid fuel stove, while useful for toasting bread nicked from the sergeants' mess, was not very good at heating the farthest reaches of the hut. But we were flight engineers, technical men, and brought our skills (!) into use. In Aylsham we were able to buy 1 KW heating elements. There was plenty of sheet dural in the workshops that could be easily cut and bent into roughly parabolic reflectors. I made a double one, one above the other. We all plugged into light sockets, the

The McPherson/Bremness crew with Liberator TT343 (W) April/May 1945. L to R: F/S Ben Buff, F/O Joe Doolin, Sgt Murdo McIver, F/L Gordon Bremness, F/O Hal Booth, Sgt Sam Leach, Sgt Roy Stott, Sgt Don Prutton *[D A Prutton]*.

only source of supply; no wonder the mains wires to the lights felt quite warm! Occasionally a fuse in the local sub-section would blow, but of course by the time the authorities came snooping for unauthorised equipment it was all stashed away. We were all warm and we survived."

The majority of 223 Squadron's aircrew, if not all, were accommodated on 3 Site. *[See airfield plan.]* The ground personnel of 9214 and 9223 Servicing Echelons and 1699 Flight occupied 1 Site.

Mervyn and his fellow Canadians, not surprisingly, found wartime British food rather a culture shock; Mervyn continues:

"Meals in the officers' mess were unforgettable, especially breakfast. I eventually gave it up as a regular meal. Fried bread with lukewarm tea was a breakfast staple. I did not like tea and the way the fried bread was presented was enough to make a person swear off eating for the rest of their life. A piece of bread was thrown into a grease-filled pan and I think that the grease was only just warm. It was then removed and slapped on to an ice cold plate and by the time the waitress presented it to you the grease had oozed out on to the plate and congealed and you were looking at a soggy mass of solidified white grease. No wonder I came home weighing only 145 pounds. Another staple was Brussels sprouts which I

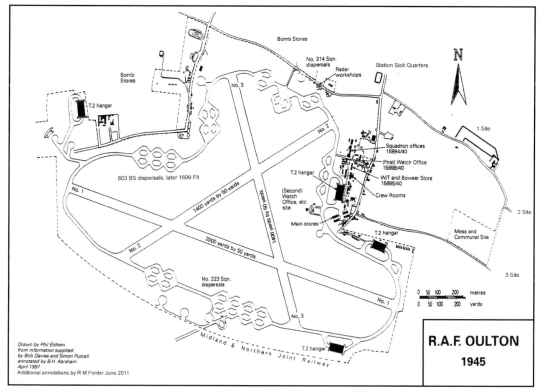

RAF Oulton site plan.

think we got with every dinner. When you travelled around the country you would see piles of Brussels sprouts in the fields. They were allowed to grow until they were extremely large and bitter. This was about the only time they did not conserve energy as they would boil the sprouts until they were almost dissolved. So along with your fried spam you would get this soggy lump of green sludge on your cold plate. It was nearly twenty-five years after the war before I was able to eat them again.

"Fortunately, after being in England for about six months I started to get parcels from home and the goodies in them were really welcome. Apparently for the first six months that we were in England, our parcels and mail had been going to India. Our first posting after Nassau was supposed to be to India but was changed to England at the last minute. I guess the military postal service only got the first notice. Initially I was not getting any letters or parcels and was only getting information from my brother Milton. My Dad started complaining to the authorities in Canada and I guess they finally got it straightened out. Then in one day I received about ten parcels and about forty letters. After all of their travels, the parcels were shapeless and contents unusable. However, after that I started to get parcels on a regular basis which helped me to survive."

In the run up to the reformation of 223 there had been discussion on the standard of the aircraft to be delivered from the USAAF to the squadron. On 30 August the Air

Ministry informed 100 Group HQ by signal that the USAAF had confirmed that operational Liberators issued to 223 Squadron would be prepared to the same standard as those to be issued to 36 BS. Unfortunately, this standard is not detailed, but it is assumed that it involved converting aircraft, previously operated on daylight missions, for the future night operations. As such this would have included the fitting of flame suppressors or dampers to the exhausts of the engine turbochargers, and modifying the cockpit lighting to minimise its visibility externally. The latter involved providing ultra violet lights which caused the radium-based paint on the instrumentation to glow.

According to Ronnie Simmons, the results were very effective and the usual practice was to turn off the ultra violet lights as the instrumentation glow remained readable for lengthy periods. Later the port side window in the nose was plated over, the astrodome was removed and the aperture also plated over; both measures to cut light emissions from the navigator's compartment. 223 Squadron Liberators also had armour plating removed from behind the pilots' seats and at the waist gunners' positions according to 'Mick' Stirrop, a waist gunner in Fg Off Morris's crew. It is not known whether this was done by the USAAF Base Air Depot at Burtonwood in Lancashire prior to delivery or subsequently at Oulton.

Meanwhile the preparation and checking out of crews continued. Apart from briefings in their specialist areas, aircrew were put through the decompression chamber with the double purpose of checking out an individual's oxygen masks and to ensure that they were suitable for flying at altitude. Flying continued as described by Sgt Peter Matthews, flight engineer in Flt Lt 'Scottie' Steele's crew:

"Once flying started we completed about twelve hours of circuits and landings, air-to-sea firing and fighter affiliation – all the usual stuff that formed a bond between crew members. It was during this period that we experienced abortive flights due to u/s (unserviceable) instruments, oxygen failure, intercom and engine failures."

Scottie Steele's crew had originated at 111 OTU, but arrived at Oulton without a flight engineer. Peter Matthew's was one of the group that had just emerged straight from the flight engineers' course at St. Athan. Peter's only experience of flying was two hours in an Airspeed Oxford during his course, and here he was about to go straight on to ops in a four-engined heavy bomber.

At Bylaugh Hall AVM Addison and his staff had been continuing the planning and development of the group's heavy squadrons to include the creation of a special Window force to fulfil its remit to provide protection for main force bomber streams. The group urgently required additional special equipment such as Dina and Carpet jammers to equip the newly-forming 223 Squadron and to extend the capability of 214 Squadron. In fact just eight days after 223 was authorised to form, Addison was urgently signalling to the Air Ministry, copied to Bomber Command and VIII USAAF:

'I see no hope of getting aircraft of 223 and 214 Squadrons equipped by your target date unless special apparatus is flown over from America. If Bomber

Command agree I propose a Liberator of 223 Squadron should proceed as soon as possible to America to collect gear. Understand Americans may also agree to send two Liberators at the same time.

'Suggest Col Scott and Major Thomson, American liaison officers attached to this HQ should proceed with flight to arrange collection of material.

'As regards our requirements for these squadrons we need 100 Carpet III and thirty-two Type AN/APR 4 receivers, and sixteen sets of Column 7 parts for the above for 214 Squadron. In addition as many Dina transmitters (AN/APT1) as possible should be added to load. Transport Command have signified their willingness to supply complete crew for our Liberator viz two pilots, one navigator, one W/Op and one F/Eng. Request you confirm these arrangements with Transport Command and VIII Air Force Pinetree and authorise Bomber Command to allow our aircraft to be sent.

'Request you also inform General McClelland in Washington of our proposals so that all possible assistance can be given to the collection of material in order to make duration of stay in America as short as possible.'

Authorisation for the flight was given by the Air Ministry by cipher message on 1 September 1944. The authorisation was sent to Transport Command HQ and info copied to 100 Group and 8th Air Force USAAF HQ. A Ferry Command crew comprising two pilots, navigator, wireless operator and a flight engineer manned the 223 Squadron

Carpet II control unit mounted for trials in a TRE B-25 Mitchell *[RSRE]*.

Liberator which departed for Patterson Field, Ohio on the same day. The 100 Group American liaison officer, Col Scott, and Col Snider of the USAAF were on board. However, there is no record of this flight taking place with a 223 Squadron aircraft or crew in the unit's RAF Form 540/541 operational record book.

Carpet III consisted of an APQ 9 transmitter and an AN/APT search receiver for jamming transmissions from the German Würzburg ground control interception (GCI) and flak gun laying radars. It was an American development of the earlier British designed Carpet II device.

Liberator VI TS533 6G-M at Oulton. Prior to joining 223 Squadron, this aircraft had flown combat missions with the USAAF's 490 BG at Eye, Suffolk, where it carried the name 'Boomerang' *[J D Oughton]*.

Dina was another jamming device developed by the Americans from the original British-designed Mandrel system. Dina was used to jam the FuG 220 Lichtenstein SN2 AI radars carried by German night fighters. This device was later reconfigured with British parts by the TRE and given the codename Piperack.

The build up of the squadron continued, with sixteen aircraft delivered to Oulton during September. They arrived in dribs and drabs throughout the month although the aircraft movement cards

Liberator VI TS534 6G-O – originally 6G-A 'Ad Lib' of 223 Squadron on the southern dispersals at Oulton *[D A G Anthony]*.

do not record fourteen of the aircraft being on the squadron's charge until 20 October; the exceptions being TS533(M) and TS534(A) which were recorded for 13 September.

On 7 September Plt Off Robert William Barrett DFM arrived from 1674 Heavy Conversion Unit (HCU) at Aldergrove in Northern Ireland, posted in to be the engineer leader. Bob Barrett was a very experienced Liberator hand, and another ex-Coastal Command veteran who had been awarded his DFM on 14 April 1944 for operations with 120 Squadron. He was always on the look-out for assistance with the restoration of his Rolls-Royce-built Derby Bentley which he kept in a field near to the aerodrome.

The crew positions in 223 Squadron Liberators and other relative data are shown opposite. The front gunner and navigator occupied the nose of the aircraft. There were two types of nose turret fitted to 223's aircraft; the more common type would appear

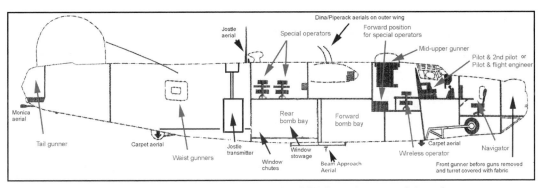

A diagrammatic layout of a Liberator fitted out with 223 Squadron special equipment.

to have been the Emerson A rounded type. The front gunner in the Emerson could not open the turret doors, as the handles were on the other side, once he was in the turret. The navigator would close the doors behind him and shut the bulkhead doors. Another comfort for the gunner was the fact that his parachute was left in the nose. Peter Witts remembered during his first trip in the front turret of the Liberator that he was very conscious of the speed down the runway and had an uneasy feeling that he would be the closest to any disaster that might occur. The other turret used was the Consolidated A6B, and was easily recognisable from its flat-fronted bevelled appearance. This is the same turret type used as a tail turret in both the squadron's H and J models. The front turret detail rapidly became academic because the decision was taken very early on to delete it. It was recognised that front guns were unnecessary at night due to the comparative rarity of frontal attacks. With the cessation of Big Ben ops in October the guns, a pair of 0.5 inch calibre Browning M2 machine guns, were removed from the front turret, and the assembly was covered with doped fabric to seal it. This was a great improvement as it gave more room for the navigator and his equipment, and the sealing eliminated draughts. The navigator sat at a table positioned forward of and below the pilot's feet facing aft. The front gunner and navigator had an escape exit in flight achieved by operating two emergency levers to open the nose-wheel doors.

Behind the pilot and co-pilot was a small compartment where the wireless operator sat at a table on the starboard side facing to starboard. His radio equipment was the standard Bomber Command transmitter receiver equipment as fitted to RAF heavy bombers, T1154/R1155; this was mounted above the table straight in front of him. Below table height, and to his left was a spool which carried a trailing aerial for the radio. This small area also contained the forward location for the special operator. He sat on the port side facing aft with his equipment mounted against the bulkhead, and this was the position used for the Big Ben ops aircraft. Fg Off Boot flew all his ops with 223 Squadron occupying this position and always operated Jostle both in the Big Ben and subsequent configurations. A second location for the special operator or operators was later created above the rear of the bomb bay, sometimes referred to as the 'loft'.

The locations of the special operators in 223 Liberators has been a difficult area of investigation, primarily because only a handful of surviving special operators responded to requests for information. Additionally, positioning and location of their special equipment has also proved impossible to confirm because of the lack of surviving internal shots of the squadron's aircraft. Further discussion of this aspect of the special operators and their equipment is covered later. What we do know however is in the roof of the compartment there was a hatch which provided an emergency exit.

Between the wireless operator and the special operator was the access to the top turret, a Martin 3C again containing two 0.5 Brownings. It is not known if any of the squadron's aircraft were fitted with the taller Martin 3D 'High Hat' turret. The mid upper gunner's feet could cause problems with fast rotation of the turret, with a chance of connecting with the unfortunate wireless operator. On one occasion Flt Lt Levy's mid upper gunner managed to break the sight glass of one of the fuel contents gauge positioned to the rear of the flight deck bulkhead behind the 2nd pilot – consternation, followed by rapid action by the flight engineer Sgt 'Taffy' Pryce cut off the flow.

Moving rearward took you down a short set of steps and into the bomb bay. These steps were removed to give the navigator and front gunner access to the nose via a tunnel attached to the starboard side of the nose undercarriage. Facing aft was a narrow catwalk bounded on either side by the original vertically-mounted bomb beams. Although 223 did not carry bombs, the beams were retained, including the bomb winches. At the forward end on the port side, racking was installed to carry some of the special equipment. Mounted on the opposite side was the small auxiliary power unit (APU) known to crews as the 'putt-putt' to provide electrical power prior to engine start. The engines could also be started from an externally provided trolley accumulator or 'trolley ack'.

The narrow access between the bomb beams prompted a change to the flight engineers' safety equipment. Whereas the rest of the crew had the standard RAF Mae West life jackets, 223 flight engineers wore USAAF life preservers which were not as bulky as the RAF item. The flight engineer was the only crew member who would routinely need to have regular access through the bomb bay. Stepping out of the rear of the bomb bay you were now in the rear fuselage. Straight ahead and in the centre of the fuselage, forward of the waist gunners' position, was the Jostle T1524 transmitter and its power supply unit. This was a substantial item weighing some 600 lb (272 kg), cylindrical in shape, about four feet six inches in height, and a similar size to a large dustbin. It was located in the position previously used for the ball turret which had been deleted by the USAAF before transfer of the aircraft to the RAF. The T1524 had specialist ground equipment for its movement, as shown in the photographs opposite. The truck was used to transport the transmitter to a specially constructed pit, into which it was lowered. The aircraft was then positioned over the pit to enable ground crew to hoist the 'Jostle' in and out of the aircraft. This system was used for both 223's Liberators and 214's Fortress. In the latter case the Jostle was mounted vertically in the bomb bay. A Jostle pit or pits were provided at each squadron dispersal area.

Returning to the B-24, forward of the Jostle and above the rear of the bomb bay was the 'loft', an area that was used to create a position for the second special operator, or both of them. However, moving aft again past the Jostle we come to the waist gunners' position. Again each gunner had a 0.5 Browning machine gun equipped with a reflector sight. The sight presented a series of rings graduated in millimetres and the wing span and speed of the attacking aircraft gave the number of rings to lay off ahead of the attacker when aiming the gun. On one occasion after an air firing exercise in the Wash area it was discovered that a round had hit the port fin, narrowly missing the rudder control. Possibly this event prompted the fitting of 'taboo' restraints in the waist positions, consisting of metal tubing mounted six inches above the bottom edge of the hatch and four inches forward of its rearward vertical edge. One can only express admiration for the waist gunners who had to stand throughout an operational sortie exposed to temperatures of 40 to 50 degrees centigrade below freezing at these open waist positions. Even though crews were equipped with electrically-heated suits, they experienced problems with the heating circuits in the suits shorting or burning out. There was a retractable airflow deflector fitted immediately forward of the waist position. The waist gunners and rear gunners were issued

A Jostle unit in the pit at Oulton, over which the Liberator was positioned to enable fitment *[RSRE]*.

A Jostle transmitter mounted on a modified US bomb truck at Oulton in April 1945 *[RSRE]*.

with Balaclava helmets to put on under their flying helmets to help combat the bitter cold. The waist hatches also provided an escape route in emergency situations.

A ventral hatch was located to the rear of the waist positions which was used by the back end crew members to access the aircraft and provided another emergency exit; the Elsan lavatory was also in this area. The crews hoped that they would not need to use it, not only for the practical difficulties of access from the front end member, but also for the immense problem of disrobing the various layers of clothing and flying kit. Mick Stirrop recalled a joke played on Vic Green, their flight engineer, during a training sortie. Vic informed his skipper Tony Morris that he was going off intercom (i/c) to use the Elsan. Whilst Vic was making his way to the rear through the bomb bay someone suggested that the skipper should exercise the controls. As poor Vic performed, the aircraft suddenly started some sharp manoeuvres to the great amusement of the crew. This amusement was quickly 'dampened' when Vic came back on i/c to announce that he had just peed all over the master compass.

The tour of the aircraft is completed with the Consolidated A6B hydraulically-driven rear turret also fitted with two 0.5 in Brownings.

One other feature of the squadron's Liberators was the retention of the American oxygen demand system, with demand-type regulators at each crew position. With the demand system, oxygen was released though the regulator as the crew member inhaled, thus sucking in the oxygen. The crews used RAF Type G or H oxygen masks with the aspiratory valves in the cheeks of the masks replaced by blanks.

Notes:
1. *Confound and Destroy* Martin Streetly, James Publishing 1985

CHAPTER FOUR

Operational Flying Begins

On 19 September, just over three weeks after reforming, Flt Lt Carrington, OC B Flight, took off at 06:45 for a Big Ben patrol on the squadron's first operational sortie in TS525 (H). A full list of all 223 Squadron's operational sorties in included at Appendix 2. Carrington had been awarded his DFC on 12 January 1943 whilst flying Lockheed Hudsons on anti-submarine and convoy patrols in the South Atlantic with 200 Squadron. Unfortunately, the crew had to leave the patrol area early because of intercom and oxygen system problems. Nothing had been seen and nothing had been picked up by the special equipment. The crew for this historic occasion comprised:

Flt Lt A Carrington DFC	Pilot
Fg Off T E Wallis	2nd Pilot
Sgt R Wade	Navigator
Sgt E Sorrell	Front Gunner
Sgt W Jewell	Wireless Operator
Sgt A A Gibbon	Flight Engineer
Flt Lt M Wheaton	Mid Upper Gunner
Fg Off L W Fairbanks	Special Operator
Flt Lt R Flint	Special Operator
Sgt G 'Dod' Nisbet	Waist Gunner
Sgt J 'Wee' Murray	Waist Gunner
Plt Off J R Wolff	Rear Gunner

Three days later it was the turn of OC A Flight, Flt Lt R E C McKnight RCAF, to fly the next sortie. Again, gremlins intervened to shorten the mission when after two hours the special equipment became unserviceable and the sortie was abandoned. The crew on this occasion was:

Flt Lt R E C McKnight RCAF	Pilot
Sgt P G Nash	2nd Pilot
Plt Off R M Wylie RCAF	Navigator
Fg Off J Burns *[Air Bomber]*	Front Gunner
Sgt R Stark	Wireless Operator
Sgt B Le Fondre	Flight Engineer

Sgt D H Thorpe	Mid Upper Gunner
Sgt G F Schutes	Waist Gunner
Sgt W Jones	Waist Gunner
Fg Off L Boot DFM	Special Operator
Plt Off W Thomson	Special Operator
Sgt C G J 'Dinkie' Brooks	Rear Gunner

Fg Off Leslie Boot had been awarded his DFM on 26 May 1942 flying as a WOp/AG in Hampdens with 61 Squadron.

The aim of the Big Ben programme was to provide twenty-four-hour coverage. The sorties were generally about five or six hours' duration, the patrol line just off shore from the Dutch coast. The aircraft were routed out over North Foreland to enable the crews to reach their operational height of 20,000 feet. The patrols were rather tedious, especially for the pilots and navigators, just stooging up and down the patrol line, although they were not always as dull as will be seen later. The crews were detailed to look for V2 launches, with evidence of any guidance transmissions to be picked up by the special equipment. The main advantage was to introduce crews to operational flying and achieving crew cohesion in a reasonably benign environment; this was particularly beneficial for those on their first tours.

Bomber Command had decreed that a Big Ben sortie would only count as half an op, which left some of the veterans rather perturbed at the prospect of a lengthy tour if this was to remain policy. Although 223's build-up of crews to full operational strength would take just over three weeks, it was significant for 100 Group and Bomber Command because it relieved 214 Squadron to resume its important Window force role. It is interesting to note that even the squadron's early operational sorties in the Big Ben phase were flown with two special operators aboard even though Jostle was apparently the only special equipment fitted. Leslie Boot was asked if he and the second special operator in his crew shared the Jostle operation. He was quite emphatic that this did not occur and that he alone operated the equipment. There was obviously little room behind the flight deck to accommodate a second operator standing with the front operator in the confined space also occupied by the wireless operator, and not forgetting the mid upper gunner's 'whirling' feet. The flight engineer also needed access to and through this area. However, it does seem logical that both operators would have helped each other in operating Jostle, especially in this early learning phase. Leslie also stated that on Big Ben sorties he would be looking at a small six to eight-inch cathode ray tube (CRT) screen to pick up possible V2 guidance transmissions which he was told would appear as blips on the screen. He was off intercom during these monitoring phases as he would also pick up signals aurally through his earphones.

Although the sorties by Flt Lt Levy and Flt Lt Stephenson on 23 and 25 September respectively were also unsuccessful because the special equipment was again u/s, the Jostle was to prove very reliable in service. Ronnie Simmons remembers:

"The briefing for Big Ben ops was indeed brief, and was done on an individual crew basis. There was vague advice that GEE was occasionally coded in the event that enemy infiltration was suspected. This was shown on the GEE receiver by the continuous flashing of the screen pulses. No one gave us any code data at our briefings and on our second operation I experienced flashing pulses with no code data. Fortunately, I had determined an accurate position beforehand and was able to decode the GEE without the data."

23 September saw the arrival of Wg Cdr H H Burnell AFC, posted in from 3 Lancaster Finishing School (LFS) to take over 223 Squadron from Wg Cdr McGlinn who had just been awarded a DFC in recognition of his earlier service with 214 Squadron. Wg Cdr Burnell was a regular serving officer who was beginning his third tour of operations. His AFC was awarded for service with his previous unit, 3 LFS.

Fg Off Alan Allnut was away in TS532 (N) early on the 23rd at 06:55 for the crew's first op, which was uneventful:

Fg Off A Allnut	Pilot
Plt Off I T Leslie RCAF	2nd Pilot
Fg Off C F Campbell RAAF	Navigator
Sgt R Tabah	2nd Navigator
Sgt E Laraway	Wireless Operator
Sgt E Manners	Flight Engineer
Fg Off S W Adamson	Special Operator
Fg Off J White	Special Operator
Sgt D Townsend	Air Gunner
Sgt J J Adams	Air Gunner
Sgt T W J Pollard	Air Gunner
Sgt J J Trail	Air Gunner

Flt Lt Mark Levy's crew in TS531 (B) relieved the earlier aircraft taking off at 11:05. The sortie was a failure with the Jostle proving u/s on reaching the enemy coast.

Flt Lt M Levy	Pilot
Fg Off C Boaden	2nd Pilot
Fg Off R A G Simmons	Navigator
Sgt J E Nicholls	Front Gunner
Sgt D Bryant	Wireless Operator
Sgt R D Pryce	Flight Engineer
Sgt N S Pearson	Mid Upper Gunner
Fg Off C A Gamble	Special Operator
Fg Off W S Stephens	Special Operator
Sgt R McEwan	Waist Gunner
Sgt W R Turpie	Waist Gunner
Fg Off A Rudd	Rear Gunner

On 25 September two more crews had their operational baptism, Fg Off V D Croft DFM,

and Flt Lt F H Stephenson DFC, deputy commander B Flight. They were airborne at 07:40 and 12:05 respectively, with Flt Lt M Levy relieving Frank Stephenson's crew from a 15:05 take-off. This was another blank day, with none of the crews seeing any V2 launches and not picking up any signals on their special equipment. Stephenson was forced to abandon his sortie early when the Jostle became u/s. Flt Lt Stephenson's DFC had been awarded on 26 February 1943 for service with 608 Squadron equipped with the Hudson V. Fg Off Val Croft received his DFM on 10 Nov 1942 while serving with 269 Squadron also flying Hudsons for operations out of Kalderdarnes in Iceland:

Fg Off V D Croft DFM	Pilot
Fg Off J Carroll	2nd Pilot
W/O J F Healy	Navigator
Sgt L J Vowler	Front Gunner
Sgt L Lucas	Wireless Operator
Sgt J M Stewart	Flight Engineer
Fg Off R G Watchorn	Special Operator
Fg Off G A Kennerley	Special Operator
Sgt J R Richards	Mid Upper Gunner (?)
Sgt R C Tofield	Waist Gunner
Sgt H C Sykes	Waist Gunner
Fg Off R P Martin	Rear Gunner (?)

Flt Lt F H Stephenson	Pilot
Fg Off D Theaker	2nd Pilot
Fg Off A H Williams	Navigator
Fg Off W Simpson	2nd Navigator
Sgt R Collins	Wireless Operator
Sgt G W Williams	Flight Engineer
Fg Off D A Boyle	Special Operator
Fg Off A W Barker DFM	Special Operator
Sgt E Longden	Mid Upper Gunner
Sgt T Wrigley	Waist Gunner
Sgt A E Tonkin	Waist Gunner
Sgt T Agnew RCAF	Rear Gunner

Fg Off Alf Barker had received his DFM for service with 207 Squadron flying Lancasters.

Fg Off Stan Woodward's crew joined the fray on the 26th flying the first sortie of the day with no sightings of V2s and nothing picked up by the special equipment. Interestingly, Fg Off Woodward gained his DFM on 26 February 1943 flying Martin Baltimores with 223 Squadron during its Middle East era; a much-respected skipper on a squadron with many experienced aircraft captains:

Fg Off S Woodward DFM	Pilot
Fg Off S F McRae	2nd Pilot

OC 'B' Flt, Sqn Ldr A J Carrington DFC and crew. Rear L to R: F/O Tom Wallis, F/O Reggie Wade, Sgt W Jewell, Sgt J 'Wee' Murray, Sgt G 'Dod' Nisbet, Sgt Alec Gibbon. Front L to R: F/L M Wheaton, W/O L T Foster, S/L A J Carrington, Sgt E Sorrell *[Tom Wallis]*.

Fg Off A McMillan	Navigator
Sgt H Harding	Wireless Operator
Sgt J F Feltwell	Flight Engineer
Fg Off C D Forrest	Special Operator
Fg Off Featherstone	Special Operator
Sgt A H Ward	Waist Gunner
W/O W Greatorex	Mid Upper Gunner
Sgt J McClaren	Waist Gunner
Sgt C L Matthews	Rear Gunner
Sgt P A Witts	Front Gunner

Canadian Fg Off J W Young's crew were the eighth to become operational, flying an uneventful second op of the day at 15:00 on 26 September. Plt Off William Williams had been awarded his DFM for service with 115 Squadron, most likely on Wellingtons:

Fg Off J W Young RCAF	Pilot
Fg Off J R Robson	2nd Pilot
Plt Off R Bass RCAF	Navigator
Plt Off J Bourque RCAF	Wireless Operator
Fg Off F S Pemberton	Air Bomber (Front Gunner?)
Sgt A Malone	Flight Engineer

Plt Off W A Williams DFM	Special Operator
Fg Off R N Godwin	Special Operator
Sgt R G Sunstrum RCAF	Air Gunner (MU?)
Sgt K Smith	Air Gunner (Waist?)
Sgt W Nolan	Air gunner (Waist?)
Sgt E J White	Air Gunner (Rear?)

The ninth and tenth crews to attain operational status were those of Fg Off Jack Brigham and Flt Lt A L Dyck RCAF, who carried out patrols on 28 September. Fg Off Brigham was an experienced bomber pilot. His navigator Fg Off Thomas was also a veteran. He had taken part in the first 1,000-bomber raid on the night of 30/31 May 1942 whilst converting to Wellingtons at 21 OTU, Moreton-in-Marsh. He then served on 38 Squadron which carried out a maritime role based in Egypt. He stayed with Wellingtons on his rest tour at 7 (Coastal) OTU at Limavady in Northern Ireland, before joining the other unsuspecting 223 Squadron candidates at 111 (C) OTU in Nassau.

Fg Off J Brigham	Pilot
Fg Off C T Reiser RCAF	2nd Pilot
Fg Off W H G Thomas	Navigator
Flt Sgt D B Johnson	Wireless Operator
Sgt D L Jones	Flight Engineer
Fg Off W S Reed	Special Operator
Fg Off L F Green	Special Operator
Sgt F J Rankin	Mid Upper Gunner
Sgt J R Denney	Waist Gunner
Sgt L S Davies	Waist Gunner
Sgt L Moran	Rear Gunner
Sgt G Nisbet	Air Gunner (Front?)

Flt Lt A L Dyck RCAF	Pilot
Plt Off J Schnarr RCAF	2nd Pilot
Plt Off E Gaiser RCAF	Navigator
Sgt T K Chung RCAF	Wireless Operator
Sgt A A Gibbon	Flight Engineer
Plt Off T Morris	Special Operator
Plt Off W H Mennell	Special Operator
Sgt G Davies	Air Gunner (Waist?)
Sgt R A D Jones	Air Gunner
Sgt E L Punnett	Air Gunner
Sgt A G V Simons	Air Gunner (Waist?)

In the period 29 September to 12 October inclusive, further new crews carried out their first squadron operations, all Big Ben sorties. This occurred in the following order:

Fg Off G Noseworthy RCAF	Pilot
Sgt A L Evens RCAF	2nd Pilot
Fg Off G Palmer RAAF	Navigator
Sgt P Buckland	2nd Navigator
Fg Off G Trail	Wireless Operator
Sgt R E Hartop	Flight Engineer
W/O J G Galley	Special Operator
W/O R E Ralph	Special Operator
Sgt W Gray RCAF	Air Gunner
Sgt D K Clark RCAF	Air Gunner
Fg Off F A Mason	Air Gunner
Sgt J Mellers	Waist Gunner
Flt Lt I McPherson	Pilot
Fg Off I T Leslie RCAF	2nd Pilot
Flt Lt A Eastman	Navigator
Sgt P S Morris	2nd Navigator
Fg Off W Doolin	Wireless Operator
Sgt D A Prutton	Flight Engineer
Fg Off H L Smith	Special Operator
Fg Off J J Denn	Special Operator
Sgt B R Buff	Air Gunner
Sgt R Stott	Air Gunner
Sgt S C R Leach	Air Gunner
Sgt H McIver	Air Gunner
W/O A Stuart	Pilot
Sgt L D Thorne	2nd Pilot
Sgt W Robinson	Navigator
Sgt D S Lightfoot	Wireless Operator
Sgt J D Moir	Flight Engineer
W/O S R Rose	Air Bomber (front gunner?)
Fg Off H E Seagrove	Special Operator
Plt Off R Fawcett?	Special Operator
Sgt C Aspinall RCAF	Air Gunner
Sgt T Skinner RCAF	Air Gunner
Sgt P Chesin RCAF	Air Gunner
Sgt J T McGregor	Air Gunner
Plt Off A E L Morris RCAF	Pilot
Plt Off M W Utas RCAF	2nd Pilot
Plt Off J Wallace RCAF	Navigator
Sgt J Bratten	Wireless Operator
Sgt V H Green	Flight Engineer

W/O J C Potter	Special Operator
W/O A C Fraser	Special Operator
Sgt W Mulligan RCAF	Air Gunner
Sgt J Parrack RCAF	Rear Gunner?
Sgt R A D Jones	Air Gunner
Sgt E Stirrop	Waist Gunner
Sgt G N Tucker	Air Gunner

Flt Lt Briscoe & crew February 1945. Rear L to R: Sgt Ken Stone, F/O 'Roxy' Hart, F/L John Briscoe, F/O Alan Love, F/S Arthur Anthony. Front L to R: Sgt Derek Wilshaw, F/S Bill Bowsher, P/O D F Roberts *[D A G Anthony]*.

Fg Off J L Briscoe	Pilot
Fg Off E A Hart	2nd Pilot
Fg Off A Love	Navigator
Sgt F D Baker	Wireless Operator
Sgt D A G Anthony	Flight Engineer
W/O D F Roberts	Air Bomber (front gunner?)
Fg Off E Chandler	Special Operator
Fg Off C E Payne	Special Operator
Sgt E Robson	Air Gunner
Sgt W L Bowsher RCAF	Waist Gunner?
Sgt D G Wilshaw	Waist Gunner
Sgt K L Stone	Rear Gunner?

Plt Off J W Thompson RCAF	Pilot
Plt Off H Radelett RCAF	2nd Pilot
Plt Off R W Johnson	Navigator
Sgt D Marsden	Flight Engineer
Flt Lt G Ellams	Wireless Operator
W/O R A Palmer	Special Operator
W/O W F Baker	Special Operator
Sgt R Wood RCAF	Mid Upper Gunner
Sgt R Porteous	Waist Gunner
Sgt E E Whittaker	Waist Gunner
Sgt G R Graham RCAF	Rear Gunner
Fg Off R Hastie	Pilot
Fg Off C R Spicer	2nd Pilot
Fg Off L Hudson	Navigator
Sgt J Brown	Flight Engineer
W/O F M Watson	Wireless Operator
Plt Off B S Beecroft	Special Operator
Sgt E D T Brockhurst	Front Gunner
Sgt C Weston	Mid Upper Gunner
Sgt P Lovatt	Waist Gunner
Sgt R C Lawrence	Waist Gunner
Sgt S A Pienaar	Rear Gunner
Fg Off T W Steele	Pilot
Fg Off N S Pickerill	2nd Pilot
Flt Lt F Freake	Navigator
Plt Off A J K Barron	2nd Navigator (front gunner)
Sgt P R Matthews	Flight Engineer
Sgt J E Dagnall	Wireless Operator
W/O R J Tanner	Special Operator
W/O O G Burtenshaw	Special Operator
Sgt W Chitticks	Mid Upper Gunner
Sgt D J Fuller	Waist Gunner
Sgt L Norwood	Waist Gunner
Sgt C G Carter	Rear Gunner

All the crews were now operational. There would be changes to these crews due to a variety of factors including illness, injury, and becoming tour-expired. Air bombers were posted out of the squadron when experience showed they were not required, with no reflection on the individuals concerned. Similarly, an air gunner would be lost when the front turret guns were deleted. The latter would be a decision by the skipper, although lots were drawn in some crews if no volunteers emerged; a sad blow for those who did not want to leave their crew.

An important announcement was received from 100 Group HQ which laid down the criteria for tours of those serving on 223 Squadron:

"A first tour would be thirty operations, and a second tour twenty. Window sorties would count as half an operation unless they were particularly hazardous with considerable penetration into enemy territory, in which case they might count as one whole sortie at the station commander's discretion."

A further decision decreed that over two hours on patrol would count as half a sortie.

6 October proved to be the squadron's most successful day so far, with six aircraft launched and five completing a successful sortie. The exception was Flt Lt Dyck who was forced to return early as the result of a fire in the starboard outer engine. Indeed, the squadron's early days were plagued with serviceability problems which impacted on both training and operational flights. This early work-up period was not without its problems as Ronnie Simmons recounts:

"10 October was our first night-time flying as a full crew at high altitude. Operation Exercise Bullseye was a complete flop for most crews. We soon discovered many problems. At that time we had a front gunner and my desk was just behind the front turret. Our front gunner kept complaining about the cold and in exasperation, the skipper told him to leave the front turret and to stand by my desk. As he opened the turret doors, the air stream swept all my papers, chart and log somewhere on the floor. The gunner had oxygen problems and soon used up the portable supply. Considerable time was lost in retrieving my papers, and nursing the young gunner to behave sensibly, so that by the time I was organised again the GEE had gone off. We were above 10/10ths cloud, and for the first and last time in my flying career I was lost. Shortly, we spotted a small gap in the clouds and made a rapid descent to find ourselves over Middleton St.George, identifiable by the DREM readout [a system of outer markers and approach lights], the GEE came back on and we were able to complete the exercise.

"The fun, however, was not over despite an excellent landing, for as we were taxiing to dispersal we saw two lights coming towards us which disappeared when about 200 yards away. We were unable of course to use our landing lights and presumed it was a truck which had pulled off onto the grass to let us by. The next thing a sharp cry was heard from our co-pilot to stop, followed by a crashing sound, and Mark Levy immediately shut down all four engines. Being closest to the bomb bay, I jumped down onto the tarmac into about a six-inch deep pond of 100 Octane fuel. We had hit and penetrated the tank of a petrol bowser with our starboard propeller. I found the driver of the vehicle perched on top of the tank looking petrified, and suggested, maybe not wisely, that he shift the…thing before we all went up in smoke. There was fortunately no fire and the outcome of the enquiry resulted in a minor endorsement in the captain's log book. Mark thereafter was known as 'Bowser' Levy.

"The navigator of one of the other crews on that exercise failed to check out the GEE co-ordinates on his set whilst leaving base. The result was that after being on the final west-bound leg home for several hours, the skipper elected to call 'Darky' *[a system for getting radio directions to steer in an emergency]* for a course home. There was no reply and after some considerable time, the English coast was seen and a safe return was made. A re-plot of the flight indicated that the 'Darky' call had been made over the middle of the Fatherland!"

Despite the priority given to Big Ben ops, the squadron's intended role had not been forgotten. Training continued to prepare for Window force tasking. In the early hours of 15 October, the squadron provided three aircraft, flown by Fg Off Woodward, Fg Off Hastie and W/O Stuart on a diversionary sweep involving a Bullseye navigation exercise by aircraft from training units. This force advanced across the North Sea and on to the continent as far as 0630 East where it lost height and returned to base. The sweep was in support of main force attacks on Brunswick and Duisburg.

On the night of 15/16 October three squadron aircraft joined the Window force for the first time, flying in support of a main force attack on Wilhelmshaven with 506 aircraft comprising 257 Halifaxes, 241 Lancasters and eight Mosquitoes. Seven heavy bombers were lost.

Progress so far had been largely uneventful, ignoring frustrations with unserviceabilities and the lack of practical results. Some of the veteran Bomber Command members of the squadron were apprehensive regarding the apparent lack of enemy reaction. Possibly this feeling was heightened as a result of the apparent 'nakedness' of operating in daylight, despite having a fighter escort. The latter were not always visible to the crews.

On 15 October Fg Off Tony Morris's crew were airborne at 10:50 in TS531 (B). They were on the usual patrol line off the Dutch coast, but a bit farther out than the expected tracks when the aircraft was struck by a burst from a flak ship. Fg Off John Wallace was hit by shrapnel, or debris, in the lower back. He received immediate attention from Sgt Vic Green, the flight engineer. The aircraft returned to base and John Wallace was admitted to the Norfolk & Norwich Hospital for treatment. This was a wake up call for those that thought ops were going to be a 'piece of cake'. The Big Ben ops continued until 24 October when Fg Off Thompson's crew brought an end to this first phase of 100 Group operations.

The introduction to Window force operations continued on the night of 19/20 October, with two sorties mounted by Flt Lt Levy and Fg Off Noseworthy.

In addition to getting to grips with the serviceability problems, the servicing and maintenance personnel together with the special fitting parties, were having a very busy month during October. The squadron had received its full unit establishment of sixteen aircraft, albeit a varied collection from different manufacturers and manufacturers block numbers. It was decided that the squadron would have a standard layout for its aircraft and work got under way during the month to achieve this. The decision to take out the front turret has already been mentioned and this major change also involved a complete reorganisation of the navigator's compartment, which included repositioning of the GEE set and control panels.

During the month 214 Squadron's aircraft had already been fitted with Dina II for jamming the Luftwaffe's AI SN2 radars. This activity commenced on 223's aircraft with the introduction of whip aerials mounted on the outer wings. The work was carried out by Oulton tradesmen with TRE designing the aerial system. Work was also completed during October to fit each of 214 and 223 Squadron's aircraft with Carpet III, each installation comprising three APQ 9 jamming transmitters and an APR 4 search receiver, which had characteristic 'arrow-head' aerials on the aircraft. The records state three jamming transmitters, but the photographs that survive showing 223 Squadron aircraft or parts of aircraft, seem to show one aerial just aft of the nose wheel and one under the rear fuselage. The Carpet transmitters were used to jam the German Würzburg radars. Part of the work involved putting a wooden floor in the rear of the bomb bay to carry the Window adjacent to the dispensing chutes. With the new arrangement, the rear bomb doors were rendered inactive. A second special operator's position was created above the rear of the bomb bay. This would appear to be the location for the Carpet and Dina operators.

A special operator's position and Jostle control panel in a 214 Squadron Fortress *[RSRE]*.

Leslie Boot operated Jostle in the forward position until the end of his tour in late February 1945 *[on aircraft TS523 (D), TS525 (H), TS529 (C), TS530 (G), TS531 (B), TS533 (M) and TT343 (K)]*. This, together with supporting evidence from Arthur Anthony, confirms that some of 223's aircraft retained a forward operating position.

Special operator F/S I Middle, who flew just three ops in late April 1945 and was trained on Jostle and Piperack, stated that when he operated Jostle it also was in the forward position. Piperack he operated in the rear position facing starboard. To add to the melting pot another special operator, Sgt Reg Smith, flew fourteen ops, mainly with Flt Lt 'Pat' Mann's crew between 28 February and 2/3 May 1945. Reg was a Jostle operator and always operated the equipment from the rear position on his own, facing forward. The sorties where he was required to operate Jostle were flown in TS519 (S), TS527 (Q), TS533 (M), TS534 (A), and TT343 (K). So what is to be made of what appears to be conflicting evidence regarding special operator positioning and the location of their special equipment? In the absence of definitive official sources, it is difficult to be certain, but the authors' view is as follows.

Leslie Boot's evidence confirms that Jostle was operated from the forward position in both the Big Ben and Window force VHF versions, as installed on the squadron's early aircraft. Limited evidence from Flt Sgt Middle, and the authors' conversations with Sgt Arthur Anthony, Flt Lt Briscoe's flight engineer, would appear to confirm that the forward position was retained for Jostle operation on at least some of the aircraft. In his book *Lucky B-24* Arthur describes a sortie when the rear special operator called up on the intercom that he was ill. This was not long after take-off so Arthur suggested to his skipper that they return to base and drop off the sick man. He advised Briscoe that they could move the front special operator to the rear position and Arthur would operate the special equipment (Jostle?) in the forward position. Apparently, Arthur was very familiar with the operation of this equipment having seen a special operator using it on many occasions.

However, this location was clearly a congested area on the aircraft and logic would support creating a second rear location for one or both special operators and their special equipments. When later aircraft were delivered it is possible that the decision was taken to position the Jostle controls to the rear. It is also logical that special operators could have operated Dina/Piperack and Carpet from this position. The same operator could quite easily have handled the operation of both, which was either on or off, that would leave the operator free to handle the more demanding Carpet. The latter required searching for frequencies to jam and then engaging one of the three jamming transmitters. As can be seen on some sorties, up to twenty frequencies could be located and jammed. It would also seem logical, and the best use of resources, for the two special operators to manage all three equipments from the rear position above the bomb bay. Certainly, waist gunners Peter Lovatt, Bob Lawrence, Leslie Matthews, Mick Stirrop and Len Davies are quite adamant that they regularly saw two special operators working above the bomb bay. From the above discussion it would appear that the forward position was retained on some of the early aircraft, with a second rear position introduced on all the squadron's aircraft. On the later aircraft it is possible that both special operators operated their special equipments from the rear position.

One final word on Jostle: The RAF's Y Service monitoring unit, based at Kingsdown in Kent, was set up to monitor enemy wireless and radio communications transmissions. In *Confound and Destroy* Martin Streetly describes the system whereby Kingsdown would transmit in code, wave meter readings that special operators were to use to jam

German night-fighter communications frequencies. These frequencies were the ones identified by the monitors. The instructions passed to 214 and 223 Squadron WOps, for onwards transmission to the Jostle operator, also notified when specific aircraft were to cease jamming. In the early months of 223 Squadron's operations, there is no mention in the operations record book (ORB) of such instructions being passed to aircraft. However, in 1945 remarks such as 'No instructions received to jam' can be seen.

In addition to this major revamp of the squadron's aircraft, a fitting party from 41 Group arrived to commence installation of direct reading compasses (DRCs), air mileage units (AMUs) and air position indicators (APIs).

Returning to the squadron's activities, an unusual incident occurred on 29 October with Flt Lt McPherson in TS521 (F) suffering the loss of the port undercarriage leg. Fortunately for the crew, this occurred during taxiing when the leg broke away. However this was not the only undercarriage problem. Mick Stirrop remembers another occasion when the nose leg would not lower on an approach to Oulton flown by Fg Off Tony Morris. An inspection by Sgt Vic Green the flight engineer, revealed that the problem was caused by misalignment of the leg in its retracted position. Vic advised that he could correct the alignment if he had a suitable lever. Mick Stirrop suggested using the barrel from one of the 0.5 Brownings. The barrel proved to be adequate for the task and the leg was lowered once the alignment had been corrected; a good example of a crew working together which saved an aircraft from significant damage.

1699 Training Flight

A change affecting crew conversion for 214 and 223 Squadrons was declared, with changes announced to 1699 Fortress Training Flight. The initial training of 223 Squadron's crews was completed during October 1944 using the three Liberators originally provided. To regularise this ad hoc arrangement, the establishment of 1669 Fortress Flight was formally changed to reflect the new training requirement with the addition of the three original aircraft. However, the new unit's strength would actually be five Liberators. Additional instructors and ground crew would be added to the unit's establishment to support the new task. The existing Fortress training commitment would be retained with an establishment of three Fortress B-17F aircraft. The revised unit would now be titled 1699 Training Flight under the command of Sqn Ldr Bellingham.

CHAPTER FIVE

Window Force Operations

Now 223 Squadron got into its operational stride, and Mervyn Utas provides us with an insight into a typical day for the squadron:

"You would rise about 07:00 and look forward with eager anticipation to your ordeal at the outdoor washrooms and then to the officers' mess for their renowned breakfast of cold fried bread and tea. After indulging you would check the daily battle order which was posted in the mess, to see if your crew would be on ops that night. The battle order would also state the briefing time which was usually in the late afternoon. Our take-off for a night operation could be anywhere from 16:00 to 03:00. If your crew were on the battle order then you usually went back to your Nissen hut and tried to get some sleep. If there was a 17:00 briefing for a 20:00 take-off then we would catch a bus from the officers' mess to the airfield about 16:00. At the briefing we would be told what our operations would be that night, given our routes, a weather briefing and an indication of what sort of anti-aircraft defences we could expect along the route and the wireless operators were given the appropriate codes. We then took buses back to the mess for a meal which, hallelujah, was accompanied by a fresh egg! Then it was back to the airfield to climb into our gear.

"Dressing for an operation was always a problem. We started with long wool/silk lined underwear, full body electrically-heated suit, battle dress trousers, white submariners' woollen sweater, battle dress blouse, electrically-heated gloves covered with leather gloves, electrically-heated socks covered with sheepskin-lined flying boots, a Mae West and a parachute harness. This was topped off with a leather helmet that contained your radio earphones and goggles, in case your windscreen was shot out. Fastened to the helmet was an oxygen mask with a long hose to plug into the aircraft oxygen system, and the microphone for the radio and intercom. Quite often one of the electric gloves or socks would develop a short circuit and would have to be disconnected. The heat was controlled by an individual rheostat *[a box was mounted at each crew position containing the rheostat control]* at each crew location which did not help too much as you would usually find that some part of you was too warm while another part was too cold. I finally, after many failures, stopped wearing the electric socks and gloves and used heavy wool socks and gloves instead. We also carried an escape kit in case we were shot down. It was in a waterproof pouch and contained some maps of Europe, some European currencies, a bit of energy food, matches and a compass.

"On a couple of trips when we were supporting Bomber Command raids on Chemnitz and Dresden we were operating near the Russian front and we were told if we got into trouble and could not get back behind our front line, to fly a short distance east to be behind the Russian lines. On these trips we were given bibs to tie over our jackets. They were covered in large notices in the Russian language that we were nice fellows and that we were on their side. We were a bit sceptical, as we had heard that the Russians were unable to read. I think if we had been in trouble we would have headed west and tried to make it behind our own lines. Dressed the way we were we would be pretty conspicuous, so I often wondered how some aircrew that had been forced to parachute into occupied Europe managed to evade the German troops. I guess most of them were picked up by the underground who would provide them with clothing that was more practical for a fugitive's tour.

"About 18:30 all the crew except the navigator would climb into the back of a canvas-covered pick-up truck for a ride to our aircraft. The navigators remained in the operations room to do their initial plotting and calculations. At the aircraft we would do a walk-round inspection and the gunners would clean their turrets. About one hour before take-off we would start up engines and do a run-up check to see that everything was working as it should. This would take about fifteen minutes and we would shut down and climb out of the aircraft. About that time the 'Sally Ann' (Salvation Army) canteen truck would arrive with the inevitable tea. We would have tea, a cigarette, pee on the tyres and then climb aboard to start up our engines for a 20:00 take-off. Often it was still daylight as we took off and the sky would be full of aircraft, as there could be 500 or 600 aircraft setting course for Germany. Once out over the Channel or the North Sea we would fire off a few rounds from all our guns to make certain that they were operating properly. As we climbed through 10,000 feet we would fasten our oxygen masks on securely and another long night would start.

"On the days that your crew were not on the battle order you would catch a bus to the airfield about 08:00. You might be required to do an air test on an aircraft that was on operations that night or you might be scheduled for a navigation training exercise. A fighter affiliation exercise with Spitfire and Mosquito aircraft was another possibility. This was hard work as you had to throw the big old lumbering B-24 into all sorts of violent evasive manoeuvres while the Spit or Mossie made a mock attack. It was fun though, since they were not really shooting at you.

"When you returned to your base after an operation, getting back on to the ground could sometimes prove to be a bit hectic. If both squadrons were operating there could be twenty-five to thirty aircraft in the air from Oulton. Everyone wanted to get home first so they did not wind up at the top of the stack. There was a certain amount of 'throttle bending' done in the race for home. As aircraft arrived back they were assigned a position in the stack. There would be four in the landing pattern at 1,000 feet above the ground, then another four at 2,000 feet and so on. There was an interval of about four minutes between aircraft landings, as we were operating initially without our navigation lights on, so everyone flew slowly and carefully to avoid a collision which unfortunately caused a lot of casualties during wartime operations. Eventually we started turning our lights on to avoid crashes. So if you were the twenty-fifth aircraft to arrive you could expect to fly around in circles for at least another ninety minutes – something you could do without after a six or seven hour operation.

"Once on the ground you were met by your maintenance crew for a report on any problems with the aircraft. Then it was back in the truck for a trip into the ops room for a debriefing. Again, if you were late getting on the ground you would have to wait for your debriefing. Fortunately, there was an urn of coffee or the RAF equivalent, but it could be made acceptable as there was a large jug of rum to spike it with. I guess this was supposed to restore your courage. What it did ensure however was that the intelligence officers did not keep you waiting too long for your debriefing as you might be a bit incoherent from too much exposure.

"Generally, they wanted to know what you had seen in the way of anti-aircraft defences, fighter attacks or aircraft going down. The navigator's log was turned in so they could plot all the aircraft positions if required. Then we would shed our flying gear and off again to the airmens' mess for another meal which would probably include another egg! If you were one of the last crews to arrive you might get an extra egg, since if any of our aircraft failed to return there would be leftovers. A ghoulish thought but we could not let an egg go to waste. Then into another bus for our ride back to Blickling Hall and our palatial Nissen hut.

"You had to be very quiet when you arrived in your hut at 03:00 or 04:00 in the morning so you would not wake the people who were asleep there as they would probably be going out on ops that night. You really could not do much in your hut but sleep after returning from ops at some ungodly hour. One morning I was sleeping after getting into bed at about 04:00. I was a bit annoyed at being woken up, but when I opened my eyes I saw the station adjutant and the station warrant officer with an open kit bag. They were at a bed across from mine and were loading everything from the locker into the kit bag. Obviously, the man was missing. Human nature is funny as we never asked if they knew if they were killed, prisoners of war or missing. We wanted to think that they had been able to safely bale out of their aircraft and were now with the underground in Europe or were prisoners of war."

A navigator's memories of briefing and debriefing are also of interest for their different slant on things together with some additional points. Andrew Barron details his experience:

"As far as the briefing was concerned I remember that we went into one of the jumbo-sized Nissen huts [possibly a Romney hut], sat at tables in crews and stood when the station commander came in. A curtain was drawn aside to reveal a large-scale (1/500,000) map of north-west Europe covered with splodges of red denoting the defended areas and with the night's routes and targets displayed. I've no idea how or when each crew was given its individual assignment. I am sure we navigators were far too busy to concern ourselves with what anybody else's task was. *[This was a specific question to Andrew to try and determine how the Window force aircraft achieved the 'formation' necessary to achieve a bomber force simulation. This is discussed later.]* They must have read out or put it up on a board because I had a note pad on which I jotted it all down. In the pad I jotted the 'way points' *[turning points]*, to use the modern term, heights, speeds, times, times and longitudes at which the special equipment had to be turned on and off, and the rates at which the different types of Window had to be dispensed. Then other items such as the GEE coding (whole numbers were added to the GEE readings to get the correct figure, in case the Germans had any GEE sets in use, diversionary aerodromes, etc. The meteorological (met) forecast was given with winds and temperatures, and sometimes we had to note them down on our log.

"The crew then dispersed to have their pre-op meal, kit up and be transported to the aircraft, whilst the navigators stayed working like the proverbial 'one-armed paperhangers'. First of all the turning points had to be marked on the chart and the tracks and distances measured and entered in the log. Then the height of the leg entered (several legs would involve a climb or descent so that had to be allowed for). True air speeds (TAS) had to be calculated and then the course and groundspeed calculated, and so giving the time of each leg. Working back from the times specified at various points (the target and designated turning points) one arrived at a set course time and an estimated time of arrival (ETA) back at base. Met winds were usually quoted at 2,000, 5,000, 10,000, 15,000 and 20,000 and perhaps 25,000 feet. If the specified height was in between the navigator had to extrapolate, or estimate, the intermediate value and temperature. The rule of thumb was two thirds of the height. When this was done the captain's of aircraft map had to be completed. Apart from the times, heights, speeds and courses etc, I guess it was up to pilots and navs what else was put on it. I always tried to put on the battle line (important if you had to bale out and were lucky enough to have a choice as to when).

"The navigators' tools were pretty simple. Pencil, Douglas protractor (about four to five inches square with a square grid engraved on it so that it was easy to line up the vectors and the grid on the chart), dividers and the Dalton computer. This wasn't a computer as we know it but a calculator, about five inches by seven and an inch or so thick. One side enabled one to mechanically solve the 'Triangle of Velocities' of track and ground speed, course and air speed, and wind velocity by means of a rotatable ground plastic screen with a square graticule and a compass rose round it. Under that was an endless belt (moved by knobs at the side) with curved speed lines and radiating drift lines. You marked the wind vector on the screen, set the roller to airspeed at the centre dot, rotated it to the required track and did a little juggle so that you got the same drift reading on the screen as against the compass rose, reading ground speed off on the endless belt at the end of the wind vector. The other side of the computer was a circular slide rule with special marks for hours etc and scales for calculating TAS according to height and temperature. All very simple and still in use to this day but it all took time. I don't remember if navigators left as they finished or if we all had to wait for the last man. Anyway when we finished it was off to kit up."

Ronnie Simmons adds:

"At the briefing we were also handed rice paper sheets giving the location and codes for the various airfields in our overall area of operation. In the event of emergency action or bale out we had to swallow these papers. All crews were given a bacon and eggs meal in the mess before take-off, known affectionately as 'the last supper'. Unfortunately, on many occasions the navigators arrived in the mess just as everyone else was finishing their meal. Quite often due to HQ uncertainties (mainly due to weather over the target areas) times and routes were changed and the navigators' preparatory works, charts, logs and captain's map had to be done over again. On these occasions the meal was over and the crews had already departed for the aircraft. I had a wonderful crew because many a time they met me with a bacon and egg sandwich as I clambered in hurriedly aboard through the bomb bay doors."

It is rather surprising to learn from 223 veterans that they had separate briefings and debriefings from 214 Squadron, especially when they would be flying together on Window force ops. Possibly, with such large crews, there was not a sufficiently large enough building available to permit joint briefings and debriefings.

Tactics

With the formation of 100 Group, Bomber Command's hand was greatly strengthened in its battle with the German defences. The introduction of the new Mandrel screen mounted by 171 and 199 Squadrons started to reduce the early warning and likely direction of main force attacks. Initially, the screen was only available over the Channel and the North Sea, but would be pushed forward on to the continent as the allied armies broke out heading for Germany. The Mandrel screen also enabled Bomber Command to confuse the Germans in a variety of ways. Apart from delaying an early sight of the attacking bomber stream(s), it could shield more than one attacking force or Window spoof force. A deliberate gap could be created in the screen by briefly stopping the transmissions from the jamming aircraft in two adjacent race track legs. The gap would expose a spoof force which would be briefly seen heading in one direction and draw defensive night fighters away from the genuine main force target tracks. After the brief pause, the false trail having been laid, the two Mandrel screen aircraft would resume jamming.

Originally, Bomber Command had used the Bullseye navigation exercise to simulate a bomber stream. The exercise employed heavy conversion units (HCU) supplemented by OTU crews, and occurred at the end of the respective courses involving flying round the UK. A modification of the exercise involved the crews flying across the North Sea towards the enemy coast line before turning back. The timing of this exercise was organised to occur prior to the launch of main force attacks. This obviously had a limited value as a feint or spoof force, but was useful when employing Window force aircraft in the formation. This was 223 Squadron's introduction to Window force operations on the night of 14/15 October when three aircraft flew at the head of the Bullseye force, although no special equipment was used.

In the early days of 100 Group, AVM Addison and his staff had been researching the employment of Window. Initial studies of its use revealed that German air defence radars were unable to distinguish between the genuine aircraft or Window bundles. The 100 Group investigations indicated that in theory it would be possible to simulate a large bomber force using a small force of aircraft dropping Window at a specific rate and pattern. The Window employed would be used to blind the German early-warning radars and night-fighter ground control communications. In his submission to Bomber Command HQ in May 1944, Addison proposed that a force of fifteen aircraft dropping Window, flying in a formation of three lanes, spread five miles apart, with a separation of twenty miles between each of the five aircraft in each lane, and dropping Window at a rate of twenty units per minute (each unit representing one aircraft), would appear as a raid of 800 bombers to the German defences[1]. This approach also called for aircraft in the formation to weave to increase the spread of the Window bundles and thus help to reduce gaps on the screen.

Sgt Leslie Matthews, an air gunner in Flt Woodward's crew, recalled a weave of up to 5 degrees either side of track at approximately 190 mph to achieve the required spread. However, members of other 223 Squadron crews when questioned about this practice did not recall or could not remember their pilots carrying it out.

For many years the authors were unable to find any instructions or details, in official documents or published works that illustrated how the formation was achieved in practice. Discussions with 223 Squadron navigators failed to throw any light on the matter, although it could be appreciated that the twenty-mile separation along the lanes could be achieved only by strict timing. It also seemed logical that the lateral separation of five miles could only be met by individual navigators being allocated to one of the parallel tracks to be entered from a designated point. The navigators agreed that this could have been the case, but they were never aware, or could not recall, being given individual routings. This perhaps, was not surprising as they remarked that they were far too busy frantically trying to complete their own preparations to bother about what other navigators were doing. However, the following plot was eventually uncovered, produced for 100 Group's navigation leader, which he had asked for as part of his running campaign to force home the importance to squadron navigators of the need for tight time keeping and accurate navigation. What it does show is a representation of the lane system. In this example, a Window patrol in the absence of main force operations on the night of 22/23 March 1945; it also shows a fanning out of the force at Point B to create eight diverging lanes to produce a much wider spread of Window. This was aimed at multiplying the apparent threat to targets in the Ruhr area[2].

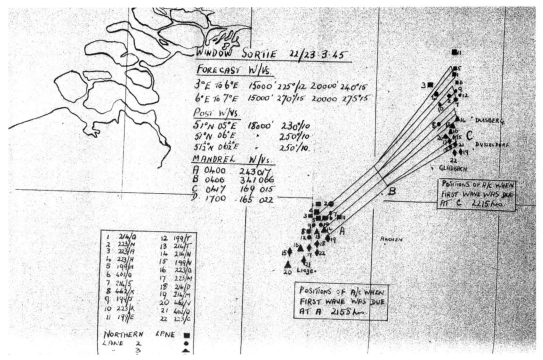

Plotted positions of aircraft for Window sortie 22/23 March 1945.

Bomber Command regularly attacked two, three or more different targets, and as another variation the Window force would operate independently, simulating another attacking force. This was usually given added authenticity by 8 Pathfinder Force (PFF) Group's Mosquito fighter bombers attacking and bombing the apparent Window force target.

Yet another valuable ploy for Bomber Command was the use of the Window force on nights when the main force was not operating at all. A Window force would operate using its special equipments to imitate a genuine main force raid, and this too could be strengthened with bombing by the Light Night Strike Force (LNSF) of 8 Group's Mosquitoes. As with a genuine raid, a Mandrel screen would be in operation, provided by 171 and 199 Squadrons, and the 100 Group Mosquito squadrons would mount high and low-level intruder patrols.

214 and 223 Squadron also provided target patrols, identified in the squadrons' operational record books (RAF Forms 540/541) as Jostle patrols. For this type of operation, the bomber support squadron aircraft would arrive in the target area at the same time as the Pathfinder force aircraft of 8 Group at approximately H (time due on target) minus five minutes. The bomber support aircraft would circle in the target area flying at 1,000 or 2,000 feet above the main force bombing height employing Jostle to jam the night-fighter control communication frequencies, Dina/Piperack to jam the night fighters' AI radar and Carpet to jam the Würzburg radars controlling the searchlights

and anti-aircraft gun-laying equipment. The aircraft would circle in the target area for a maximum of fifteen minutes before being relieved by another aircraft. This was obviously a hazardous role, not only because of the risk of night-fighter attack, but also from the attacking main force aircraft as Mervyn Utas describes:

"Our other task was to provide jamming over the target being bombed by main force. A bombing raid generally lasted from twenty to thirty minutes and we would have two or three jamming aircraft each providing about eight to ten minutes, with a bit of overlap between aircraft. The last slot was hated as you were the last aircraft to leave the target; our Liberators were slower than the main force bombers, especially after they had shed their bomb loads. It was a bit uncomfortable knowing that you were the last aircraft, and losing more ground trying to get out of Germany. Our route home was often clearly marked as the German night fighters, by that time, had established the route of the bombers leaving the target and would drop fighter flares (they hung on a parachute) along the route. Sometimes it looked like a row of street lights. If we saw it we would change our route to avoid 'Flare Road'.

"The first time we did a target we were told that main force would be bombing from 20,000 feet and that we should orbit at 21,000 feet, and we believed them. Being green we did not know that the bomber crews had a deadly fear of having bombs dropped on them by a bomber at a higher altitude. So if the bombing altitude is 20,000 feet they would add one or two thousand feet to this as a safety precaution. Halfway round our first orbit we suddenly had large aircraft shapes flashing by on either side and above. We were flying right into the middle of the main force bomber stream, but in the opposite direction. We quickly turned back in the same direction they were going and immediately climbed a couple of thousand feet.

"There were often some interesting crew interchanges when you were the first jamming aircraft over the target. We would generally arrive about a minute or two before the Pathfinders marked the target and you would be in total darkness with no searchlights or anti-aircraft fire. That minute or two would seem like an hour or two and the navigator would always be accused of getting lost and we thought we were the only aircraft in that unknown part of Germany. The navigator would hotly deny this accusation, so the wireless operator would be blamed for missing a recall signal and the fact that we were now the only allied aircraft over Germany and everyone else was back in England and safely in bed. About that time the first target indicators would go down which would trigger the enemy searchlights and anti-aircraft guns into action, and all would be forgiven as we now knew we were probably in the right spot and had company.

"The view over the target was fascinating. You could see the various coloured target indicators glowing on the ground and the bright flashes of the bombs as they struck. All around you would be bright flashes as the anti-aircraft shells exploded. If you were above clouds then the searchlights shining on the base of the clouds would illuminate them like a giant screen and from above we could see the silhouette of each bomber as it flew over the target. If the night was clear then the beams of the searchlights would be waving back and forth like a long thin pencil. Sometimes a light would catch a bomber and immediately a large number of lights would swing over to illuminate the unfortunate aircraft. They would also be sitting at the apex of this cone of light and all the anti-aircraft guns would start firing at the 'coned' aircraft. It was not often that a coned aircraft escaped."

All members of the crew were important and had their parts to play both in their individual specialisations, but also contributing to the success of a cohesive team. However, the key factor in the success of 100 Group operations was positioning and timing, and therefore the navigator was very much the key player in achieving this. First, Ronnie Simmons:

"One of the most critical pieces of data required for navigation was accurate wind speeds and direction throughout the flight. Since our only navigational aid was GEE, and it was jammed approaching enemy territory, it was essential to get as many GEE fixes as possible during the climb to operating height. The major problem was that we were climbing out from base at as slow a climb rate as possible to delay the times when we would be picked up by the German radar detectors. The wind direction veers about two degrees per 1,000 feet and the navigators were struggling to get good fixes as often as possible before our GEE sets were unusable. When we reached operational height, the resultant wind speed and direction was a composite over the climbing range and could not be used accurately for our operational altitude. The navigators therefore worked as quickly as possible attempting to see the GEE pulses through the increasing 'snow' appearing from the enemy jamming to obtain the information needed to continue the sortie by dead-reckoning navigation alone.

"Some forecast meteorological wind data was very poor. On one sortie, I do not remember which, but it was longer than a normal flight, we were on target duty requiring accurate arrival time on target. Our predicted wind speed at 23,000 feet was about 60 mph. From my GEE fixes I found to my horror that we were experiencing tail winds of about 120 mph. This meant we would be much too early and, after discussion with skipper Mark Levy, I recommended a giant dog leg across the Third Reich to kill time. We were buffeted by the early birds but arrived on time. Now came the return journey facing 120 mph winds with an economical cruising speed of only about 160 mph. It was obvious that we had to reduce altitude drastically to experience much lower wind speeds or run out of fuel. After a long discussion with Mark, I advised turning northwards towards the Frisian Islands avoiding known flak areas. We came down to about 10,000 feet and passed to the North Sea between the islands without incident. At this point we decided to head directly to base at Oulton, abandoning our flight plan. We came down to 5,000 feet and landed safely at base. There were no adverse repercussions except that five years ago the wife of one of my business colleagues talked about her experiences in the WAAF stationed at Stratton Strawless, near Norwich, where she was in charge of defence radar systems against intruders. She remembered that night because we crossed the coast at an unauthorised location and despite our identification friend or foe (IFF) transmission, Fighter Command aircraft were scrambled."

Andrew Barron's comments on navigational accuracy:

"The standard plotting chart was 1 in 2,000,000 which is about 33 mm or thirty-eight standard miles to the inch. An HB pencil, which most navigators used (I used a Hard [H] pencil which derived from my mechanical and engineering drawing training) would probably produce a line a mile wide! Working conditions were far from ideal. I reckon we had the best position in the Liberator, shut away on our own in the front, able to turn the lights up without worrying about disturbing anyone or letting any light out. We were on oxygen and I don't suppose that suited everybody's metabolism. It was bloody cold (around minus 40 degrees C) and gloves were not really an option. *[Having seen Andrew's immaculately kept navigation logs, the authors remain amazed and impressed that such neatness could be achieved in such conditions.]* The 'planes were rarely stable – I expect that 'slipstreaming' was commonplace in the bomber stream, and it is amazing how much buffeting that produces. GEE was at extreme range and subjected to heavy jamming. Some navigators were better than others in reading through the 'grass' and the 'cut' at these ranges was poor, 30 degrees, perhaps, so that errors were magnified. I was jealous of the Forts with H2S. However, we did manage on the whole."

Notes:
1. *The Second World War 1939-1945 Royal Air Force, Signals Volume VII Radio Counter-Measures.* Air Ministry 1950, reprinted by MLRS 2011.
2. Air 25/784 100 Group Report of Activities February/March 1945.

CHAPTER SIX

Operations November to December 1944

The squadron was now up to strength and contributing to the Window force. On 1/2 November it dispatched five aircraft on a Window spoof. On 2/3 November, six aircraft were launched to join the Window force diversionary feint in the direction of Osnabrück, leaving the main force track on its way to attack Düsseldorf. Similar Window force spoof or feint attacks were mounted on the nights of 4/5 and 6/7 November, to which 223 Squadron contributed five aircraft on both occasions. (Illustrated in the night bombing report route maps overleaf.) On the first of these nights, the Window force operated to draw night fighters away from the Ruhr where main force were attacking Bochum. The reverse tactic was employed on the night of 6/7 to draw night fighters to the Ruhr area whilst main force raided Koblenz and the Mittelland Canal.

9/10 November saw another variation in tactics. Main force did not operate, so a Window force was used to simulate a major attack on Mannheim. Before reaching the target, the force would retrace its steps and reform behind the Mandrel screen before emerging for a second time in support of an attack on Kassel by Mosquito fighter bombers of 8 Group. Dreadful weather, including snow, resulted in only one of 223 Squadron's aircraft completing its mission out of five aircraft originally detailed. Oulton's efforts in such difficult conditions earned congratulations for the station in a personal message from the air officer commanding, AVM Addison.

On the night of 10/11 November, 100 Group again mounted a simulated attack in the absence of main force operations. This involved a double penetration of the Mandrel screen to simulate attacks on Duisburg in the Ruhr and Koblenz in the Upper Rhine area. The squadron dispatched five aircraft, of which four completed their missions. The fifth aircraft was not so lucky, and the experience of the crew that night illustrates some of the hazards of operational flying and the spirit of skippers to complete an operation. Ronnie Simmons explains:

"Our take-offs for this night were pretty hairy. The power supply for our Libs came from No.3 engine and it required a speed of 1,400 rpm to generate power. The brakes were pneumatic with the air pressure supplied from an electric-powered compressor to a pressure storage tank. In addition, the engine fuel booster pumps were electrically operated by toggle switches which were activated on take-off. On entering the aircraft, whoever was first on through the bomb bay, started up the APU, to provide ground power for start-up procedures until ready for take-off.

"On our take-off run as we were gathering speed down the runway, the fuel boosters were activated by Joe Boaden the co-pilot, and the aircraft shot off sideways onto the grass verge; the boosters had not activated for one or more engines. We came to a stop, taxied over the grass back on to the perimeter track for another go at a take-off. No.3 engine was revved up for a few minutes to give electrical power and we were given the green for another try. The same thing happened again, but Mark was undaunted and decided to give it yet another go. Third time lucky, we got off successfully but had to abort after forty-five minutes of flight due to petrol fumes in the rear compartment and an unserviceable gun turret."

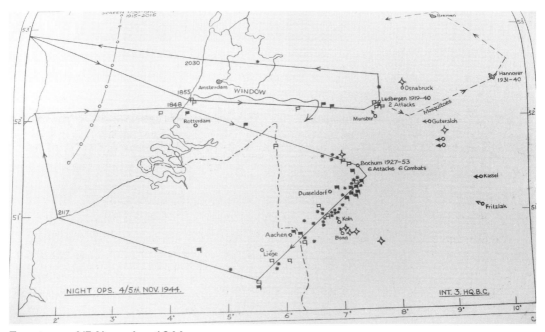

Target map 4/5 November 1944.

Main force were back in action on the night of 11/12 November with attacks on Harburg and Dortmund. To confuse the enemy defences a Window feint was mounted against Wiesbaden with six of 223's aircraft successfully completing missions. The Wiesbaden spoof appeared more credible combined with an attack on the city by Mosquitoes of 8 (PFF) Group. The latter would become a regular feature of Window feint operations.

Originally, according to a 100 Group briefing for operations on the night of 15/16 November, main force were to attack Gelsenkirchen supported by a spoof force which would split into two, directed at Düsseldorf and Koblenz. In the event main force did not operate, but the northern and southern spoofs were executed by the Window force. The squadron contributed three aircraft to both patrols. Bad weather resulted in diversions on their return for Flt Lt Briscoe from the northern patrol to Carnaby in Yorkshire, and Fg Off Morris from the southern to Foulsham in Norfolk. This was a typical operation to tire and confuse the German defences, and cause unnecessary night-fighter sorties to be mounted.

On 16 November the squadron adjutant reported that Carpet, Dina and modified

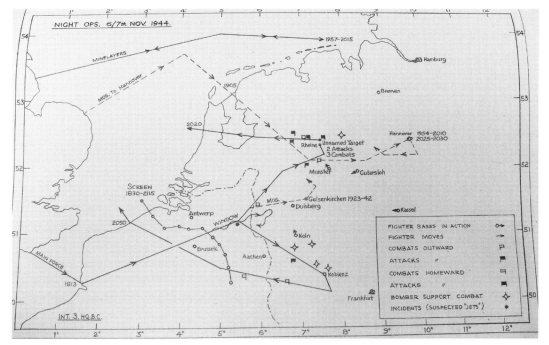

Target map 6/7 November 1944.

Jostle installations were now nearly complete on all 223's aircraft. 214 were slightly ahead of 223 in equipping their aircraft and already had Dina and Carpet installed.

Tragedy visited Oulton on the 18th when a B-24H Liberator of 406 BS belonging to 492 Bombardment Group (BG) based at nearby North Pickenham, crashed after take-off from the airfield. The aircraft had diverted to Oulton because of bad weather and was taking off to return to its base when a fuel leak was noticed from a misplaced fuel cap. The aircraft flew a tight circuit to regain the airfield but struck a tree as it came in, crashing 200 yards off the runway and burning out. The same night 223 Squadron dispatched four aircraft to join the Window force which would fly ahead of the main force. The Mandrel screen was positioned on a curved front to screen Bomber Command's tracks from Axis defences in the Netherlands and Germany. The Window force leading would emerge from the Mandrel screen in a north-easterly direction. Just to the north of Liège the Window force broke off from the main force track turning in the direction of Wiesbaden, Windowing heavily. Main force continued to its target, the oil plant at Wanne-Eickel which it attacked between 18:32 and 19:08. The Window force reached a position short of Koblenz at 18:54 when individual aircraft were briefed to turn 180 degrees and return to base. The feint attack on Wiesbaden was strengthened by thirty-one Mosquitoes from 8 Group attacking the city between 18:46 and 19:07. It proved successful, as only one Lancaster was lost. The bad weather was still causing problems and all four of 223's aircraft were diverted to Manston, Kent, on their return. At least there was a let up over Britain which permitted Flt Lt Briscoe and Fg Off Morris to return to base from their diversion airfields.

20 November was a bad day for operations. Sqn Ldr McKnight got away only to lose No.1 engine on take-off and was forced to return. The second aircraft bogged down

during take-off preventing two more from getting airborne.

Bomber Command carried out a major assault on the night of the 21/22 attacking five targets with a total of 1,345 sorties. The Window force task was to draw the enemy's attention to the south and to disguise 1 Group's attack on Aschaffenburg. The Window force would accompany the 1 Group main force as far as their turning point to the north-east. At this point the Window force would continue on the previous south-easterly track dropping Window to disguise the turn, and continuing in the direction of Karlsruhe and Stuttgart. The attention of the German defences would be further concentrated by a force of 8 Group Mosquitoes bombing Stuttgart just prior to the time of the 1 Group attack. Only 1.0% of the attacking forces were lost, including just two Lancasters from the 1 Group attack. This night was significant for 223 Squadron as it launched aircraft for the first time equipped with Jostle, Carpet and Dina jammers.

The 22nd was significant for the decision that the squadron would introduce a policy of allocating a specific aircraft to individual crews. This was an attempt to improve aircraft serviceability which was still a significant problem. Although un-serviceabilities affecting operations are recorded at Appendix 2, it has not been possible to determine the figures affecting training sorties, and the number of aircraft falling unserviceable during crew-in for operations. But just considering the number of defects recorded for operational flights gives a strong indication of the extent of the problem. The tired state and age of many of the ex-USAAF Liberators has already been mentioned. Both aircrew and ground crew were on a steep learning curve to build up experience on what for many would have been a new aircraft. The major disruption during October when the squadron set about standardising the layout and equipment fit of its aircraft, together with the rolling programme of special equipment fit, would all have contributed to the production of serviceable aircraft. It should not be forgotten that

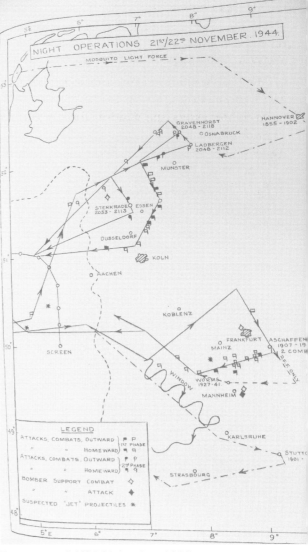

Target map 21/22 November 1944.

servicing personnel were dealing with aircraft of different production block or batch numbers, from different manufacturers' production lines. Inevitably the resulting modification state of individual aircraft must have provided a further headache for servicing activities.

On 23 November the squadron dispatched six aircraft for a Window spoof in the Cologne/south-east Ruhr area. Flt Lt Brigham failed to take off due to a failed turbocharger amplifier. The spoof was mounted to draw attention away from an abandoned main force attack on the Trondheim submarine pens, but also to continue to reduce the efficiency of German air defences in the Ruhr.

On 25/26 November there were no main force operations, so the Window force was used to stir up the German defences and force them to expend their resources unnecessarily and to reduce confidence in their raid-plotting system. The force would eventually split to cause further confusion. The squadron contributed one aircraft to the northern patrol and five to the southern patrol threatening the Frankfurt/Mainz area.

On the night of 26/27 the Window force provided a diversion to a main force raid on Munich. The spoof force broke away from the main force track to threaten Karlsruhe which was bombed by six 8 Group Mosquitoes. 223's contribution was five aircraft.

Main force mounted two attacks on the night of 27/28. No 1 Group raided Freiburg and 1 and 6 Groups hit Neuss. To confuse the enemy's raid plotting and to disperse his night-fighter assets, the Window force was tasked to break away from the 1 Group track to Freiburg and follow a new track taking them between the tracks of the two main force attacks. Six aircraft were supplied by 223.

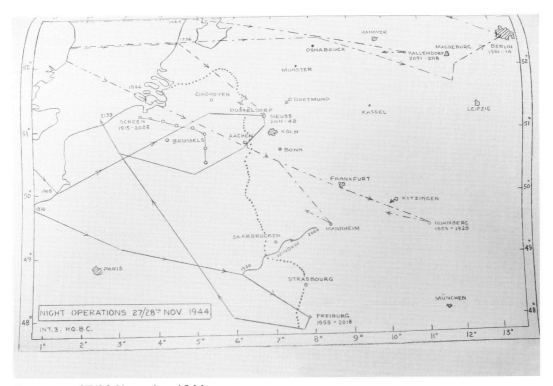

Target map 27/28 November 1944.

On 28/29 November, the main force targets were Essen attacked by 1, 4 and 8 Groups and Neuss raided by 3 Group. On this night the Window force was employed to approach the Ruhr on a wide front, splitting into three parts, just ahead of the main force to infect a large area with Window. The meteorologists forecasted a westerly wind which the Bomber Command planners hoped would extend the German defenders' confusion, with regard to possible targets, until main force aircraft had crossed the front line. 223 supplied five aircraft to support the attacks against the Ruhr targets. The squadron also dispatched two aircraft to a secondary diversion provided by a southern Window patrol. This use of the Window force to infect a large area with Window bundles was a new tactic forced on 100 Group by the German defence controllers who were becoming familiar with the normal use, particularly when employed in what were now regular attacks against targets in the Ruhr area.

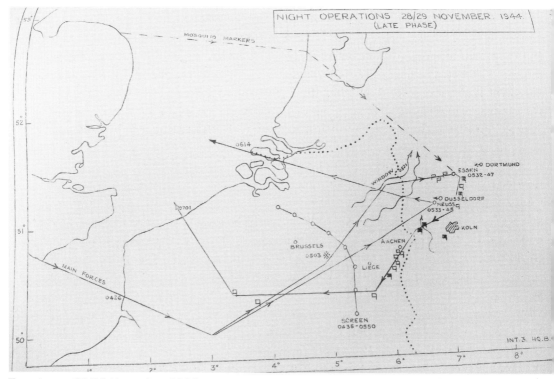

Target map 28/29 November 1944.

There were no main force operations on the night of 29/30. The Window force was used again to simulate an attack flying north-east to be interpreted by the Luftwaffe as an attack in the Münster area. This was to be carried out in conjunction with an attack by sixty-seven Mosquitoes of 8 Group heading east over Hannover, which the planners hoped would be viewed as the spoof force. Six aircraft from 223 flew with the Window force.

Just one main force attack took place on 30 November/1 December, aimed at Duisburg. Interestingly, the Mandrel screen was instructed to jam at half strength for the first ten minutes of its operation to simulate the weak screen employed the previous night for the activities of the Window force and 8 Group. The tactics of the previous night would also be repeated whereby the Window force, flying just ahead of the main force, would fly on a wide front to infect a large area with Window again sowing confusion and indecision in the defenders' minds with regard to a possible target. The squadron provided seven aircraft for this, the sixth consecutive night of operations, and all seven successfully completed their missions. The adjutant rightly recorded praise for the ground crews' excellent efforts in the face of considerable difficulties.

HQ 100 Group recorded that 223 Squadron had installed Carpet III in twelve aircraft, and Dina in nine aircraft. It also noted that one aircraft had been used for a prototype installation of Jostle. Frustratingly, this was not qualified but is assumed to refer to the fitting of an aerial winch to enable the release of a trailing aerial for use against medium frequency transmissions. This modification was intended to give 223 the same operational capability as 214 Squadron[1].

An interesting development during the month was the requirement for all flight engineers on the squadron to carry out a minimum of two hours daily in their basic trade on maintenance inspection work. No justification is given for this ruling, but it is assumed that it was part of the campaign to improve serviceability on the squadron. However it is not recorded whether the flight engineers were restricted to working on their 'own' aircraft. The flight engineers were also given flying instruction on the Link Trainer simulator during the month, together with instruction on the Liberator's A5 autopilot installation; skipper Flt Lt Jack Brigham said that for safety reasons it was not usual to use the autopilot when flying with main force. Sudden manoeuvres might be necessary if evasive action was required.

Navigators were given instruction on the long-range navigation (LORAN) aid scheduled to be fitted to the squadron's aircraft. 223 Squadron would be given priority over 214 for its fitment, recognising that its sister squadron already had the advantage of H2S.

In the latter part of the month Flt Lt Val Croft's navigator, W/O J F Healy, suffered a serious accident. Their aircraft was holding at the end of the runway while the pilots were trying to interpret the range of coloured Aldis lamp signals aimed at the aircraft from the runway control trailer. It would seem that Frank Healy dropped out through his emergency exit through the nose-wheel bay to find out. At that moment the aircraft received a recall message over the radio, and the pilot commenced to taxi back to dispersal. Unfortunately, Frank's ankle was crushed by the rim of the nose wheel as the aircraft rolled forward, and he never flew with the crew again. The squadron's ORB does not mention the accident, but records that Healy was posted to Oulton's non-effective strength on 5 December 1944. The crew then flew with a number of different navigators, but carried out twenty-two of their remaining operations with Fg Off W Simpson. According to Sgt Bill Sykes, one of Croft's waist gunners, he had an uncanny knack of giving the skipper the next course just when the flak became thick enough to taxi on; intuition perhaps? As soon as the skipper responded with "Turning now, Billy," two very relieved waist gunners turned to each other and gave the thumbs up sign! Perhaps it is not surprising that they called him 'Turning now, Billy Simpson'. Apparently, he was also well known as an inveterate cadger of cigarettes.

December 1944

The first operation for the month was another Window force spoof, comprising aircraft from 171, 192, 214 and 223 Squadrons, against the Ruhr using the wide front approach. Six aircraft were dispatched by 223. This was mounted in the absence of main force operations. To heighten the confusion four Mosquitoes from 8 Group dropped markers and bombs on Duisburg. In its intentions signal 100 Group were briefed that the Window force aircraft equipped with H2S were to switch on the equipment at 0100E and off at 0200E on the outward track. This was an experiment presumably to try and assess any German attempts to home on the transmissions. From July 1944 Bomber Command had restricted the use of H2S, instructing that it was not to be used until forty miles from enemy territory.

Similarly, in September 1944 Harris had ordered the removal of the Monica rear-warning radar from Bomber Command aircraft because of the discovery of the German Flensburg device which detected Monica transmissions[2]. The real secret to denying the enemy of an early warning of Bomber Command operations, was to prolong radio and radar silence for as long as possible on the approach to enemy territory. Whatever restrictions Bomber Command imposed, it was inevitable that some crews, for various reasons, would fail or forget to comply. It is interesting to note that both 214 and 223 Squadrons continued to use Monica, and 214 its H2S. Ignoring the navigational advantage of H2S, it is assumed the continuing use of these equipments by the two squadrons was part of the plan to increase authenticity of the Window force on spoof operations. There is also an indication that Monica was only used to an agreed plan – 223 Squadron's ORB includes references to using Monica 'as briefed'. December would see the Dina sets in 223's aircraft being replaced with Piperack. This was essentially the same equipment redesigned with British parts.

On 2/3 December 100 Group again employed the Window force on a very wide front to disguise the night's main force target in the Ruhr, Hagen. The squadron launched six aircraft for this operation thus completing its eighth consecutive night of operations. However, Fg Off Thompson was forced to return with a defective flame damper on No.4 engine. The failure of a flame damper early in the flight with a high all-up weight, normally presented the pilot with no option but to abort, notwithstanding the increased vulnerability caused by the now exposed exhaust. The failure of the flame damper required the offending engine to be shut down, thus seriously reducing the pilot's ability to maintain the required height and speed. If the failure occurred well into the flight, the same penalty generally did not apply and, although the problem engine would still be shut down, it could be restarted in an emergency or later on the return leg at the discretion of the pilot. Returning to the night's operation, Flt Lt Noseworthy was forced to take evasive action on several occasions to avoid possible attack from a suspected jet aircraft. The ORB statement suggests that the suspect jet had been picked up by special equipment. Possibly Noseworthy's aircraft already had the Monica equipment, although the ORB does not confirm it.

The Window force acted independently again on the night of 4/5 December, routed out over Le Touquet, then heading just to the north of east as far as 5055N 0620E before swinging north to threaten the Ruhr. The force discharged Window at a very high rate to cover the western part of the Ruhr. This activity was to draw attention away from the main force attacks in the south against Karlsruhe and Heilbronn. 223's contribution was seven aircraft to the Window force, whilst Flt Lt Hastie and his crew flew a Jostle (target) patrol over Karlsruhe. Flt Lt Dyck completed the majority of his Window patrol on three engines, having lost one at Gravesend on the outbound leg.

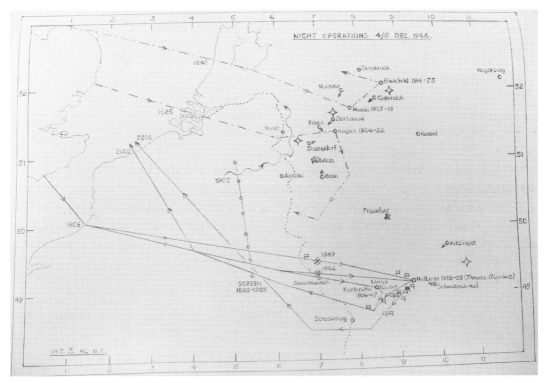

Target map 4/5 December 1944.

Soest was the main force target for the next night. The squadron sent one aircraft on a target patrol to orbit Soest, and six aircraft joined the Window force. The latter was a feint tracking towards Duisburg from Luxemburg to the north-east, passing fifteen miles north-west of the Ruhr to Rheine (NNW of Münster), returning by the same route. It proved to be a dramatic night for Fg Off Scottie Steele and his crew in TS528 (R) as described by his flight engineer, Peter Matthews:

"Our spoof was to Rheine. Approaching the turning point we were hit by flak. It sounded quite loud when the shells burst close to you. I was about to stop my Window drop, my arms were aching. Automatically, I reached for a few bundles of Type C and thrust them out. Type C was designed to confuse anti-aircraft crews and almost immediately the shells started to burst farther and farther behind us. Scottie our skipper put us into a violent corkscrew, better than any practice!

"No.4 engine started to falter and had to be feathered. We had a few holes in the fuselage which were not seen until later. Two three-engined landings on the trot was not our style but worse was to follow. On the final approach, the navigator vacated his in-flight position below and forward of the flight deck, squatting alongside the wireless operator and behind me. Flaps down, wheels down and locked. Touch-down at last. The nose wheel crunched into the deck and collapsed. The gear folded up and a section came up through the flight deck between the seats where the pilot and I were sitting. I remember reaching up to fire the Very pistol and all hell was let loose as Fire and Rescue tenders sped after us. We skidded to a halt still on the runway, still level-ISH! We did not fly in Liberator (R) again."

Although Peter says the crew did not fly in the aircraft again, the damage was not too severe. It was quickly categorised by the engineers as Cat AC, meaning that it was considered repairable on site by a contractor's working party. In the event it was repaired at Oulton by tradesmen from 67 Maintenance Unit (MU), but was not returned to the squadron until 15 April 1945.

The flight engineer was normally the man to push out the Window bundles. As Peter describes, this was hard work, particularly when the drop could last for some considerable time.

"The navigator would give the instruction to start dropping and the rate – so many bundles per minute *[normally about two bundles a minute but could be increased for high density drops]* – would be pushed through the two chutes at the rear end of the bomb bay, with a portable oxygen cylinder plugged in and electrically-heated flying suit switched on. Alone, R/T silence was maintained throughout, in total darkness, which was quite frightening."

On the high intensity Window-dropping sorties the flight engineer could be assisted by a second man, possibly one of the waist gunners. Operational requirements might involve dropping Window for periods of over an hour. The dropper(s) would work up quite a sweat, even in the extremely cold conditions. The different types of Window were easily recognisable by their different sizes and were positioned in big stacks on the available floor space in the bomb bay. The gunners at the waist positions also liked to keep some bundles of the anti-flak Window which they would hurl out of the open waist hatches on occasions when engaged by heavy flak. Arthur Anthony said that he would stuff a few anti-aircraft bundles out just as a precaution when dropping the normal MB Type Window, which covered the 70-200 Mc/s range of Freya and Lichtenstein SN2 AI radars.

6/7 December, main force mounted three major attacks on Giessen, Osnabrück and the synthetic-oil plant at Leuna near Leipzig. All three targets would be covered by Jostle patrols with 223 Squadron sending an aircraft to each of the targets. Unfortunately, Flt Lt Hastie in TS523 (D) was forced to return early with an oxygen leak. The Window force accompanied the main force attacking Leuna as far as 5155N 1025E and then diverted to 5220N 1115E, the intention being to pose a threat to Berlin as far as the German defences were concerned, thus delaying potential night-fighter attacks on the Leuna force for as long as possible. This deep penetration feint was backed up by an attack of forty-two Mosquitoes on Berlin. The diversion was successful with just five Lancasters lost

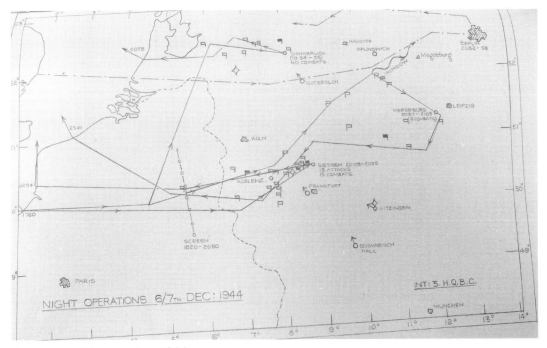

Target map 6/7 December 1944.

from an attacking force of 475 aircraft. 223 provided just two aircraft for the Window force, a third aircraft returning early whilst still in the base area with a fuel leak.

On 7 December the adjutant recorded the arrival of two 'new' aircraft for the squadron, TT340 and TT343. One of these aircraft however had already flown 380 hours!

9/10 December: Minor operations for Bomber Command with no main force attacks. It would seem that there was an original intention to mount a main force attack by 1 and 3 Groups on Leuna with the Window force providing a diversion with a feint to Koblenz. The cancellation of the attack resulted in the removal of 223's Jostle patrol aircraft from the battle order and just five aircraft were launched for the Window patrol, with Fg Off Steele returning early whilst still in the base area with a fuel leak.

On 12/13 December Fg Off Morris's crew completed the first target operation in support of the main force's major attack on Essen orbiting in the target area at 22,000 feet for seven minutes commencing at 19:30. Jostle was employed from 19:16 to 20:15. Carpet was in action for an hour from 19:18 giving intermittent jamming on seven frequencies. This night saw the squadron's first use of Piperack which was replacing Dina. Morris's special operators switched on their Piperack at 19:16. Monica was also fitted but found to be u/s. Tony Morris reported moderate to intense flak in the target area, and commented that a few fighter flares were seen but no fighters. Also no searchlights were seen. He added that marking and bombing seemed concentrated. Meanwhile the squadron dispatched six aircraft, five completed, on a Window patrol in support of the main force attack. The force took the main force route as far as 5155N 0600E where it broke away proceeding as far as 5210N 0735E arriving at 19:34. The aim was to convince the Germans that Osnabrück was the main force target. This spoof was aided by a force of forty-nine Mosquitoes which bombed Osnabrück at 19:25.

Fg Off Pocock & crew with Liberator TT343 (K). Rear L to R: Sgt E Dawes, F/O J J B Pocock, F/S E Glaze, Sgt J H Frow, Sgt R Bancroft. Middle L to R: F/S Pete Cameron, P/O R Diment, F/S J G Wookey, Sgt R New, Sgt K H Mayfield. Front U/K ground crew. *[P Cameron]*.

12 December saw the squadron finally receiving the long awaited issue of AP 2095 Pilots Notes General, and AP 1867C, D, E, F, G & J. – P.N Pilots and Flight Engineer's Notes; the latter covering Liberator Marks III, V, VI and VIII. Up to this point, the crews basically had to get by as best they could without the benefit of any formal air publications, which must have proved quite a challenge.

On 13 December Ronnie Simmons was dispatched to RAF Newmarket for a week-long course on LORAN. He recalls:

"I was volunteered by our nav leader to take a short course at Newmarket on a new navigational device known as LORAN. Our boffins designed the system to use the German guidance beam for U-Boats transmitting from Spain. After several lectures, about six of us took in a Halifax swanning around the Bay of Biscay on both a day and night flight. A set was installed in our aircraft and I was able to use it occasionally on a few sorties." *[The aircraft was TS534 (A) and the tall blade aerial mounted above the navigator's position in the nose is believed to be the LORAN aerial.]*

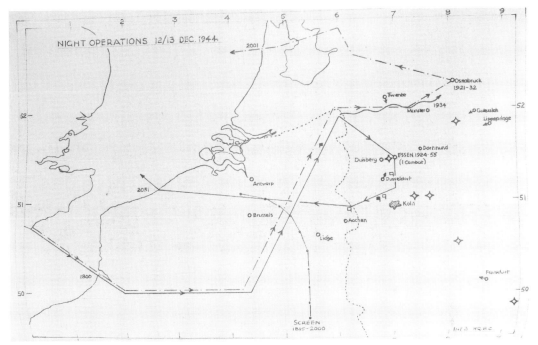

Target map 12/13 December 1944.

On 15/16 December the squadron was allocated two target patrols, one of which was cancelled, and launched four aircraft for a Window patrol in support of a main force attack on Ludwigshafen. All aircraft completed their duties, but Fg Off Steele landed heavily in TS522 (P) and suffered a nose-leg collapse, fortunately without injury to the crew. The aircraft was categorised as Cat AC and was repaired on site by 67 MU, but did not return to the squadron until 20 April 1945. W/O Stuart was forced to divert to RAF Foulsham on finding the runway blocked.

On the 17th it was decided that in future crews would be limited to eleven personnel. Guns had been removed from the front turrets and the turrets covered in doped fabric, thus removing the requirement for a front gunner. All surplus air gunners and air bombers were to be posted out.

On the night of 17/18 December the main force targets were Duisburg, Ulm and Munich. Tony Morris carried out his second target patrol in support of the Munich attack orbiting the target area for twelve minutes at 18,000 feet. It was one long night for the crew completing a nine-hour sortie. But it was not a good night for the squadron as only Flt Lt Hastie's crew completed their sortie out of the five aircraft launched on a Window patrol; engine problems and higher than forecast winds were to blame.

The main force target on 18/19 December was Gdynia on the Baltic coast. The Window force was deployed in support of an attack by 8 Group Mosquitoes on Münster. The squadron's effort was severely disrupted by a 1699 Flight aircraft that baulked on the runway, and only three aircraft were able to take off.

On 21 December, the Air Ministry highlighted to the USAAF that the squadron's aircraft strength was just fourteen against the agreed establishment of sixteen. Furthermore there were no aircraft in the pool. The reduction in strength had been caused by the crashes of TS528 (R) and TS522 (P) on 5 and 15 December, and a replacement aircraft, TT340 (U?) had recently crashed on a non-operational sortie. The latter aircraft was the only one available in the pool. The signal stated that four more operational B-24 aircraft were required, two each for the squadron and pool to restore their respective strengths[3]. For whatever reason the USAAF response was initially limited with TT343 (K) and VB852 (P) being delivered to the squadron on 8 and 20 January 1945 respectively, and VB904 (J) not arriving until 11 March.

Fog seriously affected operations over the next few days and it was the night of 21/22 before operations were flown again. Bomber Command attacked the oil refinery at Politz, and the railway yards at Cologne/Nippes and Bonn. There was still 10/10th fog but the squadron joined with 214 Squadron in dispatching aircraft on a Window spoof to the Ruhr in support of the main force attacks on Cologne and Bonn. 223's contribution was six aircraft which all completed their task. Ronnie Simmons was flying that night and remembers the conditions:

"This was an all out effort for Bomber Command due to Von Rundstedt's push in the Battle of the Bulge. I remember the airfield was fog-bound and at our briefing we were advised that we would be diverted somewhere on our return. For take-off we taxied around in the fog and turned onto the runway. We had to take off in the mist by gyro-compass on the runway heading but everyone got off safely. The sortie was to the Ruhr valley and on return we were diverted to Milltown, near Lossiemouth, in Scotland." *[Four more aircraft ended up at Milltown, and a fifth at Banff.]*

The squadron offered three aircraft for ops on the night of 22/23 December but 100 Group only called for one sortie to carry out a target operation in support of a main force attack against the railway yards at Bingen, one of the two main force attacks that night.

Following the decision to post away surplus air gunners on the 17th administrative action followed on the 23rd. They were now identified and posted to 1699 Flight to re-crew, and comprised:

Sgt P A Witts	Sgt E L Punnett
Sgt R A Jones	Sgt P Newman
Sgt L J Vowler	Sgt T W Pollard
Sgt E D T Brockhurst	

The seven were all from the thirty-eight eager boys who had joined from 10 AGS. Of them, Peter Witts was to be a very lucky man as the others were all to lose their lives on operations. Bob Jones, Pete Newman and Ted Punnett were lost on the night of 21/22 March 1945 with their new 214 Squadron crew (Flt Lt W D Allies) which they had joined on 1699 Flight. Tom Pollard failed to return with his crew (Fg Off J M Shortle DFM) on 24 February 1945. We shall hear more later of Leonard Vowler and David 'Brock' Brockhurst, who died alongside their new 223 crew. With the exception of Tom Pollard these young men died in the very last aircraft to be lost by their squadrons on the nights of 20/21 March and 21/22 March 1945 respectively. Peter was doubly lucky as he was posted away from Flt Lt W D Allies' crew, to 462 (RAAF) Squadron, before it was lost. As far as we know Peter was the only man to have flown with three 100 Group heavy squadrons, and he subsequently became a great stalwart of the RAF 100 Group Association from its formation in 1993.

The six aircraft diverted to Scotland earlier in the week returned to Oulton by 13:00 on the 23rd, but were too late to be prepared for the night's operations. However the squadron still managed to put up three aircraft for a Window patrol spoof to the Frankfurt area. Main force went to Trier and also sent a small force of Lancasters and Mosquitoes to the Gremberg railway yards at Cologne. The spoof proved to be a resounding success, as intelligence reported over 400 German night fighters being put up to oppose the feint. This was exactly the waste of German effort and resources that the Window force had been created to achieve, in addition to protecting main force.

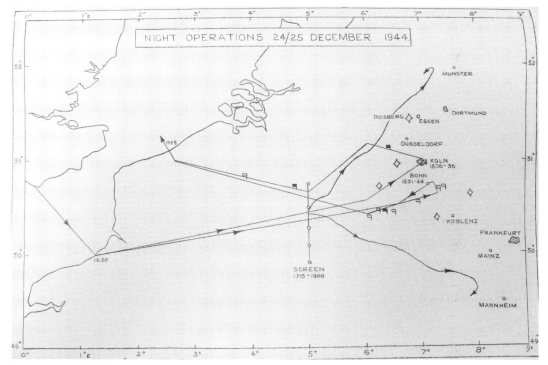

Target map 24/25 December 1944.

24/25 December. The squadron supported main force attacks against Hangelar airfield near Bonn and the Nippes railway yards at Cologne. A target patrol was flown by Sqn Ldr Carrington's crew to Hangelar, and three additional aircraft joined 214 Squadron crews in a Window force spoof on Mannheim. The latter feint was not supported by bombing but was reported as quite successful in holding night fighters of the 7th Jagd Division from arriving at the target areas. The 100 Group plan called for splitting of the Window force, which initially followed the main force route as far as 0500E, whereupon the force divided into a northern and southern patrol flying north-east and south-west respectively. To reinforce the northern patrol, Münster was bombed by two 8 Group Mosquitoes.

There was a respite from ops on Christmas Day and the Oulton station personnel and the two squadrons were able to enjoy some traditional Christmas cheer, including the officers and SNCOs serving a Christmas dinner to the airmen and airwomen.

On the 27th 223 Squadron's ORB records the interesting fact that it took six to eight men half an hour to defrost one aircraft ready for flight, and it would seem that this was the result of the required de-icing equipment not being delivered to the flights. This was an unsatisfactory drain on manpower when called on to prepare up to eleven aircraft for operations. It was back to business that evening with main force attacking the railway marshalling yards at Opladen. The squadron were asked for eight aircraft, but six were eventually launched to join a Window patrol to carry out a Window spoof in the direction of Frankfurt. The Window force followed the main force track to 0515N 0540E then broke away south-east as far as 4950N 0750E before returning home.

On the night of 28/29 the squadron contributed five aircraft to a Window force, comprising aircraft from 171, 199 and 214 Squadrons in support of attacks against railway yards at Mönchengladbach and Bonn. As for the previous night's operation, the Window force broke away from the main force track to head for Bad Kreuznach (south-west of Frankfurt). On this occasion the spoof was more heavily supported by eighty-seven Mosquitoes which bombed and marked the city. There was some excitement for Flt Lt Brigham's crew when they encountered a Ju 88 which was seen approaching them head-on at 4936N 0711E. At 19:01 they were on a heading of 244 degrees (true) at 15,000 feet when the enemy aircraft was seen at a distance of 1,000 feet, approaching at the same height. The Ju 88 broke down to port, as Jack Brigham dived to starboard. The mid upper gunner, Sgt F J Rankin, was able to fire off a short burst but did not see any hits register on the enemy. There was no return fire from the Ju 88 which was not seen again, but a short time later at 19:14 the Liberator's starboard flap was holed, possibly by friendly fire.

On 29/30 December the squadron provided a target patrol for the main force attack on the railway yards at Troisdorf, and a Window patrol contribution of four aircraft to Münster, presumably as a feint to divert attention from the other main force attack on the oil refinery and coal mines at Scholven/Buer.

The final Bomber Command operations of 1944 were mounted on the night of 30/31 December against the Kalk-Nord railway yard at Cologne, and a smaller attack against the communications pinch point at Houffalize. Fg Off Morris's crew flew a target patrol over Cologne, orbiting for eight minutes from H hour at the opening of the attack. They experienced problems with their Jostle which promptly went u/s after being switched on. Tony Morris reported that the attack appeared concentrated despite the 10/10ths cloud cover. No fighters were seen, but heavy barrage flak was put up over the target.

The 100 Group navigation officer highlighted the need for navigators to maintain an accurate track and to keep their aircraft strictly to the timings laid down for the turning points. He went on to state:

"The key to a successful Window patrol that fooled the Germans was the achievement of a regular formation of aircraft Windowing steadily. In these circumstances the enemy will react to a simulated force of 200 or more. If the Windowers are scattered they will appear to the Hun as a feint."

He circulated the following table of time keeping by the group's heavy squadrons[4]:

Squadron	Sorties Dispatched	Sorties Completed	Average Minutes Early	Average Minutes Late
223	25	22	2.0	2.5
214	20	19	1.25	3.5
199	5	4	0.5	1.0
192	7	7	1.0	0.5
171	12	10	2.0	3.0

The year ended with the squadron fully involved and contributing to Window force operations. The squadron was shaking down after its problems encountered with the rapid introduction of the various items of special equipment and the build up of experience on their war-weary Liberators. However, serviceability was beginning to improve enabling the squadron to put up a greater number of aircraft for ops. They had been fortunate that no aircraft had been lost on operations and could look forward to the new year with confidence in their ability to give a good account of themselves. Additionally, the Luftwaffe had been facing increasing difficulties in the autumn of 1944. The allied invasion of Europe had denied them their previous advantages of monitoring Bomber Command operations as their early warning radar coverage retreated, forced by the allies' advance. Fuel supplies were diminishing, forcing the Luftwaffe to conserve its usage. This had a big impact on training, which in turn resulted in aircrew arriving on front line units with less experience due to their reduced flying hours.

The war had also taken its toll on the experienced aircrew, many of whom had been flying operationally through a major part of the war – the Luftwaffe did not employ a rest tour philosophy as used by the RAF, and it is suggested that they were thus more prone to attrition caused by battle fatigue. Their exhaustion would be increased by the adverse operating conditions in the winter weather, and the constant threat provided by 100 Group's marauding Mosquito intruder activity. The formation of 100 Group had increased the challenge to the German defence controllers who not only had to deal with multiple main force attacks, but now had to differentiate between the genuine attacks and the apparent attacks provided by the Window force spoofs. The defences also had to cope with the challenge provided by the screening of main force attacks by the Window force against the background of jamming of vital early warning, anti-aircraft gun, searchlight and GCI control radars by 100 Group aircraft. By 1945 the Luftwaffe defences were severely weakened, but would still be capable of providing a significant threat to the attacking bomber forces, albeit on a reduced scale.

Notes:
1. Air25/782. 100 Group Report of Activities October /November 1944.
2. Air Ministry Monograph 1950 – Signals Vol VII – Radio Counter-Measures.
3. Air14/1070. Organisation of British and USAAF Fortress and Liberator Squadrons and 1699 Flight.
4. Air25/783. 100 Group Report of Activities December 1944/January 1945.

CHAPTER SEVEN

A New Year

January 1945

The new and final year of the war brought no let up in the pace of 100 Group operations. On 1/2 January the main force targets were the Mittelland Canal attacked at Gravenhorst by 5 Group, Vohwinkel railway yards visited by 3 Group, and 4 and 8 Groups hitting a benzol plant at Dortmund. Flt Lt John Briscoe's crew flew their first target operation over Dortmund, orbiting for twelve minutes in the target area at 23,000 feet from 19:16. Sqn Ldr Carrington was also tasked with a target operation and was sent to Gravenhorst. All was not well on this trip, as navigator Sgt Reggie Wade suffered

Flt Lt Morris & crew with Liberator TS530 (G) 'Gremlin Heaven'. Rear L to R: F/O Andrew Barron, F/S Johnny Parrack, F/L Tony Morris, F/O Mervyn Utas, F/S Vic Green. Front L to R: F/S W Mulligan, Sgt Jim Bratten, F/S Teds Sims, F/S Mick Stirrop [Andrew Barron].

104

with the loss of GEE and other navigation aids which were u/s. To add to his troubles the actual winds were found to differ from the met forecast. At the time of their Gravenhorst ETA Carrington found himself near Dortmund, with no prospect of reaching their intended target on time. But all was not lost as the crew covered the Dortmund target, orbiting at 14,000 feet for nineteen minutes from 19:09. To provide a diversion for the Ruhr target, 100 Group mounted a Window force feint towards Hamburg with 223 providing five aircraft. Fg Off Morris's crew also encountered difficulties, with his navigator Andrew Barron not having the best of days:

"The feint towards Hamburg was not a trip to remember! The rot started with the previous day. We had landed at about 23:00 off the Cologne sortie on 30 December. The next day we were detailed for a LORAN navigational training exercise, departing at 18:30, landing back at about 19:30. I was, therefore, late into the mess on New Year's Eve. Consequently, I was seriously 'hung over' from having celebrated too enthusiastically. The flame damper on No.4 engine burnt out so that it had to be shut down (to avoid leaving a highly luminous exhaust flame streaming out). No.3 engine (the remaining one on the side) was developing about half power, and I discovered a gross navigational error. At the same time we ran out of Window so curtailed our sortie by some sixty miles. We did not, however, incur any censure for aborting the trip."

The visibility on the crews' return was very poor, forcing Sqn Ldr Carrington and Fg Off Thompson to divert to RAF North Creake, and Flt Lt McPherson to divert a long way north to RAF Middleton St.George in County Durham.

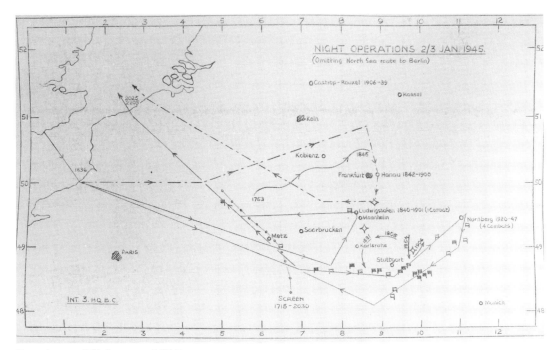

Target map 2/3 January 1945.

Bomber Command delivered two major attacks on the night of 2/3 January. 1, 3, 6 and 8 Groups struck at Nuremberg, and aircraft from 4, 6 and 8 Groups hit Ludwigshafen. To confuse the defences the Window force operated in two waves threatening Hanau in the Frankfurt area which was bombed by seven 8 Group Mosquitoes. 223 sent off two aircraft for the first patrol, and four for the second, the latter losing Flt Lt Dyck who was forced to return when the undercarriage failed to retract. The tactics were clearly successful with just an 0.8% loss rate from the 1,069 sorties flown on the night.

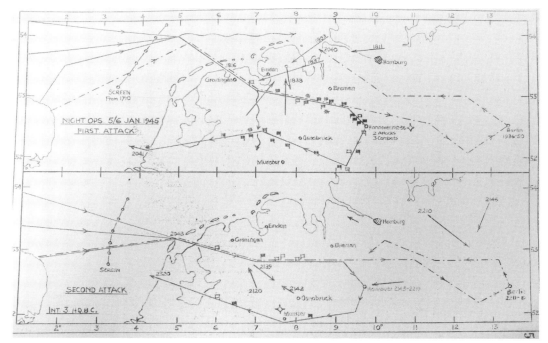

Target map 5/6 January 1945.

On 5/6 January the squadron dispatched seven aircraft in support of main force ops attacking Hannover and Houffalize, with a force of sixty-nine Mosquitoes stirring things up over Berlin. Two aircraft joined a northern Window patrol and another two for a southern Window patrol. This should have been three, but Sqn Ldr Carrington had a bomb door problem. In the event only Flt Lt Brigham completed with Flt Lt Noseworthy returning early with no power on No.3 engine. Sqn Ldr Carrington persevered and flew a target patrol over Houffalize which was apparently quiet, with no fighters or flak encountered. The remaining two aircraft did a target patrol to cover the attack on Hannover. Flt Lt Hastie reported that fighter flares were seen all the way along the route from the coast to the target; these were white flares dropped by the Germans to mark the bombers' route to guide their night fighters to the bomber stream.

6/7 January: Two aircraft were dispatched for a target patrol to cover the main force attack on Neuss. Flt Lt Croft orbited over the city for ten minutes from 18:40 at 20,000 feet, and reported moderate heavy flak with searchlights unable to penetrate the fog and low cloud. Sqn Ldr McKnight was over the target at the same time at 21,000 feet reporting negligible flak. 223 also provided three aircraft for a Window force spoof that was routed over Cologne, then east of the Ruhr, and home via southern Holland.

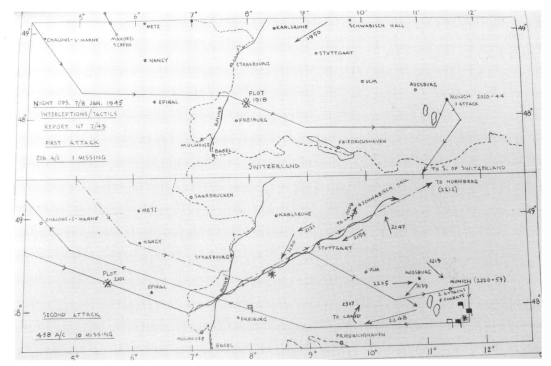

Target map 7/8 January 1945.

7/8 January saw a very heavy attack on Munich with 645 Lancasters and nine Mosquitoes, carried out in two phases. The first attack with 216 aircraft was over Munich between 20:24 and 20:44. The second attack of 435 aircraft, following a different routing, attacked the city between 22:20 and 22:59. The Window force put up by 100 Group in support of the second attack, joined the bomber stream as it turned north-east across the Rhine. Just short of Stuttgart the main force turned south-east towards the target, whilst the Window force continued on the north-east track almost to Nuremberg before breaking away to return home. Eight aircraft from 223 were detailed for operations, but only six were launched, of which five completed their missions. The night's operations, including the two-phase attack involving deep penetration sorties, could be considered successful with a loss rate of 2.1%.

Bad weather arrived with a vengeance on the 8th with bitter winds and a heavy fall of snow, and all hands were put to clearing snow to keep runways and taxiways open. Aircrew were also involved in this backbreaking task with the main runway being finally cleared on the 11th, albeit with banks of snow on both sides. Meanwhile, on the previous day the remaining air bombers were posted away following the surplus air gunners who had moved on in the previous month.

The 12th saw the arrival of the first new crew for the squadron, Fg Off A C Ball from 1699 Flight. This experienced crew, with a Bomber Command tour under their belts, was allocated to A Flight.

Operations were resumed on the night of 13/14 January with just one aircraft being launched for a target patrol over the main force objective, the railway yards at Saarbrücken. Flt Lt Dyck was circling in the target area at 17,000 feet for 15 minutes from 18:55.

The next night proved to be a record for the squadron with ten aircraft dispatched and completing their assigned duties on what was a busy night after the weather interruption. The main force targets for the night included the Leuna synthetic oil plant, the Grevenbroich railway yards and the Luftwaffe fuel depot at Dulmen near Münster. Bomber Command had planned a two-phase attack with Grevenbroich (19:30 to 19:43) and Leuna (20:47 to 21:15) being attacked during the first phase, with Mosquitoes hitting Berlin between 20:35 and 20:45. 223 supported this phase with two aircraft on a target patrol over Grevenbroich and two aircraft for a diversionary southern Window force spoof. They followed the Leuna main force route until it swung to the north-east in the direction of Frankfurt, but then broke away to the south-east to threaten Mannheim which was attacked by Mosquitoes.

For the second phase, Bomber Command attacked Leuna again (23:57 to 00:12), and sent another force to hit Dulmen to the north of the Ruhr (23:12 to 23:35). A further force of Mosquitoes would mount a second attack on Berlin. To add to the German defence controllers' confusion, a 'Sweepstake' force of 126 HCU and OTU aircraft would head across the North Sea as far as 0630E before turning back. To create more distraction 100 Group mounted a southern Window patrol which would follow the Leuna route as far as the Rhine before easing away to the north of the Leuna main force, initially towards Frankfurt, then turning abruptly north for about sixty miles, north-west and finally south-west, threatening the Ruhr then on towards Brussels and back to base. For this second phase 223 sent an aircraft to Dulmen on a target patrol, and contributed five aircraft to the southern Window patrol. All five from this patrol were diverted to RAF Woodbridge on their

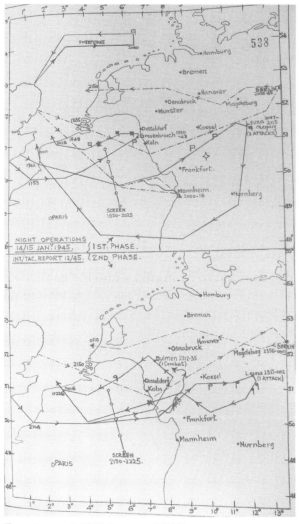

Target map 14/15 January 1945.

return due to fog, landing with the aid of fog investigation and dispersal operation (FIDO). This was a system comprising petrol-fed pipelines on both sides of the runway feeding burners. The lines of burning fuel cleared the fog from the runway, but it was a daunting sight for a crew using the system for the first time. Woodbridge in Suffolk was one of five major diversion airfields located up the east coast and equipped with an extra long and wide runway to deal with badly damaged or diverted aircraft.

This was to be a sad night for the squadron, with its first loss of an aircraft to enemy action. Flt Lt Noseworthy and his crew in TT336 (R) failed to return, and were reported as shot down to the east of Antwerp at 5107N 0438E on their return from their target patrol over Grevenbroich. Flt Lt Brigham reported seeing an aircraft shot down in the location where he had experienced light flak. At the time, the area was close to the front line and it was initially believed that the aircraft had been hit by friendly fire; in fact it would seem the likely culprit was a Ju 88.

The aircraft was struck in the tail and a fire started that was almost certainly being fed by the hydraulic fluid that powered the rear turret. It was rapidly clear that the aircraft was doomed. The crew already had a problem caused by the failure of the intercom system, which would have added to Noseworthy's difficulties in establishing the damage location, and ordering evacuation of the aircraft, aggravated by the separation of the front and back end crew members. In the event, things happened very quickly. Sgt John Mellers was manning the port waist gun when he heard the 'bang' and turned round to see the whole of the tail area on fire. Fg Off Frank Mason, the tail gunner, emerged through the flames from his turret and he together with the two special operators, W/Os Jack Galley and Bob Ralph, and the other waist gunner, Flt Sgt Don Clark, trooped down into the bomb bay. Sgt Mellers did not know why they moved forward. Presumably they had a natural instinct to get away from the flames, but they would have faced a struggle to get through the narrow gap between the vertical bomb beams as they made their way to the front bomb door exit. The squeeze would have been increased by them wearing their British Mae West life jackets and carrying their parachutes. Sgt Mellers attempted to fight the fire but the extinguisher that he located failed to work, so he hurled it into the flames. He shouted into his microphone that he was baling out just in case anyone could hear him. He tried to open the ventral hatch and found it jammed so he attempted to exit through the port waist hatch, but got stuck. He quickly switched to the starboard hatch and succeeded in clearing the aircraft. His parachute deployed and he landed in about six inches of snow with his clothes still smouldering and him suffering superficial burning.

In the cockpit, Flt Lt Noseworthy maintained control for as long as he could, but as soon as it was lost he left his seat and baled out through the top hatch, breaking his leg on the tailplane in the process. The co-pilot Sgt Evens, the wireless operator, Flt Lt G Trail, the mid upper gunner Flt Sgt W A Gray and the flight engineer Sgt Bob Hartop, would have made for the bomb bay front exit. The rear of the aircraft eventually broke away and landed just to the south side of what is now the A313 Antwerp to Liège motorway, approximately thirty miles from Antwerp. The remainder of the aircraft came down beside the Albert Canal just to the south of the small town of Meerhout, and about seven kilometres to the north-west of the tail unit.

Flt Lt Noseworthy & crew at 111 (C) OTU Nassau; lost 14 January 1945. Rear L to R: Sgt John Mellers, F/O Geoff Palmer, F/O G Noseworthy, F/O George Trail, Sgt Peter Buckland. Front L to R: Sgt Bill Gray, Sgt Les Evens, Sgt Don Clark, this poor quality picture is the only one available of the crew *[J Mellers]*.

It is likely that only Noseworthy and Mellers were successful in baling out. Fg Off Geoff Palmer, the navigator, was found and taken to hospital but was dead on arrival. Sgt Mellers was unsure on which side of the front line he had come down, but he took a chance and went to the nearest cottage. He was in luck, as the occupants arranged for some British troops to collect him within half an hour. The full crew of TT336 (R) were:

Flt Lt G Noseworthy RCAF	Pilot
Sgt A L Evens RCAF	2nd Pilot
Fg Off G R Palmer RAAF	Navigator
Flt Lt G Trail	Wireless Operator
Sgt R Hartop	Flight Engineer
Flt Sgt W A Gray RCAF	Mid Upper Gunner
W/O J G Galley DFM	Special Operator
W/O R Ralph	Special Operator
Sgt J Mellers	Port Waist Gunner
Flt Sgt D K Clark RCAF	Starboard Waist Gunner
Fg Off Mason	Rear Gunner

The night of 16/17 was a major effort by Bomber Command employing over 1,000 Lancasters against four different targets: Magdeburg, a synthetic oil plant at Zeitz near Leipzig, another synthetic oil plant at Brux in western Czechoslovakia and the benzol plant at Wanne-Eickel. Six aircraft were dispatched as part of a Window patrol to divert the defences away from the attack by 4 and 6 Groups on Magdeburg. The main force route was joined about ninety miles north of Oulton over the North Sea with the Window force flying ahead of the bombers, but diverging from their track behind the Mandrel screen at 0400E and continuing due east to Flensburg at 5445N 0900E. The feint force then returned to base following a reciprocal course. The squadron also supplied one crew for a target patrol over Wanne-Eickel.

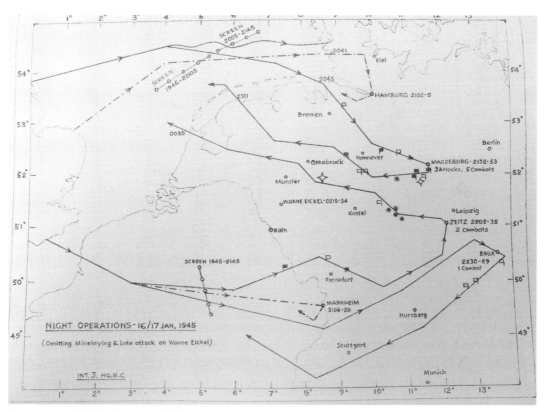

Target map 16/17 January 1945.

17/18 January: In the absence of main force operations, 100 Group mounted a deep penetration. Recent practice had involved the 100 Group Window force spoof attacks to be made on or near the main force routes, and this was simulated for the night's operation. When the spoof force reached 5010N 0710E they would drop their bombs, but instead of turning back, they would continue as far as 5030N 0820E. To increase the effectiveness of the main force deep penetration, simulation target indicators would be dropped just two minutes before the feint force reached its most easterly point. 223 contributed four aircraft to the exercise, but it was not a happy night with two crews returning early. Fg Off Steele was taken ill and returned from 5010N 0340E after three hours in the air. This was to be 'Scottie' Steele's last trip with the squadron on what had been a tour fraught with a long run of defects, flak damage and two nose-leg collapses. On a brighter note, Fg Off Ball's crew carried out their first op. However on his return he and Flt Lt McPherson were forced to divert to RAF Foulsham after a North

Creake Halifax crashed on the Oulton runway.

Fg Off A C Ball	Pilot
Fg Off L W Howell	Navigator
Fg Off F W Lomas	Flight Engineer
Fg Off J E Dow	Wireless Operator
Fg Off J Blakeley	Special Operator
Fg Off R V Piper	Special Operator
W/O W A Heaney	Air Gunner
W/O H Brown	Air Gunner
Flt Sgt E G Page	Air Gunner
Flt Sgt A G Bryant	Air Gunner

Note that this and all future new crews would not have co-pilots.

Appalling weather curtailed activities until the 21st when 100 Group again dispatched a Window force spoof in the absence of main force operations. The track was an unusually straight one from Boulogne to Bonn and return. Four aircraft were launched but unusually, no instructions were sent to the aircraft to jam with Jostle.

Main force were in action again on 22/23 January attacking a benzol plant at Duisburg, with a further attack on Gelsenkirchen. The squadron covered both sites with target patrols and sent out four aircraft on a Window patrol. The Window patrol was used to cover both attacks which were carried out in separate phases. For the first phase, 100 Group planned that the Window force would follow the main force until it was approaching the Mandrel screen when it would proceed in the direction of the target in three lines of aircraft, line abreast. In this way a moving front of twenty-five miles, six miles in depth, helped by a following wind, would saturate the target area with Window. It was thought that this would be more effective than a diversionary feint attack. The Window force would then retreat before carrying out a diversionary spoof attack in support of the main force second-phase attack.

Severe weather again prevented main force ops until the 28th on what had been a difficult time for Bomber Command. In these conditions, it is suspected that personal hygiene may have taken a dive, in view of Mervyn Utas's previous description of their outside ablution facilities! This was another two-phase attack aimed at Stuttgart. For the first phase the squadron provided four aircraft for a Window force, and two aircraft for a target patrol over Stuttgart. The Window force were briefed to follow the main force route as far as 0725E and then to break north-east towards Mainz which would be bombed by Mosquitoes. Flt Lt Croft flew a target patrol over Stuttgart to cover the second phase of the main force attack. Both phases were covered by a Mandrel screen. The first were briefed to break off after the first phase main force had passed through. They would be replaced by a second screen for the next phase attack. The first Mandrel screen played a role in the second phase by reforming, still jamming, and acting as another Window force. This was an introduction for another new crew skippered by Fg Off F T Sellars:

Fg Off F T Sellars	Pilot
Sgt P S Morris	Navigator
Fg Off J A Noble DFM	Flight Engineer
Fg Off D Geall	Wireless Operator
Fg Off F Mann	Special Operator
Fg Off A H Hobbs	Special Operator
W/O W J Ings	Air Gunner
W/O W P Duff	Air Gunner
W/O H Scott	Air Gunner
Sgt S C Thorn	Air Gunner

Fg Off Noble was awarded his DFM on 10 December 1943 for operational flying in Halifaxes with 4 Group's 78 Squadron. He was given leave on 4 February to receive the award at Buckingham Palace.

The original Window force encountered problems on the return track, when several 223 crews reported meeting Lancasters on a reciprocal heading. Apparently there had been a change to the routing of the second-phase main force which had not been communicated to Oulton.

In his monthly report the group navigation officer[1] grudgingly reported an improvement in track keeping, but added that it still could be improved. However, he considered that time keeping left much to be desired:

"Late arrival at Point A indicates that the aircraft are not setting course from base with an allowance of three minutes per flying hour in hand, or that this allowance is insufficient. Early arrival at Point A is inexcusable."

Squadron	Sorties Dispatched	Sorties Completed	Average Minutes Early	Average Minutes Late	Remarks
171	41	39	2.25	1.0	1 sortie missing
192	10	9	0.75	1.0	
199	-	-	-	-	
214	38	33	1.5	3.5	
223	49	45	2.0	1.5	
462	88	82	2.0	1.0	1 sortie missing

February 1945

On 1/2 February Ludwigshafen, Mainz and Siegen were subjected to main force attacks. A southern Window patrol was flown by five crews, and the squadron covered each attack with a target patrol.

Flt Lt Dyck & crew with Liberator TS529 (C) 'Circe' February 1945. Rear L to R: F/O W Holley (?), F/O Elmer Gaiser, U/K ground crew, F/L A L Dyck, U/K ground crew, Sgt Jamie Stewart, F/S George Davies, Sgt George Simons, W/O T K Chung. Front row, all U/K ground crew *[A G V Simons]*.

The squadron was pleasantly surprised by the unannounced return of Sgt John Mellers, shot down on the night of 14/15 January, having been flown over from Belgium. He would return to operations flying as a mid upper gunner in Flt Lt Croft's crew. That night, main force attacked Wiesbaden, Karlsruhe and Wanne-Eickel, together with a 617 Squadron attack on the U-Boat pens at Ijmuiden and Pootershaven with Tallboy bombs. The three main force tracks across French territory were roughly parallel, the central track of the Wiesbaden force was almost directly east, with the Wanne-Eickel and Karlsruhe streams on slightly divergent headings to the north and south respectively. The more northerly force broke off to the north-east at 0500E, still behind the Mandrel screen on its way to Wanne-Eickel. Shortly afterwards the most southerly stream broke to the south-east, initially hidden by the Mandrel screen on its way to Karlsruhe. To add to the Germans' disorientation, the Window force advancing along the central Wiesbaden main force track increased their Window dropping rate at 0700E and

223 Squadron flight engineers February 1945. Rear L to R: F/S Vic Green, F/S Jamie Brown, Sgt Brian Le Fondre, Sgt A Malone, Sgt Peter Matthews, F/S G Levy. Centre L to R: F/S J D Moir (?), F/O Bill Weir, F/O R W Barrett, U/K, F/S Dave Jones. Front L to R: F/S Arthur Anthony, P/O Alec Gibbon, Sgt Dennis Marsden, Sgt Jamie Stewart, F/S John Feltwell *[D A G Anthony]*.

broke away in the direction of Mannheim, simulating a large bomber force. The Window force were flying just three minutes ahead of the Pathfinders at the head of the Wiesbaden force. Mannheim would be marked and bombed to make the spoof more authentic, thus drawing the defenders' attention, and their night fighters away from the real targets.

The night could be judged a success with just 1.7% of the attacking forces being lost. The squadron's contribution to the night was five aircraft to the Window force and two for a target patrol over Wanne-Eickel; the latter orbited in the target area from 23:15 to 23:26 at 22,000 feet. An aircraft was also dispatched for a target patrol over Karlsruhe, but Flt Lt McPherson was forced to abandon his mission after suffering an electrical supply failure.

Flt Lt S B Wills was posted in to the squadron on the 3rd and was appointed to take over Fg Off Steele's crew. The crew, who had been in limbo since they lost their old skipper in mid January, were impressed with their new captain who they regarded as a great chap in both temperament and stature. However, they were in for an initial shock as Peter Matthews describes:

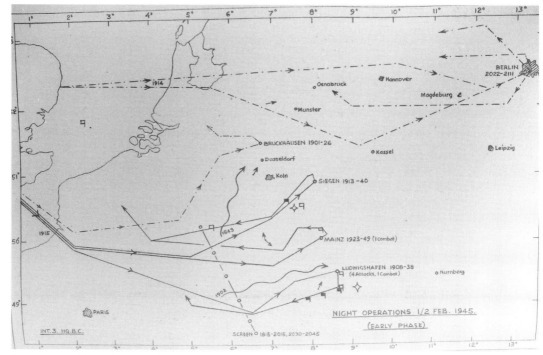

Target map 1/2 February 1945.

"1699 Flight was the conversion unit on the far side of the airfield and we were to spend three weeks there. Bill confided in us that he had lots of flying experience but only on twin-engined aircraft, mostly Oxfords. Slightly taken aback, the crew gave each other meaningful glances! For the first few hours in the B-24 TS537 (D) he was accompanied by an experienced Liberator pilot *[Fg Off Wilkinson. This took place on 5 and 6 February so no time was being lost to get the crew back to ops.]* and a skeleton crew, navigator, wireless operator and flight engineer. After just two-and-a-half hours of circuits and bumps he declared flying the Liberator as a piece of cake! The instructor got off and two days later, with four more hours under his belt, the rest of the crew were invited to join us. They were a bit tense at first! The officer commanding the training flight, Sqn Ldr Bellingham, joined us on the 14th, checked out Bill's night-flying ability and told us to go it alone. During this time the new skipper had gained the complete confidence of the shattered crew. He proved to be a great skipper and in six weeks was to become officer commanding B Flight with promotion to squadron leader."

The main force targets for the night 3/4 February were the benzol plants at Bottrop and Dortmund. A feint was mounted by the Window force to simulate an attack on Wiesbaden, being routed along the 5000N longitude to divert night fighters away. Forty-two Mosquitoes of 8 Group dropped markers on Wiesbaden to reinforce the feint. Four aircraft were contributed to the Window force and a target patrol to both target areas.

On the night of 4/5 February, 100 Group planned that the Window force would confuse the enemy by advancing on a broad front to saturate the approach route of a main force attacking the benzol plant at Gelsenkirchen with Window. The Window force would then repeat the exercise to screen the main force attack on the benzol plant at Osterfeld. A further attack on Bonn would also be carried out by main force. The squadron supported the Window force with three aircraft, and sent a target patrol to both Osterfeld and Gelsenkirchen. Two aircraft mounted target patrols over Bonn.

Operations were scrubbed due to bad weather on the 6th, which resulted in no operations being planned for the following day. On the night of 7/8 February Bomber Command launched heavy raids on German defences at Goch and Kleve, in preparation for an assault by the British Army's XXX Corps across the German frontier. To divert enemy fighters, 100 Group planned a Window force feint for which the squadron provided three aircraft. 5 Group also attacked the Dortmund-Ems Canal at Ladbergen. The squadron supported this main force raid with two target patrols. Target patrols were also flown over Kleve and Goch. Bomber Command flew 1,205 sorties on the night for a loss rate of 0.8%.

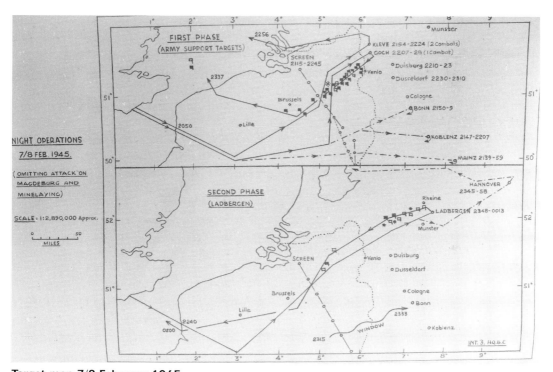

Target map 7/8 February 1945.

An improvement in the weather guaranteed another busy day on 9 February. Two oil targets at Politz and Wanne-Eickel were attacked, and main force also hit the Hohenbudberg railway yards at Krefeld. Target patrols were flown by sending a pair of aircraft to cover the attacks at Krefeld and Wanne-Eickel. A Window patrol was flown to distract the German defenders with 223 sending four aircraft in a shallow penetration to Aachen.

There were no main force operations on the following night, leaving 100 Group to stir the pot and harass the German defences. The squadron put up just two aircraft for a Window patrol.

The 11th was another dud day due to very bad weather conditions and operations were eventually cancelled. One bright spot amongst the gloom was the welcome return of Fg Off John Wallace, who had been injured by flak during the Big Ben period.

The bad weather continued throughout the next day, and operations did not resume until the night of 13/14 when Bomber Command took part in a controversial raid on Dresden. The latter was conducted in two waves and was supported by Window forces. The southern Window patrol with two aircraft from the squadron covered the first phase of the night's operations. The northern Window patrol covering the second phase, headed for the Mandrel screen from Abbeville towards Frankfurt, on an easterly heading. The patrol split after emerging from the Mandrel screen. One group of aircraft headed north-east and fanned out, increasing their Window dropping rate to saturate the Cologne area. The other group heading in a more easterly direction also fanned out with an increased Window rate to congest the Koblenz area. It is interesting to note that the majority of the northern patrol aircraft did not receive any instructions to jam with their Jostle equipment. The squadron made it a record night for operations by providing a further nine aircraft for this later force. The fact that all the crews successfully completed their missions put icing on the cake. Main force also attacked Böhlen on the same night. Just nine aircraft were lost from the 1,406 sorties flown giving a very acceptable loss rate of 0.6%.

On 14/15 February, Bomber Command operations to attack strategic targets behind the German eastern front line opposing the Russian advance continued, with a main force strike against Chemnitz. Oil was also still being targeted, with an attack on the refinery at Rositz. Another good night for 223, with nine aircraft launched to supply northern and southern Window patrols.

Poor weather on the 15th resulted in operations being cancelled on what would have been a solo Window patrol by the squadron.

Target map 13/14 February 1945.

118

The poor weather continued, with the addition of thick fog ruling out any flying. The squadron commander briefed the aircraft captains on the latest revision of tour-length policy.

"Aircrew who had completed one Coastal Command tour could still finish at thirty if they wished, but if they carried on they would be credited with two tours in Bomber Command. However, everyone doing his first tour at Oulton must carry on to thirty-six and then do an additional fourteen to complete fifty sorties for a bomber support double tour. No one who had done one tour in Bomber Command before coming to the squadron would be allowed to do a second tour at Oulton, and would have to finish at twenty."

The bad weather continued but cleared sufficiently on 18 February for the squadron to put up four aircraft for a Window patrol in support of a small force of Lancasters and Halifaxes laying mines in the German Bight. The weather forced the aircraft to divert to RAF North Creake on their return.

The night of 20/21 February was another busy night for Bomber Command with a total of 1,283 sorties being flown against a variety of targets. 100 Group contributed sixty-five RCM sorties in support of the main force operations. A force of 173 aircraft comprising 156 Halifaxes, eleven Mosquitoes and six Lancasters from 4 and 8 Groups was dispatched to attack the Rhenania Ossag oil refinery in the Reisholz district of Düsseldorf. This successful attack was achieved at the cost of four Halifaxes and one Lancaster. A second Rhenania Ossag oil refinery at Monheim was also attacked by 112 Halifaxes, ten Mosquitoes and six Lancasters from 6 and 8 Groups. This raid was also successfully completed for the loss of two Halifaxes.

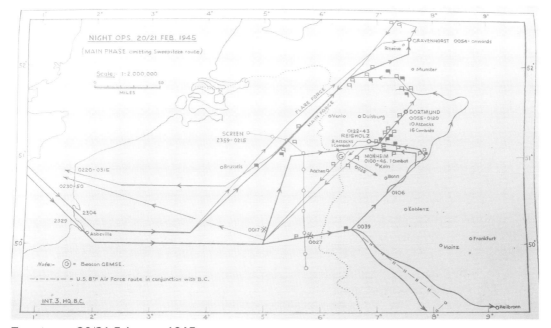

Target map 20/21 February 1945.

223 Squadron provided three aircraft for target patrols in support of the two oil targets, with the aim of jamming all Luftwaffe night-fighter communications transmissions with Jostle. The three aircraft for these operations – W/O Stuart in TS534 (A), Wg Cdr Burnell flying as co-pilot with Fg Off Morris's crew in TS530 (G), and Flt Lt Croft in TS519 (S) – were recorded airborne from Oulton at 21:58.

Flt Lt Croft & crew with Liberator TS519 (S) April-May 1945. L to R: F/S Lew Lucas, F/L L W Fairbanks, F/O Bill Weir, Sgt Ron Tofield, F/L Val Croft, F/O Des Carroll, F/S John Mellers, Sgt 'Bill' Sykes, F/S John Richards [H C 'Bill' Sykes].

W/O Stuart was over the target area from 01:25 to 01:38 at an altitude of 21,000 feet. In addition to Jostle the special operators used Carpet to jam the Würzburg radars for GCI, anti-aircraft gun laying and searchlight control on eleven frequencies. Piperack was also used to jam the night-fighter AI radars. Stuart successfully completed his task and landed back at Oulton at 04:12. Fg Off Morris's sortie was similarly uneventful. Jostle, Carpet (four frequencies) and Piperack were used, the aircraft orbiting the target area from 01:25 to 01:31 at a height of 20,000 feet. Fg Off Morris landed back at base at 04:12. Flt Lt Croft was over the target from 01:35 to 01:45 at 19,000 feet using Jostle, Carpet (five frequencies) and Piperack and returned safely to Oulton at 04:50.

154 Lancasters and eleven Mosquitoes of 5 Group were tasked with attacking a section of the Mittelland Canal near Gravenhorst. Unfortunately, the target was covered by low cloud and the attacking force was directed to abandon the operation by the master bomber. Luckily there were no aircraft losses from this abortive attack. 223

Squadron had put up three aircraft for a target patrol to support the attack. Flt Lt Briscoe in TS526 (T) was first away at 21:55, and was over the target from 01:05 to 01:10 at 13,000 feet. Jostle, Carpet (six frequencies jammed) and Piperack were employed and the aircraft landed safely back at Oulton at 03:45. Flt Lt Hastie in TS533 (M) was next away at 21:57 and was orbiting in the target area for eight minutes from 00:53 at an altitude of 12,500 feet; only Jostle and Carpet were used during the sortie, and an uneventful trip ended with a landing at 03:32. The third aircraft, Flt Lt Dyck in TT343 (K) was airborne at 21:58 but suffered an electrical supply failure at 00:52 when setting up to jam with Jostle. Carpet (three frequencies jammed) and Piperack were used before the power supply failed, which rendered all special equipment inoperable. TT343 (K) was in orbit over the target briefly from 01:01 to 01:05 at 13,000 feet before returning to land at Oulton at 03:43.

There were also a number of diversionary and minor operations to add to the problems of the German defences. Ninety-one aircraft from HCUs completed a sweep over the North Sea. Sixty-six Mosquitoes attacked Berlin and a further sixteen were sent to Mannheim. There were forty-five Mosquito patrols mounted by 100 Group and six aircraft were airborne on resistance-support operations. No aircraft were lost from these activities.

The main attack of the night, mounted by 514 Lancasters and fourteen Mosquitoes drawn from 1, 3, 6 and 8 Groups, was directed against the southern part of Dortmund. This proved to be the last major attack by Bomber Command against the city. Four Lancasters were lost from the attacking force.

223 Squadron contributed five aircraft to the Window force that flew in support of the above attacks. The force followed the southernmost main force track until it swung to the west to attack the two oil refinery targets. The Window force continued straight ahead dropping Window to disguise the main force turn. They continued to head to the north-east before hooking round to threaten Hannover then returning home north of the Ruhr. To compound the German confusion on this very busy night sixteen Mosquitoes of 8 Group bombed Mannheim and the USAAF 492 Bombardment Group accompanied the Window force with a team of thirty B-24 aircraft before breaking to the south-east to mark and bomb the Neustadt railway marshalling yards.

Fg Off Sellars was the first Window force aircraft away from Oulton in VB852 (P) at 22:18, followed by Flt Lt Woodward in TS529 (C) and Flt Lt Brigham in TS524 (O) at 22:20. Fourth away was Flt Lt Stephenson in TS527 (Q) at 22:23 with Fg Off Thompson bringing up the rear in TS520 (J) at 22:36.

This was not a good night for Thompson and his crew. For no obvious reason, the crew felt apprehensive as they walked across the dispersal to the aircraft. They were also missing their regular wireless operator Flt Sgt Rex Arnett, who had reported sick; his place had been taken by Flt Sgt Des Bryant. Last minute minor faults delayed their departure and they eventually got airborne eleven minutes after the previous aircraft. Soon after take-off the turbo supercharger on No.4 engine was found to be completely u/s. This made the climb more difficult, and to maintain height and speed it was necessary to use a higher boost and rpm settings which resulted in a significant increase in fuel consumption. However, Fg Off Thompson elected to continue the sortie and surprisingly, was only one minute late at the first turning point. The flight progressed until 01:25 when they were approximately thirty miles south-east of Dortmund at a height of 18,000 feet. Without warning the aircraft was attacked by two, possibly three, Ju 88s, according to the air gunners and the special operators in the rear of the aircraft. It would seem that Monica was not fitted, and apparently the special operators were having problems with their equipment, which may have contributed to the surprise attack. Thompson took immediate evasive action, corkscrewing to shake off the attacking aircraft. This initially appeared successful as they were left alone for a few minutes. During this period Thompson continued to weave and Window was dispensed. Meanwhile Fg Off Ron Johnson, the navigator, had gathered himself together and quickly obtained a GEE fix which showed that their evasive manoeuvres had taken them about ten miles off track.

Flg Off Thompson and crew, lost 20/21 February 1945. Rear L to R; F/S Jack Kendall, F/S Ron Wood, F/S George Graham, F/O 'Tommy' Thompson, F/S Ron Wynn, F/O Ron Johnson.
Front L to R; Sgt Ted Whittaker, F/S Rex Arnett, F/O 'Chips' Carpenter, F/S Brian Maxwell, W/O Bill Baker, W/O Ron Palmer (Carpenter had left the crew and Arnett was sick and replaced by F/S Bryant on the night.) *[R W Johnson]*.

Ron had just updated his skipper, and had given a course to bring them back on track, when they were attacked again, both from ahead and the rear. The attacks came within seconds of each other and Ron felt the strikes on the aircraft. The gunners, including mid upper gunner Ron Wood, were firing continuously. The surviving air gunners later told Ron Johnson that Wood had obtained strikes on one of their attackers and that the aircraft was forced to break away. The rear gunner was forced to evacuate his position as both the turret and his clothing were on fire. The final attack raked the aircraft from nose to tail; a violent rocking ensued and the aircraft appeared to shudder. It then dived out of control on fire, with flames and smoke in the tunnel leading to the navigator's compartment. Thompson eventually managed to regain some control briefly, and Ron Johnson heard him say over the intercom: "This is the end fellows – abandon aircraft." With the flames reaching the navigator's compartment, Ron pulled the emergency handles to open the nose-wheel doors, but they would not shift. A hefty kick did the trick and he dropped out at an estimated height of 15,000 feet into the freezing night air. Meanwhile in the rear fuselage the rear gunner, the two special operators and one of the waist gunners swiftly baled out through the ventral hatch. Ted Whittaker, the other waist gunner was last seen kneeling at the hatch putting on his parachute. By an amazing coincidence, Flt Lt Brigham was again on hand to witness the second loss of a 223 aircraft. The aircraft was seen to go down in flames with the mid upper gunner still firing. Brigham's crew also saw one of the attackers but it did not close, and TS520 was seen spiraling out of control, on fire. The five crew members baled out, and the aircraft continued its rapid descent before breaking up over the small hamlet of Dornheim.

Meanwhile the remainder of the Window force continued north-east before swinging almost due west to threaten Hannover before returning to base. Flt Lt Woodward was first back at 04:16 followed by Flt Lt Brigham 04:30. Flt Lt Stephenson and Fg Off Sellars landed shortly afterwards at 04:35 and 04:40 respectively. The 223 Squadron ORB records against the entry for TS520 – 'Believed shot down by enemy aircraft'.

Fg Off Brigham & crew with Liberator TS524 (O) March-April 1945. Rear L to R: Sgt J R Denney, Sgt Len Davies, F/O W H Thomas, F/L J Brigham, F/S Dave Jones, F/O C Reiser. Front L to R: F/S F J Rankin, Sgt L Moran, W/O D B Johnson, F/O S Reed, F/O L F Green *[L S Davies]*.

From discussions with Ron Johnson[2] it is likely that their initial attacks took place in the Plettenberg area. At the time of the attack the special operators, W/Os Bill Baker and Ron Palmer, would have been operating their Carpet and Piperack equipments. They may have also used Jostle, although only Brigham's crew, amongst the squadron's other aircraft on the Window patrol, had received instructions to jam. One of the crew, most probably the flight engineer, Sgt Ron Wynn, would have pushing out Window to deal with the night fighters' Lichtenstein AI radar, and the Würzburg gun-laying and GCI radars. The manoeuvres following the first attack had taken them off track and further south-east; they were most probably close to Schmallenberg when Ron Johnson gave his skipper the new course to get back on track. According to eyewitnesses on the ground the second combat took place over the town of Bad Fredeburg. The aircraft must have plunged in a northerly direction after this fatal attack and exploded shortly after Thompson and Kendall's efforts to briefly bring the aircraft under control to allow the survivors to bale out.

On 20 September 2000 an expedition took place, organised with the help of Richard Forder's German friends, to the crash site of TS520. Dornheim is in the Sauerland region of Germany, to the south of the town of Merschede. The intention was to locate the crash site of the aircraft and, hopefully, obtain information from any local people who might have witnessed the crash or its aftermath. The area was hilly, heavily wooded and interspersed with pasture. However much of the woodland appeared to be managed for timber production. A few kilometres along the minor roads brought us to Dornheim nestling in a fold in the hills. Probably the layout of the little hamlet had changed little since the war when it was primarily a collection of five farms and a small church. The traditional wooden frame houses made an attractive scene as we descended into its centre. We were a party of five, Bernd Klinkhardt (historian), Werner Pinn (translator – a former Ju 88 radio/radar operator), Hajo Adler (military historian and an authority on aircraft crash sites in the Hessen region) me and my wife Janice who would assist with translations. We were shortly joined by two more to complete our party, Jens Grosse-Kampmann and Werner Ruessmann, both authorities on aircraft crash sites in the Sauerland region.

When we emerged from my car, attention was drawn to the ground on the north side of the hamlet. Faced with steeply rising pastureland that led to a tree-clad summit, instinct said that this was the site we were seeking. This was shortly confirmed on the arrival of our Sauerland experts. Poignantly, but not connected with the crash, a large white painted wooden cross had been erected at the top of the pasture against the tree line.

An exploration of the hamlet, which did not take very long, revealed a dairy run by the Loeffler family. In a small shop adjacent to the dairy we found Frau Loeffler who confirmed that her husband Josef was the son of the Josef Loeffler who had written to a Sgt Irvine in March 1946 in response to his request for information concerning his friend Ted Whittaker. Sadly, Herr Loeffler was in poor health and partially sighted, but emerged from his home to give us details of the events surrounding the crash of TS520. Herr Loeffler was serving in the Wehrmacht in the Middle East at the time of the crash but had a good recall of the situation described by his father.

As we stood in the sunshine gazing up the hill at the tranquil scene, it was difficult to imagine the snow-covered ground littered with the debris of the wrecked aircraft that he portrayed. Only four major portions remained. The tailplane had come down in trees at the top of the hill to the north of the hamlet. The front fuselage was discovered on a small piece of open ground just to the east of the village. This was found to contain Fg Off Thompson and four other crew members; Flt Sgts Kendall, Wynn, Woods and Bryant. A mainplane complete with two engines came to rest just to the right of the path leading up the northern hillside, and a fuel tank described as 500 litres, 1.5 metres long by 1 metre wide, had rolled down on the southern hillside, coming to rest on open ground immediately adjacent to the east end of the hamlet. A lot of ammunition was spread over the crash site that covered some 700 metres. Another Dornheim resident Josef Schulte was a boy of fifteen when the aircraft crashed. His call up for service in the armed forces had been delayed because of illness and therefore he was an eyewitness to the events surrounding the fate of the aircraft and its crew. He recalled that the combat had taken place over Bad Fredeburg.

He remembered villagers finding the body of Sgt Ted Whittaker which had fallen to the ground some 200 metres to the rear of one of the houses that backed on to the northern hillside. Initially, they thought he was still alive as they were drawn to the figure lying in the snow. As they reached him they realised sadly that this was not so, noticing that although he was wearing a parachute it had not been deployed. It would seem that Ted had finally managed to buckle on his 'chute but the aircraft had exploded just before or just after he baled out. Herr Schulte said that the five survivors had been apprehended at the nearby villages of Fockinghausen, Osterwald, Henneborn, Sorpetal and Siedlinghausen, and that one of them had a broken foot. The latter was almost certainly Ron Johnson who had suffered frostbite after walking through the snow with only one flying boot. Werner Ruessmann was able to add that one of the survivors had been taken to the Hotel Knoche and that his mother obtained some silk from one of the parachutes. The bodies of the dead crew were taken to the Catholic cemetery at Kirchbrak and buried in shrouds without coffins. The latter was not a case of disrespect for the enemy but general practice at that time. Finally, Herr

Fg Off Ron Johnson, the navigator of Liberator TS520 which was shot down on 20/21 February 1945, with a fragment of his aircraft retrieved from its crash site at Dornheim [R W Johnson].

Schulte remarked that papers/documents were removed from the wreckage and retained by one of the villagers only to be destroyed when his house burnt down some years later.

The party then climbed the northern hillside and entered the trees at the right hand end of the hill. Approximately two thirds of the woodland had been replanted since the war, but the eastern end where the tailplane had come down still retained the original trees. This enabled us to locate the spot where the tailplane had come down, helped by the scarring still visible on some of the trees. All the wreckage had been cleared away long ago, but strolling back through the trees the author's foot caught the end of a piece of metal. Clearing away leaves and leaf mould revealed an almost complete aluminium riblet, almost certainly from the trailing edge of one of the elevators. It still carried traces of the night (black) camouflage paint. Subsequently this was presented to Ron who had it mounted and framed.

The crew on this last trip of TS520 (J) was:

Fg Off J W Thompson RCAF	Pilot
Flt Sgt J H Kendall	2nd Pilot
Fg Off R W Johnson	Navigator
Flt Sgt R Wynn	Flight Engineer
Flt Sgt D Bryant	Wireless Operator
Flt Sgt R Wood RCAF	Mid Upper Gunner
W/O W F Baker	Special Operator
W/O R A Palmer	Special Operator
Sgt E E Whittaker	Waist Gunner
Flt Sgt B Maxwell RCAF	Waist Gunner
Flt Sgt G R Graham RCAF	Rear Gunner

Ted Whittaker was a particular pal of air gunners Mick Stirrop and Leonard Vowler and the three spent their off-duty time together. Mick described Ted as very laid back, and recalled flying some ops with him as fellow waist gunners. Once airborne Ted would calmly lie down on the floor and doze whilst the aircraft climbed to operational height.

The main force targets on the night of 21/22 February were Duisburg, Worms and the Mittelland Canal at Gravenhorst. Bomber Command reported that all three targets had been successfully attacked, but at a cost. Despite 100 Group flying a total of sixty-six sorties on bomber support operations there was still a comparatively high aircraft loss rate of 3.1%. The 5 Group attack suffered most with losing 7.9% of its main force Lancasters. Three aircraft from 223 covered the Mittelland Canal attack with target patrols orbiting in the target area at 12,000 feet. Flt Lt Stephenson spent an unusually long spell of twenty-one minutes over the target from 20:32 to 20:53; possibly he had received instructions to fill a gap in the planned cover. Flt Lt Croft was 223's sole target patrol contribution to the Worms attack. Three more aircraft were dispatched on a northern Window patrol to screen the main force attack at Gravenhorst. The Window force was briefed to fan out on a broad front between 5030N 0500E and 5135N 0630E, and were timed to just precede the 5 Group attack.

The squadron's final effort for the night was carried out by Flt Lt Allnutt who joined a southern Window patrol to divert attention from the 1 and 6 Group attack on Worms. This force was briefed to follow the main force route but to advance on a broad front from 5014N 0550E to feint an attack on Koblenz, which the force marked and bombed to simulate a major attack developing.

Flt Lt Allnutt & crew with Liberator TS532 (N) March 1945. Rear L to R: Sgt Ernie Manners (?), F/O I T Leslie, F/L Alan Allnutt, F/L J R Maunsell. Front L to R; F/S E Laraway (?), F/S T J Adams (?), Sgt G N Tucker, Sgt D Townsend, Sgt J J Trail [Mrs Marjorie Munro].

The following night was limited to minor operations. In the absence of main force attacks, 100 Group planned a simulated two-phase main force attack on the Düsseldorf/Krefeld area in the Ruhr. The Window force was briefed to fly the track from north-east France to Krefeld twice in a two-hour period. The crews were instructed to fan out from 5055N 0515E and approach the Ruhr on a wide front. The force would reassemble to the west of 0400E to emerge from behind a second Mandrel screen, and repeat the first simulated attack on the Ruhr. The squadron supported the Window force with four aircraft.

The night of 23/24 February saw a major attack on Pforzheim. The squadron sent three aircraft to fly target patrols over the city at 12,000 feet, and all three were orbiting in the same period. Four more aircraft were launched to join a Window patrol spoof to Neuss. This force was joined by twenty-seven Liberators of the 492 BG North Pickenham, which simulated Parramatta and Wanganui[3] marking of the target, before bombing.

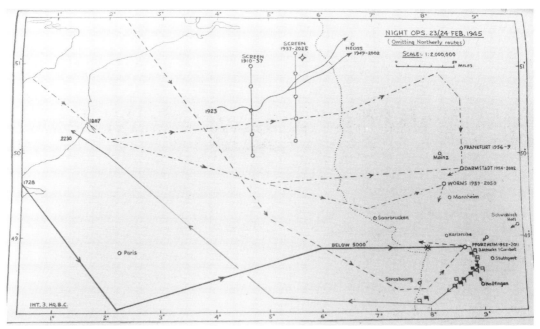

Target map 23/24 February 1945.

Flt Lt Hastie in TS523 (D) had a close encounter with a Bf 110. Peter Lovatt, the port waist gunner recorded:

"This trip was uneventful until, on the return journey, we were interrupted by a Bf 110 night fighter. It had been vectored to the general area by German GCI radar and then used its own airborne set to come up under the starboard wing of the Liberator, unseen by either Syd Piennar, the rear gunner, or Chris Weston, the mid upper gunner. It was just as well that by now the policy of using the waist gunners to drop Window had been abandoned.

"Bob Lawrence spotted the night fighter from his starboard waist position and reported its presence to Hastie. It was really too close, as if the pilot had misjudged his approach. Indeed Lawrence thought it was too close for our own safety to open fire, adding that he could almost read the instruments on the pilot's instrument panel.

"Bob tapped me on the shoulder and there was just time for me to catch a glimpse of the long greenhouse of the Bf 110's cockpit under the starboard wing. But instead of corkscrewing to starboard, the normal procedure in such circumstances, Hastie wisely chose to sideslip the Liberator to port, with everyone keeping a watchful eye.

"The German pilot, who probably was very inexperienced, had had enough. Realising he had misjudged his attack, he quickly dived away to starboard and flew off as quickly as possible, avoiding the firepower of six 0.5 inch Browning machine guns and so lived to fight another day"[4].

All seven of the aircraft launched for operations that night were diverted to RAF Carnaby on their return due to bad weather at Oulton.

Main force were not operating on the night of 24/25 which left 100 Group to waste the resources of the German defences and keep them occupied. The planners' intention was to create the conditions which would simulate a large-scale attack on a Ruhr target. The attacking force involved a Window force backed up by a Bullseye force[5]. The latter followed so far along the planned route before turning back at 0450E. The combined forces flew along the line of 0500N emerging through the Mandrel screen just before 0450E. At this point the Window force turned to the north-east headed by the Halifaxes of 462 (RAAF) Squadron which bombed the feint target of Neuss. Eighteen Mosquitoes of 8 Group also attacked Neuss. Window dropping disguised the turning back of the 'Bullseye'. Whether the German defences were convinced by the simulated main force attack or not, they attracted night-fighter opposition and, despite the Jostle, Piperack and Carpet jamming and 100 Group high and low level intruder patrols, five of the Window force aircraft were shot down. 214 Squadron lost Fg Off

Flt Lt Roy Hastie in the cockpit of a 223 Squadron Liberator *[Hastie collection]*.

J M Shortle DFM and his crew in Fortress HB805. All on board except for Flt Sgt G J E Jennings DFM were lost. One of Shortle's air gunners, Sgt T W J Pollard, had previously flown on ops with 223 and was one of the thirty-eight 10 AGS boys. But the biggest loss of the night was the four Halifaxes of 462 which failed to return to Foulsham. There were sadly only five survivors from the four crews.

223 Squadron dispatched four aircraft for the feint including a new crew captained by Plt Off N S Ayres which had arrived from 1699 Flight on 10 February. It was an experienced crew that included Sgt David Brockhurst and Leonard Vowler who had originally been posted to the training flight as surplus to squadron requirements on 15 December. We shall learn more about this crew in due course:

Plt Off N S Ayres	Pilot
W/O A E Redford	Navigator
Flt Sgt W Stanyer	Flight Engineer

Fg Off H B Hale	Wireless Operator
Flt Sgt J D Cairns	Mid Upper Gunner
W/O A C Cole	Special Operator
W/O J E Bellamy	Special Operator
Sgt E D T Brockhurst	Waist Gunner
Sgt L E Vowler	Waist Gunner
W/O S E Silvey	Rear Gunner

No main force operations were mounted on the night of 27/28 February. Again a large simulated attack was planned using Mandrel, Window and Sweepstake[6] forces, assisted by a bomber force from 492 BG in a feint attack on the German Bight area. It was felt that the German defences were becoming accustomed to feint forces approaching the Ruhr, hence this opportunity was used to move the feint further to the north. In fact two Window forces were employed with the northern formation proceeding from 5436N 0600E to 5508N 0830E, Windowing heavily. The southern formation would follow a track from 5440N 0600E to 5422N 0830E also Windowing heavily. As these formations reached their point of maximum penetration a formation of twenty-seven Liberators of the 492 BG carried out a simulated PFF attack on Wilhelmshaven and bombed it. The squadron made a significant contribution to the northern Window force launching seven aircraft, and completed a busy night by sending Flt Lt Levy to join the southern Window patrol. This proved to be a quiet night and no aircraft were lost.

Another big night followed on 28 February/1 March with the squadron again putting up eight aircraft for a Window patrol deep into southern Germany. In the absence of main force operations the Window force were supporting a feint attack on the town of Freiburg on Lake Constance. They were briefed to follow the same track as a force of twenty-two Liberators of 492 BG which bombed the railway yards at the town. The Window force passed to the south of the target to threaten Augsburg and Munich. The Germans either recognised this as a spoof or conserved their resources. No fighters were seen and another quiet night passed with just one Mosquito lost from a raid on Berlin.

The night was a debut for a new 223 skipper, Fg Off J Robson who returned to ops with his crew formerly captained by Fg Off J W Young RCAF. The full crew, who were joined by the squadron commander for the sortie, comprised:

Fg Off J Robson	Pilot
Wg Cdr H H Burnell AFC	2nd Pilot
Plt Off R W Bass RCAF	Navigator
Sgt W Nolan	Wireless Operator
Sgt A Malone	Flight Engineer
W/O O G Burtenshaw	Special Operator
Fg Off J Bourque RCAF	Air Gunner (Mid Upper?)
Sgt E J White	Air Gunner (Waist?)
Sgt A E Tonkin	Air Gunner (Waist?)
Sgt K Smith	Air Gunner (Rear Gunner?)

There was a certain amount of frustration amongst the crews of those 100 Group squadrons that did not have a bombing capability. There were some unofficial efforts to overcome this perceived shortcoming as Ronnie Simmons explains:

"The target on the night of 28 February/1 March was Munich. Many of our crews were frustrated by not being able to drop something on the Fatherland. Near our dispersal, a brick wall was being dismantled, leavings groups of mortared bricks around, weighing about 40 lb apiece. The beam gunners thought that maybe Adolph would be at home that night and received permission, unofficially of course, to give him a welcome gift. Two hunks of bricks were loaded in the beam gunners' area and, when over the centre of Munich, I gave word to let go. Accompanying this salvo apparently were a few beer bottles filled with some of the crew's kidney discharges. This proved to be a tremendous boost to the crew's morale because of the mental picture of our dumped load landing on the Fuhrer's dining table."

Len Davies also recalled some crews dropping hand grenades from the waist positions. Incidentally, apart from their air gunnery role and occasional Window-dropping role, the waist gunners also performed another useful function on an aircraft's approach to land. When the undercarriage was lowered the gunners would look to see that the yellow-painted down locks were engaged and visible on the main undercarriage. These down locks were only visible from the waist positions with a torch necessary when landing at night.

As can be seen from the squadron's operational record, efforts to improve serviceability were beginning to pay off with a much greater number of aircraft being made available for operations and a great reduction in the number of early returns. A squadron bug-bear, the failure of the engine flame dampers, was significantly reduced by the introduction of a simple modification which proved to double the life of the troublesome unit[7]. Engine issues generally had given the pilots and flight engineers a fair number of problems particularly in the squadron's early days. Possibly engine changes carried out during the period September to December 1944 had improved things, so it is interesting to see the table below which shows a comparison of engine failures per sortie for 100 Group's heavy squadrons:

Squadron	Sorties/Engine Failure
214	46/3
171	42/2
223	24/4
199	20/0
192	18/4
462	9/9

There are some interesting comparisons here with 223 Squadron's record, with its Pratt & Whitney engines, being not as bad as one might have anticipated. However, the Wright Cyclone engines of the other American aircraft in the group were proving to be twice as reliable. The fact that some of the 214 Squadron aircraft were delivered to the squadron straight off the production line in the USA would offer a possible explanation for such a difference between the two reliability figures.

Monica had given problems during the month with all aircraft fits unusable at one stage; an old problem of aerial fractures was causing the problem. The fitting of LORAN had been more successful with just five aircraft to be completed.

The squadron had enjoyed its most successful month of operations so far. A total of 121 sorties had been flown comprising thirty-three target patrols and eighty-eight Window patrols. Of these thirty-two and eighty-three had been completed, making a total of 115 successful patrols. The squadron had been active on eighteen of the twenty-eight nights including an impressive seven consecutive nights of operations.

Notes:
1. Air25/783 100 Group Report of Activities December1944/January 1945.
2. This description is based on the account given in Ron Johnson's *A Navigator's Tale* and a copy of the report Ron was requested to submit when he returned from Germany at the end of the war.
3. Parramatta was the codename for blind-dropped ground markers. Wanganui was a PFF target-marking technique when sky markers were used if visibility of the target was poor or non-existent.
4. Reproduced from Peter Lovatt's biography of his late skipper – *Ordinary Man, Super Pilot: The Life and Times of Roy Hastie DFC AE.*
5. A force of training aircraft from OTUs and HCUs also referred to as a 'Bullseye'.
6. 'Sweepstake' – later codename given to diversionary force of HCU and OTU training aircraft.
7. Air25/784. Appendix 13 to 100 Group HQ ORB Form 540, February 1945.

CHAPTER EIGHT

March 1945

On the night of 1/2 March the squadron took part in a Window spoof contributing just two aircraft. This operation which took place in the absence of main force activity was routed via Kaiserslautern and then fanning out to threaten Mannheim. No casualties resulted from this spoof.

There were no main force operations again on the following night but the squadron provided seven aircraft for another Window spoof. A Bullseye force of 70 OTU aircraft accompanied the Window force for part of the route before turning back and leaving them to continue almost as far as Bremen.

Main force were in action again on the night of 3/4 March on what proved to be an unfortunate night for the Command. Kamen and the Dortmund and Ems Canal were the targets. The squadron provided two aircraft to both targets to fly target patrols. A further two aircraft were dispatched as part of a Window patrol to cover the main force targets. On the 4th deteriorating weather eventually resulted in operations being cancelled. Fortunately, the diverted aircraft were able to return with the exception of Fg Off Ball's aircraft TS531 (B).

5/6 March. Main force were in action continuing with Operation Thunderclap. This involved a large attack on Chemnitz with a force of 754 heavy bombers and six Mosquitoes. The synthetic oil refinery at Böhlen was also hit in a separate attack using a further 248 Lancasters. The plan for the night routed the two main force attacks along the same track. The two teams were led by a Window force of twenty-four aircraft which dropped Window on a broad front to saturate the early part of the route. At 5030N 0720E the Window force broke away south-west from the main route to divert the enemy's attention. Still dropping Window they continued an approach on Mannheim which was bombed by eight PFF Mosquitoes. In a separate diversion, twenty-four Liberators of 492 BG bombed the railway yards at Wiesbaden which they marked using PFF techniques. Unfortunately, the diversionary tactics were unsuccessful. The main force split into two attacking formations to follow different tracks from a turning point just to the north-west of Halle, which the Germans initially thought was the potential target. They quickly switched their attention to Halle before concentrating on Chemnitz. The two forces were attacked on their run in to the targets with the Chemnitz formation receiving the greater attention. While the German night fighters continued their attacks along the return route of the Chemnitz force, the German GCI controllers had not appreciated that the Böhlen force was returning by a different track. Thirty-one aircraft were lost (2.5% loss rate), and 100 Group had scheduled sixty-one night fighters for high and low intruder operations. 223 Squadron put up five aircraft for the Window patrol, which, unlike main force, was a very quiet night for them, with no sign of fighter activity.

The 6th saw Flt Lt Noseworthy return to the squadron, and he was reported looking none the worse for his experiences on the night of 14/15 January, but had suffered a considerable loss of weight. He did not return to operational flying with the squadron.

Three targets were selected for main force on the 7th/8th; a heavy attack on Dessau in eastern Germany, and the oil refineries at Hemmingstedt and Harburg in the north. The two main forces designated for the oil refineries followed the same track together with a northern Window patrol, which flew at the head of the combined force. The Window force was instructed to commence dropping Window at 5520N 0941E and continue dropping as the main force split into two formations, turning to the south towards their respective targets. At this point the Window force continued on the original track to the south-east to threaten Berlin. The squadron sent two aircraft to carry out a target patrol over Hemmingstedt. Flt Lt Brigham and Flt Lt Briscoe spent fifteen minutes and thirteen minutes respectively orbiting the target. Flt Lt Briscoe reported considerable flak and many searchlights in the area.

The southern Window force was flown in support of the Dessau operation. It flew ahead of the main force commencing to drop Window as it emerged through the Mandrel screen on the main track. Still Windowing, the Window patrol passed south then east of the Ruhr before heading north to threaten and bomb Münster. To give added credibility to the feint PFF Mosquitoes were marked Münster with 'Musical' markers[1]. Again 492 BG supported the Window force, bombing Dortmund to simulate a PFF attack with Wanganui marking. 223 Squadron contributed six aircraft to this operation and all completed the operation.

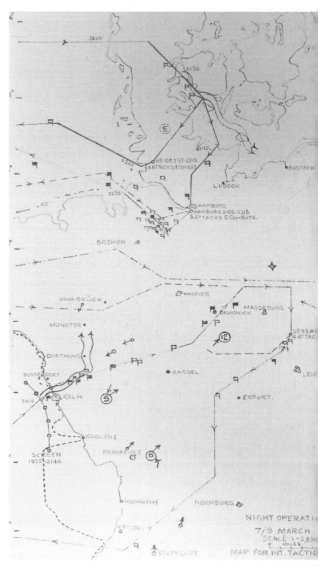

Target map 7/8 March 1945.

Bomber Command lost forty-one (3.1%) aircraft from the night's operations including Fg Off G Stewart RNZAF of 214 Squadron in Fortress KJ106 (G) missing from a target patrol over Harburg. The Command dispatched 262 Lancaster from 1 and 8 Groups and fourteen Mosquitoes of 8 Group to attack Kassel. A second main force comprising 239 Halifaxes from 4 and 6 Groups together with sixty-two Lancasters and nine Mosquitoes of 8 Group attacked the Blohm und Voss shipyards at Hamburg. The squadron supported both operations by sending a pair of aircraft on target patrols. Both pairs successfully completed their tasks.

To divert attention from the Kassel attack a Window force initially followed the track through the Mandrel screen, before following parallel and to the south of the track, then swinging to the south and approaching Dortmund on a fairly broad front to attack and bomb Dortmund. The Window force was supported by twenty-one Liberators of the 492 BG who also bombed Dortmund, simulating a Pathfinder Wanganui attack. The feint worked effectively as the German defence controllers concentrated fighters against the Window force. The main force had reached as far east as Osnabrück, where they began their turn south-east to the target, before the enemy controllers realised the true situation. Fighter attacks were negligible and the main force was never caught. The Hamburg force was equally successful and was not identified until closing on Denmark and only one combat was reported over the target.

No main force operations took place on 9th/10th, but 100 Group kept the German defences on their guard by mounting a Window spoof against Münster. Three squadron aircraft took part.

The next night saw the squadron mounting another Window feint to Münster, flying at 19,000 feet, as there were no main force operations. Four aircraft completed, including the newly-commissioned Plt Off Stuart, previously the only non-commissioned aircraft captain on the squadron. The Window force were supported by the USAAF with 858 BS simulating a PFF marking procedure on the spoof target; they marked the target with red target indicators and sky markers of green with red stars.

The benzol plants at Gelsenkirchen and Herne were the main force targets for the night of 13/14 March. The squadron contributed four aircraft to a Window force which proved uneventful until the returning aircraft were forced to divert because of a 214 Squadron Fortress which burst a tyre on landing and blocked the runway.

The main force targets on the following night included a synthetic oil refinery at Lützkendorf, and attacks on Homberg and Zweibrücken at the request of the army to hinder German troops and their equipment reaching the adjacent front line. Interestingly, the 5 Group attack on Lützkendorf proceeded without the benefit of a Mandrel screen. Possibly the planners had intended the Germans to believe that this was a spoof. The 4 and 6 Group main forces attacking Homberg and Zweibrücken approached their targets on the same track, splitting the two streams behind the Mandrel screen. Just ahead of these, a Window force started dropping Window heavily just short of the screen before heading to the north of Homberg and continuing up to Wiesbaden where they bombed the target. The spoof target was marked by fifteen Liberators of 492 BG with red target indicators and Wanganui green with red stars sky markers.

All three targets were reported to have been successfully attacked. Enemy fighters got amongst the Lützkendorf attackers and twenty Lancasters were intercepted involving eleven attacks and seventeen combats. Eight of the 5 Group Lancasters were lost to various causes. A 214 Squadron aircraft, Flt Lt H Rix in HB802 (O), one of three on target patrol over the area, was also lost.

The 100 Group spoof attack would seem to have helped the other two attacks as only two Halifaxes were reported lost from Homberg and none from Zweibrücken. 223 sent two aircraft on a target patrol over Homberg. The latter was a debut for two more crews carrying out their first operational sorties for the squadron:

Fg Off F Bowell	Pilot
W/O L R Lovatt	Navigator
W/O G Harrison DFM	Flight Engineer
Flt Lt D W Drew	Wireless Operator
Fg Off L T George	Air Gunner
Flt Sgt F A Jobson	Special Operator
Flt Sgt C Fairbairn DFM	Special Operator
Plt Off W T Berry	Air Gunner
Flt Sgt A J Polmear	Air Gunner
Flt Sgt D Copeland	Air Gunner
Flt Lt J K Mann	Pilot
Fg Off J P Hammond	Navigator
W/O R Tailford	Flight Engineer
Flt Sgt A Atkiss	Wireless Operator
Fg Off T G Hammond	Mid Upper Gunner
Fg Off R N Godwin	Special Operator
Sgt R J Smith	Special Operator
Fg Off J H McAdam	Air Gunner
Sgt I H W Rice	Air Gunner
Sgt C C Hughes	Air Gunner

The night also witnessed the first op on the squadron for Fg Off Cairney and his crew who joined Fg Off Ayres on the Window patrol:

Fg Off J W Cairney	Pilot
Fg Off R W T Tucker DFM	Navigator
Plt Off W G Howard	Flight Engineer
Fg Off J E Dow	Wireless Operator
Fg Off G A Issacs DFM	Air Gunner
W/O A Sheekey	Special Operator
W/O J Ross	Special Operator
Fg Off F R Higgins	Air Gunner
Fg Off F C Boyd DFC	Air Gunner
Sgt E Hedley	Air Gunner

Fg Off Cairney & crew. Rear L to R; F/O G Isaacs, W/O A Sheekey and W/O J Ross (or vice versa), F/O J W Cairney, F/O R W T Tucker, F/S E Hedley. Front L to R; F/O W G Howard, waist gunner, waist gunner, mid upper gunner *[W G Howard]*.

While discussing the operations on this particular night, it should also be mentioned that it became notorious for the very sad outcome for the crew of 214 Squadron Fortress HB779 (K), which also took part, flying a Jostle patrol in support of the Lützkendorf raid. On the return leg the aircraft was hit by flak, which damaged the No.2 engine, and worried about the possibility of the resultant fire taking hold, pilot Flt Lt John Wynne ordered his crew to bale out, believing that they were probably over friendly territory. After the other nine crew members had left, Wynn discovered that the fire had extinguished itself, so he elected to fly the aircraft back to England, where he made a successful landing at the 8th Air Force base at Bassingbourn in Cambridgeshire.

Regrettably, his crew were not so lucky, as they had all landed on the wrong side of the line and were quickly rounded up. Seven of them were marched into the town of Pforzheim, which had been heavily bombed a week or two before. The reception as they were marched through the town was, not surprisingly, hostile and although two of the crew managed to make their escape as they were marched on into the village of Huchenfeld, the remaining five were summarily beaten up and shot by members of the Hitler Youth. The victims were:

Fg Off Harold Frost DFM	Top Gunner
Fg Off Gordon Hall MID	Wireless Operator
Flt Lt Sidney Matthews DFC	Rear Gunner
Flt Sgt Edward Percival DFM	Waist Gunner
Fg Off James Vinall DFM MID	Flight Engineer

In addition to the skipper, those members of the crew who escaped the fate of their colleagues to be taken prisoner were:

Flt Sgt Norman Bradley DFM	Waist Gunner
Plt Off Dudley Heal DFM	Navigator
Fg Off G P 'Tubby' Pow DFC	Bomb Aimer
Fg Off Tom Tate	Special Operator

Clearly a highly experienced and decorated crew, the majority were on at least their second Bomber Command tour. Dudley Heal came from 617 Squadron, where he was awarded his DFM as part of Flt Sgt Ken Brown's crew on Operation Chastise, the dams raid in May 1943, where they were the second aircraft to attack the Sorpe Dam.

Main force were dispatched against two targets on the night of 15/16 March, visiting Hagen and the Duerag refinery at Misburg. Both attacking forces used the same outward route through the southern portion of the Mandrel screen before the Hagen force turned almost due north to attack the town. The Window force also followed the main force track as far as 5100N 0530E where it would continue heading north-west through the Mandrel screen Windowing heavily from 5120N 0600E, continuing up to Münster. To reinforce the spoof attack aircraft of 492 BG flew with the Window formation to mark Münster with green TIs, and red and green Wanganui stars; the target was bombed by both Window aircraft and 492 BG. 223 supported the night's operations by sending two aircraft on target patrol over Hagen at 22,000 feet from 20:25 to 20:37. Flt Lt Woodward reported moderate heavy and light flak in the target area and numerous searchlights on the east bank of the Rhine. Enemy fighter flares were seen just before reaching the target and for quite a long period on the return leg. Three aircraft were contributed to the Window patrol, which involved a lengthy eight-hour sortie.

214 Squadron lost Fortress HB803 (L) on a target patrol in support of the Misburg raid. Initially attacked by a night fighter they were hit by American friendly fire as they crossed the front line and were forced to abandon the aircraft. All but two of Fg Off Anderson's crew survived.

The following night, main force were in action at Nuremberg and Würzburg. The Window force was used again as a bluff to draw the Germans' attention away from the Nuremberg attack. To increase the strength of the deception the Window force was made visible to the enemy defences by its routing through the deliberately thinned northern end of the Mandrel screen. A spoof attack on Hanau was carried out with target marking and bombing by Mosquitoes of 8 Group. This attack was timed to take place just ten minutes before the main force attack on Nuremberg. The squadron put up four aircraft for the Window patrol including Flt Lt Wills who was carrying out his first op with the crew he had taken over from Fg Off Steele. Unfortunately, Wills was forced to return early with fuel and oil leaking from No.3 engine:

Flt Lt S B Wills	Pilot
Flt Lt F Freake	Navigator
Sgt P R Matthews	Flight Engineer

Flt Sgt J E Dagnall	Wireless Operator
Flt Sgt W Chitticks	Mid Upper Gunner
Fg Off W A Williams DFM	Special Operator
Flt Sgt F A Jobson	Special Operator
Flt Sgt D J Fuller	Waist Gunner
Sgt L Norwood	Waist Gunner
Flt Sgt C G Carter	Rear Gunner

The squadron also provided two aircraft for a target patrol over Würzburg. It would seem that the Window force spoof was not effective in diverting attention from the Nuremberg raid as night fighters picked up the main force route and got amongst the bombers with 1 Group losing twenty-four Lancasters from a force of 231.

Two targets were again chosen on the night of 18/9 March with a heavy attack by 324 aircraft on Witten, and a force of 277 Lancasters and eight Mosquitoes to Hanau. Both forces followed parallel tracks inland from the French coast until 5000N 0300E when the more northerly Witten stream turned north-west. The Witten force was routed clear of the northern end of the Mandrel screen before abruptly swinging through almost 90 degrees to approach Hanau from the north-west.

A Window force flying at the head of the Hanau force using the same track commenced dropping Window at 5052N 0730E and then, at 5100N 0805E continued on an easterly track threatening Kassel and disguising the Hanau force's turn to the south as it ran in on the target. The pretense stream towards Kassel was strengthened by a force of twenty-four 8 Group Mosquitoes which bombed the spoof target. The routing planned for these two attacks was well conceived, threatening a number of potential targets. This, together with the late sharp changes of course and the Window force feint was successful, and kept losses to just 1.1% of the sorties flown.

The squadron's contribution was four crews for the Window patrol, although an engine problem forced Fg Off Bowell to return to base. One aircraft was sent on a target patrol to Hanau and two over Witten.

Notes:
1. 'Musical' was normally associated with PFF marking using 'Oboe'-equipped Mosquitoes.

CHAPTER NINE

The Night of 20/21 March

20 March was just another day in Bomber Command but almost inevitably for some crews it would be a fateful one, despite the fast-fading ability of the German night-fighter force to challenge the attackers. For Fg Off Norman Ayres and his 223 Squadron crew this would be their final operation on what would be their sixth sortie after joining the squadron on 10 February from 1699 Flight, although some individuals in the crew had flown other ops with 223. The crew, whose detailed biographies are included in Appendix 5, were:

Fg Off Norman Siddall Ayres	Pilot
Warrant Officer Arnold Evans Redford	Navigator
Flt Sgt W Stanyer	Flight Engineer (not on final operation)
Sgt Dennis Marsden	Flight Engineer
Fg Off Harold Bertram Hale	Wireless Operator
Flt Sgt Joseph Davison Cairns	Mid Upper Gunner
W/O James Edward Bellamy	Special Operator
Warrant Officer Alfred Cyril Cole	Special Operator
Sgt Leonard Jack Vowler	Waist Gunner
Sgt Edward David Thornton Brockhurst	Waist Gunner
W/O Samuel Ernest Silvey	Rear Gunner

Bomber Command Operations: 20/21 March

20 March was a reasonable spring day, fair to fine with a fresh westerly wind. Norman Ayres and his crew followed the morning Bomber Command ritual of making their way to their flight office to check if they were on the battle order for the coming night's operations. They had a heightened interest in the outcome as they were scheduled for leave the next day. Air Chief Marshal Sir Arthur Harris had made his selection from a short list drawn up by his staff. This list was based on a number of factors including the Air Ministry directive on bombing policy and forecast weather conditions over Europe. Sir Arthur's decision confirmed that the synthetic oil producing plant at Böhlen near Leipzig and the Heide oil refinery at Hemmingstedt in northern Germany would be attacked. The decision resulted in eleven squadrons (35, 101, 156, 405, 419, 424, 427, 428, 431, 433, 434) drawn from 4, 6 (Canadian) and 8 (PFF) Groups being allocated to the Hemmingstedt target. This force would comprise 166 Lancasters; and they would

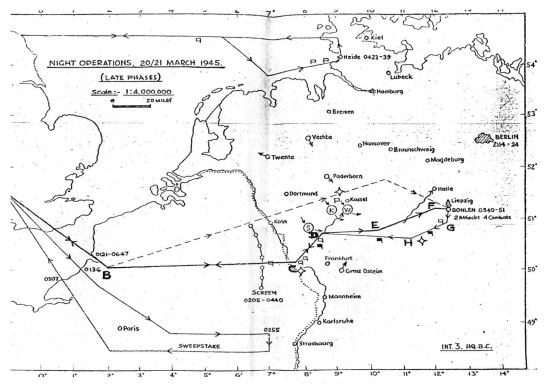

Route map showing turning points for operations on 20/21 March.

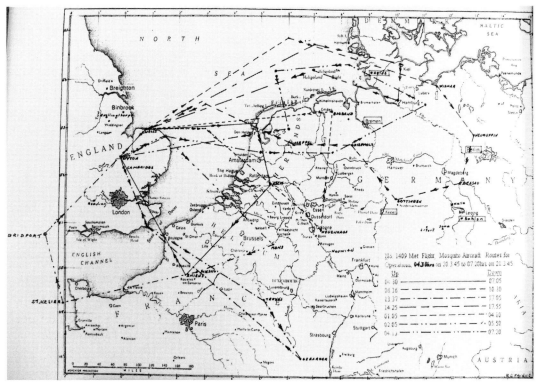

Met Flight map for 20 March 1945 [Ted Friend].

be supported by one Mosquito from 8 Group. The main attack delivered against Böhlen would be a 5 Group task using fifteen Lancaster squadrons. The group had two squadrons specialising in the Pathfinder role and they would mark the target supported by six Oboe-equipped Mosquitoes of 627 Squadron provided by 8 Group. We will concentrate on the Böhlen operation.

Bomber Command sent out the detailed instructions to the participating groups, and other organisations who needed to know, in a series of signals known collectively as the Form A. On receipt of the Form A the participating groups would issue the essential information contained in it, together with their own specialist instructions in a signal known as the Form B. Copies of the Form A and Forms B for 5 and 100 Groups can be seen at Appendix 5.

The Böhlen attack has been used by other authors as a classic example of the sophistication reached by Bomber Command tactics at the height of its powers; and showing all the main elements used to confound and confuse the enemy as to the true main force target. The main features of the night's operations and their execution will be explained as we follow the progress of the raid. The fifteen Lancaster squadrons taking part are listed below with the relevant numbers of aircraft which were dispatched:

Southern Bomber Stream
5 Group

Squadron	Station	Aircraft dispatched
44	RAF Spilsby	13 plus 3 to Halle
49	RAF Fulbeck	16
50	RAF Skellingthorpe	17
57	RAF East Kirkby	12 plus 3 to Halle
61	RAF Skellingthorpe	15
106	RAF Metheringham	15
189	RAF Fulbeck	15
207	RAF Spilsby	12 plus 3 to Halle
463 (RAAF)	RAF Waddington	16
467 (RAAF)	RAF Waddington	17
630	RAF East Kirkby	16 plus 3 to Halle
Total	166 including 12 to Halle	

Northern Bomber Stream

83	RAF Coningsby	14 (Pathfinder)
97	RAF Coningsby	14 (Pathfinder)
227	RAF Balderton	14 (Supporter) plus 1 to Halle
619	RAF Strubby	14 (Supporter) plus 1 to Halle
Total	58 including 2 to Halle	

The task of the supporter aircraft was to arrive at the target with the 83 and 97 Squadron aircraft to bomb and overwhelm the target's defences. The Böhlen attack would be aided by eleven Mosquitoes from 8 Group. Six of the Mosquitoes would assist in the marking of the target using their Oboe equipment with the remaining four aircraft used in the wind-finding role.

100 Group's participation in the night's operations was again a major one. The task laid down in the 100 Group Form B for the heavy squadrons was as follows:

Mandrel Screen
171 Squadron (code 6Y)

Flt Sgt C Dawson	Halifax NA687 (A)
Fg Off A J Brogan	Halifax NA695 (D)
W/O G W Jamieson	Halifax LK868 (J)
Fg Off E C Callon	Halifax NA673 (P)
Flt Lt W M B Dove	Halifax NA110 (Z)
Flt Sgt F M Taylor	Halifax NA106 (X)

199 Squadron (code EX)

Sqn Ldr W D Knight	Halifax PN385 (C)
Flt Lt P Chilcott	Halifax LK868 (J)
Fg Off J F Reidy RAAF	Halifax RG373 (T)
Fg Off T J Walford	Halifax NR244 (V)
Fg Off H C Broadfield	Halifax RG375 (R)
Flt Lt C Arkinstall	Halifax RG372 (P)
Fg Off A N Ward RNZAF	Halifax PN374 (N)
W/O W Sharples	Halifax RG381 (Q)

Western Window Patrol
171 Squadron

Fg Off G F Homer	Halifax LW471 (H)
Fg Off V J Townsend	Halifax NA690 (B)
Flt Lt B B Reid	Halifax NA675 (R)
Flt Lt W A Steel	Halifax PN169 (Q)

223 Squadron (code 6G)

Flt Lt Stephenson DFC	Liberator TS527 (Q)
Flt A Allnutt	Liberator TS532 (N)
Plt Off A Stuart	Liberator TS534 (A)
Fg Off F Bowell	Liberator TS525 (H)
Flt Lt A E L Morris	Liberator TS530 (G)
Sqn Ldr A Carrington DFC	Liberator TS533 (M)
Flt Lt J K Mann	Liberator VB852 (P)
Fg Off N S Ayres	Liberator TS526 (T)

Eastern Window Patrol

199 Squadron
Flt Lt A J Willis	Halifax PN375 (F)
Fg Off M Finnimore	Halifax PN376 (E)

214 Squadron (code BU)
Flt Lt G G Liles	Fortress KH999 (L)
Flt Lt W D Austin	Fortress KJ109 (V)
Fg Off D A Ingham RNZAF	Fortress KJ115 (B)
Fg Off S A Woods	Fortress KJ107 (N) returned early
Flt Lt J W Lucas	Fortress HB765 (R)

Target Patrol to Böhlen

214 Squadron
Fg Off R V Kingdon RCAF	Fortress HB785 (A)
Fg Off C J Mark	Fortress HB819 (U)
Flt Lt W D Allies	Fortress HB789 (Q)
Fg Off R V Kingdon RCAF	Fortress HB816 (F)

Target Patrol to Heide

214 Squadron
Fg Off N S Rogers	Fortress HB801 (T)

223 Squadron
Flt Lt A L Dyck RCAF	Liberator TT343 (K)

Electronic Intelligence (ELINT)

192 Squadron (code DT)
Flt Sgt F W Hobson	Halifax NA187 (U) – Böhlen
Flt Sgt A F Morley	Halifax NA182 (W) – Böhlen
Fg Off J Reay	Mosquito W4071 (K) – Böhlen
Fg Off K W Payne	Halifax PN474 (B) – Heide
Fg Off F C H Lewin	Halifax PN346 (C) – North Sea
Flt Lt A E Roach	Mosquito DZ376 (M) – Sweepstake

Piperack

192 Squadron
Fg Off C G George	Mosquito NZ797 (N) – Böhlen
Flt Lt M J Keit	Mosquito NZ997 (L) – Heide

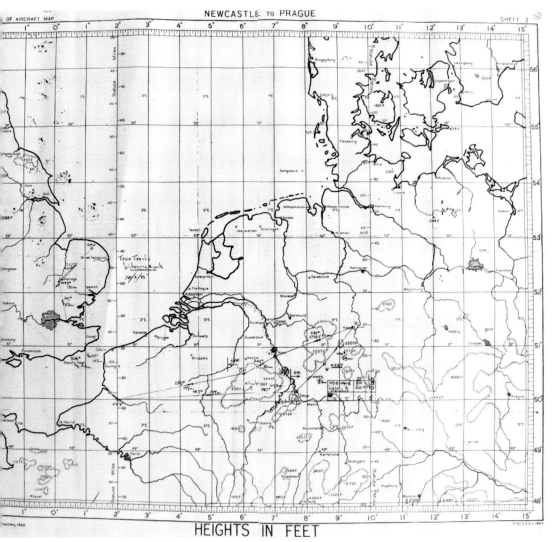

Captains of aircraft map for F/L A E L Morris *[A J K Barron]*.

In addition to the main force attack and the bomber support operations already detailed, a diversionary Sweepstake was mounted by twenty-one Halifaxes and forty-eight Lancasters drawn from 7 (Training) Group. Nine Lancasters from 1 Group were dispatched on a mine-laying task in the Heligoland area of the North Sea. To create additional confusion for the German defences and their controllers 8 Group dispatched thirty-eight Mosquitoes to bomb Berlin (ToT 21:14-21:24), twenty-seven Mosquitoes to Bremen (ToT 04:17-04:38) and a further sixteen to bomb the spoof target of Kassel.

100 Group also mounted thirty-three high level and fourteen low level intruder patrols with its Mosquito squadrons. A further eight Mosquitoes mounted anti-intruder patrols.

Fighter Command Mosquito squadrons were also in action in support of the night's operations. Low-level sorties were flown covering the Münster, Gütersloh, Paderborn, Wittmundhaven, Jever, Marx, Varel, Stade, Schleswig/Jagel and Lübeck areas. Three aircraft completed escort patrols between 02:43 and 06:52. Another aircraft acted as an escort for the Heide attackers. Two Mosquitoes were sent to patrol each of the *Quelle* (Spring or Fountain) and *Phillip* night-fighter assembly beacons, and another four patrolled the *Silberfuchs* (Silverfox) beacon just to the west of a point on the southern bomber stream track. Finally, four Mosquitoes escorted the western window force between 01:24 and 05:17.

Meanwhile back at the Bomber Command airfields, ground staff were busy with all the tasks necessary to mount the called-for operations. Ground crews worked to produce the required numbers of serviceable aircraft, and around mid-day/early afternoon any air tests required would be carried out. These would be of short duration. Preparations continued with long trails of bomb trolleys emerging from the bomb stores together with ammunition for the guns. Topping up of fuel tanks, replenishment of engine oil tanks and hydraulic systems together with the myriad other tasks to prepare an aircraft for its mission would be completed. Into the evening aircrew briefing for the operations would take place around 20:00.

At Oulton Fg Off Norman Ayres was the first 223 Squadron aircraft away at 23:22 with the squadron's remaining seven Window force aircraft all away by 23:45. 214 Squadron's target patrol aircraft bound for Böhlen and the aircraft of the eastern Window force immediately followed their sister squadron's aircraft into the air. The aircraft tasked in support of the Heide operation would take off much later.

Around about the same time, the Halifaxes of 171 and 199 Squadrons were taking off to establish the Mandrel screen at 02:05 in a slight curve between 5058N 0628E and 4940N 0640E at a height of 15,000 feet. Its location was just to the west of the existing front line, which effectively was the River Rhine. The screen would be formed using seven pairs of aircraft flying their adjacent racetrack circuits. The screen would be maintained until 04:40.

Almost immediately, main force suffered its first loss. Fg Off C A Cobern RAAF and his crew of 57 Squadron were airborne at 23:45 from their Skellingthorpe base; but ran into problems just after take-off, crashing on to a house approximately seven miles to the north of Boston. Cobern, together with the navigator, flight engineer and an air gunner were killed, and Flt Sgt W S Searby the air bomber died later from his injuries. The wireless operator and another air gunner were injured.

Sgt Ted Friend was the navigator in the 50 Squadron crew of Fg Off Neil Levy RAAF. An all SNCO crew, apart from their skipper, they had only arrived on the squadron on 11 March from 5 Lancaster Finishing School, and this was their first op. They were away at 23:53 from Skellingthorpe in Lancaster ME441 (VN-N). We shall meet them again.

Another 5 Group crew skippered by twenty-nine-year-old Rhodesian Sqn Ldr Colin Palmer were also taking off hoping to complete their first op with 619 Squadron. They had taken off for an attack on Würzburg on 16 March but were forced to abort after shutting down a failing No.1 engine and suffering overheating on the other three. They were one of two late additions to the Halle feint force. This was no novice crew; Sqn Ldr Palmer had been identified as the next CO of 44 Squadron, and had already completed a tour of operations flying Hurricanes in North Africa. The navigator, Flt Lt Leonard Raw, had considerable experience on Sunderlands flying the Transport

Command route from Lisbon to Takoradi in West Africa. Flt Lt William Graham, the wireless operator, had completed a previous Bomber Command tour on Hampdens. The flight engineer, Fg Off Frederick Ricketts had initially joined as a fitter (engines) but remustered to aircrew completing an operational tour with 625 Squadron, which had earned him a DFM. The three youngsters in the crew were all starting their operational careers. These were air bomber Fg Off David Thomas, mid upper gunner and passionate football fan Sgt Peter Wiseman and last, but not least, Sgt Jasper Miles the rear gunner, the joker in the crew who always raised spirits when the crew were up against it. They were airborne at 23:47 in Lancaster PD425 (PG-T).

The other late addition to the Halle spoof attack came from 227 Squadron based at Balderton. Fg Off Ray King RAAF and his crew were not on the original battle order and were debating how they would spend their free time when Ray was approached by another pilot who said he was due to be married the following week and asked Ray if he would take his place. Ray sought the opinion of the crew who all agreed to go as they were keen to finish their tour. They faced another decision when a new pilot on the squadron, Fg Off W H Pitts RAAF, asked Ray if he would take him with them so he could complete his 'Second Dickey' trip with them – before a new crew started operations it was customary for the pilot to do one or two ops with an experienced crew to learn the ropes. Ray was not so keen as crews were unhappy at having strangers aboard and considered them unlucky. However, Pitts who Ray had known from their school days together would not be dissuaded. The crew had been to Böhlen before on 5 March when it had proved a long nine-hour twenty-five minute flight. This time they would have the additional diversion to Halle before reaching the main target. Airborne at 23:39, fate had dealt them a deadly card.

Another 227 Squadron crew would also be involved in a night of high drama. Flt Lt Mervyn Croker RNZAF DFC was a very experienced and much-respected pilot on the squadron. He had gained a reputation for bringing home damaged aircraft, and it was a squadron joke that Balderton's hangars were full of 'Croker's crocks'. Mervyn would enhance his reputation that night. The crew, like Ray King, would fly with a 'Second Dickey', W/O Bert Allam, who would join them for this trip prior to flying ops with his own crew. Unfortunately, things got off to a bad start when intercom problems delayed their take-off, and they were eventually last away, twenty-one minutes after the previous aircraft.

The Oulton squadrons would be joined by the other bomber support squadron aircraft comprising the target and Window patrols heading for Böhlen flying some five minutes ahead of the main force. The 100 Group routeing initially took them south-west to overhead Cambridge where they turned south to cross the Thames at Gravesend to the east of London. They crossed the coast at Dungeness and made landfall on the French side of the Channel at Pointe du Haut-Banc. The main force were routed via Reading (point A), before turning south-east to cross the English coast slightly to the east of Eastbourne. They were restricted to a height of 5,000 feet until they reached 0600E. This dog leg was to assist the establishment of the bomber stream whilst minimising the visibility of a raid by the German early warning system. The French coast was crossed at 01:21 and the next turning point (B), just to the south-west of Abbeville, was reached shortly afterwards at 5000N 0200E. At this point the bomber force split into two separate formations. The two 5 Group Pathfinder squadrons, together with the two squadrons tasked as supporters, totalling a force of fifty-eight Lancasters, broke away from the rest of the Böhlen force, and its bomber support aircraft, and headed to the north-west forming the northern, flare force, stream. The main portion of the Böhlen force of 166 Lancasters, together with the two Window forces and the target patrol aircraft turned due east. Just to the south of the main force the Sweepstake force had crossed the French coast and was heading to the south-east. At 4845N 0400E they would turn due east to threaten the Strasbourg area.

The Bomber Command intention was to convince the Germans that Kassel was a main target; and the northern flare force was part of the deception – its routeing would take them round and slightly north of the city. The stream would therefore be passing through the very tip of the northern end of the Mandrel screen, and this was almost certainly intentional to give the German early warning radars partial visibility of this force. If this was the intention then it worked. The southern bomber stream was not plotted by the Germans until it was crossing the front line near Koblenz on the Rhine at 02:44[1].

At 02:30 the two pairs of aircraft flying in the two most northerly positions, one and two in the Mandrel screen, broke away from their positions and moved to 5018N 0830E and 5012N 0830E respectively. Arriving at these positions in the Frankfurt area they dropped incendiaries together with green TIs and red spot flares before returning to their original positions. A further four Halifaxes from positions 3 and 6 in the Mandrel Screen repeated this exercise at 02:40[2].

The main force aircraft climbed to a minimum height of 12,000 feet to cross the front line to minimise the risk of damage from light flak. Flt Lt Morris's navigator Andrew Barron has them crossing the Rhine at 02:43. 223 Squadron was about five minutes or so ahead. The 100 Group element of the southern stream commenced dropping Window just a few minutes before they approached the front line and switched on their special equipment as they crossed the Rhine. Window dropping ceased as they made their turn to the north-east. Almost certainly this was to ensure that the German defences picked up the turn in the direction of Kassel. The crossing of the Rhine by the southern bomber stream coincided with the Sweepstake turning back from the Strasburg area around 02:55. The German controllers had already plotted the northern stream which had been recorded in the Namur area as early as 02:07 even before it penetrated the extreme northerly edge of the Mandrel screen. This stream was also noted in the Mönchengladbach area. The German controllers concentrated their attention on the northern stream and ignored the main force. Both streams were initially assessed nominally as a force of thirty aircraft. Night fighters of the 3rd Jagd Division were alerted and Hptm Johannes Hager, the kapitän of 6th Staffel of the 2nd Gruppe of Nachtjagdgeschwader 6 (II./NJG 6), was among those scrambled from Werl airfield to the east of Dortmund.

After crossing the Rhine the southern stream turned to the north-west putting them on a direct heading for Kassel. They flew on for roughly fifty miles in the direction of Kassel before the main force and the eastern Window force turned due east at Point D

(5040N 0835E) with a sharp loss of height to between 6,000 to 8,000 feet as they completed the turn. The western Window force recommenced Window dropping as they continued on their run up to Kassel, disguising the main force turn, which was not detected by the Germans. The Window force approaching Kassel was heavily plotted and this, together with the already identified northern stream, convinced the Germans that Kassel was a genuine target, thus they concentrated at least five gruppen of night fighters against this threat. The Window force were operating HF Jostle on 3464 Kc/s from 03:27 to 04:15, Carpet on frequencies between 499 and 586 Mc/s from 02:40 to 04:16 and Piperack from 02:37 to 05:58.

The western Window force carried on up to Kassel and the four Halifaxes of 171 Squadron marked the city with red and green TIs, and dropped eight 750 lb incendiary clusters. The city was also bombed by twelve Mosquitoes of 8 Group.

Unteroffizier Walter Schneider, Hptm Johannes Hager's radio/radar operator [Walter Schneider].

Hauptmann Johannes Hager [Werner Pinn].

Hptm Hager flying in Me 110 G4, call sign C9-BC with his radio/radar operator Unteroffizier Walter Schneider and air gunner Obergefreiter Baerwald departed Werl on a Zahma Sau sortie heading for the *Schnake* (Gnat or Midge) night-fighter assembly beacon to the south of Dortmund. The report that Hager had received gave the location of the enemy bombers near Mönchengladbach flying on a course of 70 degrees. There had also been a report of another enemy formation flying to the south. As the northerly incursion was anticipated south of Dortmund, Hager immediately flew south from the city. He flew for a time on a 30 degree course and then on 150 degrees. At about 02:55 he found the bomber stream at a height of 16,400 feet in the North Hessen Edersee district. His radio/radar operator Walter Schneider, who was substituting for Hager's regular operator, picked up a contact on his SN2 radar, despite jamming interference, which were seen to be two four-engined heavy bombers flying at 15,000 feet on a course of 80 degrees. Hager immediately attacked one of the aircraft from behind and 160 feet below at 02:59. The bomber was making strong corkscrewing manoeuvres as he attacked, but after a short burst of twenty-eight rounds from his two Schräge Musik 20mm MG FF cannons the victim began to burn brightly in the port wing. The burning enemy aircraft was then observed to dive, impacting on the ground in grid square LS-MS at 03:01.[3,4]

Hager had shot down 619 Squadron Lancaster PD425 (T) flown by Sqn Ldr Colin Palmer. His air bomber, Fg Off David Thomas, lying in the nose spotted a Ju 88 approaching from ahead and below on a reciprocal course and shouted out a warning to the crew. As the aircraft disappeared from his view he heard explosions hitting the underside of the Lancaster and assumed that they had been struck by fire from the Junkers. David heard loud screaming from somewhere in the middle of the aircraft indicating that someone had been hit. He paused to check the bomb bay through an inspection flap behind him but was quickly engulfed in smoke and sparks that swept into his compartment. The flight engineer yelled something incoherently from the steps down into the bomb aimer's position just as Palmer, in the calmest of voices, called up on the intercom, "Pilot to crew, jump, jump – jump, jump". David quickly clipped on his chest parachute, and removed his flying helmet and oxygen mask that connected him to the intercom and oxygen system. He pulled up the escape hatch cover in the floor of the compartment and dropped it through the, now, open hatch. Diving head first through the hatch, clear of the aircraft he pulled the ripcord handle to release the 'chute and floated down in the darkness from 15,000 feet to make a safe landing.

The first Sgt Jasper Miles, the rear gunner, knew of the attack was a loud crash followed by Flt Lt Graham, the wireless operator, reporting a fire in the bomb bay. He was immediately aware of flames licking round his turret and remembered Palmer calling "jump, jump, jump". He rotated his turret to the beam position and exited through the turret doors to the starboard side of the aircraft. It was fortunate that he was wearing a pilot-type, sit on, parachute and not the normal chest type which would have been stowed in the fuselage on the other side of the turret doors. When free of the aircraft and drifting down on his parachute, Jasper was aware of a glow behind him and discovered his back was burning. He did not see what happened to the aircraft and the only thing he could see of the ground was a large lake (possibly the Edersee). The first clue that he was close to the ground was the branch of a tree brushing his face as he dropped into a wooded area. Apart from a smouldering flying suit and a small gash on the right hand side of his forehead he was unharmed.

Regrettably, no other members of the crew baled out. The calmness of Palmer in giving the bale out call is particularly noteworthy. When the crew practised escaping from a dummy aircraft on the ground Palmer, a large man of seventeen stone, could not get through the nose escape hatch. In giving the "jump" command he knew that he would not be able to make it to the rear door.

What of PD425? The aircraft broke up/exploded close to the village of Netze with the main portions of the wreckage falling in fields immediately north of the village; some debris including a complete mainplane landing on houses in the village. Andrew Barron's crew were still on the run up to Kassel at this point and his navigation log records the sighting of a burning aircraft on the ground at 03:03, ten to fifteen miles off the port beam.

David Thomas had always assumed that the Ju 88 had shot them down. He later appreciated that this would have been impossible when the relative closing speeds of the two aircraft are considered. The Ju 88 would have to have opened fire with Schräge Musik weaponry before he passed below the Lancaster to have had even the remotest chance of striking his victim. His approach would appear to have been purely coincidental at the time of Hager's attack. Hager and his crew would have been intently concentrating on their target and did not see the Junkers.

Almost instantly, Walter Schneider picked up another contact on his SN2 CRT and Hager identified it to the left and below them. At 03:02 he positioned himself 200 feet below another four-engined aircraft and struck again with his weapons, hitting his next victim in the starboard mainplane causing a fire. Again he reported seeing the burning aircraft impact on the ground in the same LS-MS grid square as with his first victim. The aircraft he had attacked was the 227 Squadron Lancaster flown by Flt Lt Mervyn Croker DFC RNZAF flying in PD349 (9J-G). Mervyn's aircraft had been delayed by an intercom fault, and was the last aircraft to leave. Despite the late take-off, Mervyn had obviously made up most, if not all, the deficit. Their flight up to this point had been uneventful apart from experiencing some flak as they crossed the front line. Their first knowledge of trouble was a very large bang causing a fire to break out in the starboard inner engine; this was feathered by the pilot. Wyn Henshaw, the wireless operator, reported to Mervyn that he could smell smoke which he believed was coming from the bomb bay. Instructed by Mervyn to check the bomb bay through the inspection port in the fuselage floor, Wyn was joined by the mid upper gunner, Freddy Wilcox, and they quickly confirmed the fire, which Wyn reported to his skipper. The rear gunner also confirmed the fire after rotating his turret to look up the side of the fuselage. Mervyn Croker feathered the starboard inner engine and shut it down to try and put out the fire. The fire in the bomb bay was more critical as burning hydraulic fluid was leaking over the bomb load. Mervyn gave the order to bale out, but nobody jumped. Wyn Henshaw went to the rear door, pushed it open and gave the thumbs-up sign to Freddy Wilcox to jump. Both airmen froze so Wyn reconnected his intercom lead and heard Willie Williams the rear gunner shout that the bomb load had gone down in a mass of flames.

Mervyn, having jettisoned the bomb load, cancelled the bale out order and promptly put the aircraft into a steep, spiral dive. In the attack, Bert Allam was thrown down the steps into the bomb aimer's compartment being half strangled in the process by his intercom and oxygen leads. Whilst sorting himself out he was off intercom and missed the bale out call. The bomb aimer indicated that they were to jump and they, together with the flight engineer, tried to get the nose escape hatch open. This they failed to do and as the aircraft entered its spiral dive the centrifugal forces built up and Bert was pinned to the floor and resigned himself to his fate. He was therefore very relieved when the aircraft came out of its dive and the pressure eased. Bert estimated that they pulled out of the dive at around 3,000 feet. Mervyn then carried out a few checks on the starboard inner, which was no longer on fire, unfeathered and restarted it, climbing away for a return to base. It is highly likely that it was the bomb load exploding on the ground, which Hager and his independent witness Oberfeldwebel Schellwat, had taken to be the impact of PD349 (G). It is believed that this incident also explains why there are reports in the official records of a collision in the Kassel area. What crews had witnessed was the flaming bomb load and the diving Lancaster with its fire in the starboard mainplane, particularly in view of Croker's low-level pull up.

Hager and his crew had not finished, as Schneider quickly picked up another contact on his SN2 screen at 03:10 flying at a height of 14,000 feet on a heading of 80 degrees. Hager immediately instigated an attack from the classic position behind and 60 to 100 feet below the four-engined bomber. Schneider was puzzled because he assessed the bomber was flying 60 to 90 mph slower than the other aircraft they attacked. In Schneider's words: "Suddenly, as big as a barn door, it stood before our fighter." It was so close Schneider was sure they were going to collide. Hager, it would seem, was lining up to fire with his vertically-inclined MG FF cannon as in the previous attacks, but was forced to use his forward-firing armament using fifteen rounds from his two 30 mm Rheinmetall Borsig Mk 108 20 mm cannons, and seventy-four rounds from the two 20 mm Mauser MG 151 cannons. The enemy aircraft immediately caught fire and burned fiercely along the whole fuselage and the wings, and Hager and his crew followed the burning aircraft in a steep dive up to the point of impact slightly west of Kassel at 03:11 precisely[5].

The only aircraft known to have been lost around this time, in this location, was Norman Ayres' TS526 (T) of 223 Squadron, and Andrew Barron's surviving navigation log and chart for this operation supports this. Norman's aircraft had been part of the western Window force leading the feint attack on Kassel. The two special operators, Alfred Cole and Ted Bellamy, were in the rear operators' position in the loft above the rear of the bomb bay, operating Carpet and Piperack. Dennis Marsden, the flight engineer, was busy pushing out Window. Using Andrew Barron's data the aircraft would have tracked just to the east of Kassel and when it reached a point just to the north-east of the city, Ayres would have turned the aircraft to the south-west on a heading of approximately 240/250 degrees. Thus they would have been flying on a reciprocal course to the northern bomber stream. They would also have been losing height from 18,000 feet at the turn, to around 15,000 feet some eight or nine minutes later. A firsthand account of the attack on TS526 survives in the form of a letter written by Alfred Cole, from a German hospital, to his wife:

'I was coming on leave right up to 03:00 Wednesday morning and then the aircraft I was in got a hell of a direct hit over Germany and came crashing down in flames, making a most awful noise. Some of the crew baled out but for the rest it was useless as we could not get anywhere near to the escape exit, for the machine was rolling over and over, upside down and all ways. No one spoke, but as we were thrown about all of us must have considered that we were living out our last moments. And so they were, poor lads, except your hubby, who by the grace of God still lives to recount what was my most awful experience in life yet.'

The attack on TS526 is believed to have taken place over the town of Wolfhagen about fifteen miles west of Kassel. Ayres, incredibly, managed to bring the burning aircraft under control. A witness in the village of Ippinghausen saw the aircraft passing at low level from east to west, between the village and the Weidelsburg. The Weidelsburg is a small hill with a ruined castle on its summit, a mile south of the village. The aircraft, streaming flames and making a horrendous noise, was flying over the village well below the level of the 300-metre summit. The witness Horst Willensteine recalled:

> "An air raid siren and the noise of an aircraft woke me and my mother in the early hours of the morning of 21 March 1945. Our Polish prisoner-of-war worker and I went out to the steps in front of our house. The house was on the north side of the main road through the village on its western end of Ippinghausen. Suddenly I heard a threatening roar and the loud noise of engines. We saw in the light night sky in front of us a large aircraft. The weather was clear and it was clearly recognisable. It came from the south-east from a direction between the nearby villages of Naumburg and Altenstadt. The pilot was flying at a height of about 120 metres; every part of the plane was burning and it looked like a glowing ball of fire. The aircraft flew in a gentle left-hand curve on to a westerly heading. The pilot clearly succeeded in pulling the aircraft up, we saw how it climbed higher. It was obvious that the pilot had seen the Opferberg, or he wanted to give the crew members the chance to jump out. The sucking [sic] of the air caused by the burning aircraft was very strong and in fear I ran back into the house. Very quickly the noise of the aircraft became quieter and I went outside again. There the Pole was hanging/bending over the steps area, he was very excited as the pull exerted by the aircraft had nearly dragged him away."

Clearly Ayres was looking for open ground to put the aircraft down, but sadly he was running out of time as he encountered wooded rising ground. There appeared to have been an attempt to lighten the doomed aircraft to keep it in the air for long enough to put it down under control. The wooded ground Ayres met was the Opferberg (summit 440 metres) on the Hoenscheide estate. The pilot was unable to gain sufficient altitude, and in a desperate attempt at survival Sam Silvey and Leonard Vowler baled out, probably through the ventral hatch in the rear fuselage, but were too low to make it. No one else was able to escape. Just about 200 yards short of the impact an engine, possibly the port inner, broke away from the mainplane and the aircraft crashed, the burning front portion breaking away from the rear fuselage. Tragically, all but Alfred Cole were killed. Poignantly, the translation of Opferberg is 'Hill of Sacrifice'.

The author (Richard Forder), together with Hajo Adler and Bernd Klinkhardt were able to follow the flight path of TS526 through the trees on the Opferberg by the damage still visible caused by burning fluids and/or molten metal dropping from the aircraft. Live 0.5 inch calibre ammunition was also found along the flight path indicating that it had been thrown overboard to lighten the aircraft. This ammunition was handed in to

Wreckage of TS526 on the Opferberg awaiting disposal after the war *[Mrs E Wilson]*.

the German organisation responsible for handling recovery of wartime ordinance who also swept the area to recover the remaining rounds.

There is a discrepancy in the heading given for Hager's third claim, 80 degrees. However, he had just experienced three engagements in the space of twelve minutes. The first two were on a heading of 80 degrees. So according to Hager's combat reports all three were on the northern bomber stream track. So had he mistakenly attributed the bomber stream heading instead of the reciprocal for number three? What is not in doubt is that TS526 was shot down in the area of Hager's third claim. The only aircraft from the northern stream not accounted for is the 97 Squadron Lancaster PA973 (OF-C) flown by Fg Off J D Cottman RAAF. This has been discounted for a number of reasons:

1. Consultation with German friends with their vast local knowledge and contacts in the area, only produced two aircraft crash sites on the ground for the night in question, that of TS526 and 619 Squadron's PD425 (T). It was only when the position and timing of Mervyn Croker's attack in 227 Squadron's operations record book were discovered, that is was possible to account for all three of Hager's claims.

2. The timing of Hager's kill would appear to have been too late for Cottman's aircraft. At 03:10 the northern bomber stream would have been passing to the north of Kassel and beyond. Additionally, 97 Squadron was a 5 Group Pathfinder squadron and its aircraft would have been at the head of the stream.

A further complication is a claim, in the same area as Hager's third claim, by Hptm Fritz Lau, Staffelkapitän of IV./NJG 1; Lau's claim was timed at 03:28. Unfortunately, it has not been possible to locate a copy of his combat report for this claim. The author did correspond with Fritz Lau who was most helpful but could not recall the details of his claim, however he did provide an interesting explanation of the procedure and validation process for victory claims in the German night-fighter force, which we have taken into our assessment.

Could this claim apply to either PA973 or TS526? It would seem most unlikely, as the timing would appear to be too late for either aircraft, unless either aircraft had been slowed down by problems or damage. This was not the case with TS526 as we know from Alfred Coles' letter that all was well until they were attacked and shot down. If PA973 was late there is still the problem of no corresponding local evidence of its loss in the area west of Kassel. In spite of inconsistencies Hager remains favoured as the victor of TS526. A brief biography of Hager, courtesy of Werner Pinn and his nephew Bernd Klinkhardt is included at Appendix 6.

The Kassel spoof attack had been highly successful, albeit at the cost of two aircraft and another forced to return. The German controllers were still uncertain as to the true target(s). The five or seven gruppen dispatched to counter the Kassel spoof were held in the area until 03:36 before being released to chase the Böhlen forces. Night fighters were also held to the south of the southern stream route against a perceived threat in the Frankfurt area. IV./NJG 6 were held at Beacon *Otto* in this area until released at 03:10 to chase the southern stream. Similarly, II./NJG 2 were held at Beacon *Nachtigall* (Nightingale) until 03:35 when they were given a course to Böhlen[6].

Meanwhile the Heide force was tracking across the North Sea without the protection of a Mandrel screen. This raid was poorly plotted and appeared to be largely ignored by the Germans.

The northern stream, having rounded Kassel, were on their south-easterly run to Böhlen. Sometime after 03:00, and getting close to their turn for the Halle diversion, Flt Lt Ray King, in PA259 suddenly received a "Corkscrew port, night fighter attacking from below" call from his rear gunner. Ray put the aircraft into a steep diving turn, but he was too late as cannon shells struck, and tracer whipped passed his cockpit. Ray remembers:

"The cockpit filled with smoke. I brought the Lancaster out of the dive but found difficulty in controlling the aircraft. At a quick glance, the two starboard engines were on fire, so I called for the engineer to press the fire extinguishers for them. By this time the fire had spread between the two motors and the aircraft started a diving turn. I thought, this is it and quickly called on the intercom, "Abandon aircraft, jump, jump!" twice. At the same time I thought, I have to get out last, so I pulled the pin of the seat harness in preparation and then concentrated on trying to get the aircraft out of the dive. No response from the controls. The nose came up and suddenly the aircraft rolled upside down. I remember pushing the control column forward to try and bring the nose up again, and then fell into the roof of the cockpit. The next thing I remember was the rush of cold air, so I went for the ripcord of my parachute. We were attacked at 15,000 feet but by this time had lost a lot of height.

"I have no recollection of floating down, so I guess the parachute opened just before I hit the trees. There was a vague thump and after some time I looked up and spotted my flying helmet hanging on a branch of the tree. I was suspended by the parachute about 10 feet off the ground. Fires in the forest some distance away, from the remains of our crashed aircraft, gave enough light for me to release my harness and drop to the ground."

They had come down close to the village of Schoenah just to the west of the town of Heilbad Heiligenstadt. Amazingly, Fg Off Bill Neilson, navigator; Flt Sgt W A Roots, air bomber; and Flt Sgt B T Long RAAF had also survived. Regrettably, Plt Off W H Pitts RAAF, 2nd Pilot; Sgt R W Fitton, flight engineer; and the air gunners Sgt L E Baxter RCAF and Sgt L Marshall perished. The crew had paid a high price for agreeing to substitute for another crew. Their assailant is not known.

The southern bomber stream had greatly benefited from the Kassel spoof and the other diversionary activities. Their turn to the east had been successfully screened by their dive to low level and the protection provided by the western Window force. It is also possible that the Sweepstake force may have helped in limiting the support of night-fighter support from south-west Germany to one gruppe. The stream continued uninterrupted to 5055E 1100E where the eastern Window force broke away from the main force on a north-westerly heading to threaten Halle. The Window force comprising four aircraft of 214 Squadron, and two from 199 Squadron led the twelve Lancasters up to Halle. The Fortresses operated VHF Jostle from 02:30 to 05:58, and HF Jostle on 4421 Kc/s from 03:40 to 05:50; Carpet on frequencies between 455 and 577 Mc/s from 02:50 to 05:30 and Piperack from 02:30 to 05:58. The two 199 Squadron aircraft dropped red and green TIs and four 750 lb incendiary clusters on Halle between 03:43 and 03:50. The authenticity of the attack was heightened by the bombing by the twelve Lancasters.

The Halle feint, which was well plotted, threw the German controllers as they tried to reconcile this threat and the previously plotted northern stream. The controllers were eventually reduced to specifying a possible target between Halle and Leipzig. In addition to the gruppe sent from the south and the south-east, another gruppe from the Berlin area were ordered to Leipzig. The night fighters finally caught up with main force over Böhlen.

In the leg from Points E to F, where the second spoof attack was thrown off to Halle, the main force were climbing to their bombing height of 12 to 14,000 feet. The marker squadrons indicated the target on time although the master bomber was a little late in calling in the main force to bomb. As a result of this some crews were seen to bomb and others to orbit in the target area. However, some crews in the target area may have arrived earlier than planned because of a following wind across Europe. Visibility over the target was described as hazy with a thin layer of cloud around 6,000 to 7,000 feet. This visibility would decrease with the smoke from the bombing and the German attempts to screen the plant with smoke generators. Three aircraft of 214 Squadron provided cover for the attackers. VHF Jostle was operated from 02:40 to 05:50, HF Jostle on 4421 Kc/s from 03:40 to 05:50, and on 4451 Kc/s from 03:43 to 06:19; Carpet on frequencies between 455 and 568 Mc/s from 02:37 to 05:25 and Piperack from 02:33 to 06:19. A Mosquito also operated Piperack from 03:25 to 04:10. As only three of the four 214 Squadron's Fortress aircraft circled over Böhlen during the attack it would appear that Fg Off R V Kingdon RCAF in HB785 (BU-A) was shot down before they reached the target. Kingdon and his crew had only had a brief reprieve after surviving their attack earlier in the month on the night of Operation Gisela (See Chapter 10). The aircraft was lost in the vicinity of Sulzbach am Main with no survivors.

Despite this RCM protection main force lost two Lancasters in the target area. Fg Off K W Ainsworth and his crew in Lancaster NG386 (QR-P) of 61 Squadron almost certainly fell here. An identity card for Flt Sgt A W Snelling, the wireless operator, was found near Espenhain in the Böhlen area[7]. Ainsworth was on his seventeenth op with the squadron when he was lost. There were no survivors.

Lancaster PB845 (JO-C) of 463(RAAF) Squadron flown by Fg Off Richard Stewart Bennett RAAF was also brought down in the Böhlen area. Again there were sadly no survivors. It is not known how these crews were brought down,

With the attack completed, the bombers began their long trek home pursued by night fighters, the controllers having now caught up with the true situation posed by the attacking forces. After clearing the defences the homeward-bound aircraft would have descended rapidly to a height band of 1,500 to 3,000 feet heading due south, before turning south-west at the next turning point, Point H (5032N 1120E) then finally they swung westward. At Point D they would regain their original outbound track; this was where the Kassel feint had been launched. It is possible that some crews may have cut a corner here as the next two aircraft to be lost fell to the south of this turning point.

At 0900E the retuning main force had been instructed to commence climbing to a height of not less than 8,000 feet in preparation for crossing the front line. At this time the crews would probably have seen the lightening of the skies ahead of them with the arrival of the dawn. At 04:59 Oberstleutnant Herbert Lütje, the kommandeur of IV./NJG 6 claimed a four-engined bomber. Based on the time, this could have been either the 61 Squadron Lancaster RA560 (QR-K) flown by Fg Off J Swales RAAF or Lancaster LM653 (DX-Q) of 57 Squadron flown by Flt Lt A R Palling RAAF. Initially, consultation with German friends Hajo Adler and Dirk Sohl, prompted the belief that Lütje's victim had been the 61 Squadron aircraft. However, publication of Dr Theo Boiten and Roderick Mackenzie's *Luftwaffe War Diaries* revealed that Lütje's kill had been claimed in the Friedberg area between Frankfurt and Giessen. What is known is that RA560 came down in woodland just to the north-east of Kirch Göns which lies about 14 km to the south of Giessen. LM653 fell near Kransberg which is just five km west of Friedberg. Friedberg is about 14 km due south of Kirch Göns. So it appears that Lütje's victory was most likely to have been LM653 of 57 Squadron. There were no survivors from either aircraft. Fg Off Charles Saunders, the navigator in RA560, was on his twenty-third op with Swales when they were shot down.

Just a short time later, Plt Off A N Levy in 50 Squadron Lancaster ME441 (VN-W) was approaching the front line. Thirty miles east of the Rhine Levy warned the crew of light flak ahead. About seven minutes later the aircraft, flying at 8,000 feet, was hit by intense light flak on the approach to the Remagen bridgehead. Levy instructed the wireless operator, Sgt S Chapman, to fire the colours of the day. The aircraft then went into a shallow dive and the navigator, Sgt Ted Friend, noticed that the engines were vibrating and roaring. The navigator's altimeter registered the altitude as 4,000 feet with the steady loss of height continuing. Sgt Friend therefore clipped on his parachute and, hearing nothing on the intercom, moved to the cockpit where he tried to speak to the pilot. When Levy saw him he tugged Friend's sleeve and pointed to the escape hatch in the nose. Ted moved back down into the nose where he found the air bomber, Flt Sgt D Swingler, removing the hatch. The air bomber jumped first followed immediately by Ted Friend. Ted landed safely with a few scratches that he received when passing through the branches of a tree. He was not certain of the exact position of his landing, but estimates it to be about three or four miles east of Rheinbrohl on the east bank of the Rhine. The aircraft came down close to Asbach without any other crew members escaping and all lost their lives. Flt Sgt Swingler did not survive either. It is presumed his body was found by American troops as he is buried in the American Hotton War Cemetery in Belgium.

Ted Friend could hear the sound of heavy artillery, so he lay still where he had landed until dawn when he could establish the direction of the allied lines. He hid his 'chute in a thick wood and waited until daylight, then set off in a westerly direction, climbing up through a wood that was situated on the side of a steep hill. On reaching the top he continued westwards for about one-and-a-half miles when he met some American soldiers who took him into their HQ in Rheinbrohl by the Rhine. The Americans ensured his rapid repatriation to England.

Three aircraft remained unaccounted for after all the participants in the night's operations had landed. The possible fate of Fg Off J D Cottman RAAF and his 97 Squadron crew has already been discussed. Nothing has come to light concerning the fate of Flt Lt R Miller DFM and his crew lost in Lancaster RF132 (CA-K) of 189 Squadron. They were part of the southern bomber stream to Böhlen as were Fg Off Raymond Allen Lewis and his crew of 207 Squadron who remain listed as missing in their Lancaster PA196 (EM-D). The RAF's Air Historical Branch records against PA196 state that the crew were believed to have come down in the sea. It can only be assumed that this indicates that a ditching signal had been received, but no confirmation of this has been found. Lewis and his crew were on their eleventh operation with 207 Squadron when they were lost. This was their second visit to Böhlen having taken part in the previous attack on the plant on the night of 5/6 March.

One other Lancaster, KB786 (VR-P) of 419 (RCAF) Squadron, captained by Fg Off R W Millar RCAF, was lost on the night. This was the only casualty of the Heide attack, which was largely ignored by the Germans. Reportedly shot down by a night fighter, it most probably crashed at Odderade, 7 km east-south-east of Hemmingstedt. Flt Sgt Aitken RCAF was the only survivor, being thrown clear when the aircraft exploded.

The night's operations had been a success for Bomber Command. Both oil plants had been effectively attacked and put out of commission. The tactics employed had also proved successful especially the Kassel and Halle feints, which had totally confused the

Germans. The Kassel spoof had resulted in casualties but the two feints had enabled the main force in the southern stream to reach the target almost unchallenged. The cost was thirteen aircraft, a loss rate of just 1.9%.

Aftermath

We left Flt Lt Mervyn Croker and crew returning to base after their dramatic encounter with Johannes Hager. The return proved uneventful until they reached Balderton circuit when it was discovered that the starboard undercarriage was damaged and that the leg would not lower and lock down. Mervyn gave the crew the option of baling out but there were no takers. He carried out a very skilled landing keeping the starboard mainplane up as long as possible with the aircraft coming to rest without injury to the crew. Flt Lt Croker had lived up to his reputation and added another 'crock' to the Croker collection!

David Thomas and Jasper Miles had successfully baled out of the doomed PD425. When daylight came Thomas saw open farmland stretching away to the west where his route to the allied lines lay. Escape briefings had advised resting up in the day and to travel by night to minimise detection. However, in the early morning light he could see a Fieseler Storch aircraft circling overhead, possibly on the lookout for survivors of the crash. The spotter 'plane prompted him to get on the move out of the area, notwithstanding the evasion advice. At the end of the first day, he witnessed a P-51 Mustang raking a nearby town with cannon fire and on which he also dropped his long-range tanks. After a day or so, still tramping westward, he was surprised to encounter an abandoned Ju 87 Stuka under a tree at the edge of a gently sloping field. On the fourth day he witnessed another example of allied air supremacy when he saw three or four USAAF P-38 Lightnings strafe a convoy of German troops with devastating effect. The Lightnings were accompanied by a Douglas Boston that circled overhead during the attack. After four days on the run he was eventually apprehended.

After questioning at the Dulag Luft interrogation centre at Pinneberg, which had been moved from its original location in Frankfurt, he was dispatched to the prisoner-of-war camp Stalag Luft 1 at Barth on the Baltic coast. There one of his room mates was Fg Off Bill Neilson who had successfully jumped from Flt Lt Ray King's aircraft. Interestingly, the famous USAAF fighter ace, Colonel Hubert Zemke, was the senior allied officer in the camp. The camp fell into Russian hands at the end of the war, but the prisoners-of-war were soon on their way home flying from a nearby Luftwaffe airfield; David Thomas flew home on 12 May 1945, appropriately in the bombardier's position in the nose of an USAAF B-17 Fortress.

Jasper Miles also evaded successfully but was apprehended by two Volkssturm (equivalent to the Home Guard) members who duly handed him over to the local police. He was taken to an army barracks on the Edersee. The Luftwaffe unit at the night-fighter airfield at Fritzlar was contacted to come and collect him. A truck with a driver, Luftwaffe officer and an armed escort arrived to transport him. As he climbed into the back of the vehicle Jasper noticed that it contained some equipment from an American aircraft including some 0.5in Browning machine guns, and what appeared to be RAF flying helmets. Clearly, the Germans had just been to the crash site of the 223 Squadron Liberator.

They set off on their way and the Luftwaffe officer attempted to interrogate Jasper, but his limited grasp of English made it futile. En-route they stopped to give a lift to two uniformed female Luftwaffenhelferinnen (equivalent to the Women's Auxiliary Air Force). Shortly afterwards one of the women became hysterical, pointing and shouting, "American flieger" at two USAAF Mustangs on a low-level strafe on targets of opportunity. The Germans leapt out of the truck and dived for cover leaving Jasper standing at the back of the vehicle grinning and waving at the Yanks. After an overnight stay at Fritzlar he was on his way to the Dulag Luft at Frankfurt, which was in the process of moving when they arrived. He therefore went directly to a prisoner-of-war camp at Vetzlar. At this turbulent stage of the war he was soon on his way again, this time on foot as he, and many other allied prisoners were marched away from their camps to unknown destinations. Jasper's ordeal was relatively short as they were freed by American troops and he was repatriated back to England.

The 223 Squadron Liberator TS526 had broken in two as it rushed down into the trees and impacted on the ground. The front and rear portions of the 'plane ended up some 100 yards apart with the forward fuselage continuing to burn fiercely for several hours. Debris from the crash was scattered over a wide area. The sole survivor, Alfred Cole in the rear fuselage, was knocked unconscious when the aircraft crashed. In the continuation of his letter home to his wife he wrote:

'As we hit the deck I must have lost consciousness for I remembered no more until I came round, surrounded by and trapped by a mass of twisted and torn metal. It was becoming just light by then and I looked round gingerly. I was relieved to see that there was no fire anywhere, the parts of the aircraft that were on fire had been torn off by the trees among which we had crashed; but I was horrified to see I had a dead pal *[W/O Ted Bellamy]* trapped with me. I could not move him, nor myself, so there I lay for two hours or more, yelling at frequent intervals to try and attract attention. Eventually, some Gerry farm workers came and got me out and carried me to a cart and trundled me off to a big farm. The farmer and his wife were true Nazis but could both speak English. They gave me whisky, I needed it as I was not feeling too good. I had a bed all day there, on the floor and at night I was taken in an open lorry to the hospital.'

Whilst in hospital Alfred was questioned by German officers. They told him that he was the only survivor and that those who had baled out had fouled the aircraft or their parachutes had caught fire.

The Henschel family, who lived in the Schloss Hoenscheide and owned the estate on which TS526 had crashed, had heard the crash. At first light Herr Henschel, his farm manager Herr Bals together with Bernard August, an elderly forester, set off to find the crash site. Even from a distance they could hear whimpering and groaning. As they cautiously approached Cole, he became very agitated as he thought that being an allied airman they were going to kill him. They were able to quieten him by agreeing to hide him. In addition to the body of his pal Ted Bellamy, he was also trapped by the 600 lb Jostle transmitter which had broken free during the crash. It required the use of a block and tackle to hoist the transmitter off him. They then transported him in a farm cart to the Schloss Hoenscheide. This must have been an agonising journey for him as he was suffering from a broken back, four broken ribs and a broken left leg. He was also severely bruised over virtually every part of his body. The Henschels did not live up to Alfred's description of them as true Nazis. They refused to let the Schutzstaffel (SS) take Alfred away from the house on the grounds that he was unfit to travel. Alfred apparently was reluctant to take any food offered as he feared it had been poisoned. That night he was taken in the back of an open lorry to a hospital run by nuns in the nearby town of Arolsen.

At the crash site, two more bodies were removed from the remains of the front fuselage. In addition to the bodies of Cole and Bellamy already accounted for, six more bodies were located scattered over two to three hundred yards. These included those of Sam Silvey and Leonard Vowler who were found hanging from trees by their parachutes. Contrary to the information given to Cole by the German officers in the hospital, it would appear that Sam and Leonard had jumped out very low and at the last seconds before the crash.

A Luftwaffe SNCO from the night fighter airfield at Fritzlar removed all effects and papers from the bodies before they were transported in the back of a truck to be buried in the nearby tiny hamlet of Buhle, by orders of local officials. They were buried in the small cemetery on the same morning that had seen them shot down. A local resident, Herr Faellmer, made a white painted wooden palisade fence to go round the graves and erected a white wooden cross which read 'Eight English Flyers 21 March 1945'. It should have read nine. This was to cause great anguish amongst the relatives

Graves of Ayres' crew in Buhle cemetery *[Mrs E Wilson]*.

and friends of the crew. A French prisoner-of-war who visited Cole in the Arolsen Hospital had seen the grave and told him the details. Cole was repatriated pretty quickly as the American army advanced through the area shortly after; and he was back in England at the RAF hospital at Cosford on 8 April, being debriefed on his return. The mistake on the grave marker raised the false hope that there had been a second survivor. The Air Ministry were not able to confirm the identities of those killed until October 1945. The families were in contact with each other desperate for news, and could not understand why they could not be told, especially when they knew that Cole had survived and was back in the country. Clare, Norman Ayres' girl friend, travelled out to

Germany and went to see the Bürgermeister of Wolfhagen in an attempt to find out what had happened to the crew but was also unsuccessful.

Len Davies, David Brockhurst's pal throughout their short service together, visited Mr and Mrs Brockhurst at the end of the war to pay his respects. After the loss of TS526 he had been given the unenviable task of gathering David's effects together to return to his parents. He wanted something to remember his friend by, something of little value, which would not be missed by the family. He chose a shoe brush that had David's service number on it. As he got up to leave Mr Brockhurst produced a letter from an Air Ministry department and asked Len what he should do about it. The letter requested payment of an outstanding bill of one shilling and sixpence (about eight pence today), due to deficient kit – the missing shoe brush!

Ray King had come down near the village of Schoenah. Remarkably he was undamaged apart from a sprained ankle, a gash in his right hand and a few scratches. He buried his Mae West and like his fellow evaders headed west. In the afternoon he came on two Russian prisoners-of-war who were working as farm labourers. They appeared friendly and took him to the farmhouse where he was equally well received and his wounded hand cleaned up by the farmer's wife. Any hopes of continuing his escape were dashed, however, when he was escorted to locally-based soldiers and handed over. He was then delivered to the police station at Eschwege, where he was delighted to meet up with 'Curly' Long, his wireless operator; and Bill Roots the air bomber. Curly told him that the cannon shells appeared to go through the fuselage from under the aircraft, with one going through the wireless set and hitting the armour plate behind the pilot's seat. They were soon on their way to Dulag Luft before onward transportation to Stalag Luft III at Nuremberg. On 4 April they were on the move again and marched westwards, arriving at Stalag VIIA at Moosburg, near Munich on 18 April. Their journey had not been without incident as they had suffered fatalities when their column had been mistakenly attacked by American P-47 Thunderbolts on the way. Release was a short time away when on 28 April they were freed by tanks of US General Patton's Third Army.

Notes:
1. Air24/314 Summary of Night Operations March 1945.
2. Air25/788 Interception Tactics No 70/45 dated 20/21 March 1945.
3. The account of Hager's shooting down based on his combat report together with information supplied to the author by Walter Schneider through Hajo Adler.
4. The large area night fighter organisation map for the Luftwaffe was overlaid with a grid system enabling reference to be made by a code to identify a particular square.
5. Hauptmann Hager's combat report for his third victory claim on the night of 20/21 March 1945.
6. Air 25/788 Interception Tactics No.70/45 dated 20/21 March 1945.
7. Bomber Command loss card for Lancaster N9 398.

CHAPTER TEN
The German View

As the bomber war progressed, it increasingly evolved into not only a game of strategy and deception versus response, but also a tussle between opposing scientists and engineers to find ever more sophisticated means of confusing and diverting each other's forces through electronic measures and counter-measures. Acknowledging the challenges the Luftwaffe faced as the war progressed, General der Jagdflieger, Adolf Galland stated that:

"The combination of Pathfinders' operations, the activities of 100 Group, the British advantage in radar, jamming and Window techniques combined with intelligent attacking tactics, as well as the discipline and bravery of the RAF crews, have been remarkable. We had severe problems in trying to defend Germany in the air."

It is clear that 223 Squadron and its fellow units in 100 Group enjoyed considerable success in their efforts to confuse the German defences and thus protect the main force, but it was by no means a one-sided affair. Conversations with Luftwaffe veterans have provided a quite illuminating view of how the RCM war appeared from their side. Heinz Rökker recalls the early days of the strategic bombing campaign and the Nachtjagd:

"Today people see the bombing of Germany differently from the war. They say it was not gentleman-like. We couldn't have won the war; we had too many enemies. The world was against us, which made it impossible. But we couldn't see it at the time, we had our duty and we tried to save our country from bombing.

"We came from Sicily, and flew the Ju 88. When we came back to Germany we were meant to change from Ju 88 to Me 110. Most of our group were in Parchim but some crews were ordered to go to Gilze-Rijen in Holland. Some crews who were there had already had some success with the Himmelbett system, which we would try. I only had one flight in a Himmelbett area, in Gorilla (I think) *[all the Himmelbett boxes had code names]*. But we gained experience that night, not for attacking but for exercise, as there were only four or five crews. We were given the order to fly to Berlin when there was an attack, because we couldn't just fly in these Himmelbett boxes."

With the advent of Window during the Hamburg raid in July 1943, the Luftwaffe had to make rapid changes to its methods of directing and operating the night-fighter force. Heinz again:

"With Himmelbett the fighters were led to the enemy from the ground; all over the coast. It was Kammhuber's idea and work; however when the big bomber stream came it was not as effective. It used only a small area of the ground and only one fighter. Then came Window, and when it was dropped you could not follow the fighter to the target. We began with Lichtenstein radar, then we got the SN2, with a large antenna. It was not as effective however because we were not led from the ground, we had to rely on visuals. I did not find many of the 'planes with radar, I was always on the lookout. We looked to where there were bomb bursts, so we could see where the bomber stream was. When there was a shoot down, you could see it 100 kilometres away, because it was burning in the air.

"Then there was Zahme Sau and Wilde Sau. You were always told the location of the bomber stream, and so you had to try to come in and intercept the stream. However we started from such a long distance from the bomber stream. They would only tell us when we were near, and it was not easy to find because you were underneath it. We took off when the bomber stream came over the coast. We would gather and assemble, but we didn't know in what direction or where they were flying. We never flew above 6,000 metres, although I think some others did.

"We only operated as single aeroplanes; we had no contact with others. Later on there was one night fighter who always sent signals, when he was in the bomber stream, it was mostly the captain, so you could find his location."

Peter Spoden had a similar experience of the restrictive Kammhuber Himmelbett system, and saw the transition to Wilde Sau and Zahme Sau:

"I came into missions as a night fighter in mid-1943 *[with II./NJG 5 based at Parchim in Mecklenburg for the defence of Berlin]*, but I still know the old Kammhuber line. The radar was looking for the enemy and the ground officer brought them together on a special table, and he talked to us. They had about 100 different boxes over the northern part of Germany, The Netherlands and France, and in every one, when the British came, was a night fighter. We had contact with the ground controller on VHF. He often spoke in code words, but they were very simple, 'Heading 300' and so on, then 'the distance is 3 kilometres ahead…2 kilometres …1 kilometre…you should see him now'.

"At that time, very often, there came a transmission from somebody who was in the air too, on the same frequency, and this somebody was from 100 Group over there, and 'aloop-aloop-aloop-aloop', that was the result of it. Then the contact was distorted and I lost the target. This was jamming, and that happened to me several times. We always had an alternative frequency right away and we changed over. So that was our idea when the jamming came in, and the radio operator behind me in the Messerschmitt 110 said; 'right, I will change over'. And they said, 'We hear you on the scopes', and everything was fine. These guys were pretty clever you know.

"Very often we were re-establishing communications and five or six alternative frequencies were available. This fellow must have understood my German and that of the controller; when the target was close, then he came in with the jamming. It must have been from a 'plane in the air because the ground frequencies from England were not strong enough to interrupt our ground controller.

"The Himmelbett was no longer effective since the Hamburg attack *[25 July 1943]* when the RAF brought Window in, then we were completely blind. Not only the night fighters with the Lichtenstein, but also the ground Würzburg. We had a traitor (Oberleutnant Schmitt) who diverted to England in the couple of months before Hamburg; so they checked the equipment in his Ju 88 right away. After that we adapted our tactics from the original box system to the Zahme Sau because the British no longer flew in singles, they flew in a stream."

The aircraft that Peter referred to was Ju 88R-1 360043 'D5-EV' of IV./NJG 3 which was flown to Dyce in Scotland from its base in Norway on 9 May 1943, its crew having decided to defect, thus providing the British with their first detailed understanding of the FuG 202 Lichtenstein BC AI radar with which it was fitted. Following testing at RAE Farnborough, during which the corkscrew evasion manoevre was developed, the aircraft was passed to 1426 (Enemy Aircraft) Flight at Collyweston, Northamptonshire, and today resides in the RAF Museum at Hendon. Peter again:

"Around that time Hajo Herrmann told me, only a few weeks before he died, a very tragic thing about Hamburg. Göring had said to him: 'Herrmann, this attack on Hamburg by the British is like the earthquake in Lisbon more than a hundred years ago! If we get another one like this we lose the war! Herrmann, you have to do something about it.' Therefore Herrmann came up with the Wilde Sau and we continued on with the Zahme Sau. But this was meant ground control telling us, 'all night fighters now to Berlin – attack on Berlin'. All now went to radio beacon Berta, where you have to wait for the big attack on Berlin, hoping that the British were coming.

"Over Berlin we had 213 night fighters, we saw a hell of a fire, cascades of fire even, but nothing on the ground! There were eight Mosquitoes over Berlin, and there were 250 night fighters assembled. Then I saw in the north, about 100 kilometres away, a real fire – you could see when it was clear to 200 or 300 kilometres – what was it? The enemy had sent 596 bombers over to Peenemünde (we heard this after the war); so I sped up. The controller said: 'Berlin is attacked, stay over Berlin'. A large number waited over Berlin, but not me. I went for them because I had already missed my chance in Hamburg. I opened my throttles to full power and in twenty minutes I got my first shot over Peenemünde, 18 August 1943."

Another night, 23 August 1943, was also significant in that it saw the first use of Schräge Musik upward-firing cannons by the opposing night fighters. Bomber Command losses amounted to sixty-two aircraft. Schräge Musik was devised by Hauptmann Rudi Schoenert (who finished the war with sixty-four victories) and Oberfeldwebel Mahle, and was first fitted to Do 217 night fighters. The installation consisted of a pair of steeply-inclined cannon mounted in the cockpit rear compartment of the Me 110, and also used in the Ju 88 night-fighter versions. To fire the weapons, the pilot used a special Revi gun sight mounted in the roof of the cockpit. Attacking from behind and below the pilot would position his aircraft below the enemy bomber in its blind spot. He would aim to strike the bomber in the fuel tanks located between the inboard and outboard engines, or between the inboard engine and the fuselage. Invariably fatal the Schräge Musik was a deadly weapon in the hands of an experienced Luftwaffe night-fighter pilot. Peter continues:

"When flying Himmelbett we used codenames with the ground controller. However, in Zahme and Wilde Sau we were on our own. The 'reportage' by the ground people gave all night fighters the directions of the bomber stream, however they often got it wrong. We could see the Abschüsse (shoot downs), intense flak-fire and Christbaueme (Christmas tree; the German pilots' name for RAF target indicators), and followed those with our own SN2 and Naxos radar until contact. During an attack we did not talk besides intercom with our own crew of course.

"The best help for me as a night fighter was when I had a good radio operator. He could even direct us through serious jamming by Window. The British shoved out the Window, but the 'plane always left a trail, so a good radio operator would say: 'To the right…to the left…in the middle now etc.' Then I could go into the bomber stream as well. You could distinguish between a bomber formation and a Windows spoof using SN2. After the Hamburg attack we changed to the larger antenna SN2 and we had five or six different receiving frequencies. We could find the bomber stream, through the Windowing. Mostly, it was Lancasters in the bomber stream shoving out the Window, but the stream was split in two or three different heights and directions so it was often difficult to tell."

It is believed that Luftwaffe crews could also differentiate between real aircraft radar returns and those generated by Window because of their relative speeds. Peter was well aware of the 100 Group spoof raid tactics on nights when there was no main force raid planned:

"I had more than 100 real missions. Very often when we went up nothing would happen; we were misled by fireworks [false sky markers], we were misled by those guys imitating a big stream, and it turned out to be nothing. The Brits were very clever."

Oberfeldwebel Willi Reschke was a Wilde Sau pilot, posted to JG 302 at Götzendorf on 20 June 1944, flying the Fw 190 A. In March 1945 he was transferred to JG 301, flying the Ta 152 on Defence of the Reich duties. In total he flew about seventy operational sorties, scored twenty-seven victories, and was shot down eight times:

"The Fw 190s were very easy to fly and were aerodynamically superior to the Me 109 at heights up to 5,000 metres. At heights above 5,000 metres, the performance dropped off, as well as the vertical speed (a lot). During that time I was shot down twice in an Me 109 G-6; the first time by a P-51 during the first combat flight, and the second time during take-off at Neubiberg near Munich. The other six aircraft I was shot down in were during defence protection against four-motor aircraft."

Willi was first shot down on 24 August 1944 while flying Me 109 G-6 White 10, just after claiming a B-24 near Neuhaus in Austria. On the second occasion on 29 August, he was attacked by another Me 109, and had to force-land near Uherské Hradišt in Czechoslovakia.

H2S

The use of H2S ground-mapping radar undoubtedly made a significant difference to main force bombing accuracy, but following the capture by the Germans of a virtually intact set, as described in Chapter One, it was not long before the Luftwaffe had counter-measures to use against it, and indeed to turn it to their own advantage as a means of homing in on the bomber. Peter Spoden:

"Within a very short time *[in fact several months]* of capturing the H2S set at Rotterdam, we had a receiver for H2S – Naxos. Afterwards when we were flying low the operator would say, 'I have a target now, he must be above us, he is switching on his radar…left, left, right, right…' But your boys found out very late, and of course they had switched it off then.

"The target markers had the radar on all the time; that was very brave you know. The operator said 'fly up, fly up' so I looked upwards and saw the big shadow. He could not see me below, I was too dark against the equally dark ground, but he was silhouetted for me. We could hear Monica in our head-sets but the best deal for me was Naxos and H2S. I preferred ammunition without tracers, because the other guy could see you right away when you have tracers, and it was very light over a burning town!"

Serrate

The AI radar known as Serrate, introduced in late 1943, was a very significant advantage for the RAF fighters roaming the night sky looking for the defending fighters. Heinz Rökker:

"Our enemy was the long-range night fighter – Mosquito and Beaufighter. They had a good chance of finding us because when we put on our radar they could detect it. I only ever saw one Mosquito; it was landing as at that time there were some airfields in Belgium and France being used by the English. He had his lights on and so I saw him immediately. I could only shoot him down when he was landing, not in the air; because it was faster than we were."

Peter Spoden:

"I was an ace in the American sense – I shot down ten German aeroplanes! I baled out four times and had six more complete crashes. I remember in Augsburg in March '45 only three 'planes were allowed to fly – the aces (I hate that expression) – because of fuel shortages. Against 500 bombers and more than 100 Mossies it was impossible. We were taking off with just one light, so we could see the runway, and staying very low, although landing was the same. We stayed low because the Mosquito fighters were up there waiting for us."

Cigar and ABC

The first use of ABC in September 1943, followed the earlier ground-based Cigar system in monitoring and jamming night-fighter controllers' VHF transmissions, and in a number of cases, broadcasting false messages in German in an attempt to divert the fighters away from main force's intended target. To this day there is considerable confusion about the extent to which ABC messages were used, but Peter Spoden certainly remembers them:

"Speaking in a loud German voice, the British came up at the same time, also talking to us in German. However, in some cases you could hear the British accent. The Brits have a problem with the letter 'R'; they cannot roll the 'R'. They would tell us we should all land, and the German controller would shout, 'No! No! That is the British! Stay in the air, you must not land!' In some cases, we had landed and they were mad, shouting, 'There is an attack on such-and-such, and you guys are on the ground!'

"I heard the commander, 'Poldi' Fellerer, an Austrian, made a briefing at about five or six o'clock in the evening and he said: 'Don't listen to any German masculine voices any more. Only listen to our German ladies. If you hear them it is ground control, if a girl is telling you, this is the truth, *this* is from Berlin.' They had trained up German fräulein. However in the air we were in for a big surprise; there was a German lady telling us: 'Land, land please, right away.' So we did. I have no proof, but in one of the Lancasters shot down was a female crew member, I was told it could have been her. I am not sure if this is true, because there had definitely been a feminine voice speaking to us giving us correct commands, however when we were on the ground we were asked: 'Why did you land?'

"Due to the main jamming and the dangers of obeying false commands given to us in the air, the German broadcasting system began to use music to guide us. We were mainly following Lancasters, if they were over Essen, you would hear music from Lower Land; over Munich you would hear Bavarian music; over Vienna it was the waltz. Unfortunately this was not much help."

Heinz Rökker also commented on the problem that some of the English operators had in giving themselves away by their accent:

"Sometimes we could tell straight away and we would not obey the command, they were obviously English; one I remember had a Birmingham accent!"

German Jamming

One aspect which has not really been covered so far, is the extent to which the Germans used jamming against British radar. In May 1944 a report[1] was written by Sqn Ldr H Pittendrigh of the Radar Board, summarising the effect of jamming on operations. This was compiled as a result of 'the initial employment by the Luftwaffe of airborne jammers on the 200 m/s per second band.'

'During a raid by enemy aircraft over south-west England on 15 May 1944, airborne jamming was reported for the first time. The mean bearing of the jamming changed gradually, following in general the course of aircraft approaching this country....Almost all stations south of a line, St.Twynnells (south Wales) to Walton (Essex), experienced the effects of this airborne jamming...The reduction of operational efficiency consequent upon these new tactics can be summarised by stating that two stations were almost completely jammed out at times during the period, while other stations in the south-west suffered a variable degree of restriction in operations without however being completely jammed out at any time.

'It is interesting to note that on 15 May the jamming persisted both on inward and outbound flights, while on the 16th, no aircraft plotted outwards gave a jamming signal response. Mark III IFF equipment was not seriously affected.

'On the basis of the frequency coverage as assessed and the fact that more than one transmitter appeared to be deployed to cover each operation's spot frequency, an estimate of twenty-five jammers is suggested as being in use on the first occasion, while only six were located on the second raid.

'The aircraft shot down by Exminster GCI Station was examined and the transmitter and aerial systems recovered in a damaged condition. A fuller report on this installation will, it is understood, be prepared by RAE Farnborough.'

The aircraft referred to was a Junkers Ju 188 A-2, Wnr.160089 U5+HH of I./KG 2 based at Münster-Handorf, and flown by Feldwebel Heinz Mühlberger, which was shot down en-route to Bristol by Fg Off A S McEvoy and Fg Off M N Austin in Mosquito XVII HK246 RX-V of 456 Squadron RAAF from Ford in West Sussex. The Ju 188 came down at Greenlands Artillery Range in Larkhill, Wiltshire. Mühlberger was injured and taken prisoner, but the rest of his crew perished[2]. The Germans had developed their own longwave jamming gear in an attempt to blind British radars, including Kettenhund (Watchdog) – an airborne version of the ground-based Karl jammer – with which this Ju 188 was fitted. This was a device which jammed British 'Eureka' navigation homing beacons. In addition, by 1943 the Germans had started making use of their own version of Window, which they called Düppel.

Operation Gisela

The nachtjagd was quite frequently used to go on the offensive, in modest numbers, and fly over England to seek out bombers when they were most vulnerable, returning from raids and flying low and slow as they approached their home airfields. Heinz had strong views about this:

> "By early 1943, the German long-range intruding over Great Britain should have been built up again, because it was a well-known fact that the British operational aerodromes were fully lit up during take-off and landing procedures. Furthermore, during the assembling process of the bomber stream, the bomber crews (against regulation) often switched on their navigational lights for fear of collision. To hunt them under these conditions would have been the ultimate dream of the German long-range intruders. In 1940 we were an intruder unit (although before I joined). They had much success but too many losses, so the idea was abandoned. I was first over England on 3 January 1943, taking off at 20:05. I flew to Hull, bombing an airfield with all its lights on, at 800 metres."

As the war drew to a close, and in an attempt to stem the overwhelming forces attacking German targets by day and night, the Luftwaffe increased its activity over England as far as its diminishing reserves allowed. Here they would also be less subject to jamming activity. Fg Off Henry Payne was a Stirling pilot with 299 Squadron at Shepherds' Grove in Suffolk, and he experienced one such attack on the night of 20/21 February 1945:

> "The most eventful evening of my Stirling ops, was one night I'd been on a bombing trip, somewhere in Germany. As we got back at the base, my gunner just asked for permission to unload his guns, and I agreed. Then suddenly he screams out, 'Corkscrew for Christ's sake!' which I did, exceedingly quickly, but I didn't know which way to go. Damn great cannon shells came passed my cockpit within inches. A '410 had apparently got right under my tail and had followed us all the way to England, totally undetected. Just as we were being attacked, one of 196 Squadron's Stirlings was shot down, and he was on fire on the runway. So that closed the aerodrome, meaning we couldn't land. *[The Stirling shot down was LK126 captained by Flt Lt Campbell.]*
>
> "We flew around for about ten minutes, with occasional scraps with this damn '410. He kept attacking us, but my gunner was alive then and awake, and gave me the right instructions, so we could out-manoeuvre him easily, no trouble at all. Eventually we got a message to go to Foulsham, and I still don't even know where Foulsham is today! *[Foulsham is north-west of Norwich, and was home to 462 Australian Squadron Halifaxes at the time.]* My navigator found it on a chart, and we flew there, landed, but were most unwelcome, because they were all getting ready for a peaceful day, and our Stirlings descended upon them."

This activity reached a final crescendo on the night of 3/4 March 1945, when the Luftwaffe dispatched a force of up to 200 Ju 88 night fighters (opinions vary with regards to the actual number), across the North Sea at very low level, to intercept returning bombers. The Bomber Command main force operations had been successful that night, but it was early on the morning of Sunday 4th that the nachtjagd attacked. Heinz Rökker was one of the crews involved:

"At the end of the war we were told we should fly over England because there was no defence against the bombers. Many of the flyers put on their lights as they landed so it was easy for us to find them. During the whole war I never saw a single 'plane with lights on in Germany. But here I spotted one with lights on, and I tried to shoot him down, but the distance was too great. I could see him very well and I was beneath him, but I was too low. After my attack he switched off his lights so I could no longer see him and he landed safely. I think he had a lot of luck; I didn't hit him with the Schräge Musik!

"At that time the towns were lit up too; Norwich, Grimsby and Lincoln. Although I was never too sure where I was! We would fly very low over the sea, because we couldn't be detected by radar. It was horrible to fly so low, only 100 metres over the sea. You always thought you might hit the water but we had equipment to detect the height. *[The Ju 88 was equipped with a Siemens & Halske FuG 101 radio altimeter.]* When we saw the coast we had to 'pull up' and then we flew at 1,000 metres and there was nothing, no flak, no night fighters. At last I dropped bombs on an airfield. I fired with my forward cannons and all was lit up, so we shot at the light – immediately the light would go out. Unfortunately we could only stay over England for one hour.

"They obviously thought we wouldn't come. We saw the town was full of light and we saw a tram; we were that low! I saw at a very far distance, another German night fighter shoot down one English 'plane. I couldn't see what make it was, because you just saw tracer from underneath then you saw it burning, possibly it was a Lancaster or Halifax."

Operation Gisela cost Bomber Command twenty aircraft lost, with others being damaged, while the Luftwaffe losses amounted to about forty, although almost all of these were a result of crashes on the way home due to adverse weather conditions and poor navigation at low level. These were losses, especially of crews, that the Germans could ill-afford at this late stage in the war. Andrew Barron, a navigator with 223 Squadron, witnessed one of the 100 Group aircraft that was a victim of an intruder while in the circuit at Oulton:

"On the night of Gisela we got to the circuit just when a Fortress *[of 214 Squadron]* was being shot down. I only learned recently when I was talking to my old co-pilot in Canada that they had seen this night fighter. Presumably, he hadn't seen them or if he had, he was on the tail of the B-17 so he ignored us. As far as I was concerned, I just got the order: 'Course for Brawdy' so he got 270 as the 'off you head' sort of 'head west, young man' and then about twenty minutes later, I got a fix, found a wind and did the job properly."

A follow-up night-fighter operation was flown the following night, but on a much smaller scale, and with very little success.

One noteworthy result of Gisela was the loss of the last German aircraft to be brought down on British soil. Hptm Johann Dreher's Ju 88 G-6 D5-AX of 13./NJG 3 had shot down two 158 Squadron Halifaxes approaching Lissett, before flying over to nearby Elvington, occupied by Free French Halifax squadrons. Having narrowly missed a 347 Squadron Halifax on approach, and unable to find any other aircraft in the circuit, Dreher began strafing road traffic while circling for another attack, but his aircraft hit a tree and crashed into Dunnington Lodge farmhouse at 01:58, resulting in the loss of all five crew members and three people in the house.

By this time the Luftwaffe was in significant decline and rapidly becoming less effective as a fighting force. Heinz Rökker:

"I had a meeting with Hermann Göring when I got my Oakleaves *[to his Knight's Cross]*. I had to go to Carinhall, near Berlin, where he was living during the war. It was near the end of the war, March 1945. He came out of the door with all his entourage, gave me the award and shaking hands, said 'keep up the good work and don't make waves'.

"We had no gasoline, but we had plenty of aeroplanes. Therefore only a few crews were allowed to start; usually ones with a greater success rate. Only three or four machines would fly; we had twelve altogether in our gruppe. We still had new crews coming in however; younger crews, but they only had experience flying by day. They couldn't gain any more because there was no gasoline for training. Consequently we had many losses from the young crews. I always had the same crew. For example, my *funker* (radio operator) and I were together right from the beginning until the very end.

"My last flight was on 15 April, it was an attack coming from an island to the north of us. We got the order to start and we knew the direction but the order was just to fly, and after half an hour we got the order to land again; in the meantime the bombing had finished. We were only a short range from England, and we thought the bombers would fly to another town, but we saw nothing."

Peter Spoden:

"As a night fighter you only got the Iron Cross when you had at least four successes. The Ehrenpokal (Honour Goblet) you got with ten, the Golden Cross with fifteen and the Ritterkreuz (Knight's Cross) with twenty-five! If you were not dead before! Herbert Lütje was geschwaderkommodore in NJG 6 since 13 September 1944. He told me (I was the commander of the group I./NJG 6), to defend the airport at Munich-Schleissheim in a ground battle against US troops on 28 April 1945, but I did not. I saw these young boys, the American soldiers, were coming across the field towards us, and I stood up and waved with some white cloth; that was the best decision I ever made. By the way, the American boys waved right back with their helmets!"

During the closing stages of the war, the Luftwaffe pressed a night-fighter variant of the Me 262 into service. Fitted with both FuG 218 Neptun combined AI and reverse-warning radar and the already well-established FuG 350 Naxos centimetric radar homing equipment, flight trials were started at Erprobungsstelle (Test Centre) E-Stelle Werneuchen, near Berlin, October 1944, but it was not until April 1945 that about ten examples were delivered to 10./NJG 11, primarily for use in a Wilde Sau role in the defence of Berlin against the ever-present 'Serrate' Mosquito, and most of the thirteen such aircraft claimed by the Luftwaffe during the closing months of the war fell victim to the Me 262. Kurt Welter ended the war with twenty-five night victory claims against Mosquitoes, of which nine were achieved in both radar and non-radar equipped '262s. The Me 262 B-1a/U1 night fighter was clearly a formidable opponent of the Mosquito, but there were far too few and too late. When talking about his favourite Ju 88 Peter Spoden said:

"Of course, I would have loved the Me 262 NJ version!"

A night-fighter variant of the Arado Ar 234 jet bomber, the Ar 234 C to be fitted with FuG 245 centimetric AI radar, was also tested at E-Stelle Werneuchen, but did not progress beyond the prototype stage. FuG 245 was itself an evolution of FuG 240 Berlin, of which only around thirty sets had been completed before the end of the war. This radar had an internally-mounted adjustable dish antenna to dispense with aerials and thus reduce drag on the aircraft. Allegedly based on captured British equipment, it had a range of up to 5,000 metres and the operator was provided with a single screen displaying both the height and the range of the target.

This design was further developed into the FuG 244 and FuG 245 Bremen radars which were intended to provide a panoramic view of the whole bomber stream through a horizontal sweep of 100 degrees, but again only prototypes were completed.

Notes:
1. Air14/3229 ORS General Correspondence 4 Group.
2. *The Luftwaffe Over The Bristol Area*, Fishponds Local History Society.
   Bristol Past website www.fishponds.org.uk

CHAPTER ELEVEN

End Game:
22 March to 7 July 1945

21 March was a fine day and soon the crews would learn that the main force would be attacking two targets again. 5 Group would be attacking Deutsche Erdoelwerke oil refinery at Hamburg across the North Sea and 1 Group would hit a benzol plant at Bochum in the Ruhr. 100 Group supported the northern attack with two Window forces which flew ahead of main force on the same track as far as the German coast. The northern Window force commenced Window dropping from 5420N 0800E and broke off the route at 5420N 0808E continuing east as far as Kiel, which they bombed with TIs and incendiaries. The southern Window force turned south on a heading for Bremen with 5 Group at 5420N 0808E, and began Window dropping at 5355N 0827E. The Window force continued towards Bremen leaving to break away and attack Hamburg at 5345N 0830E. Bremen was then bombed with TIs and incendiaries. The main force attack on Hamburg occurred between 03:55 and 04:15.

223 provided a single aircraft for the northern Window patrol but supported the southern patrol with seven aircraft. It was a long, eight-hour trip for the crews but uneventful. Regrettably, 214 lost an aircraft, Flt Lt Allies in Fortress KJ112 (J), their second in successive nights; thankfully however this would be their last loss of the war. The loss was also felt on 223 as three of Allies' air gunners, Sgts Pete Newman, Bob Jones and Ted Punnett, were former 223 and 10 AGS. Another ex-223 air gunner, Sgt Peter Witts, had also been a member of Allies' crew, but luckily had been posted out to join 462 (RAAF) Squadron. There were no survivors. Four aircraft were lost from the Hamburg attack from a force of 151 Lancasters, plus the 214 aircraft.

Main force rested on the night of 22/23 March, apart from minor operations, leaving 100 Group to keep the pot boiling as far as the German defences were concerned. A Window patrol was mounted to carry out a spoof attack on the Ruhr, protected by a Mandrel screen disposed between 5130N 0525E and 5047N 0628E at 17,000 feet. When the patrol reached 5052N 0536E they fanned out to advance on a broad front as far as a line between 5140N 0635E to 5116N 0640E. The pretense was strengthened by six Mosquitoes of 8 Group who marked Bochum with red bursting TIs. 223 dispatched seven aircraft on this patrol which proved to be quiet and uneventful.

On 23 March 100 Group supported the main force attack on the town of Wesel in anticipation of the Rhine crossing by ground forces the next day. Seven aircraft from 223 joined a Window patrol which flew at the head of the main force formation. The patrol saturated the approach to the target, the target itself, and the early part of the return route with Window. A diversion was provided by a Sweepstake force which was routed towards the Frankfurt area. 223's crews had another quiet patrol without incident, apart from Flt Lt Ball who returned whilst still in the base area with an undercarriage that would not retract.

The squadron were not in action again until the night of 27/28 March. With no main force operations taking place the squadron also had a quiet night contributing just two aircraft on a Window patrol over Bremerhaven. The patrol was successful in that it prompted reaction by three gruppen of night fighters, but 100 Group operated without any losses. The night marked the debut of Flt Lt Wills, flying with Fg Off Steele's former crew.

A quiet period for the squadron continued on the night of 30/31 March with just four aircraft required for an uneventful Window patrol in the Hamburg area.

The operational requirements section (ORS) report on losses and interceptions in the month of March makes interesting reading. The report stated that the proportion of heavy bombers returning damaged by night fighters had increased to 0.6% having been 0.4, 0.3 and 0.2 in the previous three months. They added that these increased successes were mainly sporadic and confined to the nights of 5/6, 7/8, and 16/17 when one or more of the attacking formations were contacted in force by night fighters. Generally, however the night fighters' reaction was uncertain, being frequently led astray by the feint forces; the report added that neither tactics nor counter-measures had been altered during the month and offered the following factors as reasons for the increase in damage:

1. Possible receipt of warning earlier than was indicated by the first plots broadcast.
2. Correctly guessing, either from weather conditions, the positioning of the Mandrel screen, or from other factors, the most likely position of the initial penetration by bomber forces.
3. Better co-ordination between fighter divisions.
4. More restraint shown by controllers in making their initial fighter dispositions, thereby preventing all the available forces in the fighter division from being committed to a wrong move before a clear appreciation of the situation had been obtained[1].

This report indicates the success of 100 Group feint attacks, exemplified by the Böhlen operation on the night of 20/21 March.

Returning to Oulton, the LORAN installations in the aircraft of both 214 and 223 Squadron were proving unsatisfactory. The decision was made to remove the installations temporarily, pending the outcome of an investigation by TRE[2].

April 1945

Bad weather blighted the first day of April and flying did not begin until the 2nd when a total of ten aircraft, together with four from 214, were sent on a Window patrol feint attack against Hamburg; all successfully completed this operation in the absence of main force activity. The feint prompted a reaction by three gruppen of night fighters, wasting valuable fuel in the process.

Operations were cancelled on the 3rd so the squadron resumed activities the following day. This was a big effort by Bomber Command with main force in action against three targets. A force of 327 Lancasters from 3 and 6 Groups were sent to attack the synthetic oil plant at Leuna in the Leipzig area. The Rhenania oil installation at Harburg near Hamburg was hit by a force of 327 heavy bombers from 4 and 6 Groups. 258 Lancasters from 1 Group were sent against an oil refinery at Lützkendorf. This very busy night also included a force of thirty Lancasters mine laying in the Oslo fjord and the Kattegat. Proceedings were completed with nuisance attacks by thirty-five Mosquitoes on Berlin and thirty-one to Magdeburg.

100 Group operated their biggest effort of the war on this night, dispatching a total of 136 aircraft on a variety of tasks. 223 made a significant contribution sending a target patrol aircraft to both Leuna and Lützkendorf; and launching ten aircraft for the Window patrol in support of the Leuna attack. The Window force flew just ahead of the main force as far as 1100E, the point where 3 and 6 Groups turned for the run in on Leuna. The Window force continued on the original heading in the direction of Berlin at 5207N 1228E, the aim being to hold night-fighter assets in the north-east. The Mosquito attacks on Berlin and Magdeburg went in at 22:42 and 22:31 respectively, their timings being close to the attacks on Magdeburg and Leuna which were attacked at 22:31 and 22:35. The defences also had to cope with the attack on Hamburg which was timed to begin at 22:42. The Bomber Command tactics proved successful as only two Lancasters were lost from the Leuna raid, and three heavies from the Hamburg attack. The Lützkendorf attack, which went in much later at 01:24, did not have the benefit of a Mandrel screen or a major Window force diversion, and suffered the loss of six Lancasters.

All but one of the squadron's aircraft returned safely, but bad weather forced all the returning aircraft to land at diversion airfields. Flt Lt Dyck was forced to abandon his sortie because of a fuel leak and was instructed by 100 Group to land at the French airfield at Juvincourt. The problem was quickly resolved and the aircraft refuelled. They then had a problem starting one of the engines the next day, which amazingly Dyck solved by swinging the propeller of the recalcitrant engine – spinach for breakfast perhaps?[3]

No ops on 5 April, but the exciting news for the squadron that they were scheduled to be re-equipped with Fortresses. There was also the news that a double bomber support tour originally set at fifty ops, would now be reduced to forty-five.

The poor April weather continued causing the abandonment of flying on the 6th. And the following evening was no better, the squadron put up a single aircraft to fly a target patrol over the Molbis oil plant near Leipzig.

Following the news of the squadron's conversion to the Fortress, it was announced that Sqn Ldr McKnight RCAF, Flt Lt Bremness RCAF and Flt Lt Wills would be the first to convert to the new type.

The 8th April was another busy day for Bomber Command, with attacks being mounted on the Hamburg shipyards by 440 heavy bombers, and a 5 Group raid with 231 Lancasters on the oil refinery at Lützkendorf. To support these raids 100 Group put

Sqn Ldr Wills & crew with Fortress KJ114 (B) April-May 1945. Rear L to R: F/S Eric 'Ginger' Dagnall, F/S Peter Matthews, S/L Bill Wills, F/S Joe Walters. Front L to R: F/S Wilf 'Bunny' Chitticks, F/S Les Norwood, F/S Cyril Carter, F/S Den Fuller, F/S Horace Brain *[Peter Matthews]*.

up Window patrol feints for both attacks. Additionally, target patrols were also sent.

The northern Window patrol flying at the head of the main force on the same track, were accompanied by a small bombing force of twenty-four Halifaxes of 4 Group and twelve Liberators of 492 BG as far as 1000E where main force turned south to carry out the attack on Hamburg. The Window force, together with the 4 Group and 492 BG aircraft, continued the original main force heading to Travemunde on the Baltic coast which was bombed. The Window force then continued as far as 5338N 1125E threatening Berlin.

For the Lützkendorf attack, the southern Window force followed the 5 Group track to 1115E and continued the main force heading when the 5 Group aircraft turned south-west on their run in to the target. The Window force diversion carried on as far as 5155N 1155E where red flares and TIs were dropped. This was followed ten minutes later by an attack of seventy-one Mosquitoes from 8 Group bombing Dessau.

223 contributed eleven aircraft with target patrols to both main force targets. Three aircraft were sent to the southern Window patrol and six put up for the northern force. The aircraft did not return unscathed, with Sqn Ldr Carrington's aircraft shot up by flak, putting out No.1 engine and causing other damage. Flt Lt Roy Hastie returning from a target patrol over Hamburg was also struck by flak. His waist gunner, Peter Lovatt describes the incident:

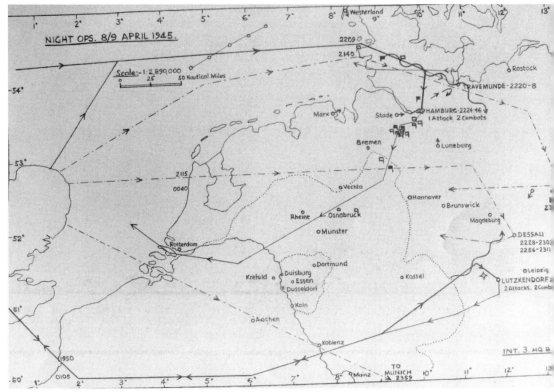

Target map 8/9 April 1945.

"Coming home, the German flak around Hamburg was extremely accurate at 22,000 feet and hit our aircraft severely damaging No.2 engine, so its propeller had to be feathered. As No.2 drove the pumps transferring fuel from the reserve tanks to the other engines, Roy Hastie realised that fuel for the return flight would be very limited. A debate was held, to which I listened with interest, whether or not to fly to the diversion airfield, Juvincourt, in the middle of France. This was rather isolated, and nowhere near a town of any size. It had been a German night-fighter station and was not known for its high standard of comfort and hospitality. In the end it was decided we would try and make for base.

"We threw everything overboard, into the North Sea, as many guns and as much ammunition as we could, and conserved fuel by using the leanest of mixtures. Roy Hastie got the aircraft back to Oulton, only to be told to divert because of bad weather. Despite his protests, we were sent to RAF Barford St.John in Oxfordshire. This was not far away, but the extra distance certainly added to the pilot's problems. Barford was a Mosquito training station and they clearly liked their sleep. The Liberator arrived overhead to find not a single light showing below. Firing a red Very cartridge or two provoked some reaction and the airfield lights were, reluctantly, switched on.

"With his usual superb airmanship Roy landed his much larger aircraft on the unfamiliar runway. As he taxied in to the dispersal the three working engines cut out, their fuel exhausted. It had been a close run thing."[4]

Flt Lt Hastie & crew with Liberator TS524 (O). Rear L to R: F/S Jamie Brown, F/L Roy Hastie, Sgt Chesney Weston, Sgt Bob Lawrence, Sgt Peter Lovatt, F/O 'Soapy' Hudson. Front L to R: W/O F M Watson, F/S Sydney Pienaar *[Hastie collection]*.

Just to add to the squadron's aircraft serviceability problems, Fg Off Pocock flying in a new aircraft VD245 (R) turned into a hole after landing, resulting in the aircraft being categorised Cat AC (repairable on site but not by the operating unit).

Bomber Command were out in force again on the night of 9/10 April sending 591 Lancasters of 1 and 3 Groups to attack Kiel. A Window force accompanied the main force on the same track as far as 0810E when it broke away to the south-east and continued up to Stade, which was marked by Wanganui red and green stars and green TIs by aircraft from 492 BG. The target was then bombed by twenty-two Halifaxes of 4 Group. The map on page 180 shows the positions of the Window force aircraft at two positions in the run up to their diversionary spoof target, revealing the use of the 'lane' system for spreading Window. This diversion achieved its aim of protecting the Kiel attackers and only one Lancaster was lost. The squadron put up three aircraft for the Window patrol.

On the following night Bomber Command's main effort was directed at the Plauen railway yards, mounted by a force of 307 Lancasters from 1 Group. A smaller force of seventeen Lancasters was directed against railway yards at Leipzig. These attacks were launched without the benefit of a Mandrel screen, and the two main force formations following parallel tracks across Germany before breaking away to attack their separate targets, thus spreading the German defences thinly. To add to the confusion a small force of Mosquitoes attacked Chemnitz which was neatly located between the two main

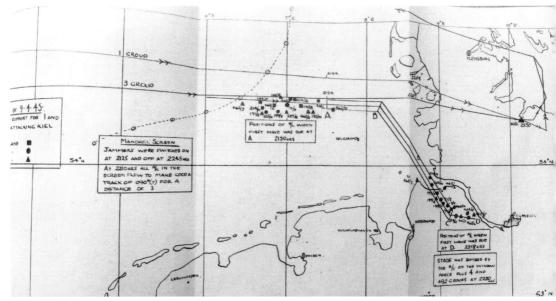

Target map 9/10 April 1945.

force objectives. 100 Group contributed by sending a Window patrol with the 5 Group force following the same track as far as 1100E before breaking north-east to carry out a feint attack on Dessau at 22:45. Aircraft of 492 BG accompanied the Window force and bombed the feint target. 100 Group's intention was to hold night fighters under No.1 Fighter Division in the north. The Plauen force escaped without loss but the small 5 Group attack lost seven Lancasters.

223 sent a target patrol aircraft to Plauen and contributed three aircraft to the Window patrol. All returned safely, although Fg Off Bowell was forced to land in France short of fuel.

The squadron was not in action again until the night of the 13/14 April when main force visited Kiel with 482 heavy bombers. A minor operation was also mounted against Boizenburg by a small force of twenty Halifaxes and eight Mosquitoes. The Mandrel screen was in action, forming a reversed L-shaped line to protect both attacks. The squadron sent a target patrol in support of the Kiel attack, and mounted a Window patrol feint to strengthen the diversionary attack on Boizenburg. For the latter the Window force was accompanied again by aircraft from 492 BS which joined the Halifaxes and Mosquitoes in bombing the target. Just three aircraft were lost from both targets.

The next night saw a big effort against Potsdam by 500 Lancasters from 1 and 3 Groups. A small diversionary raid was also made against Cuxhaven in northern Germany. No Mandrel screen was employed for the main attack. 100 Group supported the Potsdam raid with target patrols and two Window patrols.

The two Window forces followed the main force track as far as 1145E when they broke to the north-east and south-east respectively. Only one Lancaster was lost from the night's operations. 223 supported operations by sending a target patrol aircraft to Potsdam, and supplying four aircraft to the southern Window patrol. Fg Off Sellars had an interesting return, being forced to land at Woodbridge with his port wing on fire.

On 15/16 April, 223 Squadron dispatched four aircraft on an uneventful Window patrol in support of a minor operation by four Mosquitoes which attacked the airfield at Lechfeld.

On the following night the squadron supported main force attacks on railway yards at Pilsen and Schwandorf. The squadron also sent four aircraft as part of a southern Window patrol in support of a minor operation against Gablingen airfield.

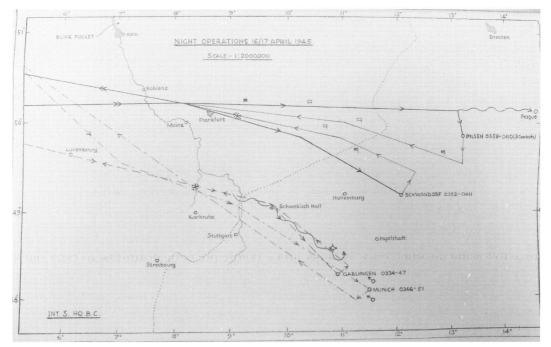

Target map 16/17 April 1945.

On the 17th 223 received the good news that a tour had now been reduced from thirty-three to thirty ops. In the evening the squadron was in action again sending one aircraft on a target patrol to support the only main force attack of the night on the railway yards at Cham. Four more aircraft were dispatched to join a Window patrol supporting an attack by forty-three Mosquitoes on Ingolstadt airfield. For Sqn Ldr Carrington, who flew on the Window patrol this would be his last op with the squadron.

For the night of the 18th/19th the squadron was hoping to make history by launching its first operational sortie in a Fortress flown by Flt Lt Wills. Unfortunately, the No.4 engine became u/s and the sortie was abandoned at 5039N 0140E. Operations that night were in support of a sole main force attack by 5 Group on the railway yards at Komotau, with 223 contributing just two aircraft to a diversionary Window patrol.

On the following night Flt Lt Bremness had better luck, and took Fortress KJ121 (B) on a quiet Window spoof into Denmark accompanied by three other aircraft from the squadron. The spoof was mounted in the absence of major main force ops.

Main force were not operating on the night of 22/23 April, but 100 Group harassed the enemy by mounting three separate Window patrol operations to which 223 dispatched seven Liberators and two Fortresses. It was a celebratory occasion for Flt Lt Frank Stephenson and Flt Lt Val Croft DFM, who both completed double tours.

Flt Lt Stephenson & crew with Liberator TS527 (Q) February 1945. Rear L to R: F/L Frank Stephenson, F/S Glyn Williams. Front L to R; Sgt Tommy Agnew, W/O Reg Collins, F/L D A Boyle, F/S Ted Longden, F/L Alf Barker, F/L Hugh Williams, F/O Dave Theaker *[S/L E Longden]*.

23/24 April saw the squadron take part in a Window patrol spoof on Lübeck via Hamburg to divert attention away from an attack on Kiel by sixty Mosquitoes. 223's contribution was three aircraft.

The next night was low key again with just four aircraft sent on a Window patrol to the Munich area in the absence of main force activity. The only drama of the night was encountered by Flt Lt Mann and his crew who were shot up by flak in TS527 (Q).

The rest of the month was free of ops. Poor weather, including snow on one day contributed to a rather miserable end to the month. On the 25th the first completely new Fortress crew captained by Plt Off Bob Belton arrived on the squadron from 1699 Training Flight. Frustratingly, they had arrived too late to fly on operations. The arrival of new Fortresses caused serious overcrowding at Oulton despite parking five of the redundant Liberators at Swannington.

It will have been noted that there were a number of operations during the month when the Mandrel screen had not been employed. Instead Mandrel-equipped aircraft had flown with the main force stream on deeper penetrations to help confuse the enemy plotters.

In the 100 Group monthly summary of activities for April it mentions the RCM School and states that No.5 Course was then in progress.[5] This is the first and only reference found in official documents that mentions a formal course for special operators. It will be remembered from Fg Off Leslie Boot's recollections, that this formal training was not available when 223 Squadron was formed.

In the same summary the group navigation officer was still hammering home to the squadrons the need for good time keeping. He commented that a good standard of track keeping had been maintained throughout the month, but that 'time keeping is not a cause for congratulations'. He published the following table for Window sorties during the month:

Sqn	No Det	No Comp	% within 30 secs	% Late	Ave Mins Late	% Early	Ave Mins Early
171	51	47	36	38	2.5	26	1.8
192	31	30	56	24	1.9	20	2.5
199	70	65	40	26	1.4	34	2.5
214	34	31	13	36	2.2	51	2.2
223	76	72	33	30	3.1	37	1.9
214	116	111	43	30	2.4	27	1.6

223 Squadron navigators April-May 1945. Rear L to R: F/O Glyn Thomas, P/O R A Tabah, F/O Ronnie Simmons, F/O Alex McMillan, F/L Hugh Williams, F/O Alan Love, F/O Reg Wade, W/O L R Lovatt, U/K. Front L to R: F/O Elmer Gaiser, F/O 'Soapy' Hudson, F/L P F O'Leary, Sgt Phillip Morris, F/L Freddie Freake, F/O Bob Wylie, F/O Andrew Barron [A G V Simons].

Bearing in mind the group navigation officer's view that it is far easier to lose time than to gain it, the 223 navigators had not done so well during April. Possibly the introduction of new crews may have influenced this.

May 1945

The month also opened with a day of dreadful weather and no flying was possible. The next day saw a maximum effort and the squadron put up all nine crews that were available for a Window spoof to Kiel. The squadron's effort comprised four Fortresses and five Liberators with the following crews taking part for the last operation of the war:

Fg Off J W Cairney	Pilot	Fortress
Fg Off R Tucker	Navigator	
Plt Off W G Howard	Flight Engineer	
W/O A Sheekey	Wireless Operator	
Fg Off G Isaacs	Mid Upper Gunner	
Fg Off T Baines	Special Operator	
W/O J Ross	Special Operator	
Fg Off F Higgins	Waist Gunner	
Fg Off F Boyd	Waist Gunner	
Flt Sgt E Hedley	Rear Gunner	
Flt Lt G Bremness RCAF	Pilot	Fortress
Fg Off H Booth RCAF	Navigator	
Sgt D Prutton	Flight Engineer	
Fg Off W Doolin	Wireless Operator	
Fg Off L Rendle	Special Operator	
Fg Off F Rowe	Special Operator	
Flt Sgt R Stott	Mid Upper Gunner	
Flt Sgt B Buff	Waist Gunner	
Sgt H McIver	Waist Gunner	
Flt Sgt S C R Leach	Rear Gunner	
Fg Off A Stuart	Pilot	Liberator
Plt Off R Wade	Navigator	
Flt Sgt W Stanyer	Flight Engineer	
Flt Sgt D Lightfoot	Wireless Operator	
Fg Off R Fawcett	Special Operator	
Fg Off D Oakley	Special Operator	
W/O C Aspinall RCAF	Air Gunner	
W/O T Skinner RCAF	Air Gunner	
W/O P Chesin RCAF	Air Gunner	
W/O J Parrack RCAF	Air Gunner	

Flt Lt A E L Morris RCAF	Pilot	Liberator
Fg Off A J K Barron	Navigator	
Flt Sgt V Green	Flight Engineer	
Flt Sgt J Bratten	Wireless Operator	
Fg Off A Knight	Special Operator	
Sgt W R Legge	Special Operator	
Sgt E Stirrop	Mid Upper Gunner	
Flt Sgt A H Ward	Waist Gunner	
Sgt J McClaren	Waist Gunner	
Sgt C L Matthews	Rear Gunner	
Flt Lt J K Mann	Pilot	Liberator
Fg Off J P Hammond	Navigator	
W/O R Tailford	Flight Engineer	
Flt Sgt A Atkiss	Wireless Operator	
Flt Sgt D J Cornish	Special Operator	
Sgt R J Smith	Special Operator	
Fg Off T G Hammond	Mid Upper Gunner	
Plt Off J McAdam	Air Gunner	
Sgt C C Hughes	Air Gunner	
Sgt I H Rice	Air Gunner	
Fg Off J Robson	Pilot	Liberator
Fg Off W Simpson	Navigator	
Flt Sgt A Malone	Flight Engineer	
Flt Sgt W Nolan	Wireless Operator	
Sgt S Dodd	Special Operator	
Sgt C S Ward	Special Operator	
Fg Off J Bourque RCAF	Mid Upper Gunner	
Flt Sgt R Sunstrum RCAF	Waist Gunner	
Flt Sgt E White	Waist Gunner	
Sgt K Smith	Rear Gunner	
Fg Off F Bowell	Pilot	Liberator
W/O L R Lovatt	Navigator	
W/O G Harrison	Flight Engineer	
Flt Lt D Drew	Wireless Operator	
W/O C Fairbairn	Special Operator	
Flt Sgt F A Jobson	Special Operator	
Fg Off L T George	Air Gunner	
Fg Off W T Berry	Air Gunner	
Flt Sgt A Polmear	Air Gunner	
Flt Sgt D Copeland	Air Gunner	

Sqn Ldr R E C McKnight RCAF	Pilot	Fortress
Plt Off P G Nash	2nd Pilot	
Fg Off J G Morris	Navigator	
Flt Sgt B Le Fondre	Flight Engineer	
Flt Sgt R Stark	Wireless Operator	
Fg Off W Thomson	Special Operator	
Fg Off W Lane	Special Operator	
Flt Sgt D H Thorpe	Mid Upper Gunner	
Flt Sgt G F Schutes	Waist Gunner	
Sgt W Jones	Waist Gunner	
Flt Sgt C G J Brooks	Rear Gunner	
Flt Lt S B Wills	Pilot	Fortress
Flt Sgt P S Morris	Navigator	
Sgt P R Matthews	Flight Engineer	
Flt Sgt J Dagnall	Wireless Operator	
W/O R Housden	Special Operator	
Flt Sgt W Chitticks	Mid Upper Gunner	
F/S H J Brown	Air Gunner	
Flt Sgt D J Fuller	Waist Gunner	
Sgt L Norwood	Waist Gunner	
Flt Sgt C G Carter	Rear Gunner	

Everyone had an uneventful trip with the exception of Fg Off Stuart. He was the first to take off at 21:25 in VD249 (T) but was forced to return early from 5310N 0250E from 10,000 feet at 21:47. Landing at 22:20, the crew quickly transferred in to a replacement aircraft TS538 (V). In their determination to complete the op they flew directly to reach Point A but, not surprisingly, were unable to make up the lost time.

This proved to be the last op for the squadron although the war was not officially over until 7 May when the armistice was signed. VE-Day was formally declared on the following day to great rejoicing throughout Great Britain. No doubt amongst the squadron there was a mixture of feelings with the initial joy of victory and survival being balanced by quiet reflection on comrades lost, together with a measure of uncertainty about the future. All aircraft were grounded; no doubt the 'powers that be' were taking wise precautions against celebrations getting out of hand.

On 11 May flying resumed with the opportunity being taken to fly ground crew on the so-called 'Cook's Tours' over the Ruhr and Rhine areas, so they could see the result of their contribution. The route flown was: Oulton-Gravesend-Dungeness-Calais-Aachen-Duren-Cologne-Essen-Dortmund-Dunkirk-Dover-Gravesend-Oulton. These trips were an eye opener for both aircrew and ground crew and no doubt all were taken aback at the huge scale of damage incurred on the German cities. At the time they would have seen this as deserved retribution. Andrew Barron recalled the unusual sight of the glittering reflections of the sun from the areas of broken glass.

These trips continued to be flown through the remainder of the month, and some normal training flights resumed. On the 13th a stand down was declared, and a Service of Thanksgiving for the victory over Germany was held in one of the aircraft hangars.

The disposal of Liberators continued, with aircraft being flown into storage at 51 MU at Lichfield. Turbulence occurred amongst the crews with the posting out of veteran members of the squadron, including the first of the Canadians. Newcomers continued to arrive through the month and during the following month of June including an influx of new, Fortress-trained, crews from 1699 Flight. With the exception of Plt Off Bob Belton, and Flt Sgt Walter Gatenby's crew listed below, it has not been possible to identify and list the crews for the other Fortress captains:

Flt Sgt W E Gatenby	Pilot
Fg Off C Smith	Navigator
Sgt J Thomas	Flight Engineer
Sgt R V P Perry	Wireless Operator
Fg Off W McDonald	Special Operator
W/O A Baxter	Special Operator
Sgt A C D Reid	Mid Upper Gunner
Sgt F Monger	Waist Gunner
Sgt L Harper	Waist Gunner
Sgt W H Tucker	Rear Gunner

The following Fortress aircraft captains for the post-war period, as far as it is possible to establish, are listed by flight:

A Flight		B Flight	
Fg Off C A Boaden	Ex-Liberator	Plt Off R O Belton	
Plt Off B G Churcher		Fg Off F D Carroll	Ex-Liberator
Plt Off K Reynolds (?)		Fg Off J J B Pocock	Ex-Liberator
Plt Off L Roullier		Flt Sgt W E Gatenby	
Fg Off T Wallis	Ex-Liberator	Flt Sgt J Hastings	
Flt Sgt E Boyes		Flt Sgt W D James	
		W/O J Thorpe	

Towards the end of the month, the squadron prepared its aircraft for a major exercise aptly codenamed Post Mortem. This exercise involving German personnel and a large number of RAF observers was held to try and establish the effectiveness of the Bomber Command tactics and radio counter-measures against the German air defence system. The exercise was held in northern Germany and scheduled to begin on 25 June and run until 5 July, and involved aircraft from 1, 3, 8 and 100 Groups. Initially, the first sorties were flown without 100 Group participation, presumably for comparison purposes. As the exercise progressed the succeeding tests introduced the various elements of 100 Group capability, starting with the effectiveness of the Mandrel screen and continuing with the other capabilities including Window, Jostle, Carpet and Piperack, and the Window force was exercised. Despite the artificiality of some aspects

223 Squadron B Flight Fortress captains June 1945. L to R: F/O F D Carroll, W/O J Thorpe, F/O J J B Pocock, P/O R O Belton, F/S W D James, F/S W E Gatenby, F/S J Hastings *[W E Gatenby]*.

223 Squadron A Flight Fortress captains May 1945. L to R: P/O Tom Wallis, P/O Cyril 'Joe' Boaden, U/K, U/K, F/S E Boyes, U/K. Two of the U/K are P/O L Roullier & P/O B G Churcher *[W E Gatenby]*.

of the tests, they did confirm the capability of Window. The observers also commented that the combination of Window and airborne jamming made the close control of enemy night fighters impossible, due to the interference with W/T and R/T communications. For a detailed account of the Post Mortem exercise readers are referred to Martin Streetly's excellent account in his book *Confound and Destroy – 100 Group and the Bomber Support Campaign*. 223's first sorties on Post Mortem were flown on 28 June.

On 4 July Wg Cdr Burnell flew the last of the Liberators to Gatwick. Trips to the Ruhr were still taking place, and the first WAAFs to participate were flown on the 9th.

On 12 July Wg Cdr Burnell relinquished command of the squadron and replaced Gp Capt Dickens as station commander at Oulton. Sqn Ldr Van Der Bok DFC from 214 Squadron became the new CO of 223. Wg Cdr Burnell was subsequently killed in a flying accident on 14 November 1945 while piloting a Lancaster on an air test. This, always sad, period in the dying days of any squadron ended on 29 July 1945 when the squadron disbanded. Like many of the high-number squadrons it has never been reformed.

Notes:
1. Air24/314 Operational Requirements Section (Bomber Command) Report No.125 – Losses and Interceptions of Bomber Command Aircraft March 1945.
2. Air25/784 Appendix 3 to 100 Group Operational Record Book RAF Form 540. Report of Activities for March 1945.
3. Interview with Ralph Tailford, Flt Lt Dyck's flight engineer, 26 March 2003.
4. Reproduced from Peter Lovatt's book *Ordinary Man, Super Pilot: the Life and Times of Roy Hastie DFC AE*.
5. Air 25/785 Appendix 3 to 100 Group Operational Record Book RAF Form 540. Report of Activities for April 1945.

Epilogue

The bomber war had started from small beginnings in 1939; with a force that had little experience of night flying, and operating the first generation of 'heavy' bombers. These aircraft had little in the way of navigation or bombing aids. Early raids were carried out with crews finding their own way to the target, and their unsophisticated equipments were found wanting by the devastating Butt Report produced in late 1941. The report exposed the failure of bombing accuracy of those aircraft that found the target. This should not denigrate the spirit and bravery of those early crews who did their best with what they had. This startling revelation was the catalyst for a remarkable development of the truly formidable force that Bomber Command eventually became. The arrival of Sir Arthur Harris as a resolute and determined commander of Bomber Command coincided with the introduction of the new heavy bombers. This, together with the arrival of the new navigational and bombing aids described in Chapter One, heralded a new era for the bomber offensive.

Development was not idle in Germany. The early work of Hauptmann Wolfgang Falck, which eventually led to the formation of dedicated night-fighter units, produced the Luftwaffe's equally formidable arm. Again, we have described the initial barrier of the Kammhuber belt, and the establishment of the radar-controlled flak and searchlight batteries to defend major targets; together with the provision of early-warning radars, and radar-directed night fighters. These developments, which greatly strengthened the German defences, were assisted by the very effective German Y (listening service) which provided additional intelligence from the gift of failures in the allies' radio/wireless discipline.

Through 1943 and into 1944 Bomber Command suffered increasingly heavy losses from the greatly strengthened and capable German defences, not least from the introduction of the deadly Schräge Musik attacks. The airborne RCM protection provided in a small way by early Mandrel and ABC equipment was a start, but the formation of the dedicated 100 Group was a key factor in reducing what was becoming an unacceptably high loss rate in aircraft and trained crews.

Could or should 100 Group have been formed earlier than December 1943? Ideally yes, but not all the crucial equipments that proved so effective were available at that time. The Mandrel screen only became of real benefit when it was able to operate over Europe as opposed to off the enemy coast. Window, which was an essential feature, was not

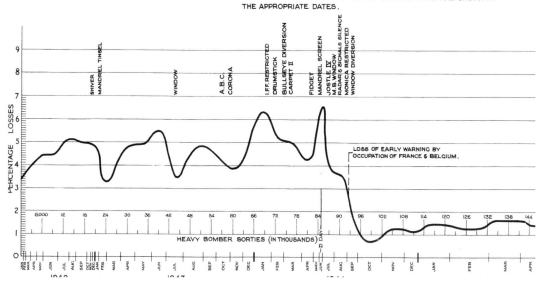

Bomber Command aircraft loss rate chart, showing the impact of various counter-measures as the war progressed [Sir Arthur T Harris Despatch on War operations 23 February 1942 to 8 May 1945].

released for use by Bomber Command until July 1943, and even then only after much debate. A most interesting chart, reproduced from Sir Arthur Harris's Dispatch on War Operations shown above, reveals the effect on the Bomber Command loss rate against German targets by the introduction of various equipments and policies. Without exception, there is a fall in loss rate with each introduction of a new measure, but equally it displays a rise again as the Germans took remedial action. The huge drop in loss rate after the D-Day landings are strongly affected by Bomber Command's withdrawal from attacking Germany to hit French targets in support of the invasion. A further drop in the rate can be partly attributed to the gradual loss of Germany's early-warning radar capability as the allies advanced.

By the autumn the loss rate had sunk well below 2%, never to rise significantly after that. Desperate fuel shortages also weakened the ability of the night-fighter force to counter the RAF's tactics of multi-targeting, strengthened by the use of diversionary forces and the very effective Window force spoofs. Another crucial factor was 100 Group's capability to jam the night-fighter controller's MF and VHF communications systems.

It is perhaps surprising that the Luftwaffe was still able to mount the defence it did considering the overwhelming forces it was fighting against. The remaining veteran night-fighter crews were still a dangerous adversary to the very end, given the opportunity; and it shows up the deficiencies in the higher levels of Luftwaffe command that some of these crews were wasted on daylight operations.

What of 223 Squadron? They had entered the battle in unfortunate circumstances, operating in a new type of aircraft, many of which in a war-weary condition. The Big

Ben operation, which proved ultimately to have been an unnecessary diversion, had some advantage in binding crews together and providing breathing space to gain experience with the Liberator before serious operations over Germany began. The hard work by air and ground crews to overcome the initial aircraft and equipment serviceability problems paid off, and by the end of 1944 they were playing their full part in Window and target patrol operations. They, together with 214, as the only Jostle-equipped squadrons, provided the crucial night-fighter communications jamming capability. They were extremely lucky considering their role, that they only lost three aircraft on operations; anyone transmitting information is at risk of being monitored and tracked. Over the same period, 214 Squadron operating in the same role lost twelve aircraft. People have asked why this should be. One important difference between the two squadrons was the H2S equipment fitted to 214's Fortresses. As we have already recorded, the Germans were able to home in on H2S transmissions, so almost certainly this is the answer.

We hope this book adds to the growing awareness of the important role that 100 Group heavy squadrons played in the bomber war. To those members of 223 Squadron that we have met or corresponded with through the years, we extend our gratitude for your help and respect for what you achieved.

Abbreviations

ABC	Airborne Cigar	Hptm	Hauptmann	Sgt	Sergeant
AC	Aircraft	HQ	Headquarters	SNCO	Senior Non-Commissioned Officer
AGS	Air Gunnery School	IFF	Identification Friend or Foe		
AGT	Airwork General Trading	IA	International Alloys	SOC	Struck Off Charge
AI	Air Interception	IAS	Indicated Airspeed	SofTT	School of Technical Training
Air Cdre	Air Commodore	I/C	Intercom	SS	Schutzstaffel
AMU	Air Mileage Unit	JG	Jägdgeschwader (Fighter Wing)	TAMU	Transport Aircraft Modification Unit
API	Air Position Indicator				
APU	Auxiliary Power Unit	KG	Kampfgeschwader (Bomber Wing)	TAS	True Air Speed
AVM	Air Vice-Marshal			TI	Target Indicator
BG	Bombardment Group	KGr	Kampfgruppe (Bomber Group)	TNA	The National Archives
BS	Bombardment Squadron			TOT	Time on Target
BS	Bomber Support	LFS	Lancaster Finishing School	TR	Transmitter Receiver
C-in-C	Commander-in-Chief	Lt	Lieutenant	TRE	Telecommunications Research Establishment
CO	Commanding Officer	Mc/s	Megacycles per second		
CRD	Civilian Repair Depot	MHz	Megaherz	UE	Unit Establishment
DFC	Distinguished Flying Cross	MID	Mentioned in Despatches	UK	United Kingdom
DFM	Distinguished Flying Medal	MT	Motor Transport	U/S	Unserviceable
DRC	Direct Reading Compass	MU	Maintenance Unit	USAAF	United States Army Air Force
DSC	Distinguished Service Cross	NCO	Non-Commissioned Officer	VHF	Very High Frequency
EFTS	Elementary Flying Training School	NJG	Nachtjagdgeschwader (Night Fighter Wing)	WAAF	Womens' Auxiliary Air Force
				Wg Cdr	Wing Commander
ELINT	Electronic Intelligence	NJRF	Nacht Jagd Raum Führer (Night Fighter Control Room)	Wnr	Werk Number (manufacturer's serial number)
E-Stelle	Erprobungsstelle (Test Centre)				
ETA	Estimated Time of Arrival	OBE	Order of the British Empire	W/O	Warrant Officer
F/Eng	Flight Engineer	ORB	Operations Record Book	WOp/AG	Wireless Operator/Air Gunner
Fg Off	Flying Officer	OTU	Operational Training Unit		
FIDO	Fog Investigation and Dispersal Operation	PFF	Pathfinder Force	W/T	Wireless Telegraphy
		Plt Off	Pilot Officer	WWII	World War Two
Flak	Fliegerabwehrkanone (anti-aircraft gun)	PRU	Photographic Reconnaissance Unit	ZG	Zerstörergeschwader (Heavy Fighter Wing)
FLB	Flying Log Book	RAAF	Royal Australian Air Force		
Flt Lt	Flight Lieutenant	RAE	Royal Aircraft Establishment		
Flt Sgt	Flight Sergeant	RAF	Royal Air Force		
FuG	Funkgerät (W/T equipment)	RCAF	Royal Canadian Air Force		
FuMG	Funkmessgerät (Radar set)	RCM	Radio (and Radar) Counter-Measures		
GCI	Ground Controlled Interception				
		RDF	Radio Direction Finding		
Gerät	Apparatus	RFC	Royal Flying Corps		
Gp Capt	Group Captain	RN	Royal Navy		
GPO	General Post Office	RNAS	Royal Naval Air Service		
GR	General Reconnaissance	RNZAF	Royal New Zealand Air Force		
HCU	Heavy Conversion Unit	RoS	Receipt of Spares		
HF	High Frequency	R/T	Radio Telephony		

Select Bibliography & Sources

Bibliography

Ausbildung und Einsatz eines Nachtjagers im II. Weltkrieg: Heinz Rökker. Taschenbuch, 2006.
Coastal Support and Special Squadrons of the RAF and their Aircraft: J D R Rawlings. Janes, 1982.
Confounding the Reich: Martin W Bowman & Tom Cushing. Patrick Stephens, 1996.
Confound and Destroy: Martin Streetly. MacDonald & J, 1979.
Enemy in the Dark: Peter Spoden. Ceberus, 2003.
Gefechtsstand of Jägdabschnittsführer Dänemark. Colonel Michael 'Ses' Svejgaard www.gyges.dk
German Secret Flight Test Centres: Heinrich Beauvais et al. Midland Publishing, 1996.
History of the German Night Fighter Force: Gebhard Aders. Franklin Watts, 1980.
Honour the Air Forces: Michael Maton. Token, 2010.
Mighty Eighth War Diary: Roger Freeman. Weidenfeld Military, 1980.
Nachtjagd War Diaries: Dr Theo E W Boiten & Roderick J Mackenzie. Red Kite, 2008.
RAF Bomber Command Losses: W R Chorley. Midland, 1996.
RAF Squadrons: Wing Commander C G Jefford MBE BA RAF (Ret'd). Crowood Press, 2001.
Royal Navy Aircraft Serials and Units: Ray Sturtivant and Gordon Page. Air Britain, 1992.
Secret Squadrons of the Eighth: Pat Carthy. Ian Allen, 1990.
Despatch on War Operations 23 February to 8 May 1945: Sir Arthur T Harris. Frank Cass, 1995.
Squadron of Deception: Stephen Hutton. Schiffer Publishing, 2004.
The Bomber Command War Diaries: Martin Middlebrook & Chris Everitt. Midland Publishing, 2011.
War Prizes: Phil Butler. Midland Publishing, 2006.
The Luftwaffe Over The Bristol Area, Fishponds Local History Society. Bristol Past website
   www.fishponds.org.uk
The Second World War 1939-1945 Royal Air Force, Signals Volume VII Radio Counter-Measures.
   Air Ministry 1950, reprinted by MLRS 2011

Official Sources in The National Archives
Air14/1070   Organisation of British & USAAF Fortress & Liberator Sqns & 1699 Flt
Air14/3229   ORS General Correspondence 4 Group
Air14/2971   100 Group Statement of Daily Intentions
Air14/3412   Bomber Command Reports on Night Operations
Air24/314   Summary of Night Operations March 1945
Air24/314   HQ Bomber Command Operational Requirements Section. Report No.125 –
             Losses and Interceptions of Bomber Command Aircraft March 1945
Air25/172   HQ Bomber Command Preliminary Warning Order Form A 20 March 1945
Air25/782   100 Group Report of Activities October/November 1944
Air25/783   100 Group Report of Activities December 1944/January 1945
Air25/784   100 Group Report of Activities February/March 1945.
Air25/788   Interception Tactics Report No.70/45, Part II Night of 20/21 March 1945
Air27/series Squadron Operational Record Books RAF Forms 540/541
Air Ministry Form 78 – Aircraft Movement Cards.
RAF Museum Bomber Command Loss Cards.

APPENDIX ONE
100 Group Order of Battle

Squadron	Equipment	Station	First 100 Group operation
23	Mosquito VI	Little Snoring	July 1944
85	Mosquito II	Swannington, West Malling	June 1944
141	Beaufighter II, Mosquito II	West Raynham	December 1943
157	Mosquito XIX	Swannington, West Malling	May 1944
169	Mosquito II	Little Snoring	January 1944
171	Halifax III	North Creake	September 1944
192	Halifax III & V, Mosquito IV, Wellington X	Foulsham	December 1943
199	Stirling III, Halifax III	North Creake	May 1944
214	Fortress II & Fortress III	Sculthorpe, Oulton	April 1944
223	Liberator IV & VI & Fortress III	Oulton	September 1944
239	Beaufighter II, Mosquito II	West Raynham	January 1944
462 RAAF	Halifax III	Foulsham	January 1945
515	Mosquito VI	Little Snoring	March 1944
36 USAAF	B-24H & J	Cheddington	August 1944
803 USAAF	B-17F & G, B-24H & J	Sculthorpe, Oulton	June 1944

223 Squadron Operations

Date	Main Force Operations	Duty	Aircraft Launched	Remarks
19.9.44	Not connected	Big Ben	S/L Carrington TS525 (H)	Left patrol early because I/C and O2 u/s. No visuals, no blips.
22.9.44	Not connected	Big Ben	F/L McKnight TS534 (A)	Jostle u/s.
23.9.44	Not connected	Big Ben	F/L Allnutt TS532 (N)	No vis.
			F/L Levy TS531 (B)	S/E u/s at enemy coast.
25.9.44	Not connected	Big Ben	F/L Stephenson TS533 (M)	No visuals, no blips. Jostle u/s. Abandoned patrol when vis became bad.
			F/O Croft TS531 (B)	No visuals, no blips.
			F/L Levy TS531 (B)	No visuals, no blips.
26.9.44	Not connected	Big Ben	F/O Woodward TS534 (A)	No visuals, no blips.
			F/O Croft TS533 (M)	
			F/L Stephenson TS531 (B)	2 blips while on ground.
27.9.44	Not connected	Big Ben	F/L Levy TS533 (M)	2 sightings, no blips.
			F/O Young TS531 (B)	Late on patrol. No signals, no blips.
27/28.9.44	Not connected	Big Ben	F/O Woodward TS533 (M)	No signals, no blips.
28.9.44	Not connected	Big Ben	F/O Brigham TS529 (C)	Returned early. No.2 engine u/s. Front & rear turrets u/s.
			F/L Dyck TS533 (M)	No signals, no blips.
29.9.44	Not connected	Big Ben	F/O Noseworthy TS529 (C)	No signals, no blips.
			F/O Brigham TS533 (M)	Late TO – various failures. 1 sighting.
			F/L McPherson TS529 (C)	Gyro failure.
29/30.9.44	Not connected	Big Ben	F/L Stephenson TS529 (C)	1 sighting.
30.9.44	Not connected	Big Ben	F/L Allnutt TS523 (D)	3 signals, no blips.
1.10.44	Not connected	Big Ben	W/O Stuart TS531 (B)	
			F/L Carrington TS531 (B)	
2.10.44	Not connected	Big Ben	P/O Morris TS534 (A)	
			F/L McPherson TS531 (B)	
			F/O Noseworthy TS519 (S)	
2/3.10.44	Not connected	Big Ben	F/O Young TS534 (A)	Nav instrument u/s. Diverted to Woodbridge.
3.10.44	Not connected	Big Ben	F/O Briscoe TS533 (M)	
			F/O Croft TS519 (S)	
			F/O Allnutt TS531 (B)	1 sighting.
			F/L Dyck TS522 (P)	Returned early, weather.
4.10.44	Not connected	Big Ben	F/O Woodward TS519 (S)	
4/5.10.44	Not connected	Big Ben	F/O Young TS531 (B)	Engine failure. 2 sightings from same site.
			S/L Carrington TS522 (P)	

Date	Main Force Operations	Duty	Aircraft Launched	Remarks
5.10.44	Not connected	Big Ben	F/L McKnight TS533 (M) F/L Stephenson TS534 (A)	No sightings. 2 sightings.
5/6.10.44	Not connected	Big Ben	F/O Croft TS522 (P)	No visual sighting. 1 weak blip.
6.10.44	Not connected	Big Ben	F/O Young TS522 (P) P/O Morris TS531 (B) F/O Briscoe TS529 (C) F/L Dyck TS534 (B)	No visuals or blips. 2 visuals. Original a/c u/s. No visuals or blips. No.4 engine fire.
6/7.10.44	Not connected	Big Ben	F/L McKnight TS529 (C) F/O Noseworthy TS534 (A)	Original a/c u/s. 2 visuals. O2 mask u/s. No visuals or blips.
7.10.44	Not connected	Big Ben	F/O Thompson TS524 (O) F/O Hastie TS533 (M) F/O Allnutt TS534 (A)	1 sighting. 1 sighting. No visuals or blips.
9.10.44	Not connected	Big Ben	F/O Hastie TS519 (S)	1 visual.
10/11.10.44	Not connected	Big Ben	W/O Stuart TS531 (B) F/O Brigham TS532 (N)	No visuals or blips. No visuals or blips.
11.10.44	Not connected	Big Ben	F/O Hastie TS534 (A)	No visuals or blips.
12.10.44	Not connected	Big Ben	F/O Steele TS531 (B)	No visuals or blips.
13.10.44	Not connected	Big Ben	F/O Briscoe TS532 (N)	Complete electrical failure. 1 large blip on screen for approx 5 seconds, about 50 Megacycles. No audio.
14.10.44	Not connected	Big Ben	F/O Steele TS534 (A) F/O Thompson TS531 (B) F/O Steele TS531 (B)	Engine trouble.
14/15.10.44	Duisburg	Bullseye Window Patrol	F/O Woodward TS523 (D) F/O Hastie TS525 (H) W/O Stuart TS522 (P)	
15.10.44	Not connected	Big Ben	P/O Morris TS531 (B)	Hit by flak over Rotterdam. Navigator F/O Wallace fairly seriously wounded.
15/16.10.44	Wilhelmshaven	Window Patrol	F/O Allnutt TS525 (H) F/L McKnight TS523 (D) S/L Carrington TS519 (S)	No special equipment used. No special equipment used. No special equipment used.
17.10.44	Not connected	Big Ben	F/O Briscoe TS519 (S)	Recalled early because of weather. A/C fired on twice by heavy flak – not hit but a/c shaken.
18.10.44	Not connected	Big Ben	F/O Steele TS531 (B)	Early return. Mid-upper gunner ill. 2 visuals.
19.10.44	Not connected	Big Ben	F/O Hastie TS523 (D) F/O Briscoe TS522 (P)	No sightings or blips. No sightings or blips.
19/20.10.44	Stuttgart Nuremberg	Window Patrol	F/L Levy TS534 (A) F/O Noseworthy TS532 (N)	
22.10.44	Not connected	Big Ben	F/L McPherson TS532 (N)	No visuals or blips.
23/24.10.44	Essen	Window Patrol	F/L McKnight TS534 (A) F/O Croft TS519 (S) F/O Morris TS524 (O) F/L Levy TS523 (D) F/O Briscoe TS522 (P)	Jostle u/s. Jostle on. Early return. Mid-upper turret perspex split. Early return. Delayed by bad weather, unable to catch up with main stream.
24.10.44	Not connected	Big Ben	P/O Thompson TS532 (N)	No occurences

Date	Main Force Operations	Duty	Aircraft Launched	Remarks
26/27.10.44	Minor ops. 42 Mosquito patrols. 10 Lancasters mine laying off Heligoland	Window Patrol	F/L Levy TS534 (A)	Jostle used.
			F/O Hastie TS529 (C)	Jostle used.
			F/L Stephenson TS519 (S)	Jostle used.
			F/O Young TS532 (N)	Early return. Did not leave local area, no turbo pressure.
30/31.10.44	Cologne	Window Patrol	F/O Brigham TS519 (S)	Window, Jostle on. No Dina or Carpet carried. Reported twin vapour trails climbing almost vertically.
			F/O Young TS520 (J)	Window, Jostle on. No Dina or Carpet carried.
			F/L Dyck TS534 (A)	Window, Jostle on. No Dina or Carpet carried.
31.10.44	Cologne	Window Patrol	F/O Steele TS531 (B)	Window, Jostle on. No Dina carried.
			F/L Woodward TS520 (J)	Window, Jostle u/s – no HT supply.
			F/O Morris TS523 (D)	Window, Jostle on.
1/2.11.44	Homberg 1 Nov Oberhausen 1/2 Nov	Window Patrol	F/L Croft TS523 (D)	Window, Jostle on.
			F/L Brigham TS534 (A)	Window, Jostle on.
			F/L Allnutt TS524 (O)	Window, Jostle and GEE u/s.
			F/L Hastie TS531 (B)	Window, Jostle on.
			W/O Stuart TS529 (C)	Early return, engine failure.
2/3.11.44	Düsseldorf	Window Patrol	F/L Levy TS534 (A)	Window, Jostle not used, 80v AC failure.
			F/L Woodward TS520 (J)	Window, Jostle.
			F/O Steele TS525 (H)	Window, Jostle.
			F/L Stephenson TS524 (O)	Window, Jostle.
			F/L Dyck TS531 (B)	Window, Jostle.
			W/O Stuart TS523 (D)	Early return, navigation error.
4/5.11.44	Bochum Dortmund-Ems Canal	Window Patrol	F/L McKnight TS531 (B)	Window, Jostle.
			F/L Allnutt TS523 (D)	Window, Jostle.
			F/O Young TS529 (C)	Window, Jostle.
			F/O Morris TS520 (J)	Window, Jostle.
			F/O Hastie TS525 (H)	1 jet aircraft seen.
6/7.11.44	Mittelland Canal Koblenz	Window Patrol	F/O Noseworthy TS529 (C)	Window, Jostle.
			S/L Carrington TS524 (O)	Window, Jostle.
			F/O Steele TS533 (M)	Window, Jostle on but no indicator. Lights u/s?
			F/L Dyck TS520 (J)	Jostle.
			F/L Woodward TS531 (B)	Jostle.
9/10.11.44	Wanne-Eickel and minor ops	Window Patrol	F/L Briscoe TS522 (P)	Jostle VHF and Window.
			F/L McKnight TS529 (C)	Early return. Delayed changing aircraft and could not catch up.
10/11.11.44	Castrop-Rauxel synthetic oil refinery and minor ops	Window and Jostle Patrol	F/L Stephenson TS534 (A)	Window and Jostle.
			F/L Woodward TS520 (J)	Window, Jostle u/s.
			F/L Dyck TS530 (G)	Window and Jostle.
			S/L Carrington TS526 (T)	Window, Jostle, Carpet and Dina.
			F/L Levy TS529 (C)	Late take-off due to electrical failure. Returned early because rear compartment filled with petrol fumes.
11/12.11.44	Harburg Rhenania-Ossag oil refinery Dortmund-Hoesch benzin synthetic oil plant	Window Patrol	F/L McKnight TS531 (B)	Window, Jostle.
			F/L Croft TS526 (T)	Window, Jostle not used.
			F/O Young TS528 (R)	Window, Dina intermittent, Carpet not used because special operator trying to service Dina.
			W/O Stuart TS534 (A)	Window, Jostle intermittent due to pressure leak.
			F/L Allnutt TS520 (J)	Window, Jostle.
			F/L Brigham TS529 (C)	Window, Jostle u/s due to loss of pressure. Window, Jostle.

Date	Main Force Operations	Duty	Aircraft Launched	Remarks
15/16.11.44	Dortmund oil plant Minor ops	Window Patrol	F/L Noseworthy TS533 (M)	Window, Jostle VHF.
			F/L Dyck TS531 (B)	Window, Jostle VHF.
			F/O Steele TS528 (R)	Early return, engine trouble.
			F/O Morris TS530 (G)	Window, Jostle VHF. Weather diversion, Foulsham.
			F/L Briscoe TS522 (P)	Window, Jostle VHF. Weather diversion, Carnaby.
				Window, Jostle VHF. Weather diversion.
18/19.11.44	Wanne-Eickel oil plant	Window Patrol	F/L Hastie TS525 (H)	Window, Jostle. Weather diversion, Manston.
			P/O Thompson TS529 (C)	Window, Jostle, Carpet & Dina. Mandrel u/s after 3 minutes. Weather diversion, Manston.
			S/L Carrington TS526 (T)	Window, Jostle, Carpet & Dina. Mandrel u/s after 3 minutes. Weather diversion, Manston.
			F/L Croft TS533 (M)	Window, Jostle u/s (alternative Mandrel u/s for part of patrol). Weather diversion, Manston.
20/21.11.44	Koblenz	Window Patrol	F/L McKnight TS525 (H)	No.1 engine lost power on take-off
21/22.11.44	Aschaffenburg railway yards and lines. Castrop-Rauxel oil refinery. Sterkrade synthetic oil refinery. Mittelland Canal. Dortmund-Ems Canal	Window Patrol	F/O Steele TS533 (M)	Window, Jostle u/s after take-off.
			F/L Hastie TS529 (C)	Window, Jostle.
			F/L McPherson TS534 (A)	Window, Jostle. Carpet and Mandrel u/s from take-off.
			F/L Briscoe TS524 (O)	Window, Jostle, Carpet and Dina.
			P/O Thompson TS523 (D)	No.2 engine flame damper u/s.
23/24.11.44	Gelsenkirchen Nordstern oil plant. Minor ops	Window Patrol	F/L McPherson TS534 (A)	Window, Jostle. Carpet did not jam, could pick nothing up. No Dina, Mandrel u/s.
			W/O Stuart TS529 (C)	Window. Only Jostle used and carried. A/C returned from near Aachen with No.1 engine u/s (no oil pressure) and another nearly u/s.
			F/O Morris TS530 (G)	Window. Only Jostle used and carried.
			S/L McKnight TS525 (H)	Window, Jostle, Carpet on but went u/s – aerial shorting? No Dina carried.
			F/L Briscoe TS533 (M)	Window, Jostle. No other special equipment carried.
			F/L Allnutt TS524 (O)	Window, Jostle, Carpet and Dina.
25/26.11.44	Minor ops	Window Patrol	S/L Carrington TS533 (M)	Window, Jostle.
			F/O Morris TS530 (G)	Window, Jostle.
			F/L Stephenson TS527 (Q)	Window, Jostle, Carpet and Dina.
			F/L Brigham TS524 (O)	Window, Jostle, Carpet and Dina.
			F/O Thompson TS534 (A)	Window, Jostle.
			F/O Steele TS522 (P)	Late take-off due to oil leak. Dropped Window.
26/27.11.44	Munich	Window Patrol	S/L McKnight TS525 (H)	Window, Jostle, Carpet and Dina.
			F/L Levy TS534 (A)	Window, Jostle and Carpet.
			F/O Morris TS530 (G)	Window, Jostle and Carpet.
			F/L Noseworthy TS533 (M)	Window. Jostle on but went u/s when air pressure dropped.
			F/L Allnutt TS524 (O)	GEE u/s. Long trip so credited with full op.
28/29.11.44	Freiburg, Neuss	Window Patrol	F/O Steele TS534 (A)	Window, Jostle. Carpet u/s.
			F/L Dyck TS531 (B)	Window, Jostle and Carpet.
			W/O Stuart TS530 (G)	Window, Jostle and Carpet.
			P/O Thompson TS520 (J)	Window, Jostle, Carpet and Dina. Saw jet aircraft.
			F/L Briscoe TS533 (M)	Window, Jostle.
			F/L Brigham TS524 (O)	Early return. GEE u/s, but credited with ½ op.

Date	Main Force Operations	Duty	Aircraft Launched	Remarks
28/29.11.44	Essen, Neuss	Window Patrol	S/L Carrington TS533 (M)	Window, Jostle not used.
			F/L Woodward TS525 (H)	Window, Jostle, Carpet and Dina.
			F/L Hastie TS523 (D)	Jostle u/s, lack of pressure. Carpet, nothing heard, no jamming Window. Could not use Jostle and Carpet because alternator on No.2 engine u/s before take-off.
			F/O Morris TS530 (G)	Window, Jostle, Carpet and Dina.
			P/O Thompson TS520 (J)	Window, Jostle and Dina. Carpet, no jamming.
			F/L Allnutt TS527 (Q)	Early return. Intercom failure.
			F/L Levy TS534 (A)	
29/30.11.44	Dortmund Duisburg	Window Patrol	F/L Levy TS534 (A)	Window, Jostle and Carpet.
			F/L Dyck TS531 (B)	Window, Jostle. Carpet did not jam, nothing picked up.
			W/O Stuart TS523 (D)	Window, Jostle, Carpet and Dina.
			S/L McKnight TS525 (H)	Window, Jostle, Carpet and Dina.
			F/O Steele TS520 (J)	Window, Jostle, Carpet and Dina.
			F/L Noseworthy TS527 (Q)	Early return. Rear turret u/s. Short caused guns to fire themselves.
1.12.44	Minor ops	Window Patrol	S/L McKnight TS525 (H)	Window, Jostle, Carpet and Dina.
			F/L Levy TS534 (A)	Window, Jostle and Dina.
			F/L Noseworthy TS524 (O)	Window, Jostle and Dina. Carpet no jamming. No.3 engine problem at end of patrol; returned on 3 engines.
			P/O Thompson TS520 (J)	Took off, circled airfield and returned with port outer feathered.
			F/O Steele TS528 (R)	Intercom failure.
			F/L Woodward TS525 (H)	Window, Jostle, Carpet and Dina.
2/3.12.44	Hagen	Window Patrol	F/L Dyck TS531 (B)	Window, Jostle and Carpet.
			F/L Levy TS534 (A)	Window, Jostle and Carpet.
			F/L Hastie TS523 (D)	Window, Jostle, Carpet and Dina.
			F/L Noseworthy TS519 (S)	Window, Jostle u/s, Carpet and Dina.
			F/O Young TS528 (R)	Window, Jostle and Dina. Carpet nothing heard, no jamming.
			P/O Thompson TS520 (J)	Returned, flame damper on No.4 engine u/s.
4/5.12.44	Karlsruhe Heilbronn	1. Window Patrol	F/L Dyck TS531 (B)	Window, Jostle and Carpet. Dina not fitted.
			P/O Thompson TS520 (J)	Window, Jostle, Carpet and Dina.
			F/L Brigham TS528 (R)	Window, Jostle and Dina. Carpet no jamming.
			F/L Stephenson TS524 (O)	Window, Jostle u/s from take-off, Carpet no jamming, Dina.
			F/L Briscoe TS526 (T)	Window, Jostle and Dina. Carpet no jamming.
			F/L McPherson TS533 (M)	Window and Carpet. No other SE carried.
			F/O Steele TS522 (P)	Returned 4 minutes after setting course. Leak from No.2 tank.
		2. Jostle Patrol	F/L Hastie TS523 (D)	Jostle, Carpet and Dina. Very little flak; no searchlights or fighters.
5/6.12.44	Soest	1. Window Patrol	F/O Steele TS528 (R)	Window, Jostle and Carpet. No transmissions on Dina.
			F/L Morris TS520 (J)	Window and Carpet. Jostle u/s 9 minutes after take-off due to power failure.
			F/L Levy TS534 (A)	Window, Jostle and Carpet.
			F/L Noseworthy TS533 (M)	Window, Jostle, Carpet and Dina.
			F/L Briscoe TS527 (Q)	Window, Jostle, Carpet and Dina.
			F/L Woodward TS529 (C)	Window, Jostle, Carpet and Dina.
		2. Jostle Patrol Soest	S/L McKnight TS523 (D)	Jostle, Carpet and Dina. Circled target 21:20-21:35 at 23K feet. Moderate heavy flak but no fighter reaction noticed in target area. Bombing appeared to be well concentrated.

Date	Main Force Operations	Duty	Aircraft Launched	Remarks
6/7.12.44	Leuna Osnabrück Giessen	1. Window Patrol	P/O Thompson TS522 (P)	Landed Manston short of fuel.
			F/L Croft TS533 (M)	Sortie abandoned in base area – fuel leak.
			F/L Briscoe TS525 (H)	Window, Jostle, Carpet and Dina.
		2. Jostle Patrol Giessen	F/L Stephenson TS527 (Q)	Jostle, Carpet and Dina.
		3. Jostle Patrol Osnabrück	F/L Woodward TS529 (C)	Jostle, Carpet and Dina. No TIs or Sky Markers seen. Only 1 fighter seen, 1 A/C seen shot down. Flak moderate.
		4. Jostle Patrol Leuna	F/L Hastie TS523 (D)	Early return, oxygen leak.
9/10.12.44	Minor ops	Window Patrol	F/L Brigham TS519 (S)	Window, Jostle, Carpet and Dina.
			F/L Stephenson TS527 (Q)	Window, Jostle, Carpet and Dina.
			W/O Stuart TS531 (B)	Window, Jostle, Carpet no jamming. Three 214 a/c switched on their H2S on crossing French coast.
			P/O Thompson TS520 (J)	Returned at 18:56 at 18K feet – problems with flame damper.
			F/L Levy TS534 (A)	Returned at 19:06 at 20K feet – runaway booster feed in rear turret.
12/13.12.44	Essen Minor ops	1. Jostle Patrol Osnabrück	F/O Morris TS520 (J)	In target area 1930-1937 at 22K feet. Jostle, Carpet and Piperack. Intermittent to jamming on 7 frequencies. Flak moderate to intense. Few fighter flares seen, no fighters.
		2. Window Patrol	F/L Hastie TS523 (D)	Window, Jostle, Carpet and Piperack. No Monica.
			S/L Carrington TS525 (H)	Window, Jostle, Carpet and Piperack. No Monica.
			F/L Croft TS527 (Q)	Window, Jostle, Carpet, Piperack and Monica.
			F/L Brigham TS519 (S)	Window, Jostle, Carpet, Piperack and Monica.
			F/O Steele TS522 (P)	Returned while still in base area – fuel leak.
			F/L Allnutt TS526 (T)	Jostle H/J button frozen solid. Carpet intermittent jamming. Piperack only 1 transmitter serviceable, Monica u/s.
15/16.12.44	Ludwigshaven	1. Window Patrol	F/O Steele TS522 (P)	Window, Jostle on but believed u/s.
			F/L Hastie TS523 (D)	Window, Jostle, Carpet, Piperack and Monica.
			F/L Allnutt TS526 (T)	Window, Jostle, Carpet and Piperack. No Monica fitted.
		2. Patrol	W/O Stuart TS520 (J)	Window, Jostle, Carpet, Piperack and Monica.
			F/L Croft (TS519 (S)	Jostle, Carpet, Piperack and Monica.
17/18.12.44	Duisberg Ulm Munich	1. Window Patrol	F/L Hastie TS523 (D)	Window, Carpet and Piperack.
			F/L Croft TS526 (T)	Returned early – oil leak in No.3 engine.
			W/O Stuart TS520 (J)	Returned early – u/s flame dampers on Nos. 3 & 4 engines.
			F/L Dyck TS529 (C)	Returned early – behind ETA due to strong winds.
			F/L Stephenson TS527 (Q)	Returned early – behind ETA due to strong winds.
		2. Jostle Patrol Munich	F/O Morris TS530 (G)	Jostle, Carpet, Piperack and Monica. Orbited in target area at 18K feet. Flak and searchlights, but no fighters. 9 hr trip.
18/19.12.44	Minor ops	Window Patrol	F/L Woodward TS529 (C)	Window, Jostle, Carpet and Piperack. Monica u/s.
			F/L Allnutt TS519 (S)	Window, Jostle, Carpet and Piperack. Monica not fitted.
			F/L Dyck TS530 (G)	Window, Jostle, Carpet, Piperack and Monica.

Date	Main Force Operations	Duty	Aircraft Launched	Remarks
21/22.12.44	Pölitz Cologne/Nippes Bonn	Window Patrol Ruhr	F/L Hastie TS519 (S)	Window, no Monica fitted. Weather diversion to Banff.
			F/L Briscoe TS524 (O)	Window, Jostle not used, Carpet, Piperack. Diverted Milltown.
			F/L Woodward TS529 (C)	Window, Jostle, Carpet, Piperack. Diverted Milltown.
			F/L Croft TS520 (J)	Window, Jostle, Carpet, Piperack. Diverted Milltown.
			S/L McKnight TS523 (D)	Window, Jostle, Carpet, Piperack. Diverted Milltown.
			F/L Levy TS530 (G)	Window, Jostle, Carpet, Piperack. Diverted Milltown.
22/23.12.44	Koblenz Bingen	Jostle Patrol Bingen	F/L Allnutt TS532 (N)	Window, Jostle, Carpet and Piperack. Monica u/s.
23/24.12.44	Trier Cologne/ Grimberg Minor ops	Window Patrol	F/L Allnutt TS525 (H)	Window, Jostle, Carpet and Piperack. No Monica fitted.
			F/L Dyck TS534 (A)	Window, Jostle, Carpet intermittently, Monica.
			F/L Noseworthy (TT336 (R)	Window, Jostle. Piperack and Monica u/s.
24.12.44	Hangelar airfield Cologne/Nippes	1. Window Patrol	F/L Hastie TS523 (D) F/L Woodward TS529 (C)	Window, Carpet, Piperack.
			F/L Croft TS532 (N)	Window, Jostle u/s, Carpet, Piperack. No Monica fitted.
		2. Jostle Patrol	S/L Carrington TS525 (H)	Jostle, Carpet and Piperack. Monica not used. Moderate flak, no fighters seen.
27/28.12.44	Opladen	Window Patrol	S/L McKnight TS525 (H)	Window, Jostle, Carpet, Piperack. Monica not fitted.
			F/L Levy TS530 (G)	Window, Jostle, Carpet, Piperack, Monica.
			F/L Woodward TS529 (C)	Window, Jostle, Carpet, Piperack. Monica not fitted.
			F/L Croft TS532 (N)	Window, Jostle, Carpet, Piperack. Monica not fitted.
			F/L Briscoe TS533 (M)	Window, Jostle, Carpet and Piperack.
			F/L Dyck TS531 (B)	Window, Jostle, Carpet, Piperack, Monica.
28/29.12.44	Mönchen- gladbach Bonn Oslo fjord	Window Patrol	F/L Brigham TS532 (N)	Window, Jostle, Carpet, Piperack. Monica u/s. Ju88 approached head on and mid upper gunner returned fire. Starboard flap holed by allied flak.
			S/L Carrington TS533 (M)	Window, Jostle u/s, Carpet, Piperack. Monica not fitted.
			F/O Morris TS530 (G)	Window, Jostle, Carpet, Piperack and Monica.
			W/O Stuart TS531 (B)	Window, Jostle, Carpet, Piperack and Monica.
			F/L McPherson TS525 (H)	No.4 engine smoking on take-off. Impossible to maintain height so returned to base.
29/30.12.44	Scholven/Buer Troisdorf	1. Jostle Patrol Troisdorf	S/L McKnight TS530 (G)	Jostle (interference with I/C and communications), Carpet and Piperack.
		2. Window Patrol Münster	F/L Briscoe TT336(R)	Window, Jostle, Carpet, Piperack and Monica.
			F/O Thompson TS520 (J)	Window, Jostle, Carpet and Piperack.
			F/L Dyck TS531 (B)	Window, Jostle, Carpet, Piperack and Monica.
			F/L Allnutt TS532 (N)	Window, Jostle, Carpet and Piperack.

Date	Main Force Operations	Duty	Aircraft Launched	Remarks
30/31.12.44	Cologne/Kalk Houffalize	1. Jostle Patrol Cologne	F/O Morris TS532 (N)	Jostle u/s, Carpet, Piperack, Monica u/s. Heavy flak over target, no fighters seen.
		2. Window Patrol	W/O Stuart TS531 (B)	Window, Jostle, Carpet and Piperack. Monica u/s.
			S/L Carrington TS533 (M)	Window, Jostle, Carpet and Piperack. Monica not fitted.
			F/L Briscoe TS519 (S)	Window, Jostle u/s, Carpet and Piperack. Monica u/s.
			F/L Woodward TS529 (C)	Window, Jostle, Carpet and Piperack. Monica not fitted.
			F/L McPherson TT336 (R)	Window, Jostle, Carpet, Piperack and Monica. No fighters seen, accurate heavy flak.
1/2.1.45	Gravenhorst Vohwinkel Dortmund	1. Jostle Patrol Gravenhorst	S/L Carrington TS533 (M)	Jostle, Carpet and Piperack. Monica not fitted. GEE & other nav aids u/s & drifted off target. Landed North Creake.
		2. Jostle Patrol Dortmund	F/L Briscoe TS526 (T)	Jostle, Carpet and Piperack.
		3. Window Patrol	F/L Woodward TS529 (C)	Jostle, Carpet and Piperack.
			F/L Allnutt TS532 (N)	Jostle, Carpet and Piperack.
			F/O Morris TS530 (G)	Jostle, Carpet and Piperack.
			F/O Thompson TT336 (R)	Jostle u/s, Carpet no frequencies heard, Piperack. Landed North Creake.
			F/L McPherson TS531 (B)	Jostle, Carpet and Piperack. Landed Middleton St.George.
2/3.1.45	Nuremberg Ludwigshaven	Window Patrol	W/O Stuart TS520 (J)	Jostle, Carpet and Piperack.
			F/O Morris TS530 (G)	Jostle, Carpet, Piperack and Monica.
			F/L Woodward TS529 (C)	Jostle, Carpet, Piperack and Monica.
			F/L Allnutt TS532 (N)	Jostle, Carpet and Piperack.
			F/L Briscoe TS526 (T)	Jostle, Carpet and Piperack.
			F/L Dyck TS519 (S)	Returned after circling airfield, unable to retract undercarriage.
5/6.1.45	Hannover Houffalize Minor ops to Berlin	1. Northern Window Patrol	F/L Allnutt TS532 (N)	Jostle not used, Carpet, Piperack. Monica abandoned.
		2. Southern Window Patrol	F/L McPherson TS531 (B)	Jostle, Carpet and Piperack.
			F/L Brigham TS524 (O)	Jostle, Carpet and Piperack. Monica not fitted.
			F/L Noseworthy TT336 (R)	Returned early, No.3 engine no power.
		3. Jostle Patrol Hannover	F/L Hastie TT336 (R)	Jostle, Carpet and Piperack. No Monica fitted. Fighter flares in evidence all the way along the route.
		4. Jostle Patrol Houffalize	F/L Stephenson TS527 (Q)	Jostle, Carpet and Piperack.
			S/L Carrington TT336 (R)	Jostle, Carpet nothing to jam, Piperack. No fighters, no flak.
6/7.1.45	Hanau Neuss Spoof op to Kassel	1. Jostle Patrol Neuss	F/L Croft TT336 (R)	Jostle, Carpet. No Monica fitted. Moderate heavy flak.
			S/L McKnight TS531 (B)	Jostle switched off because of interference with Carpet and intercom. Piperack. Negligible flak.
		2. Window Patrol Cologne	F/L Levy TS534 (A)	Jostle u/s, Carpet and Piperack.
			F/L Morris TS533 (M)	Jostle, Carpet and Piperack. Monica not fitted.
			W/O Stuart TS532 (N)	Jostle, Carpet and Piperack. Monica abandoned.

Date	Main Force Operations	Duty	Aircraft Launched	Remarks
7/8.1.45	Munich	Window Patrol	F/L Allnutt TS532 (N)	Jostle, Carpet and Piperack.
			F/L McPherson TS533 (M)	Jostle, Carpet and Piperack. Monica not fitted.
			F/L Stephenson TS527 (Q)	Jostle, Carpet and Piperack. Landed Manston, engine problems.
			F/L Dyck TS531 (B)	
			F/L Hastie TS523 (D)	Returned early, No.2 engine oil pressure.
			F/L Brigham TS524 (O)	Jostle, Carpet and Piperack. Window, Jostle u/s, Carpet, Piperack and Monica.
13/14.1.45	Saarbrücken	Jostle	F/L Dyck TS529 (C)	Jostle, Carpet and Piperack. Very little flak.
14/15.1.45	Leuna Dülmen	1. Jostle Patrol Grevenbroich	F/L Brigham TS524 (O)	Jostle u/s, Carpet. Monica not fitted.
			F/L Noseworthy TT336 (R)	Failed to return, shot down east of Antwerp.
		2. Southern Window Patrol	F/L Woodward TS529 (C)	Jostle, Carpet and Piperack. Monica abandoned.
			F/L Hastie TS523 (D)	Window, Carpet and Piperack.
		3. Jostle Patrol Dülmen	F/L Levy TS534 (A)	Jostle, Carpet and Piperack. Diverted Woodbridge.
		4. Northern Window Patrol	F/L Morris TS530 (G)	Window, Jostle u/s, Carpet, Piperack. Diverted Woodbridge.
			S/L McKnight TS525 (H)	Window, Jostle, Carpet, Piperack. Diverted Woodbridge.
			F/L Briscoe TS533 (M)	Window, Jostle, Carpet, Piperack. Diverted Woodbridge.
			F/L Allnutt TS532 (N)	Window, Jostle, Carpet, Piperack. Diverted Woodbridge.
			F/L Stephenson TS519 (S)	Window, Jostle, Carpet. Diverted Woodbridge.
16/17.1.45	Magdeburg Zeitz Brüx Wanne-Eickel	1. Window Patrol	S/L Carrington TS533 (M)	Window, Jostle, Carpet, Piperack.
			F/L Morris TS530 (G)	Window. No special equipment used, No.2 generator u/s.
			S/L McKnight TS525 (H)	Window, Jostle switched off, interference with intercom.
			F/L Briscoe TS532 (N)	Window, Jostle, Carpet, Piperack.
			F/L Croft TS519 (S)	Window, Jostle, Carpet, Piperack.
			F/L Hastie TS523 (D)	Window, Carpet and Piperack.
		2. Jostle Patrol Wanne-Eickel	F/L Woodward TS529 (C)	Jostle, Carpet and Piperack.
17/18.1.45	Minor ops	Window Patrol	F/L McPherson TS523 (D)	Window, Jostle, Carpet, Piperack, Monica. Diverted Foulsham.
			F/O Ball TS520 (J)	Window, Jostle, Carpet, Piperack, Monica. Diverted Foulsham. Returned early, pilot unwell.
			F/O Steele TS519 (S)	Returned early, No.1 engine turbo & flame damper.
			F/L Brigham TS524 (O)	
21/22.1.45	Minor ops	Window Patrol	F/L Croft TS519 (S)	Window, Carpet and Piperack.
			F/L Levy TS534 (A)	Window, Jostle no message to jam, Carpet and Piperack.
			F/L McPherson TS520 (J)	Window, Carpet and Piperack.
			F/L Morris TS531 (B)	Window, Jostle no message to jam, Carpet and Piperack. Returned on three engines.
22/23.1.45	Duisburg Gelsenkirchen	1. Window Patrol	F/L Hastie TS526 (T)	Returned early, Smoke & fumes in a/c from No.2 engine.
			F/O Ball TS532 (N)	Window, Carpet, Piperack and Monica.
			F/L Briscoe TS524 (O)	Window, Carpet, Piperack and Monica.
			F/O Sellars TS519 (S)	Window, Carpet, Piperack and Monica.
		2. Jostle Patrol Duisburg	F/L Woodward TS529 (C)	Jostle, Carpet, Piperack and Monica.
		3. Jostle Patrol Gelsenkirchen	S/L Carrington TS533 (M)	Jostle, Piperack. All special equipment failed due to u/s generator.

Date	Main Force Operations	Duty	Aircraft Launched	Remarks
28/29.1.45	Stuttgart	Window Patrol	W/O Stuart TS525 (H)	Window, Carpet and Piperack. Returned early due to fuel and oil leaks and flame damper trouble.
			F/L Dyck TT343 (K)	Window, Jostle u/s, Carpet, Piperack and Monica.
			F/O Sellars TS526 (T)	Window, Carpet, Piperack and Monica. Returned early & landed Woodbridge with fluctuating boost on all engines.
			S/L Carrington TS524 (O)	Window, Carpet, Piperack and Monica.
		Jostle Patrol	F/L Hastie TS523 (D)	Jostle, Carpet and Piperack.
			F/L Allnutt TS532 (N)	Jostle, Carpet, Piperack and Monica.
			F/L Croft TS519 (S)	Jostle, Carpet and Piperack. Monica not used.
			F/L Croft TS519 (S)	Jostle, Carpet and Piperack. Monica not used.
1/2.2.45	Ludwigshaven	Window Patrol	F/L Croft TS527 (Q)	Window, Jostle, Carpet, Piperack and Monica.
			F/L Dyck TS531 (B)	Window, Jostle not used, Carpet, Piperack and Monica.
			S/L McKnight TT343 (K)	Window. Special equipment not used, small fire on board.
			F/L Levy TS534 (A)	Window, Jostle interference, Carpet no signals to jam, Piperack and Monica.
			F/O Ball TS524 (O)	Window, Jostle not used, Carpet, Piperack and Monica.
		Jostle Patrol Mannheim	F/L Allnutt TS532 (N)	Window, Jostle not used, Carpet, Piperack and Monica.
		Jostle Patrol Siegen	F/L Hastie TS523 (D)	Jostle, Carpet and Piperack.
		Jostle Patrol Mainz	W/O Stuart TS530 (G)	Jostle, Carpet and Piperack.
2/3.2.45	Wiesbaden	Jostle Patrol Wanne-Eickel	S/L Carrington TS532 (N)	Returned early and landed at Woodbridge.
	Karlsruhe	Wanne-Eickel	F/L Woodward TS529 (C)	Jostle, Carpet and Piperack. Monica u/s.
		Window Patrol Mannheim	F/L Hastie TS532 (D)	Window, Jostle and Piperack.
			F/L Levy TS525 (H)	Window, Jostle, Carpet, Piperack and Monica.
			F/O Ball TS524 (O)	Window, Jostle went u/s, Carpet, Piperack and Monica.
			F/L Croft TS527 (Q)	Window, Carpet, Piperack and Monica.
			F/O Sellars TS526 (T)	Mission abandoned with oxygen problem.
		Jostle Patrol Karlsruhe	F/L McPherson TT343 (K)	Mission abandoned, failure of 20v AC supply.
3/4.2.45	Bottrop Dortmund	Window Patrol	F/O Thompson TS524 (O)	Window, Carpet and Piperack.
			F/O Sellars TS526 (T)	Window, Carpet, Piperack and Monica.
			F/L Allnutt TS532 (N)	Window, Carpet and Piperack.
			W/O Stuart TS527 (Q)	Window, Carpet and Piperack.
		Jostle Patrol Bottrop	S/L McKnight TS530 (G)	Jostle, Carpet not used as swamped by Jostle, Piperack.
		Jostle Patrol Dortmund	F/L McPherson TS 520 (J)	Jostle, Carpet and Piperack.

Date	Main Force Operations	Duty	Aircraft Launched	Remarks
4/5.2.45	Bonn Osterfeld Gelsenkirchen	Window Patrol	F/L Woodward TS529 (C)	Window, Jostle, Carpet and Piperack. Monica not fitted.
			F/O Ball TS524 (O)	Window, Carpet, Piperack and Monica.
			F/L Levy TT343 (K)	Window, Jostle no instructions to jam, Carpet, Piperack and Monica.
		Jostle Patrol Osterfeld	F/L Croft TS527 (Q)	Jostle, Carpet and Piperack.
		Jostle Patrol Gelsenkirchen	F/L Allnutt TS532 (N)	Jostle, Carpet and Piperack.
		Jostle Patrol Bonn	F/L Dyck TS532 (D)	Jostle, Carpet, Piperack and Monica.
			S/L Carrington TS533 (M)	Jostle, Carpet, Piperack and Monica.
7/8.2.45	Goch Kleve Dortmund-Ems Canal	Jostle Patrol Kleve	W/C Burnell TS529 (C)	Jostle, Carpet and Piperack.
		Jostle Patrol Hassum	F/O Thompson TS520 (J)	Jostle, Carpet and Piperack.
		Jostle Patrol Ladbergen	F/L Allnutt TS532 (N)	Jostle, Carpet and Piperack.
			F/L Dyck TS527 (Q)	Jostle, Carpet and Piperack.
		Window Patrol	F/L Brigham TS524 (O)	Window, Jostle not used, Carpet and Piperack. Monica not fitted.
			S/L McKnight TT343 (K)	Window, Jostle not used, Carpet and Piperack.
			F/L McPherson TS523 (D)	Window, Jostle not used, Carpet and Piperack.
8/9/2/45	Pölitz Wanne-Eickel Krefeld	Jostle Patrol	F/L McPherson TS531 (B)	Jostle no instructions to jam, Carpet and Piperack.
		Hohen-budberg	F/L Briscoe TS532 (N)	Jostle, Carpet and Piperack.
		Jostle Patrol Wanne-Eickel	S/L Carrington TS533 (M)	Jostle, Carpet and Piperack.
			F/O Ball TS524 (O)	Jostle no readings, Carpet and Piperack.
		Window Patrol	F/L Woodward TS530 (G)	Window, Jostle, Carpet and Piperack.
			F/L Morris TS523 (D)	Window, Jostle no brief to jam, Carpet and Piperack.
			F/O Thompson TS520 (J)	Window, Jostle no brief to jam, Carpet and Piperack.
			F/L Stephenson TS527 (Q)	Window, Jostle, Carpet and Piperack.
10/11.2.45	Minor ops	Window Patrol	F/L McPherson TS523 (D)	Window, Jostle, Carpet and Piperack.
			F/L Brigham TS532 (N)	Window, Jostle, Carpet and Piperack.
13/14.2.45	Dresden Böhlen	Southern Window Patrol	S/L McKnight TS343 (K)	Window, Jostle u/s, Carpet and Piperack.
			F/L Allnutt TS532 (N)	Window, Jostle and Carpet. Very quiet, no fighters.
		Northern Window Patrol	W/O Stuart TS534 (A)	Window, Jostle, Carpet and Piperack.
			F/O Thompson TS520 (J)	Window, Jostle went u/s, Carpet and Piperack.
			F/L Brigham TS524 (O)	Window, Jostle no instructions to jam, Carpet and Piperack.
			F/L McPherson TS529 (C)	Window, Jostle no brief to jam, Carpet and Piperack.
			F/L Morris TS530 (G)	Window, Jostle no brief to jam, Carpet and Piperack.
			F/L Stephenson TS527 (Q)	Window, Jostle no brief to jam, Carpet and Piperack.
			S/L Carrington TS533 (M)	Window, Jostle no brief to jam, Carpet and Piperack.
			F/L Hastie TS523 (J)	Window, Carpet and Piperack.
			F/L Briscoe (TS526 (T)	Window, Jostle no brief to jam, Carpet and Piperack.

Date	Main Force Operations	Duty	Aircraft Launched	Remarks
14/14.2.45	Chemnitz Rositz	Northern Window Patrol	F/L Dyck TS531 (B)	Window, Jostle, Carpet and Piperack.
			F/L McPherson TS523 (D)	Window, Jostle not used, Carpet and Piperack.
			F/L Allnutt TS343 (K)	Window, Jostle not used, Carpet and Piperack.
			S/L Carrington VB852 (P)	Window, Jostle, Carpet and Piperack.
			F/L Hastie TS529 (C)	Window, Carpet and Piperack.
		Southern Window Patrol	F/L Morris TS530 (G)	Window, Jostle not used, Carpet and Piperack.
			W/O Stuart TS534 (A)	Window, Jostle, Carpet and Piperack.
			F/L Briscoe TS532 (N)	Window, Jostle not used, Carpet and Piperack.
			F/L Stephenson TS533 (M)	Returned early, No.2 engine failure with runaway propeller.
18.2.45	Minor ops	Window Patrol	S/L McKnight TS534 (A)	Window, Jostle u/s, Carpet, Piperack u/s. Diverted North Creake.
			F/O Thompson TS529 (C)	Window, Carpet and Piperack. Diverted North Creake.
			F/O Sellars TS526 (T)	Window, Jostle, Carpet and Piperack. Diverted North Creake.
			F/L Croft TS519 (S)	Window, Carpet and Piperack. Diverted North Creake.
20/21.2.45	Dortmund Düsseldorf Monheim Mittelland Canal	Jostle Patrol Reisholm & Monheim	W/O Stuart TS534 (A)	Jostle, Carpet and Piperack.
			W/C Burnell (F/L Morris) TS530 (G)	Jostle, Carpet and Piperack.
			F/L Croft TS519 (S)	Jostle, Carpet and Piperack.
		Jostle Patrol Gravenhorst	F/L Dyck TT343 (K)	Jostle u/s, Carpet and Piperack.
			F/L Hastie TS533 (M)	Jostle and Carpet. Piperack not used.
		Northern Window Patrol	F/L Briscoe TS526 (T)	Jostle, Carpet and Piperack.
			F/L Woodward TS529 (C)	Window, Carpet and Piperack.
			F/L Brigham TS524 (O)	Window, Jostle, Carpet and Piperack.
			F/O Sellars VB852 (P)	Window, Carpet no signal received to jam, and Piperack.
			F/L Stephenson TS527 (T)	Window, Carpet and Piperack.
			F/O Thompson TS520 (J)	Shot down by fighters SE of Dortmund.
21/22.2.45	Duisburg Worms Mittelland Canal	Northern Window Patrol	W/O Stuart TS534 (A)	Window, Carpet and Piperack.
			F/L Brigham TS524 (O)	Window, Carpet and Piperack.
			F/L Briscoe TS526 (T)	Window, Carpet and Piperack.
		Jostle Patrol Gravenhorst	S/L McKnight TT343 (K)	Jostle, Carpet and Piperack.
			F/L Hastie TS529 (C)	Jostle, Carpet and Piperack.
			F/L Stephenson TS527 (Q)	Jostle, Carpet and Piperack.
		Jostle Patrol Worms	F/L Croft TS519 (S)	Jostle, Carpet and Piperack.
		Window Patrol South	F/L Allnutt TS533 (M)	Window, Jostle, Carpet and Piperack.
22/23.2.45	Minor ops	Window Patrol	F/L Dyck TS534 (A)	Window, Carpet and Piperack.
			F/L Woodward TS533 (M)	Window, Carpet and Piperack.
			F/L Morris TT343 (K)	Window, Carpet and Piperack.
			F/O Sellars TS519 (S)	Window, Carpet and Piperack.
23/24.2.45	Pforzheim Horten	Window Patrol Spoof to Neuss	F/O Ball TS534 (A)	Window, Carpet, Piperack. Diverted Carnaby.
			F/L Hastie TS523 (D)	Window, Carpet, Piperack. Diverted Carnaby.
			F/L Croft TS519 (S)	Window, Carpet, Piperack. Diverted Carnaby.
			F/L Brigham TS524 (O)	Returned early; No.1 flame damper burnt out, oxygen leak.
		Jostle Patrol Pforzheim	S/L McKnight TT343 (K)	Jostle, Carpet, Piperack. Diverted Carnaby.
			F/L Briscoe VB852 (P)	Jostle u/s, Carpet, Piperack. Diverted Carnaby.
			F/L Stephenson TS527 (Q)	Jostle, Carpet, Piperack. Diverted Carnaby.

Date	Main Force Operations	Duty	Aircraft Launched	Remarks
24/25.2.45	Minor ops	Window Patrol Neuss	F/L Woodward TS529 (C) P/O Ayres TS523 (D) F/L Morris TS530 (G) F/O Sellars TS524 (O)	Window, Jostle, Carpet, Piperack. Window, Carpet, Piperack. Window, Carpet, Piperack. Window, Carpet, Piperack.
27/28.2.45	Minor ops	Northern Window Patrol	F/O Ayres VB852 (P) F/O Ball TS530 (G) F/L McPherson TT343 (K) S/L Carrington TS533 (M) F/O Sellars TS519 (S) F/L Brigham TS524 (O) F/L Woodward TS529 (C)	Window, Jostle, Carpet, Piperack. Window, Carpet, Piperack. Window, Jostle, Carpet, Piperack. Window, Carpet, Piperack. Window, Carpet, Piperack. Window, Jostle, Carpet, Piperack. Window, Carpet, Piperack.
		Southern Window Patrol	F/L Levy TS534 (A)	Window, Carpet, Piperack.
28.2/1.3.45	No Main Force ops	Window Lake Constance	F/L Levy TS534 (A) F/L Hastie TS523 (D) F/L McPherson TS529 (C) W/C Burnell (F/L Young) VB852 (P) F/L Morris TS530 (G) F/L Croft TS533 (M) S/L McKnight TT343 (K) F/O Sellars TS532 (N)	Window, Jostle, Carpet, Piperack. Window, Carpet, Piperack. Window, Jostle, Carpet, Piperack. Window, Carpet, Piperack. Window, Carpet, Piperack. Window, Carpet, Piperack. Window, Carpet, Piperack. Returned after take-off, flames from No.1 & No.2 engines.
1/2.3.45	Minor ops	Window Patrol	F/O Ball TS523 (D) S/L Carrington TS532 (N)	Window, Jostle, Carpet, Piperack. Window, Carpet, Piperack.
2/3.3.45	No Main Force ops	Window Patrol Spoof	F/O Sellars TS526 (T) F/L McPherson TS531 (B) F/L Levy TS534 (A) F/L Woodward TS529 (C) F/L Stephenson VB852 (P) F/L Brigham TS524 (O) F/L Croft TS532 (N)	Window, Carpet, Piperack. Window, Carpet, Piperack. Window, Carpet, Piperack. Window, Carpet, Piperack. Window, Carpet, Piperack. Window, Carpet, Piperack. Window. Returned early, No.3 engine fire.
3/4.3.45	Kamen Dortmund-Ems Canal	Window Patrol	F/L Hastie TT343 (K) F/O Ball TS531 (B)	Window, Carpet, Piperack. Window, Carpet, Piperack. Attacked & damaged by Ju 88 during landing. Diverted Woodbridge.
		Jostle Patrol Kamen	F/L Morris TS530 (G) F/L Allnutt TS519 (S)	Jostle, Carpet, Piperack. Landed Brawdy. Jostle, Carpet, Piperack. Damaged over base, landed Brawdy.
		Jostle Patrol Ladbergen	W/O Stuart TS529 (C) S/L Carrington TS533 (M)	Jostle, Carpet, Piperack. Jostle, Carpet, Piperack.
5/6.3.45	Chemnitz Böhlen	Window Patrol	F/L Woodward TS529 (C) F/L Levy TT343 (K)	Window, Carpet, Piperack. Window, Jostle no instructions to jam, Carpet, Piperack.
			P/O Ayres VB852 (P) F/L Croft TS519 (S) F/O Sellars TS527 (Q)	Window, Jostle, Carpet. Window, Carpet, Piperack. Window, Carpet, Piperack. No.4 engine u/s, landed Woodbridge.
7/8.3.45	Dessau Hemmingstedt Harburg	Southern Window Patrol	F/L Hastie TT343 (K) F/L Allnutt VB852 (P) F/L McPherson TS529 (C) F/L Croft TS519 (S) S/L Carrington TS533 (M) F/L Morris TS530 (G)	Window, Jostle, Carpet, Piperack. Window, Carpet, Piperack. Window, Jostle, Carpet, Piperack. Window, Carpet, Piperack. Window, Carpet, Piperack. Window, Carpet, Piperack.
		Jostle Patrol Hemmingstedt	F/L Brigham TS524 (O) F/L Briscoe TS526 (T)	Jostle, Carpet, Piperack. Jostle, Carpet, Piperack

Date	Main Force Operations	Duty	Aircraft Launched	Remarks
8/9.3.45	Hamburg Kassel	Jostle Patrol Hamburg	F/O Sellars VB852 (P) P/O Ayres TS519 (S)	Jostle, Carpet, Piperack. Jostle, Carpet, Piperack.
		Jostle Patrol Kassel	F/L Dyck TS526 (T) F/O Ball TS530 (G)	Jostle, Carpet, Piperack. Jostle, Carpet, Piperack.
9/10.3.45	Minor ops	Window Patrol Spoof to Ruhr	F/L Levy TS534 (A) F/L Woodward TS533 (M) F/L Allnutt VB852 (P)	Window, Jostle, Carpet, Piperack. Window, Carpet, Piperack. Window, Jostle, Carpet, Piperack.
10/11.3.45	Minor ops	Window Patrol Spoof to Münster	P/O Stuart TS534 (A) F/L Dyck TT343 (K) F/L Croft TS519 (S) S/L Carrington TS533 (M)	Window, Carpet, Piperack. Window, Carpet, Piperack. Window, Carpet, Piperack. Window, Carpet, Piperack.
13/14.3.45	Gelsenkirchen Herne	Window Patrol	F/L Briscoe TS526 (T)	Window, Jostle, Carpet, Piperack. Diverted Swannington.
			F/L Stephenson TS519 (S) F/L Hastie TS524 (O) S/L McKnight TS534 (A)	Window, Carpet, Piperack. Diverted. Window, Carpet, Piperack. Diverted. Window, Jostle, Carpet, Piperack. Diverted.
14/15.3.45	Homberg Lützkendorf Zweibrücken	Window Patrol Homberg	F/O Cairney TS524 (O) F/O Ayres VB852 (P)	Window, Carpet, Piperack. Jostle, Carpet, Piperack.
		Jostle Patrol Homberg	F/O Bowell TS534 (A) F/L Mann TS527 (Q)	Jostle, Carpet, Piperack. Jostle, Carpet, Piperack. Landed Manston short of fuel.
15/16.3.45	Hagen Misburg	Jostle Patrol Hagen	F/L Ball TS534 (A) F/L Woodward TS529 (C)	Jostle, Carpet, Piperack. Jostle, Carpet, Piperack.
		Window Patrol	S/L Carrington TS519 (S) F/O Sellars VB852 (P) F/L Allnutt TS524 (O)	Window, Jostle, Carpet. Window, Jostle, Carpet, Piperack. Window, Jostle u/s, Carpet, Piperack.
16/17.3.45	Nuremberg Würzburg	Window Patrol	P/O Stuart TS529 (C) F/L Stephenson TS532 (N) F/L Briscoe TS526 (T) F/L Wills TS519 (S)	Window, Carpet, Piperack. Window, Carpet, Piperack. Window, Carpet, Piperack. Returned early, No.3 engine petrol & oil leak.
		Jostle Patrol Würzburg	F/L Levy TS534 (A) F/L Dyck TT343 (K)	Jostle, Carpet, Piperack. Jostle, Carpet, Piperack.
18/19.3.45	Hanau Witten	Window Patrol	F/O Ball TS525 (H) F/L Levy TS534 (A) F/L Briscoe TS526 (T) F/O Bowell TS527 (Q)	Window, Carpet, Piperack. Window, Carpet, Piperack. Window, Carpet, Piperack. Returned early from base area, No.2 engine problem.
		Jostle Patrol Hanau	F/L Woodward TS529 (C)	Jostle, Carpet, Piperack.
		Jostle Patrol	S/L McKnight TT343 (K) F/O Cairney TS524 (O)	Jostle no request to jam, Carpet, Piperack. Jostle no request to jam, Carpet, Piperack.
20/21.3.45	Böhlen Hemmingstedt	Window Patrol Kassel	F/L Stephenson TS527 (Q) F/L Allnutt TS532 (N) P/O Stuart TS534 (A) F/O Bowell TS525 (H) F/O Morris TS530 (G) S/L Carrington TS533 (M) F/L Mann VB852 (P) F/O Ayres TS526 (T)	Shot down SW of Kassel by Hptm Johannes Hager.
		Jostle Patrol Hemmingstedt	W/C Burnell (F/L Dyck) TT343 (K)	

Date	Main Force Operations	Duty	Aircraft Launched	Remarks
21/22.3.45	Bochum Hamburg	Northern Window Patrol	S/L McKnight TT343 (K)	Window, Carpet, Piperack. 1 a/c seen shot down
		Southern Window Patrol	F/L Ball TS534 (A)	Window, Jostle, Carpet, Piperack.
			F/L Woodward TS529 (C)	Window, Carpet, Piperack. Hit by flak.
			F/L Morris TS530 (G)	Window, Carpet, Piperack.
			F/L Croft TS533 (M)	Window, Jostle, Carpet, Piperack.
			F/L Allnutt TS532 (N)	Window, Carpet, Piperack.
			F/L Brigham TS525 (H)	Window, Carpet, Piperack.
			F/L Briscoe VB852 (P)	Window, Jostle, Carpet, Piperack.
22/23.3.45	Minor ops	Window Patrol	P/O Stuart TS534 (A)	Window, Carpet, Piperack.
			F/O Bowell TS525 (H)	Window, Jostle u/s, Carpet, Piperack.
			F/L Dyck TT343 (K)	Window, Carpet, Piperack.
			F/O Cairney TS532 (N)	Window, Carpet, Piperack.
			F/L Stephenson TS527 (Q)	Window, Carpet, Piperack.
			S/L Carrington TS533 (M)	Window, Jostle, Carpet, Piperack.
			F/L Croft TS529 (C)	Window, Carpet, Piperack.
23/24.3.45	Wesel	Window Patrol	F/L Hastie TS529 (C)	Window, Carpet, Piperack.
			F/L Morris TS530 (G)	Window, Carpet, Piperack.
			F/L Brigham TS533 (M)	Window, Carpet, Piperack.
			F/L Allnutt TS532 (N)	Window, Carpet, Piperack.
			F/L Mann VB852 (P)	Window, Carpet, Piperack.
			F/L Ball TT343 (K)	Returned after 20 minutes, unable to retract undercarriage.
24/25.3.45	Minor ops	Window Patrol Spoof	F/L Dyck TS530 (G)	Window, Carpet, Piperack.
			F/O Ball TS525 (H)	Window, Carpet, Piperack.
			S/L McKnight TT343 (K)	Window, Carpet, Piperack.
			P/O Stuart TS533 (M)	Window, Carpet, Piperack.
			F/O Cairney TS532 (N)	Window, Carpet, Piperack.
			F/L Briscoe VB852 (P)	Window, Carpet, Piperack.
			F/L Croft TS519 (S)	Window, Carpet, Piperack.
27/28.3.45	Minor ops	Window Patrol	F/O Robson VB852 (P)	Window, Carpet.
			F/L Wills TS519 (S)	Window, Carpet. Diverted North Creake, bad weather.
30/31.3.45	Minor ops	Window Patrol	F/L Levy TS534 (A)	Window, Carpet, Piperack.
			F/L Woodward TS529 (C)	Window, Carpet, Piperack.
			F/O Sellars VB852 (P)	Window, Carpet, Piperack.
			F/L Stephenson TS527 (Q)	Window, Carpet, Piperack.
2/3.4.45	Minor ops	Window Patrol Spoof on Hamburg	F/L Hastie TS525 (H)	Window, Carpet, Piperack.
			F/L Morris TS530 (G)	Window, Carpet, Piperack.
			F/L Briscoe VB852 (P)	Window, Carpet, Piperack.
			F/L Brigham TS519 (S)	Window, Carpet, Piperack.
			P/O Stuart TS534 (A)	Window, Jostle no request to jam, Carpet, Piperack.
			F/O Bowell VB904 (J)	Window, Carpet, Piperack.
			F/L Mann TS533 (M)	Window, Jostle, Carpet, Piperack.
			F/O Pocock TS531 (B)	Window, Carpet, Piperack.
			F/L Allnutt TS532 (N)	Window, Carpet, Piperack.
			S/L McKnight TT343 (K)	Window, Carpet, Piperack.

Date	Main Force Operations	Duty	Aircraft Launched	Remarks
4/5.4.45	Harburg Leuna Lützkendorf	Jostle Patrol Leuna	F/L Wills TS533 (M)	Jostle, Carpet, Piperack.
		Jostle Patrol Lützkendorf	F/L Stephenson TS527 (Q)	Jostle, Carpet, Piperack.
		Window Patrol	F/O Cairney TS532 (N)	Window, Carpet, Piperack.
			F/L Levy TS534 (A)	Window, Jostle, Carpet, Piperack.
			F/L Ball TT343 (K)	Window, Carpet, Piperack.
			P/O Stuart TS525 (H)	Window, Carpet, Piperack.
			F/L Brigham TS524 (O)	Window, Jostle, Carpet, Piperack.
			F/O Sellars VB852 (P)	Window, Carpet, Piperack.
			F/L Woodward TS529 (C)	Window, Carpet, Piperack.
			F/O Bowell VB904 (J)	Window, Carpet, Piperack.
			F/L Croft TS519 (S)	Window, Carpet, Piperack.
			F/L Dyck TS531 (B)	Window, Carpet, Piperack. Fuel leak, abandoned op diverted Juvincourt.
7/8.4.45	Molbis	Jostle Patrol	F/L Morris TS530 (G)	Jostle, Carpet, Piperack.
8/9.4.45	Hamburg Lützkendorf Hamburg	Jostle Patrol	F/L Hastie TS530 (G)	Jostle, Carpet, Piperack. Flak damage No.2 engine, diverted Barford St.John due to weather.
		Jostle Patrol Lützkendorf	F/L Croft TS519 (S)	Jostle, Carpet, Piperack. Diverted due to weather.
		Southern Window Patrol	F/L Levy TS534 (A)	Window, Carpet, Piperack.
			S/L Carrington TS525 (H)	Window, Carpet, Piperack. Flak damage No.1 engine. Weather diversion.
			F/L Ball TT343 (K)	Window, Carpet, Piperack. Weather diversion.
		Northern Window Patrol	F/L Woodward TS529 (C)	Window, Carpet, Piperack. Weather diversion Wickenby.
			F/L Mann TS532 (N)	Window, Carpet, Piperack. Weather diversion Ludford Magna.
			F/O Sellars VB852 (P)	Window, Carpet, Piperack. Weather diversion.
			F/L Stephenson TS527 (Q)	Window, Carpet, Piperack. Weather diversion.
			F/O Pocock VD245(R)	Window, Carpet, Piperack. Weather diversion.
			F/L Dyck TS531 (B)	Window, Carpet, Piperack. Weather diversion.
9/10.4.45	Kiel	Window Patrol	F/O Cairney TS527 (Q)	Window, Carpet, Piperack.
			F/L Brigham TS532 (N)	Window, Carpet, Piperack.
			F/O Robson VB904 (J)	Abandoned op due to lateness caused by changing weather.
10/11.4.45	Leipzig Plauen	Window Patrol Leipzig	F/L Morris TS529 (C)	Window, Carpet, Piperack.
			F/L Mann TS519 (S)	Window, Jostle, Carpet, Piperack. Diverted Foulsham.
			F/O Bowell TS531 (B)	Window, Carpet, Piperack. Landed France short of fuel.
		Jostle Patrol Plauen	F/O Sellars TS532 (N)	Jostle u/s, Carpet, Piperack.
13/14.4.45	Kiel	Jostle Patrol Kiel	F/L Stephenson TS527 (Q)	Jostle, Carpet, Piperack.
		Window Patrol	F/L Hastie TS523 (D)	Window, Carpet, Piperack.
			F/L Ball TS534 (A)	Window, Jostle no request to jam, Carpet, Piperack.
			F/O Robson TS532 (N)	Window, Carpet, Piperack.
			F/L Croft TS519 (S)	Window, Carpet, Piperack.

Date	Main Force Operations	Duty	Aircraft Launched	Remarks
14/15.4.45	Potsdam	Jostle Patrol Potsdam	S/L Carrington TS527 (Q)	Jostle, Carpet, Piperack.
		Southern Window Patrol	F/L Levy VB904 (J)	Window, Jostle, Carpet, Piperack.
			F/O Sellars VB852 (P)	Window, Jostle, Carpet, Piperack. Landed Manston port wing on fire.
			F/L Mann TS519 (S)	Window, Jostle, Carpet, Piperack. Attacked by Ju 88.
			F/O Bowell TS523 (D)	Returned unable to climb, landed Woodbridge.
15/16.4.45	Minor ops	Window Patrol Lechfeld	F/L Brigham TS533 (M)	Window, Jostle, Carpet, Piperack.
			F/L Hastie VB904 (J)	Window, Carpet, Piperack.
			P/O Stuart TT343 (K)	Window, Jostle no request to jam, Carpet, Piperack.
16/17.4.45	Pilsen Schwandorf	Jostle Patrol Pilsen	F/L Briscoe TS533 (M)	Jostle, Carpet, Piperack.
		Jostle Patrol	F/L Croft TS519 (S)	Jostle, Carpet, Piperack.
		Southern Window Patrol	F/O Bowell TS534 (A)	Window, Jostle, Carpet, Piperack.
			F/O Pocock VB904 (J)	Window, Jostle, Carpet, Piperack.
			F/L Ball TT343 (K)	Window, Carpet, Piperack.
			W/C Burnell (F/L Stephenson) TS527 (Q)	Window, Jostle, Carpet, Piperack.
17/18.4.45	Cham	Window Patrol Ingolstadt	F/O Robson VB852 (P)	Window, Jostle u/s, Carpet u/s.
			S/L Carrington TS533 (M)	Window, Jostle, Carpet, Piperack not used.
			F/L Levy VB904 (J)	Window, Jostle, Carpet, Piperack not used.
		Jostle Patrol Cham	F/L Briscoe TS519 (S)	Jostle, Carpet.
18/19.4.45	Komotau	Window Patrol	P/O Stuart TS532 (N)	Window, Jostle no request to jam, Carpet.
			F/O Sellars VD249 (T)	Window, Jostle, Carpet.
		Jostle Patrol Komotau	F/L Wills Fortress KJ118 (H)	1st Fortress op. Abandoned No.4 engine u/s.
19/20.4.45	Minor ops	Window Patrol	F/L Stephenson VD249 (T)	Window, Jostle no request to jam, Carpet, Piperack.
		Spoof into Denmark	F/O Pocock TS521 (F)	Window, Jostle, Carpet, Piperack.
			F/L Brigham TS532 (N)	Window, Jostle, Carpet, Piperack.
			F/L Bremness Fortress KJ121 (B)	Window, Jostle no request to jam, Carpet.
22/23.4.45	Minor ops	Window Patrol	F/O Sellars VB852 (P)	Window, Carpet, Piperack.
			F/L Stephenson TS527 (Q)	Window, Carpet, Piperack.
			F/O Robson TS533 (M)	Window, Carpet, Piperack.
			F/L Levy TS519 (S)	Window, Carpet, Piperack.
			F/L Wills Fortress KJ118 (H)	Window, Carpet, Piperack.
		Central Window Patrol	F/L Brigham TS532 (N)	Window, Jostle, Carpet, Piperack.
			F/O Stuart TS521 (F)	Window, Jostle, Carpet, Piperack.
		Eastern Window	F/L Bremness Fortress KJ121 (B)	Window, Jostle, Carpet, Piperack.
			F/O Cairney VD249 (T)	Returned early, electrical failure.
23/24.4.45	Kiel	Window Patrol	S/L McKnight Fortress KJ118 (H)	Window, Jostle, Carpet, Piperack.
		Spoof on Lübeck	F/O Pocock TT 343 (K)	Window, Jostle no signals to jam, Carpet, Piperack.
			F/O Cairney TS530 (G)	Window, Jostle, Carpet, Piperack.
24/25.4.45	Minor ops	Window Patrol Munich	F/O Sellars VB852 (P)	Window, Carpet.
			F/L Mann TS527 (Q)	Window, Jostle, Carpet. Shot up by flak.
			F/L Brigham TS532 (N)	Window, Carpet. Returned early, fuel leak.
			F/L Bremness Fortress KJ121 (B)	Window, Carpet.

Date	Main Force Operations	Duty	Aircraft Launched	Remarks
2/3.5.45	Kiel	Central Window Patrol Spoof	S/L McKnight Fortress KJ118 (H)	Window, Jostle, Carpet, Piperack.
			F/L Wills Fortress KH998 (C)	Window, Jostle, Carpet, Piperack.
		Kiel	F/O Cairney Fortress KJ113 (D)	Window, Carpet, Piperack.
			F/L Bremness Fortress KJ121 (B)	Window, Carpet, Piperack.
			F/O Stuart VD249 (T)	Returned early, unable to make up time after delayed take-off.

APPENDIX THREE
223 Squadron Personnel

1. Squadron Executives August 1944 to July 1945

Squadron Commanders

Wg Cdr D J McGlinn (temporary OC)	23 August-22 September 1944
Wg Cdr H H Burnell DSO AFC	22 September 1944-11 July 1945

*Assumed command of RAF Oulton with effect from
12 July 1945. DSO awarded 21 September 1945 for
service with 223 Squadron.*

Sqn Ldr R Van der Bok DFC and bar	12 July-29 July 1945

OC A Flight

Sqn Ldr R E C McKnight DFC	29 August 1944-16 June 1945

*DFC awarded 16 November 1945 for
service with 223 Squadron.*

OC B Flight

Sqn Ldr A J Carrington DFC	29 August 1944-25 April 1945
Sqn Ldr S B Wills	26 April 1944-19 June 1945

Adjutant

Flt Lt B James	27 August 1944-28 May 1945
Flt Lt A L West	1 June 1945-

Navigation Leader

Flt Lt D J Furner DFC	30 August-30 September 1944

*DFC awarded 12 November 1943 for service with
214 Squadron.*

Flt Lt P F O'Leary DFC	1 October 1944-

*DFC awarded 16 February 1945 for service with
223 Squadron.*

Engineer Leader

Flt Lt R W Barrett DFM	7 September 1944-

Gunnery Leader

Fg Off J R Wolff	28 August-19 September 1944
Flt Lt W Wells DFC	19 September 1944-

Also Fighter Affiliation Officer

Signals Leader

Flt Lt J H Cook DFM	July 1945

Special Signals Leader

Flt Lt N V O O Haveland	20 September 1944-

Special Signals (Ground) Officer

Fg Off J A Golder   19 September 1944-1 January 1945

Also Radar, with posting of Plt Off G J Malik
on 20 November 1944

Radar Officer (Air)

Plt Off G J Malik   10 October-20 November 1944

Special Signals (Ground) and Radar under
Fg Off J A Golder

2. Sergeant Air Gunners Posted from 10 AGS to 223 Squadron, September 1944

Brockhurst E D T	Nisbet G
Davies LS	Norwood L
Denney J R	Pollard T W J
Dobson E	Punnett E L
Fuller D J	Simons A G V
Jones R A D	Smith K
Jones W	Stirrop E
Lawrence R C	Stone K L
Lovatt P	Sykes H C
Matthews C L	Tonkin A E
McEwan R	Trail J J
McGregor J T	Tucker G N
McIver H	Turpie W R
McLaren J	Vowler L J
Moran L	Whittaker E E
Morton F G	Wilshaw D G
Murray J	Witts P A
Newman P	Wrigley T
Nicholls J E	Tofield R C

3. Decorations Awarded For Service With 223 Squadron[1]

DSO

Wg Cdr Harold Hamlyn Burnell AFC	21 September 1945[2]
Flt Lt Stanley Woodward DFM	21 September 1945

DFC

Sqn Ldr Ralph Edwin Caldwell McKnight	16 November 1945
Flt Lt Alan Allnutt	22 May 1945
Flt Lt Jack Brigham	26 October 1945
Flt Lt John Leigh Charlton Briscoe	16 November 1945
Flt Lt Mark Levy	6 November 1945
Flt Lt Anthony Edward Lloyd Morris	21 September 1945

Notes:

1. Details of awards drawn from *Honour The Air Forces – Awards to the RAF & Dominion Air Forces During WWII*, Michael Maton. Token Publishing Ltd, Honiton, 2004.
2. Date of promulgation of the award in the *London Gazette*.

4. Squadron Personnel Who Flew Liberator Operations

Notes:

1. Crews are listed in order of starting operations with the squadron.
2. Individuals are listed in the order they flew with the crew.
3. Total operations flown with the crew are shown in brackets after each name. This number applies to take-offs for operations, and does not take account of early returns or credits for half-operations, which are listed in Appendix 2.
4. Rank shown is the highest held during their operational flying period.
5. Air gunner's position in the aircraft detailed where known, i.e. F (front), M (mid upper), W (waist) and R (rear).
6. Air bombers are listed, but their actual crew function is uncertain; could be air gunner, navigation assistant or possibly Window dropper.
7. * after the name indicates Royal Canadian Air Force (RCAF). ** indicates Royal Australian Air Force (RAAF).

Captain	2nd pilot	Navigator	Wireless Operator	Flight Engineer	Special Operator	Air Gunner	Air Bomber
S/L A	F/O T E Wallis (25)	P/O R Wade (31)	F/S W Jewell (33)	P/O A A Gibbon (33)	F/O L W Fairbanks (8)	F/S E Sorrell (28)	
Carrington OC	W/C H H Burnell (2)	F/O H Booth* (1)	F/S F Brannigan (1)	Sgt R Hartop (1)	F/O R Flint (23)	Sgt G Nisbet (32)	
B Flt (34)	Sgt J Kendall (1)	F/L F Freake (1)			F/O H L Smith (1)	Sgt J Murray (33)	
1st op 19.9.44	F/O J Schnarr* (1)	W/O L R Lovitt (1)			F/O J J Denn (1)	F/O J R Wolff (R) (9)	
Last 17/18.4.45					F/O T Morris (1)	F/L M Wheaton (23)	
					F/O R Watchorn (1)	Sgt R Stott (1)	
					W/O L T Foster (20)	F/S E Longden (1)	
					W/O R J Tanner (1)	F/S T Agnew* (5)	
					F/L N V O O Haveland (2)	F/S D J Fuller (2)	
					Sgt W R Legge (1)	F/S F J Rankin* (2)	
					W/O A C Cole (1)	Sgt K Smith (1)	
					F/S J Walters (1)	F/L W Wells (1)	
					F/S J Goudie (1)	F/S D K Clark (1)	
						F/S J Mellers (1)	
						Sgt A E Tonkin (1)	
						F/O T F Sherry (2)	
						F/O G Trail (1)	

Captain	2nd pilot	Navigator	Wireless Operator	Flight Engineer	Special Operator	Air Gunner	Air Bomber
S/L R E C	F/S P G Nash (31)	F/O R M Wylie* (28)	F/S R Stark (29)	F/S B Le Fondre (29)	F/O L Boot (24)	F/S G F Schutes (M) (30)	F/O J Burns (14)
McKnight* (31)	F/O A C Ball (1)	F/O L W Howell (1)	F/O R V Piper (1)	P/O A A Gibbon (1)	F/O W Thomson (22)	F/S D H Thorpe (W) (30)	
1st op 22.9.44		F/L P F O'Leary (1)	F/O J E Dow (1)	F/O L W Lomas (1)	Sgt J H Hinton (1)	Sgt W Jones (W) (30)	
Last 2/3.4.45		F/O E Gaiser* (1)			W/O L T Foster (1)	Sgt C Brooks (R) (30)	
See also Fortress					F/O J Blakeley (1)	Sgt E L Punnett (1)	
ops list					F/L N V O O Haveland (1)	F/S E G Page (1)	
					F/O W H Mennell (1)	F/S A G Bryant (1)	
					F/O W V Lane (1)	F/O W G Holley* (1)	
					F/O L F Rendle (1)	Sgt J T McGregor (1)	
					W/O T A Hughes (1)		

F/L A Allnutt (38) 1st op 23.9.44 Last 2/3.4.45	P/O I T Leslie* (32) F/O J Robson (3) F/O J Schnarr* (1) F/S P G Nash (1)	F/O C F Campbell** (13) F/S R Tabah (7) plus 6 as 2nd nav F/O R Bass* (3) F/O R M Wylie* (1) F/O H Booth* (1) F/O J R Maunsell (19)	F/S E Laraway (38)	Sgt D Manners (37) Sgt D Marsden (1) F/O J White (23) P/O T Morris (1) F/O H L Smith (1) F/O R Flint (1) F/O H E Snelgrove (3) W/O R J Tanner (1) F/L L W Fairbanks (5) F/O A Williams (2) F/O W S Stephens (1) F/O G A Gamble (1) Sgt J R Bancroft (2) Sgt E J Downs (1) Sgt W R Legge (1) W/O R J Housden (2) W/O T A Hughes (1)	F/O W Adamson (24)	W/O S E Millbank (1) F/O R N Godwin (2) Sgt R G Smith (2) F/O A L Haynes (1)	F/S D Townsend (29) F/S T J Adams (38) Sgt T W J Pollard (13) Sgt J J Trail (36) F/O J R Wolff (R) (1) Sgt G N Tucker (28) F/S R Stott (1) Sgt H McIver (1) F/S T Skinner* (1) Sgt J T McGregor (1) Sgt L Norwood (1) F/S G F Schutes (2) F/S C G J Brooks (1) F/S J Mellers (1) Sgt J R Denney (1) Sgt D G Wilshaw (1) Sgt R McEwan (1) Unidentified (1)
F/L M Levy (36) 1st op 23.9.44 Last 22/23.4.45	F/O C Boaden (34) F/O D Theaker (1)	F/O R A G Simmons (36)	Sgt D Bryant (7) F/O W Bridgeman (28) Unidentified (1)	F/S R D Pryce (31) Sgt D Marsden (2) F/S A Malone (1) Unidentified (2)	F/O C A Gamble (23) F/O W S Stephens (21) P/O E P Youngs (1) F/O J J Denn (2) W/O R J Housden (2) F/O R N Godwin (2) Sgt E J Downs (1) F/L L W Fairbanks (5) W/O C Fairbairn (5) F/O T Davies (1) F/O A S Knight (2) W/O T A Hughes (1) Sgt J R Bancroft (1) F/S D G Ridgway (1) F/S S Dodd (1) F/S C S Ward (1) W/O D L Wynn (1)		F/O A Rudd (R) (17) Sgt J E Nicholls (35) Sgt R McEwan (28) Sgt W R Turpie (35) F/S N S Pearson (34) F/O J R Wolff (R) (10) Sgt K Smith (1) Unidentified (1)

Captain	2nd pilot	Navigator	Wireless Operator	Flight Engineer	Special Operator	Air Gunner	Air Bomber
F/L V D Croft (39)	F/O F Carroll (36)	W/O J F Healy (8)	F/S L Lucas (34)	Sgt J M Stewart (2)	F/O G Watchorn (25)	Sgt L J Vowler (7)	F/S E J Saddington (2)
1st op 25.9.44	F/O J Robson (2)	F/L A H Williams (1)	F/L J H Cook (1)	F/O W C Weir (35)	F/O G A Kennerley (25)	F/S J R Richards (R) (38)	
Last 16/17.4.45		F/O W Simpson (2)	F/S D S Lightfoot (1)	Sgt J D Moir (1)	F/O H E Snelgrove (1)	Sgt R C Tofield (W) (39)	
		plus 7 as 2nd nav	F/S F Brannigan (1)	F/O R C Diment (1)	F/O F Mann (1)	Sgt T H Sykes (W) (39)	
		F/O H Booth* (2)	F/S W Nolan (2)		W/O A C Cole (1)	F/O R P Martin (25)	
		Unidentified (3)			F/O L W Fairbanks (4)	F/O G Trail (1)	
					F/O A Williams (4)	Sgt R McEwan (1)	
					F/O L F Green (1)	F/S J Mellers (M) (7)	
					F/O R N Godwin (1)	F/S T Agnew (R) (1)	
					W/O R J Housden (2)	F/S L O'Brennan (1)	
					F/S D J Cornish (1)	F/S F J Rankin* (1)	
					F/S D Hunter (1)	Sgt S J Murray (1)	
						F/S D H Thorpe (1)	
						P/O J R McAdam (1)	

Captain	2nd pilot	Navigator	Wireless Operator	Flight Engineer	Special Operator	Air Gunner	Air Bomber
F/L F Stephenson (32)	F/O D Theaker (29)	F/L A H Williams (28)	W/O R E Collins (31)	F/S G W Williams (27)	F/O A W Barker (23)	F/S E Longden (M) (32)	F/S E J Saddington (1)
1st op 25.9.44	W/C H H Burnell (1)	F/O W Simpson (2)	F/S F Laraway (1)	Sgt D Marsden (4)	F/O A Boyle (24)	Sgt T Wrigley (W) (18)	
Last 22/23.4.45	F/O J Schnarr* (1)	plus 7 as 2nd nav		Unidentified (1)	F/O A Williams (1)	Sgt A E Tonkin (W) (25)	
		F/O R Bass* (2)			Sgt R J Smith (1)	F/S T Agnew* (W) (21)	
					F/S H Brain (3)	W/O W Greatorex (M) (1)	
					F/S J Walters (3)	F/S D J Fuller (2)	
						Sgt R McEwan (2)	
						F/O L I George (2)	
						Sgt L T O'Brennan (10)	
						Sgt C L Matthews (R) (1)	
						F/S C Brooks (R) (1)	
						F/S G F Schutes (2)	
						W/O F J Rankin* (1)	
						F/S I C Rice (2)	
						F/S C C Hughes (1)	
						Sgt J R Denney (1)	
						Sgt L S Davies (1)	
						F/S D Townsend (3)	
						Unidentified (3)	

Captain	2nd pilot	Navigator	Wireless Operator	Flight Engineer	Special Operator	Air Gunner	Air Bomber
F/L S Woodward (40)	F/O S F McRae (39)	F/O A McMillan (40)	F/S H Harding (40)	F/S J F Feltwell (39)	F/O C D Forrest (24)	Sgt A H Ward (W) (35)	
1st op 26.9.44	W/C H H Burnell (1)			Sgt B Le Fondre (1)	F/O A Featherstone (26)	Sgt J M McClaren (W) (40)	
Last 8/9.4.45					F/O H L Smith (1)	Sgt C L Matthews (R) (40)	

F/O J W Young* (9)

1st op 27.9.44
Last 2/3.12.44
Note: crew reappeared on ops 28 Feb/1 Mar 1945 with F/O J Robson as captain

F/O J Robson (9)   F/O R W Bass* (8)   F/S W Nolan (9)   Sgt A Malone (9)

F/W Simpson (1)

P/O W A Williams (6)
F/O R N Godwin (7)
F/O D A Boyle (2)
F/O W A Barker (2)

F/O J Borque* (9)
F/S R G Sunstrum* (9)
Sgt K Smith (R) (9)
Sgt E J White (W) (9)

F/O A Williams (1)
W/O O G Burntenshaw (10)
W/O R J Tanner (9)
F/O R N Godwin (2)
F/O A S Knight (2)
W/O T A Hughes (1)

W/O W Greatorex (M) (35)
Sgt P A Witts (F) (11)
Sgt F G Morton (3)
Sgt R McEwan (W) (1)
F/O J Bourque* (2)
Sgt G N Tucker (1)
F/S D H Thorpe (1)
Unidentified (1) possibly Sgt A H Ward

F/O F S Pemberton (9)

F/L J Brigham (33)   F/O C T Reiser* (33)   F/O W H G Thomas (30)   W/O D B Johnson (32)   F/S D L Jones (32)

1st op 28.9.44
Last 24/25.4.45

F/O H Booth* (1) plus 2 as 2nd nav
F/S R Tabah (1)
F/S P S Morris (1)

W/O T K Chung* (1)   Sgt D Marsden (1)

F/O W S Reed (24)
F/O L F Green (25)
F/O C E Payne (3)
P/O R Fawcett (2)
Sgt J K Chapple (1)
Sgt S Dodd (1)
Sgt J R Bancroft (1)
W/O R J Thouseden (1)
F/S J Goudie (1)
F/S D Hunter (2)
Sgt H Waugh (1)

W/O F J Rankin* (M) (29)
Sgt J R Denney (W) (32)
Sgt G Nisbet (F) (2)
Sgt L S Davies (W) (32)
Sgt L J Vowler (F) (2)
Sgt P Newman (F) (5)
F/S A J Polmeardam (1)
F/S D J Fuller (W) (1)
W/O T K Chung* (M) (1)
F/S D H Thorpe (1)
F/S L O'Brennan (1)

Captain	2nd pilot	Navigator	Wireless Operator	Flight Engineer	Special Operator	Air Gunner	Air Bomber
F/L A L Dyck* (36) 1st op 28.9.44 Last 8/9.4.45	P/O J Schnarr* (19) Sgt A Levens* (1) Sgt J Kendall (3) Sgt L D Thorne (1) F/O E Reiser* (1) F/O G Bremness* (1)	P/O E Gaiser* (35) F/O L Hudson (1)	W/O T K Chung* (36)	P/O A A Gibbon (1) Sgt G Levy (5) Sgt J M Stewart (29) Unidentified (1)	P/O T Morris (26) P/O W H Mennell (25) F/O J J Denn (1) W/O T Foster (1) F/O W A Williams (2) W/O C Fairbairn (1) F/S E A Jobson (1) F/O R N Godwin (2) Sgt R J Smith (1) F/O L F Rendle (2) F/O F Rowe (2) F/S E J Downs (3) W/O J R Bancroft (1)	P/O W Holley* (W) (30) F/S G Davies (R) (33) Sgt R A D Jones (F) (2) Sgt E L Punnett (W) (7) Sgt A G V Simons (29) F/S K A Exelby (M) (25) Sgt B L Collings (1) Sgt L J Vowler (1) Sgt E E Whittaker (W) (1) Sgt R McEwan (1) W/O P Chesin* (1) Sgt K Smith (1) Sgt L Moran (1) W/O T Skinner* (2) F/S L O'Brennan (1) F/S T Agnew (1) F/O L I George (1) W/O F J Rankin* (2) F/S A J Polmeardam (1) F/S D Copeland (1) W/O W A Heaney (1) W/O H Brown (1) F/S D J Fuller (2) Unidentified (1) possibly F/S Exelby	
F/O G Noseworthy* (14) 1st op 29.9.44 Last 14/15.1.45 shot down	Sgt A L Evens* (14)	F/O G Palmer** (14) Sgt P Buckland (5) 2nd nav	F/O G Trail (14)	Sgt T R Hartop (14)	W/O J G Galley (13) W/O R E Ralph (13) W/O R J Tanner (1)	Sgt W Gray* (M) (12) Sgt D K Clark* (W) (14) F/O R A Mason (R) (12) F/S J Mellers (W) (14) Sgt T C G Carter (R) (1) Sgt P Newman (W) (1) F/L J H Cook (R) (1) F/O W Doolin (1)	
F/L I McPherson (23) 1st op 29.9.44 Last 7/8.3.45	F/O I T Leslie* (1) F/O G Bremness* (22)	F/L A Eastman (1) F/S P S Morris (2) plus 2 as 2nd nav	F/O W Doolin (17) F/S J E Dagnall (3) F/S W Nolan (1)	F/S D A Prutton (23)	F/O H L Smith (19) F/O J J Denn (19) W/O L T Foster (1)	F/S R R Buff (W) (17) F/S R Stott (M) (21) F/S S C R Leach (R) (21)	

F/O A Stuart (34)
1st op 1.10.44
Last 2/3.5.45

F/S L D Thorne (34)

Sgt W Robinson* (5)
F/O W Simpson (3)
F/S R Tabah (22)
plus 1 as 2nd nav
F/S P S Morris (1)
F/L F Freake (1)
P/O R Wade (2)

F/O A Love (1)
F/O H L Booth* (19)

F/S D S Lightfoot (33)
F/S R Arnett* (1)

F/S J D Moir (32)
F/L R W Barrett (1)
W/O W Stanyer (1)

Sgt D Bryant (2)

F/O T Morris (1)
W/O R J Housden (1)
Sgt J R Bancroft (2)
Sgt E J Downs (2)

F/O H E Snelgrove (23)
P/O R Fawcett (32)
F/O J J Denn (1)
F/L N V O O Haveland (1)
W/O J E Potter (1)
F/O R N Godwin (1)
F/O A S Knight (1)
F/S I Middle (1)
F/S W C Meyrick (1)
F/S J Goudie (1)
F/O D Oakley (1)

Sgt H McIver (W) (23)
Sgt F G Morton (3)
Sgt L Moran (1)
Sgt K L Stone (1)
Sgt R McEwan (3)
Sgt H L Smith (1)
F/O J R Wolff (2)

W/O C Aspinall* (32)
W/O T Skinner* (31)
W/O P Chesin* (30)
Sgt J T McGregor (31)
Sgt E E Whittaker (1)
F/S B Maxwell* (1)
F/S D K Clarke* (1)
Sgt K Smith (1)
Sgt E J White (1)
F/S W L Bowsher* (1)
F/S D J Fuller (1)
W/O J Parrack* (1)

W/O S R Rose (10)

Captain	2nd pilot	Navigator	Wireless Operator	Flight Engineer	Special Operator	Air Gunner	Air Bomber
					F/L A E L Morris (40)		P/O M W Utas* (38)
P/O J Wallace (3)	F/S J Bratten (40)	F/S V Green (36)	W/O J E Potter (25)	F/S W Mulligan* (31)	P/O D Copeland (12)	W/O J Parrack* (31)	
1st op 2.10.44	W/C H H Burnell (1)	F/O A J K Barron (36)		Sgt D Marsden (1)	W/O A C Fraser (25)	Sgt R A D Jones (1)	
Last 2/3.5.45		F/O W Simpson (1)		F/S G W Williams (1)	F/O S W Adamson (1)	F/S E Stirrop (37)	
				F/S A Malone (1)	F/O W A Williams (1)	Sgt G N Tucker (3)	
				F/S B Le Fondre (1)	W/O W F Baker (1)	F/S T E Sim* (32)	
					W/O A C Cole (3)	Sgt B L Collings (1)	
					W/O J E Bellamy (1)	Sgt L S Davies (2)	
					F/O A L Haynes (1)	F/S T Agnew* (2)	
					W/O R J Tanner (1)	Sgt E E Whittaker (1)	
					W/O O G Burtenshaw (1)	F/S B Maxwell (1)	
					Sgt W R Legge (4)	F/S D J Fuller (2)	
					W/O J Ross (1)	F/L W Wells (1)	
					W/O T A Hughes (1)	F/O W Holley* (2)	
					F/O T Baines (1)	F/S G Davies (2)	
					F/S F A Jobson (1)	Sgt A G V Simons (1)	
					F/O A Knight (1)	W/O F J Rankin* (2)	
						Sgt L Moran (1)	
						Sgt E Hedley (1)	
						F/S P Cameron (1)	
						F/S A H Ward (1)	
						Sgt C L Matthews (1)	
						Unidentified (1)	

Captain	2nd pilot	Navigator	Wireless Operator	Flight Engineer	Special Operator	Air Gunner	Air Bomber
F/L J Briscoe (37)	F/O E A Hart (35)	F/O A Love (34)	F/S D A G Anthony (36)	F/S F D Baker (18)	F/O E Chandler (26)	Sgt E Dobson (3)	F/S E J Saddington (1)
1st op 3.10.44	F/O D Theaker (1)	F/O G Palmer** (1)	F/S D L Jones (1)	Sgt W Nolan (3)	F/S W L Bowsher* (W) (36)	Sgt S G Wilshaw (W) (32)	
Last 17/18.4.45	F/O C Reiser* (1)	F/O J P Hammond (1)	F/O C E Payne (23)	Sgt T D Bryant (1)	F/O R N Godwin (1)	Sgt K L Stone (R) (34)	
		F/S J E Dagnall (2)		F/L J H Cook (4)	F/O G A Gamble (3)	W/O D F Roberts (M) (25)	
		F/O W H G Thomas (1)		F/O W Doolin (3)	W/O J Ross (1)	F/S F Brannigan (6)	
				F/S R Arnett* (3)	W/O J E Bellamy (1)	F/L W Wells (1)	
				F/O D S Johnson (1)	F/O L F Rendle (7)	F/S T Agnew* (1)	
				Unidentified (2)	F/O F Rowe (6)	Sgt G Nisbet (1)	
				possibly F/S Baker	F/O W A Williams (1)	F/S D K Clark* (1)	
					W/O R J Housden (1)	F/S W Chitticks (1)	
						F/S K A Exelby (1)	
						F/O T F Sherry* (2)	
						P/O W T Berry (1)	
						F/S E Longden (2)	

P/O J H McAdam** (1)
Sgt J J McGregor (1)
W/O F J Rankin* (1)
Sgt L Moran (1)
Sgt J R Denney (1)
Sgt L S Davies (1)
F/S D J Fuller (1)
F/O J Bourque* (1)

F/O R D Carpenter (10)

Sgt R E Porteus (W) (1)
F/S R M Wood* (18)
F/S G R Graham (17)
F/S B Maxwell* (19)
Sgt B L Collings (1)
F/S D K Clark* (2)
Sgt J T McGregor (1)
F/S T Agnew* (1)

Sgt E D T Brockhurst (F) (18)
F/S C Weston (M) (41)
Sgt P Lovatt (41)
Sgt R C Lawrence (W) (41)
F/S S A Pienaar (R) (40)
Sgt K Smith (1)

W/O R A Palmer (15)
W/O W F Baker (20)
F/S P B Clarke (2)
F/O R N Godwin (1)
F/O W A Williams (1)
F/L L W Fairbanks (1)

P/O B S Beercroft (29)
F/O E P Youngs (27)
F/O C E Payne (1)
F/O L Boot (2)
F/O W S Stephens (2)
W/O R J Tanner (1)
W/O O G Burtenshaw (1)
W/O J Ross (1)
Sgt W R Legge (2)
F/O R N Godwin (3)
W/O R J Housden (1)
F/O W A Williams (1)
Sgt J K Chapple (1)
F/S W T Weston (1)
F/O W Lane (1)
F/S D J Cornish (1)

Sgt D Marsden (1)
F/S R Wynn (18)
Unidentified (1)
possibly F/S Wynn

F/S J Brown (38)
F/S A Malone (1)
Sgt D Marsden (2)

F/L G Ellams (2)
F/S R Arnett* (16)
F/S D Bryant (2)

P/O F M Watson (34)
F/S D S Lightfoot (1)
F/S J E Dagnall (1)
F/O W Bridgeman (4)
F/S R Stark (1)

F/O H T Radclett* (1)
F/O H L Booth* (1)
F/S P S Morris (2)

F/O R W Johnson (17)
Sgt J Kendall (19)

F/O L Hudson (40)
F/O R M Wylie* (1)

F/O C R Spicer (40)
F/O J Robson (1)

F/O J W Thompson* (20) 1st op 7.10.44 Last 20/21.2.45 shot down

Unidentified (1)
F/L R Hastie (41) 1st op 7.10.44 Last 15/16.4.45

Captain	2nd pilot	Navigator	Wireless Operator	Flight Engineer	Special Operator	Air Gunner	Air Bomber
F/O T W Steele (17) 1st op 12.10.44 Last 17/18.1.45 Crew returned to ops 16/17.3.45 with S/L S B Wills as captain	F/O N S Pickerill (6) F/O J Robson (4) F/O D Theaker (2)	F/L F Freake (15) F/O A J K Barron 5 as 2nd nav F/O W Simpson (2)	F/S J E Dagnall (17)	Sgt P R Matthews (17)	W/O R J Tanner (17) W/O O G Burtenshaw (17)	F/S W Chitticks (M) (17) F/S D J Fuller (W) (16) Sgt L Norwood (W) (15) Sgt C G Carter (R) (17) Sgt R A D Jones (W) (1) Unidentified (2)	
F/O A C Ball (20) 1st op 17/18.1.45 Last 16/17.4.45	F/O J J B Pocock (2)	F/O L W Howell (20)	F/O J E Dow (20)	F/O L W Lomas (18) W/O W Stanyer (1) Unidentified (1) possibly F/O Lomas	F/O J Blakeley (20) F/O R V Piper (20)	W/O W A Heaney (20) W/O H Brown (18) F/S E G Page (20) F/S A G Bryant (20) Sgt K Smith (1) F/S C R Leach (1)	
F/O F T Sellars (21) 1st op 22/23.1.45 Last 24/25.4.45	-	F/S P S Morris (21)	F/O D Geall (21)	F/O J A Noble (21)	F/O F Mann (20) F/O A H Hobbs (18) F/O J E Dow (1) Sgt S Purvis (1) F/S I Middle (1) F/S H Waugh (1)	F/S S C Thom (21) W/O W P Duff (21) W/O H Scott (21) W/O W J Ings (19) Sgt J Murray (1) Sgt J T McGregor (1)	
F/O N S Ayres (6) 1st op 24/25.2.45 Last 20/21.3.45 shot down	-	W/O A E Redford (6)	F/O H B Hale (6)	W/O W Stanyer (3) Sgt D Marsden (3)	W/O J Bellamy (6) W/O A C Cole (6)	F/S J D Cairns (M) (6) Sgt L J Vowler (W) (6) Sgt E D T Brockhurst (W) (6) W/O S E Silvey (R) (6)	
F/O J Robson (7) 1st op 28.2/1.3.45 Last 2/3.5.45	W/C H H Burnell (1)	F/O R W Bass* (6) F/O W Simpson (1)	F/S W Nolan (7)	F/S A Malone (7)	W/O O G Burtenshaw (1) Sgt J R Bancroft (1) Sgt E J Downs (1) W/O C Fairbairn (1) F/O W Lane (1) F/S D S Hunter (1) W/O D L Wynne (1) F/S I Middle (1)	F/O J Bourque* (7) F/S E J White (7) Sgt A E Tonkin (1) Sgt K Smith (6) F/S R G Sunstrum* (6)	

F/O J W Cairney (8) 1st op 14/15.3.45 Last 23/24.4.45 See also Fortress ops list	-	F/O R W Tucker (8)	W/O A Sheekey (8)	P/O W G Howard (8)	W/O J Ross (8) W/O R J Housden (1) F/O J Blakeley (1) Sgt R J Smith (1) F/S W T Weston (1) Sgt W R Legge (1) F/S S Purvis (2) Sgt S Dodd (2) Sgt D J Cornish (1) Sgt C S Ward (1)	F/O G A Isaacs (M) (7) F/O F R Higgins (W) (8) F/O F Boyd (W) (6) Sgt E Hedley (R) (8) F/O J E Dow (1) Unidentified (2)
F/O F Bowell (10) 1st op 14/15.3.45 Last 2/3.5.45	-	W/O L R Lovitt (10)	F/L D W Drew (6) F/S F Brannigan (3) Unidentified (1)	W/O G Harrison (10)	F/S F A Jobson (10) W/O C Fairbairn (10)	F/O L I George (9) F/O W T Berry (10) F/S A J Polmear (10) F/S D Copeland (10) Unidentified (1)
S/L S B Wills (3) 1st op 16/17.4.45 Last 4/5.4.45	-	F/L F Freake (3)	F/S J E Dagnall (3)	Sgt P R Matthews (3)	F/O W A Williams (1) F/S F A Jobson (1) Sgt W R Legge (1) F/O W V Lane (1) F/O L F Rendle (1) F/O F Rowe (1)	F/S W Chitticks (M) (3) Sgt L Norwood (W) (3) F/S D J Fuller (W) (3) F/S C G Carter (R) (3)
F/O J J B Pocock (5) 1st op 2/3.4.45 Last 23/24.4.45	F/L J Schnarr* (1)	F/S E Glaze (5)	F/S K H Mayfield (5)	P/O R C Diment (5)	Sgt J R Bancroft (5) Sgt E J Downs (4) F/S S Dodds (1)	F/S P Cameron (R) (5) F/S J G Wookey (M) (5) Sgt W H Frow (W) (5) Sgt R H New (W) (5)

5. Squadron Personnel Who Flew Flying Fortress Operations

Captain	2nd pilot	Navigator	Wireless Operator	Flight Engineer	Special Operator	Air Gunner	Air Bomber
F/L S B Wills (3) 1st op 18/19.4.45 Last 2/3.5.45 See also Fortress ops list	-	F/L F Freake (2) F/S P S Morris (1)	F/S J E Dagnall (3)	Sgt P R Matthews (3)	F/S J R Bancroft (1) F/O W Lane (1) W/O R J Housden (1)	F/S W Chitticks (3) F/S H J Brown (3) Sgt L Norwood (3) F/S D J Fuller (3) F/S C G Carter (3)	
F/O G Bremness* (4) 1st op 19/20.4.45 Last 2/3.5.45	-	F/O H E Booth * (4)	F/O W Doolin (4)	Sgt D A Prutton (4)	F/O L F Rendle (4) F/O F Rowe (3) W/O R J Housden (1)	F/S S C R Leach (4) F/S B Buff (4) Sgt H McIver (4) F/S R Stott (4)	
S/L R E C McKnight (2) 1st op 23/24.4.45 Last 2/3.5.45	P/O F G Nash (2)	F/O J G Morris (2)	F/S R Stark (2)	F/S B Le Fondre (2)	F/O W Lane (2) F/O W Thomson (1)	F/S G Schutes (2) F/S D H Thorpe (2) F/S C G J Brooks (2) F/S W Jones (2) F/S H Brown (1)	
F/O J W Cairney (1)	-	F/O W R Tucker (1)	W/O A Sheekey (1)	P/O W G Howard (1)	F/O T Baines (1) W/O J Ross (1)	F/O G Isaacs (1) F/O F Boyd (1) F/O F Higgins (1) F/S E Hedley (1)	

APPENDIX FOUR

223 Squadron Liberators

Note: The data in this table has been compiled from Air Ministry 27 Aircraft Movement Cards and the flying log books of 223 Squadron aircrew. USAAF model identification and USAAF codes and names courtesy of the late J D Oughton.

RAF Serial	USAAF Serial & Model	USAAF Units, Codes & Names	223 Sqn Codes & Names	Taken on Charge	Movement and Events Dates in RAF Service
TS519	41-29568 B-24H-15-CF	850 BS, 490 BG *WHY WORRY*	S	20 Oct 44 223 Sqn	4/5 Jul 45 to AGT Gatwick, 9 May 46 to 6 MU, 7 Jul 48 to J Dale & Co for Scrap.
TS520	41-28868 B-24H-15-DT	851 BS, 490 BG S3-Q *DEVIL'S STEPCHILD*	J	20 Oct 44 223 Sqn	Failed to Return (FTR) from op 20/21 Feb 45.
TS521	42-52483 B-24H-15-FO	835 BS, 486 BG H8-M *TWENTIETH CENTURY WOLF*	F	20 Oct 44 223 Sqn	30 Oct 44 Cat AC, 18 Jan 45 RoS (67 MU), 8 Apr 45 223 Sqn, 8 Jun 45 AGT Gatwick Cat B, 19 Mar 46 51 MU, 12 Mar 47. Sold to International Alloys (IA).
TS522	42-52712 B-24H-15-FO	832 BS, 486 BG 3R-D	P 223 Sqn	20 Oct 44	16 Dec 44 Cat AC, 27 Dec 45 RoS (67 MU), 20 Apr 45 223 Sqn, 7 Jun 4551 MU, 12 Jun 45 AGT Gatwick Cat B MI. 8 Mar 46 51 MU, 12 Mar 47. Sold to IA.
TS523	42-52620 B-24H--15-FO	487 BG *SMOKEY JOE*	D *DEAD BEAT*	20 Oct 44 223 Sqn	15 May 45 Shawbury, 18 May 45 RAF Kirkbride, 10 Jul 45 Lockheeds, 30 Jan 46 51 MU, 12 Mar 47. Sold to IA.
TS524	42-52573 B-24H-15-FO	835 BS, 486 BG H8-G	O	20 Oct 44	25 May 45 51 MU, 30 May 45 223 Sqn MI Rootes, 9 Apr 46 Blythe Bridge to 51 MU, 12 Mar 47. Sold to IA.
TS525	42-52771 B-24H-15-FO	487 BG *MY BABY*	H	20 Oct 44 223 Sqn	9 Apr 45 FB Cat AC, 16 Apr 45 RoS (67 MU), 11 Jan 46 Cat AC 54 MU, 7 Feb 46 Ex RoS, 21 Mar 46 51 MU , 12 Mar 47. Sold to IA.
TS526	42-52572 B-24H-15-FO	487 BG	T 223 Sqn	20 Oct 44	20/21 Mar 45. Missing.

RAF Serial	USAAF Serial & Model	USAAF Units, Codes & Names	223 Sqn Codes & Names	Taken on Charge	Movement and Events Dates in RAF Service
TS527	42-52591 B-24H-15-FO	487 BG	Q	20 Oct 44	25 May 45 51 MU, 15 Jun 45 AGT Gatwick, 18 Ju 45 Cat B Rootes MI RIW, 4 Feb 46 CRD Scottish Aviation, 26 Feb 46 51 MU, 12 Mar 47. Sold to IA.
TS528	42-52731 B-24H-15-FO	832 BS, 486 BG 3R-M 493 BG THE SPIRIT OF LSU	R	20 Oct 44 223 Sqn	5 Dec 44 Cat AC, 16 Dec 44 RoS (67 MU), 15 Apr 45 223 Sqn, 15 May 45 Shawbury, 18 May 45 Kirkbride, 14 Jul 45 AGT Gatwick M I, 18 May 46 to 12 MU, 3 Jun 47 SOC.
TS529	42-94856 B-24H-20-FO	850 BS, 490 BG 7Q-V LADY KESSLER	C CIRCE	20 Oct 44 223 Sqn	25 May 45 51 MU, 20 Jun 45 Cat B MI AGT Gatwick, 5 Feb 46 Mods RAF Tempsford, 16 Mar 4 51 MU, 12 Mar 47. Sold to IA.
TS530	42-94981 B-24H-20-FO	80 BS, 490 BG 7Q-B 833 BS, 486 BG 4N-O NOBLE EFFORT	G GREMLIN HEAVEN	20 Oct 44 223 Sqn	30 May 45 51 MU, 15 Jun 45 MI AGT Gatwick, 18 Feb 46 Tempsford, 15 Mar 46, 12 Mar 47. Sold to IA.
TS531	42-51529 B-24J-5-FO		B, A	20 Oct 44 223 Sqn	3 /4 Mar 45 Cat AC/FB, 12 Mar 45 RoS Scottish Aviation, 30 Mar 45 223 Sqn, 7 Jun 45 Cat AC, 13 Aug 45 223 Sqn, 7 Sep 45 Cat B MI AGT Gatwick, 4 Mar 47 SOC.
TS532	44-40350 B-24J-160-CO	861 BS,493 BG Q4-D	N	20 Oct 44 223 Sqn	26 May 45 51 MU, 11 Sep 45 Recat E, 14 Dec 45 SOC.
TS533	44-40457 B-24J-165-CO	493 BG; 490 BG BOOMERANG	M	13 Sep 44 223 Sqn	26 May 45 51 MU, 16 Jun 45 32 MU, 26 Jun 45 Cat B MI 32 MU, 12 Oct 45 Scottish Aviation, 14 Dec 45, 18 Jan 46 1 TAMU Tempsford, 20 Mar 46 51 MU, 12 Mar 47. Sold to IA.
TS534	44-10574 B-24J-65-CF		A, O AD LIB	13 Sep 44 223 Sqn	7 Jun 45, 51 MU, 10 Jun 45 MU, 26 Sep 45 MI 32 MU, 10 Nov 35 Lockheeds, 14 Nov 45 1 TAMU, 18 Jan 46 51 MU, 12 Mar 47 Sold to IA Mar 47 SOC.
TS535	42-94813 B-24H-20-FO	18 BS, 34 BG 8I-E 4 BS Q6-Z	A, B	20 Oct 44 1699 Flt	11 Apr 45 223 Sqn, 19 May 45 12 MU, 13 Jul 45 Cat B MI AGT Gatwick, 16 Apr 46 12 MU, 3 Jun 47 SOC.
TS536	42-94771 B-24H-15-FO	391 BS, 34 BG 3L-N then 3L-H WINNIE	W	26 Oct 44 1699 Flt	11 Apr 45 223 Sqn, 25 May 45 RoS Scottish Aviation, 9 Jun 45 223 Sqn, 9 Kjun 45 12 MU, 11 Jun 45 MI AGT Gatwick, 23 May 46 51 MU, 12 Mar 47. Sold to IA.
TS537	42-94847 B24H--20-FO	848 BS, 490 BG MISS ME	X, D	25 Aug 44 1699 Flt	4 May 45 12 MU, 11 Apr 45 223 Sqn, 20 Jun 45 AGT Gatwick Cat B MI, 21 Mar 6 51 MU 12 Mar 47. Sold to IA.

RAF Serial	USAAF Serial & Model	USAAF Units, Codes & Names	223 Sqn Codes & Names	Taken on Charge	Movement and Events Dates in RAF Service
TS538	44-10594 B-24J- 65-CF	36 BS	V, A, B	25 Aug 44 1699 Flt	11 Apr 45 223 Sqn, 5 May 45 RAF Kirkbride, 7 May 45 12 MU, 29 Jun 45 Tempsford, 8 Oct 45 Tempsford Mods, 11 Oct 45 86 Sqn Odiham then Oakington, 7 Jul 48. Sold to J Dale & Co.
TS539	44-10611 B-24J-70-CF		Y, C	25 Aug 44 1699 Flt	11 Apr 45 223 Sqn, 7 Ma 45 RAF Kirkbride, 4 May 45 12 MU, 2 Jul 45 Lockheeds, 28 Sep 45 Mod Unit Tempsford, 19 Oct 45 86 Sqn, 6 Apr 4 FA Cat AC, RoS Scottish Aviation, 30 Jul 46 Ex RoS, 27 Sep 46 51 MU, 17 Dec 46 SOC (Broken Down.)
TT336	44-10597 B-24J-65-CF		R	29 Nov 44	14 Jan 45 FTR, Cat E/FB.
TT340	42-94797 B-24H-20-FO	849th BS, 490th BG W8-R *WISHBONE*	U?	8 Dec 44 223 Sqn	19 Dec 44 Cat AC, "0 Dec 44 RoS (67 MU), 15 May 45 223 Sqn, 16 Jun 45 51 MU, 29 Jun 45 AGT Gatwick, 3 Jul 45 Cat B MI, 22 May 46 12 MU, 3 Mar 47 SOC.
TT343	42-52350 B-24J-5-DT		K, W *KAY*	10 Dec 44 223 Sqn	13 Jun 45 51 MU, 20 Jun 45 AGT Gatwick, 24 Jun 45 53 Sqn, 17 Jan 46 Cat AC, Feb 46 53 Sqn, 18 Apr 46 51 MU, 3 Mar 47 SOC.
VB852	42-50744 B-24J-1-FO		P	20 Jan 45 223 Sqn	13 Jun 45 51 MU, 23 Jun 45 Lockheed Renfrew, 25 Jun 45 51 MU, 29 Jun 45 Tempsford, 30 Nov 45 206 Sqn, 27 Apr 46 12 MU, 4 Jun 47 SOC.
VB904	42-52766 B-34H-15-FO	487 BG *CUBBY*	J	11 Mar 45 223 Sqn	14 Jun 45 51 MU, 26 Jun 45 AGT Gatwick, 29 Jun 45 RIW MI, 21 Mar 46 51 MU, 12 Mar 47. Sold to IA.
VD245	42-52681 B-24H-15-FO	833 BS, 486 BG 4N-H *LADY FROM HELL*	R	22 Mar 45 223 Sqn	9 Apr 45 FB Cat AC, 27 Apr 45. SOC.
VD249	44-10533 B-24J-60-CF		T	27 Mar 45 223 Sqn	14 Jun 45 51 MU, 22 Jun 45 Lockheeds Renfrew, 27 Jun 45 51 MU, 29 Jun 45 Tempsford, 220 Sqn, 28 Nov 45 12 MU, 3 Jun 47 SOC.

Key:

AC	Aircraft	DT	Douglas/Tulsa
AGT	Airwork General Trading	FB	Aircracft accident/incident from operational flying
Cat AC	For repair by contractors working party. (Contractors works.)	FO	Ford/Willow Run
		MI	Major Inspection
Cat B	Damaged but repairable at RAF Maintenance Unit or contractors works.	NT	North American/Dallas
		RIW	Repairable in Works
CF	Consolidated/Fort Worth	TAMU	Transport Aircraft Modification Unit
CO	Consolidated/San Diego		
CRD	Civilian Repair Depot		

The Crew of Liberator TS526 & Raid Documentation 20/21 March 1945

Fg Off Norman Siddall Ayres – Pilot

Norman was born on 14 June 1920 in the Wadsley parish in Sheffield to Edmund and Sarah Ayres. There was early tragedy in the family when his siblings Edmund and Ruth were lost to childhood illnesses. Norman was therefore a much-loved only son. He enjoyed a normal and happy childhood, making friends easily growing up in the village-style atmosphere that characterised Sheffield before the war. He started his education at Marcliffe Road Junior and Infants School where he showed early promise. In the three years from 1930 he attended Hillsborough Council Boys' School where he continued to do well. According to Edmund Rhodes, a contemporary, Norman's build was on the plump side and he inevitably acquired the nickname 'Fatty'. His good results continued

[C Bramley].

and he was lucky enough to gain a place at the Sheffield Central School starting in September 1933. It was at this time that the school moved to newly-built premises at Bents Green, located in the south-west fringe of the city. Here it was renamed High Storrs Grammar. Unfortunately, his nickname followed him as he was still a heavily-built lad of average height. He was an active boy despite his tubbiness and proved to be good at sport. It would appear that his chemistry master, Mr Alf Ridler, saw Norman's potential and was impressed by his enthusiasm and drive; he noted his leadership qualities and selected him as captain of Goff's House. It would appear that his liveliness did not endear him to all members of the teaching staff. Norman maintained his academic progress obtaining passes in all subjects when he sat his matriculation set by the Northern Universities Joint Matriculation Board in the summer of 1937, while he was in the upper stream of Form IVB in his final year.

Although the Great Depression was over, jobs were not easy to find. Norman sat and passed the entry examination for the Civil Service, but did not appear to have taken up employment with them. Now in his late teens he had shed his excess weight and become a presentable young man. He acquired a motor bike and like many youngsters of his age had developed an interest in aviation. It was probably around this time that his parents moved the family home to 41 Eskdale Road at Hillsborough, close to the Sheffield Wednesday football ground. He had also learned to drive, and in the run up to the outbreak of war he was employed by British Chemicals Ltd in Sheffield as a lorry driver. This may have been a temporary job while he waited for call up, as he was also recorded as working as a garage attendant during this period.

One of his closest pals during his boyhood was his cousin Vincent G Siddall. By 1939 they were under no illusions regarding the prospects of another war with Germany and decided to enlist, but disagreed initially on their choice of service. Norman, with his aviation interest, was drawn to the Auxiliary Air Force, but Vincent preferred the army. The key issue for both men was that they should stay together, and so they joined the Territorial Army on a four-year engagement in the locally-based 231 Field Park Company, Royal Engineers, on 3 May.

On 1 September 2078298 Sapper Ayres and Vincent were embodied for wartime service and posted to 142 Officer Cadet Training Unit (OCTU) Royal Engineers at Malta Barracks in Aldershot on 6 October. Norman saw Vincent on arrival but did not have an opportunity to speak with him. Ironically, notwithstanding their plan to serve together, Vincent was soon posted away. Norman stayed with the unit as clerk and also assisted with exercises carried out by the OCTU officer cadets. However, Norman soon became disillusioned with his army service, and clearly regretted not following his original ambition to join the RAF. Salvation finally came with the promulgation of an order permitting army personnel to apply for transfer to the RAF for aircrew duties. Norman put in his application on 12 December 1940 giving his first choice as pilot, followed by observer and then wireless operator/air gunner. Things moved relatively quickly; having successfully passed the Aircrew Selection Board and medical tests he was accepted and directed to report to 9 Reception Wing at the Aircrew Receiving Centre, Aberystwyth on 10 May 1941.

He spent just seven days at the reception wing before starting his training with 6 Initial Training Wing (ITW) also located at Aberystwyth. His stay at ITW ran from 17 May to 5 July and he enjoyed comfortable quarters, being accommodated in the Marine Hotel. He then moved north to Sealand, near Chester, to begin his flying training with 19 Elementary Flying Training School (EFTS) on 6 July. Here he would fly the de Havilland Tiger Moth and was soon completing his first flight with Flt Lt Hill in N6879 on 8 July. He made his unforgettable first solo in T7283 on 7 August and was up for twenty minutes, achieving this landmark in eleven hours and fifty minutes. At the end of the course he received the assessment, 'Average', in his flying log book; and had flown a total of fifty-six hours and twenty-five minutes including twenty-five hours and five minutes solo.

From 4 October to 23 December he graduated to flying the twin-engined Airspeed Oxford at 14 Service Flying Training School (SFTS) at Lyneham in Wiltshire. He continued his training on Oxfords at 6 SFTS, Little Rissington and successfully qualified for the award of his flying badge on 21 February 1942. His flying hours had risen to a total of 144.55 of which eighty-one hours and fifty-five minutes were solo including, three hours and forty minutes at night.

After a short spell of leave he attended 10 Course at the Beam Approach Training (BAT) Flight based at Ipswich airport from 10 to 18 March.

A move closer to operational flying came with his arrival at 21 Operational Training Unit (OTU) at RAF Moreton-in-Marsh on 24 March. The unit were responsible for training crews for Wellington squadrons. The assembled aircrew formed themselves into crews and Norman joined Sgt Reynolds's crew as 2nd Pilot. Their training on the Wellington took them through to 25 June when they participated in the third and last of Sir Arthur Harris's ground-breaking 1,000-bomber raids. Normally, a crew at OTU at this time would finish their training by completing a leaflet-dropping sortie over enemy territory to give them an experience of operational flying. The target was the north German port of Bremen; so quite a formidable baptism for embryo crews, and it was perhaps not surprising that twenty-three aircraft of the forty-eight that were lost on the raid were from OTUs.

Leave followed this 'graduation' sortie before the crew returned to Moreton-in-Marsh on 3 July, this time joining 1446 Ferry Flight. They would be with the flight until 27 July to prepare for their posting to an operational Wellington squadron in the Middle East which would involve them ferrying a new aircraft, Wellington IC HX529. The crew carried out two oil and fuel consumption flights in the aircraft before their departure on 22 July. The initial part of the flight took them down to RAF Portreath in Cornwall which would be the departure point for their ferry flight. The aircraft was fully refuelled while the crew waited for weather clearance for the trip. This came on the 25th and they set off for the long eight-hour twenty-five-minute flight to Gibraltar, arriving on the 26th, Norman flying as 1st Pilot for four hours. The next leg of their trip, on the same day took them from Gibraltar to Khanka in Egypt. Finally, on the 27th they continued to Landing Ground (LG) 224 (Cairo West) where their delivery task was completed.

Interestingly, Norman did not remain with Sgt Reynolds's crew but was posted on 31 July to 104 Squadron based at Kabrit close to the Great Bitter Lake. His first op with the squadron took place on 3 August when he flew as 2nd Pilot to Flt Sgt Williams bombing Tobruk in Wellington DV606. Norman's sixth op was also to Tobruk with Flt Sgt Williams in DV606, but was much more dramatic with the aircraft hit by flak over the target. Both engines failed, with one on fire. Fortunately, all five crew members were able to bale out. Norman was probably flying the aircraft at the time as he was the last man to bale out seventy miles south-west of Wadi Natrun. The crew walked for over fifty miles with just half a bottle of water between them before being spotted by an Air Sea Rescue Wellington (fifty-four years later his cousin Charles Bramley still had the pebble that Norman had sucked to keep his saliva flowing). Norman duly received his caterpillar badge awarded to aircrew who had successfully baled out by parachute.

Norman had completed a total of thirty-three ops by the time he left 148 Squadron in December 1942. He was briefly posted to 37 Squadron, also flying Wellingtons, on 14 December. This would appear to have been a vehicle to get him to his next posting as he only made two flights with 37, the second was a trip to Malta where his new squadron, 104, had a detachment. He joined 104 on 24 December and was now an aircraft captain with his own crew flying Wellington II aircraft. He completed thirteen more ops, making a total of forty-six before becoming tour expired in April 1943. On 1 May he received promotion to the rank of flight sergeant.

His repatriation to the UK was done in style, no troopship for Norman. He departed Cairo in BOAC Short 'C' Class flying boat G-ADYB 'Corsair', under the command of Commandant H M L Slover. It must have been quite a fascinating journey: Cairo-Wadi Halfa-Khartoum-Malakal-Laropi-Stanleyville-Coquahatville-Leopoldville-Libreville-Lagos. At Lagos he changed aircraft to a BOAC Sunderland captained by Commandant Rose. The remaining route was Lagos-Freetown-Bathurst-Port Etienne-Lisbon-Foynes and arriving at Poole on 26 June.

His new posting after leave was to 82 OTU based at Ossington in Nottinghamshire. Having completed an operational tour he was now 'screened' from operations and would pass on his valuable experience in training others. Before starting his duties he attended a short ten-day course at 93 Group's Screened Pilots School at Church Broughton. The course prepared him for his future instructional role. Returning to Ossington he commenced his training duties instructing embryo crews on Wellington IIIs and Xs. This continued until the end of August 1943 when he was switched, or volunteered, to fly Miles Martinets for fighter affiliation training with the Wellington crews and a few target-towing duties for the benefit of the air gunners. Norman obviously enjoyed the freedom of his new role, particularly the excitement provided by fighter affiliation, flying simulating enemy fighter attacks to train the Wellington crews in evasive tactics. The latter would include the gut-wrenching but effective 'corkscrew' whereby the pilot would put the bomber into tight descending turn then reversing the turn into a climb before repeating the process until the attacking fighter was lost or abandoned the attack. Normally, the air gunner who spotted the attacking fighter would give the pilot the call "corkscrew port (or starboard), go". Pity the poor navigator trying to hold on to his disappearing pencils, charts, Dalton computer etc. Norman continued his Martinet duties until the end of February 1944 when he received a posting to 3 Flying Instructors School (FIS) at Lulsgate Bottom near Bristol. He was now a warrant officer, having received promotion on 1 February. Although reporting warm weather, Norman remarked that most people had colds. He had a bad cough himself, and a sore throat which he put down to spending all day learning the instructors' 'patter' – the formal instruction method used when training pupils in the air. This information was included in one of the many letters he wrote to his wider family (his mother was one of five Siddall sisters) during his service. He also remarked about the unusual and amusing presence of a gypsy encampment right in the middle of the camp.

At Little Horwood, Norman received a more comprehensive programme of flying instructor training than he had received at Church Broughton. This might account for his limited period as an instructor there. His training on 58 Course was carried out on Oxfords between 17 March and 22 April when he was pronounced qualified as a multi-engine instructor. However, he was categorised as 'Below Average' as an instructor retaining his 'Average' grading as a pilot. It may be significant that he continued flying at 3 FIS until 11 June.

As a fully-qualified flying instructor he was posted to 85 OTU at Husbands Bosworth, Leicestershire, another Wellington training unit. He arrived on 12 June for what was to be a six-month tour. His final flight with the unit took place on 7 December. Whilst at Husbands Bosworth he met a contemporary from his old school in Sheffield, a navigator, Warrant Officer Arnold Redford. During his time on the unit he had also met wireless operator Warrant Officer Alfred Cole, flight engineer Flt Sgt W Stanyer and an air gunner Flt Sgt Joe Cairns. They were all experienced campaigners on the staff of the OTU. Whether they were all due to return to ops after screening is not known, or whether they had got together and volunteered, but on 20 December they were all posted to 1699 Training Flight at RAF Oulton to provide the nucleus of crew destined to join 223 Squadron.

Warrant Officer Arnold Evans Redford – Navigator

A Sheffield boy like his skipper, Arnold was born in the parish of Norton on 14 October 1921. Remembered by a distant cousin Mrs Josephine Mitchell as a nice, steady, and quiet boy, he was fond of music, singing and playing the piano. His family home was on the Chesterfield Road, one of the main thoroughfares leading out of the city to the south. He initially attended Meersbrook School before gaining a place at High Storrs Grammar School where he was in the year below Norman Ayres. After leaving school he was employed in the Nunnery Coal Office in Duke Street, working as a clerk. He enlisted in the RAF, volunteering for aircrew duties at 2 Reception Centre at Aberystwyth on 10 April 1941. After initial processing and appearing before 7 Aircrew Selection Board on the 11th he was placed on reserve and told to report back on 21 June. On arrival at 1 Reception Wing he resumed the induction process but a referral to hospital delayed his transfer to 6 ITW until 12 July. He just missed Norman who left the ITW on the 5th although they might have bumped into each other in the town. Completing ITW successfully Arnold had been accepted for observer training which he would undertake in America. He eventually set sail for the USA arriving at the Pan American Airways Navigation School in Miami on 11 October 1941. This was an American training establishment which took allied airmen for training as part of the Arnold Scheme. Apparently the school was full when Arnold arrived so he was sent to Canada to 31 Personnel Depot (PD) to kick his heels until a place on a course was available. He returned to Miami to begin his navigation course on 5 December. Successfully completing the course, he returned to 31 PD in Canada on 20 March 1942 prior to his return to 3 Personnel Reception Centre in England which he reached on 8 April.

Navigating in the clear blue skies over Miami was not a complete preparation for flying in the complex weather systems over Europe, and so on his return to England he was posted to 3 (Observers) Advance Flying Unit (O) AFU at Bobbington near Wolverhampton on 13 June. The unit was equipped with Anson and Oxford aircraft, and after acclimatising to UK flying conditions Arnold moved on to 12 OTU, a Wellington unit at Chipping Warden in Oxfordshire. At Benson he made up a crew with Sqn Ldr J C Giles. With their initial crew training completed they moved on to 1651 Heavy Conversion Unit, based at Waterbeach near Cambridge, on 1 November where they converted to the Stirling. Here they were joined by a flight engineer and extra air gunner. Finally, after the long trail of training Arnold and his crew moved to their operational squadron on 8 December 1942.

Sqn Ldr Giles was an experienced pilot who had recently returned from India, and had been posted to 90 Squadron as the new flight commander of A Flight. The squadron was based at Bottesford in Nottinghamshire, but was about to move to Ridgewell, Suffolk at the end of December. Arnold's first op took place on 21 January 1943 and involved mine laying. This was considered to be a relatively risk-free operation and quite often was used to blood new crews. 'Risk free' was relative to normal bombing operations. Aircraft were lost on mine-laying sorties, particularly if they strayed over flak ships or shore defences or had the misfortune to be picked up by a night fighter. Arnold visited a variety of heavily-defended targets including two trips to Berlin before he completed his tour. On the night of 3/4 June Giles and his crew completed a mine-laying sortie. In view of Arnold's future role with 100 Group it is interesting to note that the 90 Squadron ORB records that their aircraft used Mandrel during the sortie. His skipper Sqn Ldr Giles was promoted to Wg Cdr and took over command of the squadron on 13 July. He was promoted to flight sergeant on 8 August, just prior to his posting from operations to 84 OTU at Desborough in Northamptonshire equipped with Wellingtons, which took place on 16 September 1943. His screening as a navigator instructor continued when he was posted to another Wellington OTU, 85, at Husbands Bosworth on 15 June 1944. 'Red' as he was now nicknamed in the service would have been delighted to meet up again with Norman his fellow Sheffielder.

Flt Sgt W Stanyer – Flight Engineer

Flt Sgt Stanyer was one of the five posted into 1699 Flight from 85 OTU. He trained as part of Ayres' crew as they completed their conversion to the Liberator prior to their posting across the airfield to 223 Squadron on 10 February 1945. He took part in the first three of the crew's operational flights and then was replaced by Sgt Dennis Marsden. The reason for the change is not known. Although little is known of Stanyer he was almost certainly starting his second tour of operations. It is possible that he may have suffered an accident or some other medical problem. He is not recorded as being posted from the squadron and indeed returned to fly two more operations right at the end of hostilities with the rank of warrant officer.

Sgt Dennis Marsden – Flight Engineer

Dennis Marsden was born in the family home at 35 Eastgate, Worksop in Nottinghamshire on 22 May 1925, the son of coal miner Richard and his wife Clara Marsden. The family later moved to 18 Potter Street. The Marsdens with a family of seven sons and a daughter were well known in Worksop, and the male members noted for their interest in coarse fishing. Dennis attended Central School in the town leaving at sixteen. It is not known what his employment was after leaving school but it would have been of short duration as he most likely joined the RAF in 1943. Nothing is known of his early service until he was posted to St.Athan in South Wales in 1944 for flight engineer training. The would-be flight engineers were allocated to the various types of aircraft they were to be trained on. Dennis got the Liberator and amongst his fellow trainees were six other young men who would also complete the course successfully and be posted with him to 223 Squadron. They were Bob Hartop, also to lose his life, Alex Gibbon, Ernie Manners, Peter Matthews, Jamie Stewart and Don Prutton. The course was no pushover and the seven would have to work very hard to assimilate all the complexities of the various systems, fuel management and fault finding, etc. – it was a very intensive course. The seven duly arrived at Oulton on 2 September direct from St.Athan and were allocated to the same Nissen hut. Dennis did not get allocated to a crew on arrival but flew odd sorties with a number of different crews and had flown twelve when he joined the Ayres' crew for ops on the night of 8/9 March 1945. He was on his fifteenth operational sortie on the night of 20/21 March. Peter Matthews and Don Prutton remembered him as a friendly, cheerful lad, quite fond of the girls and an enthusiastic attendee of the local dances.

Fg Off Harold Bertram Hale – Wireless Operator

Norman's wireless operator was a Londoner, the son of a tailors' cutter Alec Hale and his wife Frances, and was born at 34 Allfarthing Lane in Wandsworth on 19 November 1921. He was educated at nearby Emmanuel Pubic School from 1930 to 1937. He entered his father's tailoring profession after leaving school and worked for S Pewson (Tailors) at 25 Bank Street, W1. He was not known to have a particular interest in aviation but volunteered for aircrew duties, possibly influenced by the Battle of Britain which was at its height at that time. He attended 9 Aircrew Selection Board on 25 August 1940 where he was recommended for training as wireless operator/air gunner. The next day he was enlisted in the RAF at 2 Reception Centre at Cardington. Harold was then called forward to 9 Reception Centre at Stratford-upon-Avon arriving on 6 September. The training machine was under stress at this time and he was temporarily posted to Farnborough on 23 October, before being moved again to 10 Reception Centre at Scarborough to finish his basic training.

[Mrs Doris Hulbert].

At last his specialist training started with a move to 3 Wing of 2 Signals School at Yatesbury near Calne in Wiltshire on 29 March 1941. The first phase of his training complete on 18 July, he was given a holding posting to RAF Southend. He remained at Southend until 4 November when he was recalled to Yatesbury to complete the wireless operator element of his training which he achieved in March 1942. A temporary holding post at 4 Signals School at Madley in Herefordshire followed, until his air gunnery course formed at 8 AGS at Evanton, way up in the north of Scotland. He started the course on 10 April 1941 and successfully completed it at the end of May, now a fully fledged WOP/AG.

He now moved to the last step in his training before joining an operational squadron. On 2 June he arrived at 10 OTU at Abingdon in Oxfordshire, whose task was to train bomber crews on the Armstrong-Whitworth Whitley. Harold flew the majority of his flights at the unit as a wireless operator, with only three as an air gunner, as a member of Sgt Harry Gumbrell's crew. Normally, the crew would have completed their OTU training with a leaflet-dropping sortie over enemy territory. However, their training coincided with a time of great concern over the high loss rate of shipping due to the German U-Boat attacks. As an emergency measure, a large anti-submarine flight was formed at St.Eval in Cornwall, six miles north-east of Newquay, manned by graduating OTU crews. Their role was to carry out patrols over the Western Approaches and the Bay of Biscay. 10 OTU's detachment to St.Eval commenced on 4 August with twenty-six Whitley Mark V aircraft modified with air to surface vessel (ASV) radar and equipped to carry depth charges.

This was a tough assignment and some long flights were made on convoy patrols and anti-submarine sweeps. Extra fuel tanks were fitted in the fuselage to extend their range and endurance, and sorties of nine to twelve hours duration were flown on some occasions and eight operations were flown, including an early return, before their return to Abingdon at the end of September. On these sorties they carried four depth charges and twenty-nine half-pound practice bombs. As a sop to their Bomber Command allegiance they were briefed to drop the practice bombs on a rocky outcrop off the Cornish coast. Their sorties were not without incident. During a convoy patrol on 4 September they were attacked by two Ju 88s, who broke off the attack before any critical damage was done. This was particularly fortunate as they were briefed to ditch if they met a Ju 88 rather than attempt the impossible and fight it off. It is assumed that the enemy aircraft were short of fuel. On 7 September they were forced to return with a starboard engine failure. On the 9th they were attacked, again this time by three Arado seaplanes without sustaining damage and claimed one Arado shot down, which was later confirmed.

The crew had now completed their OTU course and were posted to 101 Squadron in 1 Group, based at Holme-on-Spalding Moor, north-east of Goole. The squadron were operating Wellington III aircraft but were in the process of converting to the Lancaster. The crew were promptly dispatched on 16 October to 1654 HCU at Wigsley in Nottinghamshire to the west of Lincoln. The unit was equipped with both the Manchester and its successor the Lancaster; the crew flew in both types during their conversion but mainly the Lancaster. Five of their fifteen flights with 1654 were flown with Fg Off Henry Maudslay who would later win fame as one of Guy Gibson's skippers with 617 Squadron's attack on the German dams. Sadly, Henry Maudslay and his crew did not return from the attack. Completing their conversion on 6 December 1942, the crew rejoined 101.

The first few days on the squadron were occupied with practice bombing, night-flying tests, formation flying and cross-country navigational exercises before they were deemed fit for ops. Their first op to the Ruhr was not a success, as they were forced to return early with a u/s rear turret; they were also fired on by a British vessel, and had to use the emergency system for lowering the undercarriage on landing.

Harold remained with Harry Gumbrell's crew until 1 March 1943 when he joined Sgt Stancliffe's crew. Harry remembered Harold as a quiet, reserved, man. In fact the only time he remembered him getting excited was when he successfully picked up a

German ground controller's transmission and jammed it with his Tinsel microphone: "Yippee, I've got one." Harry added that Harold was nicknamed 'Sonnie' after the well-known English theatre and cinema actor of the day.

On 25 May Harold and his new crew moved to another Lancaster squadron, 12 based at Wickenby in Lincolnshire. He only stayed a comparatively short time with his new squadron, finishing his first operational tour on 25 June 1943. He had completed twenty-six ops including the seven completed sorties on loan to Coastal Command. He was commissioned at the end of the tour as a pilot officer.

Harold's rest tour was completed initially with 82 OTU at Ossington between 30 June 1943 and 10 September 1944, before spending brief spells with two other OTUs 86 and 83. He received his posting to 1699 Flight at Oulton on 8 November 1944. On 2 September, just before his departure from Ossington, he married his girl friend Doris Sands at St.Paul's church, Hammersmith. He may well have come across Norman Ayres during his service with 82.

Flt Sgt Joseph Davison Cairns – Mid Upper Gunner

Flt Sgt Joe Cairns was born in Northumberland and grew up in the Ashington area where it is believed he went to school. An aviation enthusiast as a boy, he was a keen member of his ATC unit. It is not known when he joined the RAF, but it was probably in 1942. He was selected for air gunnery training and qualified successfully at 4 AGS at Morpeth, conveniently close to his home. The course lasted from 1 August to 11 September 1943 using Anson aircraft. His end of course report identified him as keen and a good worker but needing further air experience, the latter was an odd comment which almost certainly applied to all the trainees at this stage in their training. He achieved a creditable 77.3% in the course examination, and had completed twenty-one hours and twenty-six minutes in the air.

[Mrs E Wilson].

He quickly moved on to an OTU, reporting to 14 at Market Harborough, Leicestershire which was equipped with the Wellington I/C. He arrived on 14 September and joined Sgt H W Hill's crew, who would spend just fourteen days at the OTU. From 20 to 30 October Joe was based at Skellingthorpe near Lincoln on an air gunnery refresher course. The unit used Wellington X aircraft and the detachment may have been designed to give him the extra air experience the AGS claimed he needed.

The next step towards operations saw the crew attending 1654 HCU at Wigsley. The crew arrived at the unit on 22 October and spent the rest of the year converting to the Lancaster.

New Year's Day was the start of their operational career, with a move to 630 Squadron at East Kirkby in Lincolnshire. Joe's skipper Hill was now a commissioned pilot officer and the crew had been supplemented with a flight engineer and an extra gunner. Between 5 January and 24 May 1944, Joe and his crew would complete thirty-one operations, visiting some of the toughest targets over Europe including five to the formidable 'Big City', Berlin. Joe had flown 230 hours on operations and at just nineteen years of age was already a veteran.

His rest tour, as a screened air gunner, was taken at 85 OTU at Husbands Bosworth, which he joined on 20 June 1944 after a well-earned spell of leave. He would meet his future skipper, W/O Norman Ayres, at the unit and flew with him on a number of occasions. His sister, Mrs Wilson, remembers Joe chaffing at the frustration and boredom of life on a training unit, and being very keen to get back to operations. So, after six months of rest, Joe reported to Oulton in mid-December with his 85 OTU contemporaries on their way to join 1699 Flight.

W/O James Edward Bellamy – Special Operator

[Michael Bellamy].

James Edward Bellamy, known as Ted by his RAF pals, was born at Doncaster on 12 May 1911. His parents moved south and ran an off licence at Sutton in Surrey before moving to Norfolk during the 1930s. Ted met and married his wife, Catherine, in Norfolk, getting married in June 1936; their only son, Michael was born in 1938. Notwithstanding having a wife and young child, Ted enlisted in the RAF volunteering for aircrew duties. Appearing before 12 Aircrew Selection Board on 4 September 1940 he was recommended for training as a wireless operator/air gunner. Officially enlisted on 9 September at 9 Reception Centre at Blackpool, he was sent home to await further instructions. These followed fairly shortly and he was told to report to Waddington, near Lincoln, on 23 October where he was employed until the training system could accept him.

He was called forward to 10 Reception Centre on 30 May 1941 to commence his basic training. This was completed by the end of August when he was given another holding posting at Binbrook in Lincolnshire whilst he awaited his specialist wireless course. A long wait ensued before he was finally instructed to report to 2 Signals School at Yatesbury. This initial phase of his wireless training was completed in two months, and he was then moved to 8 AGS at Evanton for the air gunnery element of his training. The four-week course was completed successfully, and he was moved to 11 OTU, Bassingbourn in Cambridgeshire. The training completed on Wellingtons, Ted was posted to 115 Squadron, equipped with the same type, on 14 October 1942, where he crewed up with Sgt G P Finnerty. The squadron was based at East Wretham in Ted's adopted county, so he would be reasonably close to home for periods of leave.

Their first op in Wellington III Z1696 was an anti-climax as they were forced to return early and bring their two 1,500-lb mines back with them. However, things settled down and the crew went on to complete ten successful operations, mainly mine-laying sorties, with their last Wellington sortie in X3878 being completed on 3 February 1943.

On 1 March 1943, the squadron started their conversion to Lancaster II aircraft. Only a handful of squadrons were equipped with this version of the Lancaster as only 300 were built. Essentially the same as the Marks I and III versions, it differed in having Bristol Hercules VI radial engines in place of the usual Rolls-Royce Merlins. Another recognition feature of the Mark II was its bulged bomb doors.

The crew were joined by a flight engineer and an extra air gunner and, with conversion to the new type complete they were airborne for their first Lancaster op on 29 March. Unfortunately, they very quickly encountered stability problems with the aircraft and were forced to jettison their bomb load safely at Rushford, and landed just twenty minutes after take-off. The crew went on to complete another eleven operations by the time their tour ended at the beginning of July 1943. Finnerty was commissioned during this phase and also awarded a well-deserved DFM. His skipper recalled that Ted was used to man the astrodome when the presence of enemy fighters was suspected and also over the target to provide another pair of eyes. He also remembered that the crew teased Ted about his dislike of flak and searchlights – surely he was not alone! On one occasion, he called Ted up on the intercom to come into the cockpit to witness the amazing inferno of fires on the ground, exploding bombs, target markers, not forgetting the flak and searchlights. Poor Ted apparently took one look at this unforgettable scene, promptly cried "bloody hell" and dived back into his curtained-off compartment. The crew never let him forget it.

Ted's ground tour after operations saw him return to 11 OTU at Bassingbourn which he moved to on 3 July. Shortly after his arrival, on the 17th, he received promotion to flight sergeant. He was to remain at Bassingbourn as a screened wireless operator until his posting to 1699 Flight on 20 December 1944, by which time he had received further promotion to the rank of W/O.

Warrant Officer Alfred Cyril Cole – Special Operator

A very experienced and senior member of the crew, he was also from the same area as Norman Ayres and 'Red' Redford, having been born and brought up in Chesterfield, just ten miles to the south of Sheffield. He was born on 6 November 1908. He was an early volunteer for aircrew duties and was recommended for training as a wireless operator/air gunner after his initial assessment on 8 April 1940. His enlistment took place at 3 Recruit Centre, Padgate, near Warrington in Lancashire. The following day he was placed on the reserve to await a call forward when a place on a training course became available. This was surprisingly quick and he was instructed to report to 3 Electrical & Wireless School (3 E & WS), near Calne in Wiltshire, located at Compton Bassett.

He completed his specialist wireless operator training at 3 Wing, 2 Signals School, Yatesbury from 11 October to 4 November 1940. It was now time for the gunnery element of his training, and this was undertaken at 5 Bombing & Gunnery School at Jurby on the Isle of Man. He arrived on 29 November, completing the course successfully on 18 January 1941. He was now a sergeant and entitled to wear the air gunners flying wing badge. He was awaiting a posting to an OTU, but again he was made to wait until a course was available. This waiting time was spent at Martlesham Heath and 6 Anti-Aircraft Co-operation Unit (6 AACU) at Ringway, now the site of Manchester airport.

On 22 March he duly reported to 12 OTU at Benson, Oxfordshire, to train on

Wellingtons. This hurdle completed, he finally moved to 214 Squadron based at Stradishall in Suffolk on 25 August 1941. He was now a member of Flt Lt R Hilton's crew and employed as an air gunner. Their first op was to Bremen in Wellington X9939 on the night of 21/22 October; but due to bad weather and problems with navigation Flt Lt Hilton was not certain that the designated target had been hit.

Alfred only completed four ops with Hilton before joining the crew of Plt Off E D Baker RCAF. He was with Baker's crew on the night of 11/12 January 1942 when they were tasked with ten other squadron aircraft to attack the German battle-cruisers *Scharnhorst* and *Gneisenau* in Brest harbour dropping six 500-lb semi-armour piercing (SAP) bombs. He was to complete eleven operational flights with Baker before the crew suffered a bad landing after being damaged by flak during an attack on Kiel. The aircraft's hydraulic

[Mrs Jennie Taylor].

system had been damaged and Baker elected to carry out a landing with the undercarriage retracted on their return to base. Unfortunately, the aircraft caught fire and burnt out, but luckily all the crew escaped, although two suffered broken arms and one a broken nose. Alfred's broken arm was a serious injury, and he was admitted to the RAF Hospital at Ely. It is likely that he also had broken ribs and a damaged shoulder. Although he was discharged from Ely on 4 April Alfred was to suffer continuing problems with his injuries and was in and out of hospital on several occasions up to 23 July. On that date he was transferred to the aircrew dispatch centre at Hoylake in the Wirral and he may have been at the recuperation centre there. His service record is unclear at this point and there is an undated reference of a posting to Chedburgh. His old squadron 214 had moved there in October 1942 so it is possible that he returned to them in a ground capacity, as it would appear unlikely that he had regained his flying medical category at this time. However, he did return to operations with the squadron, now equipped with Stirlings.

1943 opened with good news for Alfred; he was promoted to flight sergeant. He flew on his first op with his new crew skippered by Sgt E Challis in R9242 on 1 March 1943 to attack St.Nazaire. He did a second op with Challis on 5 March, target Essen, but then joined the crew of Sgt J W Evans RCAF. His first sortie with Evans was a trip to Berlin, in BF381 on 27 March. He was to fly nine more ops with Evans, the last being against Bochum in the Ruhr on the night of 13 May. Fortunately, for Alfred, a bout of flu prevented him from flying with his crew on the night of 23 May 1943 when they failed to return from a raid on Dortmund. The aircraft was presumed lost at sea off the Dutch Frisian Islands and there were no survivors.

Alfred got on well with his Canadian skipper who stayed with him during a spell of leave in April 1943. They obviously let their hair down and were both in disgrace as far as Mrs Cole was concerned when they dug up the access road at the back of the Cole home after a session in a local pub.

Alfred's first tour of operations had been flown initially in a bomber, equipped with minimal navigational and bombing aids, and through winter weather conditions. Bomber Command was beginning to get into its stride under Sir Arthur Harris, but many crews were still pioneering bomber ops in the period before the better equipped and more effective new generation of heavy bombers would dominate. Alfred and his contemporaries in this period deserve our respect.

With his first tour now judged to be completed, he was posted back to 12 OTU on 29 June 1943. The unit was now located at Chipping Warden, six miles to the north-east of Banbury. The unit's role was still to prepare bomber crews for the Wellington squadrons. After a frustrating period he had got his flying category back.

He spent eighteen months with the unit before being posted to 85 OTU at Husbands Bosworth on 5 June 1944. He arrived as a W/O having been promoted to the rank on 1 January 1944. He too would meet up with Norman Ayres, with whom he flew on a number of occasions and his future crew mates on 223 Squadron. While serving at Husbands Bosworth he was interviewed for a commission. When asked why he wanted it he replied, "because I deserve it". This obviously did not impress, and he did not get the commission. His subsequent move to 1699 Flight took place on 20 December 1944; he was the oldest member of the crew and had just turned thirty-six when he reported to the flight.

Sgt Leonard Jack Vowler – Waist Gunner

Leonard Vowler was one of the thirty-eight air gunners posted from 10 AGS to 223 Squadron when it reformed in 100 Group in August 1944. He was a Devonshire lad, born at Bickleigh near Tiverton on 2 October 1923, the son of Mr J H Vowler. He worked on the family farm before volunteering for service in the RAF. Like many of his contemporaries he was a keen member of his local ATC unit. On 4 April 1942 he appeared before 8 Aircrew Selection Board and was recommended for training under the pilot, navigator, air bomber (PNB) scheme. Although Leonard was keen to enlist, he feared that his employment as a farm worker would be a bar to his joining up, and that his father would not sanction it. With the help of his brother he effectively eloped from the farm and eventually enlisted at Oxford on 11 November 1942, mustering as an aircraft hand/PNB. He was initially placed on reserve, and had to wait until 27 April 1943

[R E Vowler].

before he reported to 1 Aircrew Reception Centre (ACRC). He was at the centre for just over three weeks before being selected to attend a preliminary aircrew training wing under a recently-introduced scheme designed to improve the standard of education of aircrew candidates. He started the course on 22 May before being posted to an aircrew dispatch centre (ACDC) to await his next move. He finally made it to 7 ITW at Newquay on 4 December 1943 and at long last would start his aircrew training.

Unfortunately, Leonard's progress was to be halted again once his ITW course had finished. He was shuffled between the ACDC and a couple of temporary postings while the authorities decided his fate. Sadly, the various delays resulted in his recategorisation for air gunner training. The training machine had now reached a stage where there was a surplus of pilots, and so Leonard and a number of his fellow PNB candidates were given little option but to accept the remustering. So, probably with very mixed feelings, Leonard reported to 10 AGS Walney Island on 1 July 1944 to join 96 Air Gunnery Course. He successfully completed the course with an examination score of 80.1% and joined his fellow air gunners on their journey to 223 Squadron overnight on 1/2 September 1944. It had been a long and frustrating trail for Leonard following his appearance before the aircrew selection board back in April 1942. Leonard was to fly sixteen ops with a number of crews before being posted to 1699 Flt for recrewing on 15 December.

Sgt Edward David Thornton Brockhurst – Waist Gunner

We now come to the young airman I knew all those years ago who started me (Richard Forder) on the long trail which has culminated in this book. David, or 'Brock' as he was known on the squadron, was born at Turkey Tump, Llanwarne, Herefordshire on 19 August 1925. He was the second son of John William and Edith Louisa Brockhurst. His father had originally been employed as gamekeeper by Major Davy of Lyston Court, but lost his job after suffering a serious injury to his right hand. On leaving he obtained work as a postman, one of six based at Wormelow Post Office.

David briefly attended the small school in nearby Llanwarne, before moving to the County Primary at Much Birch. Sadly, just after his seventh birthday, the family was struck by tragedy with the loss of David's elder brother Leonard, who was killed in a motor-cycle accident on 22 September 1932 aged just seventeen. Her son's death had a devastating effect on Edith Brockhurst's health and she would remain an invalid for the rest of her life.

[L S Davies].

David was a bright young lad who delighted his friends and family by gaining a place at Hereford High School for Boys where he joined Form II at the start of the autumn term in 1937. Stanley Smith, the Wormelow sub-postmaster's son, remembers his talent for music, and recalled that he was a very willing and helpful lad who was always ready to help out at the post office during his school holidays. He was noted for being happy and well mannered; characteristics that were also mentioned by my aunt Mrs Violet Smith of Lyston, and Mr and Mrs George Holley of Much Dewchurch. Mr Holley recalled him riding round energetically on his red sports bike, but always prepared to stop and pass the time of day before dashing on his way.

He was in Form V when he left the high school in July 1942 obtaining his Cambridge School Certificate in english literature, french, oral french, maths and physics. A Mortimer House boy, he had been a member of the school's orchestral society and played as a first violinist. After leaving school he worked in a Hereford radio shop – which he obviously had an interest in as the new occupiers of the family home, after the death of his parents, found a large pile of old *Practical Wireless* magazines in the house. David was also a keen member of the Hereford ATC squadron which he joined with George Holley's brother.

David enlisted in the RAF on 3 May 1943 obtaining a recommendation as a PNB candidate, but was sent home on reserve awaiting a place in the training machine. His decision to join the RAF must have been one of deep regret and apprehension for his parents. David was very good with his mother who spent her daytime hours lying on a sofa. When he was at home he would play the piano for her, and carry her upstairs to bed at the end of the day, Eventually, on 22 November he was called forward with his friend Len Davies to 32 Receiving Wing, 2 Aircrew Reception Centre at Regents Park in London where they were accommodated in one of the blocks of flats overlooking Lords cricket ground, taking their meals in the London Zoo restaurant. Their initial processing and basic training was completed on 18 December, and they moved on immediately to begin the next phase at 2 ITW located in Downing College, Cambridge. The training system was working smoothly and they were on their way again on 25 March 1944 to begin their flying training at 16 EFTS at Burnaston, near Derby; now the site of the Toyota car factory.

Flying training on the Tiger Moth proceeded satisfactorily with the benefit of the summer flying conditions. Len and David had both achieved solo standard when the blow fell. Due to a surplus of pilots the decision had been made that the flow of trainees would be curtailed. David and Len were among the victims of this policy decision, and they had little option but to accept remustering to air gunner. Their time at Burnaston was terminated on 23 May and there followed a hiatus before they were allocated a place with fellow PNB casualties on 96 Air Gunnery Course at 10 AGS, Walney Island; the course running from 11 July to 1 September 1944. Len and David together with 36 other air gunners, all graded above average, were immediately posted to 223 Squadron arriving at Oulton on 2 September. Len was allocated to Flt Lt Jack Brigham's crew and would fly a total of 35 ops on the squadron. David initially joined Flt Lt Roy Hastie and flew 18 ops with him before being reassigned to 1699 Flt to form a new crew.

W/O Samuel Ernest Silvey – Rear Gunner

The crew was completed by Sam Silvey a very experienced air gunner and at twenty-eight, one of the more senior figures. A native of Buckinghamshire he was born at the family home, 3 Albert Street, High Wycombe on 16 November 1916, the only son of William Burnett and Florence Isabel Silvey; a sister completed the family. His father worked in the local furniture industry as a wood machinist. Sam was educated at High Wycombe Priory School which he left at fourteen to work in Brazil's grocery shop. He worked there for three years before moving to a butcher's shop also owned by Brazil's. Mr G W Hoing, a boyhood friend, recalled that Sam was a confirmed bachelor and was very fond of his local pub The Antelope. He was also a keen musician and played the clarinet in the High Wycombe town band.

[W G Hoing].

Sam's RAF service commenced when he enlisted at 1 Recruit Centre at Uxbridge on 30 April 1940. He was quickly passed on to 4 Recruit Centre on 4 May where he did his basic training. It is not known if he volunteered for aircrew on joining, or if this was done later. His next move took him to 3 Wing, 1 School of Technical Training at Halton, which might suggest that he had enlisted in a ground engineering trade. However, it is possible that it was a holding posting until he was called forward to enter an ITW, but it is interesting that he was promoted to temporary corporal rank on 5 June. After a lengthy stay at Halton he was posted on 25 October 1941 to the recently formed 14 ITW at St. Leonards-on-Sea. The course was successfully completed and his next move took him back to Uxbridge for specialist training at 1 Air Armament School where he arrived on 13 December.

His stay at Uxbridge was brief, and he was on his way to 9 AGS at Llandwrog near Caernarvon on 3 January 1942. However, the gunnery school was due to close in June, so Sam transferred to complete his course at 3 AGS at Castle Kennedy, close to Stranraer, at the beginning of May 1942. His gunnery course, flying in Whitley and Lysander aircraft, finished on 20 August.

His first operational squadron was 149 equipped with Stirlings at Lakenheath in Suffolk. Sam is recorded as joining the squadron on 31 August 1942, and flew his first operation in Flt Lt M W Hartford's crew. Unfortunately, the sortie had to be abandoned as the aircraft could not gain height above 8,000 feet. His next op on 4 September was successful, with a long trip to attack Bremen, flying as the mid upper gunner. He flew with Hartford's crew on a total of fourteen operations with a further five that resulted in early returns for various reasons. On 30 December Hartford was attached to 26 OTU, and his crew was attached to 1651 HCU at Waterbeach. The crew, with a few changes, were now to fly with Sqn Ldr D S Robertson, with whom Sam flew a further five operations, plus one early return after losing the port inner engine.

His first operational tour completed, Sam was posted to 26 OTU at Wing in Buckinghamshire on 6 April 1943 to start his screened tour. He did a year at Wing, apart from a month's attachment to 7 AGS at Stormy Down, before being posted to 85 OTU at Husbands Bosworth on 20 June 1944. He enjoyed a six-month stay at the OTU before joining Ayres, Cole, Cairns and Stanyer at 1699 Flt at Oulton on 20 December.

FROM H.Q. 100 GROUP   201930A
TO FOULSHAM   WEST RAYNHAM   LITTLE SNORING   NORTH CREAKE   OULTON
   SWANNINGTON   MASSINGHAM   SWANTON MORLEY

INFO H.Q.B.C.   H.Q.F.C.   12 GROUP
SECRET QWM BT

A. FORM 'B' NO. 347.

B. 20 MARCH 1945

C. BOMBER TARGETS AND ROUTES (OTHER GROUPS)

GP.	NOS.	TARGET.
1	11L (ABC)	GQ 1644
5	200L)	GQ1514A
	12M)	
6	110L)	GQ 1644
	90 HX)	
8	48L)	MARKERS ON GQ 1644
	1M)	

ROUTES:- GQ1644 - BASE - WHITBY - 5430N 0400E - 5430N 0530E - 5355N
         0700E - TGT - 5413N 0910E - 5430N 0900E - WHITBY - BASE

         GQ1514A BASE - READING - 5000N 0200E - 5010N 0740E - 5040N
         0835E - 5040N & 1010E - 5110N 1200E - TGT - 5050N 1220E 5035N
         5040N 0835E - 5010N 0740E - 5000N 0200E - READING - BASE. 11206

         GQ1514A MARKERS. BASE - READING - 5000N 0200E - 5033N 0553E-
         5111N 0820E - 5137N 1023E - TGT - 5050N 1220E - 5032N 1120E-
         5040N 0835E - 5010N 0740E - 5000N 0200E - READING - BASE.

D. INTENTION MY A. 665 RKX REFERS.

F. SQUADRONS REQUIRED FOR OPERATIONS :- 171 - 199 - 214 - 223 - 462 -1
   ///// 462 - 192 - 85 - 157 - 515 - 23 - 169 - 239 - B.S.D.U.

G. H. K. AND L.

7/171)   ANGEL
8/223)
4/171)
5/462)   WINDOW
2/199)
5/214)

5/214)
1/223)   JOSTLE

2/192   PIPERACK

X 9/192   SPECIAL INVESTIGATION.

7/515)
7/ 23)   LOW INTRUDER

2/BSDU)
8/157)
8/ 85)   HIGH INTRUDER
3/515)
8/239)
6/169)

2/169)
2/239)
2/ 85)   ANTI INTRUDER STANDBY
2/157)

M. TIMES OF BOMBER ATTACKS. GU 1044 H - 0430 HRS TOT H - H+7
GQ 1514A H= 0345 HRS TOT H - H+7

N. GEE INFORMATION. SEE SIGNALS FORM 'B'
(2) SCRAM DIVERSIONS.
   TANGMERE - 169 - 239 - 192 MOS.
   BLACKBUSHE - 23 - 515 - B.S.D.U.
   ODIHAM 85 - 157
   TARRANT RUSHTON 214 - 223
   EXETER 192 - 462
IN P THORNEY ISLAND 199 - 171
BT 201930A
IN N. CC N. (1) GEE INFORMATION

INPARA C. CC GP   TARGETS ETC.
IN ROUTES 2ND. PARA CWA 5040N... 0835E 5032N 1120E 5040N ETC.
SAME PARA LINE 2 INSERT AFTER 1220E...
IN NEAT PARA CWA 5137N... 1023E
CC IN PARA M LINE 1 H- H+7
HART K WITH R OCAKMIN
QUOTING NR NOS.
K

JWIO
EDR   MSM   R FOR EDR 31/20   HBC127/20   EDR 33/20 R2010/20 GN AR
SWM   R2019234 2010A PC   HBC   R202020A BW
RAY   R2020T0A JW   RDT   R202012A NB
SNO   R202012A GAS   GPL   R202010A F MARCH
NCK   R202012A GR
FLS   R202013A MH
OUL   R202012A MLW
SNG   R202015A MW

A copy of the 100 Group Form B sourced from Air25/784.

This copy of the 5 Group Form B was given to Richard Forder by the late Bert Allam, 2nd Pilot in Lancaster PD349.

STAND BY FOR EMERGENCY BCST FORM A
V HBC   HBC104/20 00   FORM A   FORM A   FORM A

GPA B522 GPC B561 GPD B213 GPE B207 GPF B986 GPG B85 GPH B279
ABG B662 OTG B62 EDR B915

NRV T 38 GROUP
OIPNT T VIIITH USAF   IX USAF ADVANCED
IAH T 11 GROUP   HQ FIGHTER COMMAND   AIR STAFF SHAEF FORWARD

AIR STAFF SHAEF MAIN   HQ 2ND TAF MAIN   2 GROUP BLA   1ST TAC AF

FROM HQ BOMBER COMMAND 201025A
TO 1 3 4 5 6 7 8 11 38 91 92 100 GROUPS

HQ FIGHTER COMMAND   AIR STAFF SHAEF FORWARD   AIR STAFF SHAEF MA

VIIITH USAF   IX USAF ADVANCED   HQ 2ND TAF MAIN   2 GROUP BLA

1ST TAC AF
SECRET QQY BT

AC 605 20 MAR SECRET   PRELIMINARY WARNING ORDER

                                            PROVISIONAL H HOURS
1 GP   11 ABC GQ16444 COOKIE
       10 L   GARDENING ROSEMARY   0330

3 GP   DAYLIGHT ALREADY ORDERED

4 GP   DAYLIGHT ALREADY ORDERED

5 GP   200 L   GQ1514A COOKIE   0345
       NO 9 SQDN GN5852 TALLBOY   1700
              (038H 120V ON 77/1)

6 GP   100 H   GQ1644 BUFFER   0330
       100 L   GQ1644 COOKIE   0330

8GP   TO MARK GQ1644
       MOSQUITOS WHITEBAIT AND DIVERSION TARGET

100 GP SUPPORT FOR GQ1644 AND GQ1514A

BT 201025A

TOD 1040A RW AR

This copy of AC 605 for 20th March shows the information given, the time on this, 201025A gives the time of issue as 1025 on the 20th. ABC stood for Airbourne Cigar which was the code name for the system for jamming German radio broadcasts, the wartime equivalent of today's Electronic Countermeasures. Gardening was laying mines at sea and Rosemary was in the Heligoland area. A "Cookie" was a 4000lb bomb and indicated the type of bomb load.

STAND BY FOR EMERGENCY BCST FORM A
V HBC   HBC104/20 00   FORM A   FORM A

GPA B522 GPC B561 GPD B213 GPE B207 GPF B986 GPG B85 GPH B279
ABG B662 OTG B62 EDR B915

NRV T 38 GROUP
OIPNT T VIIITH USAF   IX USAF ADVANCED
IAH T 11 GROUP   HQ FIGHTER COMMAND   AIR STAFF SHAEF FORWARD

AIR STAFF SHAEF MAIN   HQ 2ND TAF MAIN   2 GROUP BLA   1ST TAC AF

FROM HQ BOMBER COMMAND 201025A
TO 1 3 4 5 6 7 8 11 38 91 92 100 GROUPS

HQ FIGHTER COMMAND   AIR STAFF SHAEF FORWARD   AIR STAFF SHAE

VIIITH USAF   IX USAF ADVANCED   HQ 2ND TAF MAIN   2 GROUP BLA

1ST TAC AF
SECRET QQY BT

AC 605 20 MAR SECRET   PRELIMINARY WARNING ORDER

                                            PROVISIONAL H HOURS
1 GP   11 ABC GQ16444 COOKIE
       10 L   GARDENING ROSEMARY   0330

3 GP   DAYLIGHT ALREADY ORDERED

4 GP   DAYLIGHT ALREADY ORDERED

5 GP   200 L   GQ1514A COOKIE   0345
       NO 9 SQDN GN5852 TALLBOY   1700
              (038H 120V ON 77/1)

6 GP   100 H   GQ1644 BUFFER   0330
       100 L   GQ1644 COOKIE   0330

8GP   TO MARK GQ1644
       MOSQUITOS WHITEBAIT AND DIVERSION TARGET

100 GP SUPPORT FOR GQ1644 AND GQ1514A

BT 201025A

TOD 1040A RW AR

This copy of AC 605 for 20th March shows the information given, the time on this, 201025A gives the time of issue as 1025 on the 20th. ABC stood for Airbourne Cigar which was the code name for the system for jamming German radio broadcasts, the wartime equivalent of today's Electronic Countermeasures. Gardening was laying mines at sea and Rosemary was in the Heligoland area. A "Cookie" was a 4000lb bomb and indicated the type of bomb load.

Bomber Command Form A.

Copies of the Bomber Command Form A for the night of 20/21 March 1945, redrafted with appropriate comments, and given to Richard by Ted Friend, the sole survivor from Lancaster ME441.

VZ GPN
  GPH
EMERGENCY B/CAST FORM A
V HBC HBC 105/ 20A

EMERGENCY B/CAST
Y HBC HBC105/20 '00' FORM A   FORM A   FORM A
GPA B524 GPC B562 GPD BZXX GPD B214 GPG B208 GPF D708 GPH B280
EDR B917
PNT T 8TH USAAF (DOF1)
RC AORE T 325 RECCE WING.

FROM HQ BOMBER COMMAND 201100A
TO 1 3 4 5 6 8 100 GROUPS   8TH USAAF (DOF1)

325 RECCE WING
  SECRET QQY BT

AC 606 20 MAR SECRET

                    TARGETS AND AP'S FOR NIGHT 20/21 MAR

GQ1644 030H 039V ON ILLUST. 54/2 TO COMPLETE DESTRUCTION OF REFINERY.

GQ1514A TO COMPLETE DESTRUCTION OF SYNTHETIC OIL SECTION OF PLANT
        THE ESSENTIAL INSTALLATIONS ARE WITHIN THE AREA BOUNDED
        THE FOLLOWING POINTS ON ILLUSTRATION 14/8:-
        062H 084V - 064H 048V - 064H 035V - 062H 035V - 062H 041V - 058H 041V
        058H 046V - 062H 046V

GN 5852 TO DESTROY THE BRIDGE AT 038H 120V ON ILLUSTRATION 77/1

BT 201100A

The operations staff would work out the route and timing over the targets allocated to each group, select the aiming points and decide the tactics to be employed by the Bomber Support aircraft with their radar and radio countermeasures.

BC 110/20 ' 00 ' FORM A   FORM A   FORM A
S GPC B564 GPD B'2F GPE B211 GPF B920
GH B282 RRG B664 OTG B64 EDR B920
QFC AIR STAFF SHAEF FORWARD   AIR STAFF SHAEF MAIN

TAF MAIN 2 GROUP BLA 1ST TAC AF
H USAF IX USAF ADV
38 GROUP

D BOMBER COMMAND 201124A
4 5 6 7 8 38 91 92 100 GROUPS   HQ FIGHTER
ID AIR STAFF SHAEF FORWARD AIR STAFF SHAEF MAIN
SAF IX USAF ADV 2ND TAF MAIN 2 GP BLA 1ST TAC AF
QQY BT

20 MAR SECRET   ACTION SHEET

UP   NOS   TARGET
      10 L   GARDENING ROSEMARY

1

G - BASE - WHITBY - 5430N 0400E - 5430N 0530E - 5355N 0700E
- GARDEN - 5430N 0530E - WHITBY - BASE.

2

ING - H HOUR AT 0700E 0330 HRS

3

GHT AND RADAR RESTRICTIONS - AS FOR AIRCRAFT DETAILED ON GQ

1124A

2 CWA ON H HOUR AT
150A ES

ext ACTION SHEET, AC 609, was sent out at 1210 hrs. which gave details of how the
on the Bohlen Synthetic Oil Plant and the Heide Oil Refinery were to be carried out. This
llowed at 1217 hrs. by AC 610 orders for a Sweepstake Exercise carried out by crews who
still under training at the Heavy Conversion Units of No. 7 Group, it was intended to be a
sion which helped to confuse the enemy defences, and also was very good training for
tions.

TOP OF SHEET AS OTHERS

QQY BT   FORM A

0 MAR SECRET   ACTION SHEET

TAKE EXERCISE TONIGHT 20/21 MARCH

EFFORT. MAXIMUM EFFORT FROM 7 GROUP

ASE - READING - 4935N 0140E - 4840N 0400E - 4840N 0700E - 4825N
00E - 4820N 0200E - READING - BASE

HOUR AT 4840N 0700E IS 0255 HRS ATTACK TO BE SPREAD EVENLY
ER 4 MINS

AIRCRAFT TO KEEP BELOW 5000 FEET UNTIL 4915N 0230E OUTWARD
AND TO CLIMB TO 15000 FT BY 4840N 0510E AIRCRAFT TO LOSE HEIGHT
RAPIDLY TO BELOW 5000 FT FROM 4840N 0700E UNTIL 4820N 0200E ON
RETURN THEREAFTER HEIGHTS AT AOC'S DISCRETION

NCE IS TO BE MAINTAINED UNTIL 4840N 0510E WHEN H2S IS TO BE
ON UNTIL 4840N 0700E WHEN IT IS TO BE SWITCHED OFF FOR
OF THE FLIGHT

TYPE MB TO BE DROPPED AT 5 BUNDLES PER MINUTE FROM
840N 0600E - 4840N 0700E OUTWARD

AOC'S DISCRETION AFTER READING ON RETURN

RW AIR

TOP OF SHEET AS OTHERS.
FORM A
SECRET QY BT
AC609 20 MAR SECRET   ACTION SHEET
GROUP   NOS   TARGET
1   11L ABC   GQ1644   BOMB LOAD COOKIE
5   200L   GQ1514A   "   " COOKIE
     12M
6   110L   GQ1644   "   " COOKIE
     90H   GQ1644   "   " COOKIE
8   48L MARK   GQ1644
     1M
NOTE 1
    H HOUR GQ1644 - 0400
            GQ1514A - 0345
NOTE2
    TOTS   GQ1644 H - H+7
           GQ1514A H - H+7
           AIRCRAFT TO BE SPREAD EVENLY THROUGHOUT THE ATTACK
NOTE 3
    MARKING GQ1644 - FULL PFF
             GQ1514A - 5 GROUP
NOTE4
    AIMING POINT - GQ1644 030H O39V ON ILLUST. 54/2

NOTE 5
HEIGHT RESTRICTIONS - WEATHER PERMITTING AIRCRAFT ATTACKING GQ1644
ARE
    TO REMAIN BELOW 5000FT TO 0520E AND ARE NOT TO CLIMB ABOVE 12000FT
    FROM 0530E TO TARGET WHEN BOMBING HEIGHT WILL NOT BE ABOVE 10000FT
    AND MAY BE DETAILED LOWER BY MASTER BOMBER ON LEAVING COAST
    AIRCRAFT WILL DESCEND TO 3000FT AS EARLY AS POSSIBLE AND CROSS THE
    NORTH SEA AT THIS HEIGHT

NOTE 6
RADAR AND SIGNALS SILENCE TO BE MAINTAINED AS FAR AS 0630E ON GQ1644
FOR TARGET GQ1514A RADAR AND SIGNALS SILENCE IS TO BE OBSERVED UP TO
0600E

NOTE 7
ROUTES GQ1644 BASE - WHITBY - 5430N 0400E - 5430N 0530E - 5355N 0700E - TGT -
5413N
           0910E - 5430N 0900E - WHITBY - BASE

        GQ1514A - BASE - READING - 5000N 0200E - 5010N 0740E - 5040N 0835E - 5040N -
            1010E - 5110N 1200E - TGT - 5050N 1220E - 5032N 1120E - 5040N 0835E -
            5010N 0740E - 5000N 0200E - READING - BASE

        GQ1514A (MARKERS)
            BASE - READING - 5000N 0200E - 5033N 0553E - 5111N 0820E - 5137N
            1023E - TGT - 5050N 1220E - 5032N 1120E - 5040N 0835E - 5010N -
            0740E - 5000N 0200E - READING - BASE
BT 201210A
C IN NOTE 7 2ND PARA CWA 5050N 1220E - 5033N 1120E
TOD 1257A CW
M+ AS FOR K WITH R

AC 611 at 1315 hrs revised the timing of the attack on the Heide oil refinery.

TOP OF SHEET AS OTHERS

SECRET QQY BT
                          ACTION SHEET
AC611 20 MAR SECRET

REF MY AC608 TOXXX AC608 OF TODAYS DATE NOTE 2 H HOUR
IS NOW 0400 HRS AT 0700E

REF MY AC609 OF TODAYS DATE NOTE 1 H HOUR FOR GQ1644
IS NOW 0430 HRS
BT 201315A

In addition to providing the markers for the attack at Heide Mosquitos of No. 8 Group, the
Path Finder Force were to attack three targets, Whitebait (Berlin), Salmon (Bremen), and Kassel
(Bream) as detailed on AC612.

TOP OF SHEET AS OTHERS.

SECRET QQY BT
                          ACTION SHEET
AC612 20 MAR SECRET

GROUP   NOS   TARGET
8   38   WHITEBAIT
PFF   27   SALMON (FEINT ATTACK)
PFF   17   BREAM   (FEINT ATTACK)

NOTE 1
' H ' HOURS : WHITEBAIT : 2120 HRS SALMON : 0420 HRS BREAM : 0310 HRS

NOTE 2
ROUTEING :
WHITEBAIT : BASE - HAPPISBURG - 5240N 0400E - TGT - 5214N 1325E - 5155N 1155E -
            5210N 0650E - 5245N 0440E - 5300N 0100E - BASE
SALMON   : BASE - 5300N 0045E - 5430N 0400E - 5430N 0530E - TGT - 5256N 0850E -
            5240N 0750E - 5310N 0620E - 5250N 0440E - 5300N 0100E - BASE
BREAM :   BASE - CAMBRIDGE - HASTINGS - 5010N 0200E - 5015N 0725E - TGT -
9MOS   5200N 0710E - 5205N 0510E - 5245N 0400E - 5300N 0100E - BASE
BREAM :   BASE - CAMBRIDGE - HASTINGS - 5022N 0838E - 5032N 0907E - TGT -
8MOS   5200N 0800E - 5200N 0500E - HAPPISBURG - BASE
BT 201737A

2 TOD 1815/20 FB. AR

The final signal from Bomber Command HQ. For this nights ops came at 2340 hrs, AC616
cancelled the 90 Halifaxes on standby for Heide and changed the Time over Target (TOT).

TOP OF SHEET AS OTHERS   ACTION SHEET
AC616 20 MAR 45   SECRET

REF MY AC609 OF TODAYS DATE DELETE 90H ON GQ 1644

NOTE 2 TOT FOR GQ 1644 WILL NOW BE H - H+4
BT 202340A
TOD 0009A KF AR
STNS AS FOR K

Hauptmann Johannes Hager

Brief Biography of Hauptmann Johannes Hager, Knight's Cross

Johannes Hager was born in Pretzier on 16 August 1920, the eldest of three brothers who all survived World War II. Johannes did very well at school, achieving an excellent result in his arbitur. He was also a very good sportsman. Like many of his contemporaries, before the war he was a keen glider pilot and his ambition was to become a professional pilot. It is not known when he joined the Luftwaffe, but he apparently took a particular interest in, and increased his skill in early experiments with the Schräge Musik installation of inclined cannon.

In 1943 he was shot down near Koblenz while testing a new radar. He took to his parachute but struck the tailplane with his leg as he left the aircraft. He lost consciousness and his 'chute did not fully deploy. However he was saved by landing in a tree. The injury to his leg was such that the hospital he was taken to proposed amputation. He refused, and as a result of this he spent nearly seven months in hospital, but his leg was saved.

He collected souvenirs from his aerial victories, including a section of aircraft skin from an enemy night fighter which featured forty kill symbols. His first victory was achieved on 14 February 1943 flying with II./NJG 1, his unit for the remainder of the war. He flew ninety-nine operations, of which two were daytime sorties. He was credited with six victories on the night of 21/22 February 1945, receiving the Knight's Cross on 12 March 1945. His score at the end of the war was forty-seven night, and two day victories. His claims on the night of 20/21 March 1945 were his final victories of the war. After the war he worked in the building industry and died on 2 September 1993 aged seventy-three years.

Note:
Biographical details supplied by Werner Pinn and Bernd Klinkhardt.

Hager's combat reports for the night of 20/21 March 1945.

Index